McGraw-Hill's Criminal Law for Paralegals

The McGraw-Hill Paralegal List

WHERE EDUCATIONAL SUPPORT GOES BEYOND EXPECTATIONS.

Introduction to Law & Paralegal Studies
Connie Farrell Scuderi
ISBN: 0073524638
© 2008

Introduction to Law for Paralegals
Deborah Benton
ISBN: 007351179X
© 2008

Basic Legal Research, Second Edition
Edward Nolfi
ISBN: 0073520519
© 2008

Basic Legal Writing, Second Edition
Pamela Tepper
ISBN: 0073403032
© 2008

Contract Law for Paralegals
Linda Spagnola
ISBN: 0073511765
© 2008

Civil Law and Litigation for Paralegals
Neal Bevans
ISBN: 0073524611
© 2008

McGraw-Hill's Torts for Paralegals
ISBN: 0073376930
© 2009

McGraw-Hill's Real Estate Law
for Paralegals
ISBN: 0073376957
© 2009 Publishes 01/04/08

Legal Research and Writing
for Paralegals
Pamela Tepper and Neal Bevans
ISBN: 007352462X
© 2009

Wills, Trusts, and Estates for Paralegals
George Kent
ISBN: 0073403067
© 2008

The Law Office Reference Manual
Jo Ann Lee
ISBN: 0073511838
© 2008

The Paralegal Reference Manual
Charles Nemeth
ISBN: 0073403075
© 2008

The Professional Paralegal
Allan Tow
ISBN: 0073403091
© 2009 Publishes 01/01/08

Ethics for Paralegals
Linda Spagnola and Vivian Batts
ISBN: 0073376981
© 2009

Family Law for Paralegals
George Kent
ISBN: 0073376973
© 2009

McGraw-Hill's Criminal Law for Paralegals
Lisa Schaffer and Andrew Wietecki
ISBN: 0073376965
© 2009

McGraw-Hill's Law Office Management
for Paralegals
ISBN: 0073376949
© 2009

Legal Terminology Explained for Paralegals
Edward Nolfi
ISBN: 0073511846
© 2009

For more information or to receive desk copies, please contact your McGraw-Hill Sales Representative.

McGraw-Hill's Criminal Law for Paralegals

Lisa Schaffer
Contributing Author

Andrew Wietecki
Contributing Author/Editor

McGraw-Hill
Higher Education

Boston   Burr Ridge, IL   Dubuque, IA   New York   San Francisco   St. Louis
Bangkok   Bogotá   Caracas   Kuala Lumpur   Lisbon   London   Madrid   Mexico City
Milan   Montreal   New Delhi   Santiago   Seoul   Singapore   Sydney   Taipei   Toronto

McGraw-Hill
Higher Education

CRIMINAL LAW FOR PARALEGALS

Published by McGraw-Hill, a business unit of The McGraw-Hill Companies, Inc., 1221 Avenue of the Americas, New York, NY, 10020. Copyright © 2009 by The McGraw-Hill Companies, Inc. All rights reserved. No part of this publication may be reproduced or distributed in any form or by any means, or stored in a database or retrieval system, without the prior written consent of The McGraw-Hill Companies, Inc., including, but not limited to, in any network or other electronic storage or transmission, or broadcast for distance learning.

Some ancillaries, including electronic and print components, may not be available to customers outside the United States.

This book is printed on acid-free paper.

3 4 5 6 7 8 9 0 QVS/QVS 15

ISBN   978-0-07-337696-7
MHID   0-07-337696-5

Vice president/Editor in chief: *Elizabeth Haefele*
Vice president/Director of marketing: *John E. Biernat*
Sponsoring editor: *Natalie J. Ruffatto*
Developmental editor II: *Tammy Higham*
Marketing manager: *Keari Bedford*
Lead media producer: *Damian Moshak*
Media producer: *Marc Mattson*
Director, Editing/Design/Production: *Jess Ann Kosic*
Project manager: *Marlena Pechan*
Senior production supervisor: *Janean A. Utley*
Designer: *Marianna Kinigakis*
Cover and interior design: *Pam Verros*
Cover image: © *Steven Robertson/iStockPhoto*
Media project manager: *Mark A. S. Dierker*
Outside development house: *Beth Baugh*
Typeface: *10.5/13 Times New Roman*
Compositor: *Aptara, Inc.*
Printer: *Quad/Graphics*

Library of Congress Cataloging-in-Publication Data

Schaffer, Lisa.
   McGraw-Hill's criminal law for paralegals / Lisa Schaffer, contributing author ;
  Andrew Wietecki, contributing author/editor.
     p. cm. — (The McGraw-Hill paralegal list)
   Includes index.
   ISBN-13: 978-0-07-337696-7 (alk. paper)
   ISBN-10: 0-07-337696-5 (alk. paper)
   1. Criminal law—United States. 2. Criminal procedure—United States. 3. Legal
assistants—United States—Handbooks, manuals, etc. I. Wietecki, Andrew. II. Title.
III. Title: Criminal law for paralegals.
   KF9219.S334 2009
   345.73—dc22

                     2007043015

The Internet addresses listed in the text were accurate at the time of publication. The inclusion of a Web site does not indicate an endorsement by the authors or McGraw-Hill, and McGraw-Hill does not guarantee the accuracy of the information presented at these sites.

About the Authors

Curriculum Technology

Curriculum Technology works with McGraw-Hill on several projects related to the paralegal series. Curriculum Technology serves education organizations and publishing companies by providing a source of intellectual property development, media, technology, as well as consultation and research.

Lisa Schaffer, JD, MBA

Contributing Author

Lisa Schaffer earned a Bachelor of Arts in History from the University of California, Los Angeles; her Juris Doctorate in law from Chapman University School of Law; a Masters in Business Administration from Chapman University; and an Advanced Management Certificate and an Executive Management Certificate from the University of California, Riverside.

Lisa worked in the legal industry for over 20 years in a variety of positions for law firms that specialized in the areas of criminal law, real estate law, corporate law, and personal injury. She served as in-house counsel for regulatory compliance in the legal affairs department of National Water & Power, Inc., doing business in 43 states.

Lisa has taught a variety of courses in paralegal studies for InterCoast Colleges over a period of five years. She was offered and accepted the position of director of education. She was later promoted to school director of the Riverside campus before accepting the position of chief administrative officer for all campuses.

Lisa also has served as an assistant vice president in the accreditation and licensing department for Corinthian Colleges, Inc.

Andrew Wietecki, JD, MPA

Contributing Editor/Author

Andrew Wietecki earned a Bachelor of Arts in English from St. Thomas Aquinas College; a Masters in Public Administration from the Graduate School at Hamline University; and his Juris Doctorate in law from Hamline University School of Law.

Andrew was born and raised in New York City. He has been in the education business for 13 years, having practiced real property law before that. He has taught at the high school level in New York City as well as instructing college-level paralegal students. He has been academic dean, legal program chair, and a college instructor for the past 11 years. Currently, Andrew works in the education field with Curriculum Technology producing a wide variety of learning tools while also tutoring children in English skills.

Amy Eisenhower, JD, BS
Contributing Writer

Amy Eisenhower earned a Bachelor of Science in English from Wayne State College in Wayne, Nebraska, and her Doctorate in Jurisprudence from the University of South Dakota in Vermillion, South Dakota.

Amy was born in Nebraska and has spent much of her life there. She currently resides in Grand Island, Nebraska. Amy is a member of both the South Dakota and the Nebraska State Bars.

Amy taught five years of high school English before attending law school. She is currently employed as assistant general counsel for Credit Management, Inc. She has been with Curriculum Technology for approximately a year and a half as a senior consultant.

Rastin Ashtiani
Contributing Writer

Rastin Ashtiani earned a Bachelor of Arts in Psychology from the University of California at Irvine and a Doctorate in Jurisprudence from Chapman University School of Law in Anaheim, California.

Rastin was born in Los Angeles, California, has spent much of his life in the Los Angeles area, and currently resides in Orange County, California. Rastin has worked with the Orange County District Attorney's office and also has worked at the law offices of Dyke Huish. Rastin has been with Curriculum Technology for approximately a year as a consultant for both paralegal and legal projects.

Preface

Criminal law is an exciting and thought-provoking area of law that each one of us has given some consideration to in the past. Many Americans are either victims of criminal acts themselves or know of a friend or family member who has been victimized. We live in a nation that is obsessed with crime, criminal behavior, and criminal laws. The media offer a vast selection of television programming and film production covering crime-driven stories. As each year transpires, we continue to build more jails, more prisons, and more penitentiaries to house a continuing surge in the felonious population.

This text covers the basic groundwork for the criminal justice system and sets forth the substantive and procedural rights of a criminal defendant. Additionally, we examine the general components of the criminal act, covering the major crimes against people, property, and habitation. Along with the elements of particular crimes, the text discusses the available defenses.

We then turn to the criminal prosecution process and have included three adjacent chapters beginning with pretrial proceedings, moving on to the actual trial against the defendant, and finishing with sentencing and post-trial proceedings. This approach helps the student get a firm grasp on how the criminal procedure works.

Paralegals often play a crucial part in criminal proceedings because they contribute so much to the discovery of evidence that may be favorable to the defendant or prosecution. A paralegal may conduct interviews of witnesses or compile police reports that may be used at the time of trial. Moreover, many paralegals conduct legal research and assist in developing the legal theories that the defendant will rely on as part of his/her defense. These examples are only a partial list of the many roles a paralegal may play.

McGraw-Hill's Criminal Law for Paralegals contains 14 chapters along with two appendixes. In providing a hands-on approach to learning, each chapter has a recent, applicable case opinion along with many ancillaries, including charts, tables, figures, and exercises to aid in the student's development.

TEXT DESIGN

Pedagogy

This text has numerous features that take advantage of the varying learning styles that students use to gain knowledge. Students who apply their newly acquired knowledge often retain it much better than those who do not. So we have designed the chapters to assure students the opportunity to learn the appropriate legal concepts and the necessary vocabulary, develop their legal reasoning skills, and demonstrate their knowledge of the material. Each chapter contains the following features:

- **A Day in the Life of a Real Paralegal**—A scenario of what a usual day is like for a paralegal at his/her position, often with a practical application designed to help students build a specific skill set.
- **Case Fact Pattern**—A simple fact pattern with story and outcome.
- **Research This**—Hands-on assignment designed to develop his/her research skills.

- **Eye on Ethics**—Student is presented with ethical issue(s) related to the subject of the chapter.
- **Surf's Up**—Hands-on research presenting the student with numerous Web sites by which to *surf* and gather material.
- **Practice Tip**—Alerts the student to a nuance of law or caveat to a rule.
- **Case in Point**—A significant case designed to expand on the topics discussed in the chapter.
- **Portfolio Assignment**—Student is given an assignment by which to begin, create, and add to a portfolio.
- **Vocabulary Builders**—Crossword puzzles for the student to complete using vocabulary words found in each chapter.

The text is written in clearly presented language that engages the student's interest, and presents information in a variety of styles.

OTHER LEARNING AND TEACHING RESOURCES

Supplements

The **Online Learning Center (OLC)** is a Web site that follows the text chapter by chapter. OLC content is ancillary and supplementary germane to the textbook—as students read the book, they can go online to review material or link to relevant Web sites. Students and instructors can access the Web sites for each of the McGraw-Hill paralegal texts from the main page of the Paralegal Super Site. Each OLC has a similar organization. An Information Center features an overview of the text, background on the author, and the Preface and Table of Contents from the book. Instructors can access the Instructor's Manual, PowerPoint presentations, and Test Bank. Students see the Key Terms list from the text as flashcards, as well as additional quizzes and exercises.

Acknowledgments

Finally, special thanks need to be given to the reviewers who provided invaluable feedback during the steps to completion of the final draft.

Ernest Davila
San Jacinto College

Darren Defoe
Andover College

Jane Breslin Jacobs
Community College of Philadelphia

Jennifer Labrozzi
Tidewater Tech

Steven Mallery
Eagle Gate College

Kathryn L. Myers
Saint Mary-of-the-Woods College

Richard Patete
Keiser College

Kathleen Reed
University of Toledo

Debbie Vinecour
SUNY–Rockland

Debbie Wicks
Pittsburgh Technical Institute

Walkthrough

McGraw-Hill's Criminal Law for Paralegals offers students an exciting way to learn about many different crimes and their elements, beginning with the different sources of criminal law and proceeding right through to the last step of a criminal trial, "Sentencing and Post-Trial Procedures." The text has numerous built-in, hands-on assignments with a variety of exercises and cases to help the student learn and enjoy the study of criminal law. The pedagogy of the book applies three main goals:

- Learning outcomes (critical thinking, vocabulary building, skill development, issues analysis, writing practice).

- Relevance of topics without sacrificing theory (ethical challenges, current law practices, technology application).

- Practical application (real-world exercises, practical advice, portfolio creation).

CHAPTER OBJECTIVES

Upon completion of this chapter, you will be able to:

- Understand the origins of criminal law.
- Explain the differences between civil and criminal law.
- Define the term *crime* and the theories of punishment associated with it.
- Identify the classifications of crimes.
- Discuss jurisdiction in criminal law.

Criminal law is the area of law that is perhaps most familiar to the layperson. Television shows that are based in criminal law blanket the television networks. Salacious criminal trials such as those for O.J. Simpson and Michael Jackson are plastered across the news. Ordinary citizens are asked to serve on jury trials that deal with people being tried for committing crimes. With this exposure, people have become familiar with the basic aspects of criminal law. This chapter will seek to supplement the paralegal student's basic knowledge of criminal law and provide an overview of this important area of the law.

Chapter Objectives

Introduce the concepts students should understand after reading each chapter as well as provide brief summaries describing the material to be covered.

A Day in the Life of a Real Paralegal

Presents scenarios depicting what a usual day is like for practicing paralegals and provides practical application designed to help students build a skill set to prepare for a career as a paralegal.

A DAY IN THE LIFE OF A REAL PARALEGAL

Fran loves working as a criminal law paralegal. Recently, she was given an assignment to research and investigate a client's (Pedro) killing of a police officer. Pedro was arrested and is currently being held downtown at the county jail. The supervising attorney gave Fran the following fact pattern based on the client's viewpoint of the killing:

Pedro was walking down the street on his way to the local grocery store to pick up some items for dinner. Pedro lives in a rough area downtown and often carries a small handgun, for which he has a license. He hears a commotion in the alley between two apartment buildings. Pedro walks slowly down the alley and sees a man and a woman struggling over a knife. The man is grabbing the woman when Pedro walks toward them. The man, holding the woman with one hand, turns toward Pedro with the knife and begins to walk toward Pedro. Pedro becomes afraid, takes out the gun, and shoots the man. The man turns out to be an undercover police officer who was apprehending the woman who had just robbed a liquor store and was fleeing the scene with a deadly weapon.

Fran immediately begins to outline the case with facts from Pedro. Fran must determine what issues are present including the charges pending against Pedro, any defenses Pedro may have, and finding any witnesses that haven't come forward as yet.

Research This

Gives students the opportunity to investigate issues more thoroughly through hands-on assignments designed to develop critical research skills.

RESEARCH THIS

The California Supreme Court has wrestled with the issue of when life begins in various cases. Two cases that involve this issue are *Keeler v. Superior Court*, 470 P.2d 617 (Cal. 1970), and *People v. Davis*, 872 P.2d 591 (Cal. 1994). Research both cases. How did the courts rule in each of these cases? When is a fetus considered a human being according to both courts?

Practice Tip

Presents different nuances of the law and caveats to rules to alert the student to the intricacies of the law.

PRACTICE TIP

Credit card fraud occurs when a defendant, intending to defraud the owner, obtains title to personal property through use of a stolen or an unauthorized credit card. Check fraud occurs when a defendant, intending to defraud the owner, obtains title to personal property through the use of stolen checks or a check drawn on an account without sufficient funds.

CASE FACT PATTERN

Timothy gets a thrill from starting fires. He loves to watch them burn. He has set numerous fires during his life just to watch them burn. Timothy lives in Southern California, which is an area that has been prone to violent wildfires that spread rapidly because of the Santa Ana winds that blow through the area from time to time. Parts of Southern California have been devastated by wildfires in the past, and these fires have caused significant damage and injuries.

Timothy has set wildfires before just for the thrill. One day, the Santa Ana winds began blowing heavily through the Riverside County area of Southern California. Some of the gusts clocked speeds of 80 mph. Timothy was thrilled with the weather conditions. He knew that if he set a fire today, it would spread rapidly due to the winds. The thought of the fire burning made his heart pound with excitement.

Armed with an incendiary device as well as gasoline, Timothy drove up into the Esperanza Canyon area of the county near the desert. The area was heavily vegetated with dry brush as the area had not received much rainfall the previous year. Timothy drove to a somewhat desolate area and started the fire. As he watched it burn, he felt the thrill of the destruction.

The winds whipped the fire up rapidly. Fueled by dry brush and high dry winds, the fire spread through thousands of acres. Firefighters made various stands against the fire, only to retreat as it advanced fiercely and rapidly. Five firefighters drove rapidly to a house to try to save it from destruction. On the way, the fire overtook them and they died. The fire charred over 40,200 acres, or 63 square miles, before it was finally contained and extinguished. Arson investigators were brought in to make a determination as to the cause of the fire. It was determined that the fire was caused by arson and Timothy had been seen by witnesses fleeing the scene.

After a thorough investigation by arson investigators as well as the FBI and local police, Timothy was arrested and charged with arson as well as felony murder due to the fact that the firefighters lost their lives as a result of Timothy's actions.

EYE ON ETHICS

The prosecutor is an officer of the court. As such, he/she is responsible to protect and serve the judicial system. A prosecutor is required to turn over evidence to the defense attorneys so the defense attorneys can properly prepare the defense of their client. Every person is entitled to a proper and adequate defense. If the prosecution fails to turn over evidence to the defense, the entire case against the defendant can be in jeopardy and may be dismissed. It is very important for prosecutors to act ethically and to be diligent in dealing with the turning over of evidence to the defense. To withhold evidence in a criminal matter is a serious ethical offense. Paralegals who work for prosecutors must be very aware of these requirements as it is the paralegal who is often gathering evidence that is ultimately going to be provided to the defense.

SURF'S UP

In order to learn more about complicity, visit the following Web sites:

- www.judiciary.state.n.j.us/criminal
- www.law.cornell.edu
- www.kentlaw.edu
- www.lawspirit.com
- www.freedictionary.com
- www.answers.com
- www.quizlaw.com.

Case Fact Pattern

Describes simple fact patterns and asks students to apply concepts learned from the chapter to understand the legal issues at hand.

Eye on Ethics

Recognizes the importance of bringing ethics to the forefront of paralegal education. It raises ethical issues facing paralegals and attorneys in today's legal environment.

Surf's Up

Presents students with numerous and varied Web sites to "surf" and gather additional information on the important legal concepts and issues discussed in each chapter.

Chapter Summary

Provides a comprehensive review of the key concepts presented in the chapter.

In order to convict a person of a crime, the prosecutor must prove the elements of the crime beyond a reasonable doubt. Each crime consists of four basic elements: actus reus—a guilty act; mens rea—a guilty mind; concurrence—a guilty act and guilty mind that exist at the same time; and causation—a harmful result.

An act involves physical behavior by the defendant. The mental process of the crime is not part of the act. Only the physical act that gives rise to the crime is considered the actus reus. The actus reus is known as the evil act of the defendant. The actus reus of a crime causes a social harm that constitutes the crime. The actus reus of a crime is important because it enables society to make inferences regarding the defendant's state of mind based on her actions. However, in order for the actions of the defendant to qualify as the actus reus of a crime, the defendant must have committed voluntary actions.

Voluntary acts are necessary in order for the defendant's actions to be considered a criminal act. A voluntary act is an act that is done with a conscious exercise of free will. It includes muscular contractions that are willed by the defendant. The law will not punish an involuntary act such as a reflexive movement or spasm. Likewise, criminal liability will not attach for acts performed while a defendant is unconscious or sleepwalking. Therefore, in order for a defendant to be blameworthy, she must have committed a voluntary act.

Summary

Key Terms

Used throughout the chapters are defined in the margin and provided as a list at the end of each chapter. A common set of definitions is used consistently across the McGraw-Hill paralegal titles.

Key Terms

Aggravated robbery	Owner
Asportation	Personal property
Carjacking	Possession
Commingling	Puffing
Conversion	Real property
Counterfeiting	Receiving stolen property
Embezzlement	Robbery
Extortion	Signatory
False pretenses	Tangible property
Fiduciary	Theft
Forgery	Title
Intangible property	Trade secret
Larceny	Trespassory taking
Larceny by trick	Uttering

Review Questions and Exercises

Emphasize critical-thinking and problem-solving skills as they relate to criminal law. The Review Questions focus on more specific legal concepts learned in each chapter. The Exercises introduce hypothetical situations and ask students to determine the correct answers using knowledge gained from studying topics in each chapter. Both sets of questions are found at the end of each chapter.

Review Questions

1. What is the definition of a homicide?
2. List the differences between justifiable and excusable homicide.
3. Why is it difficult to determine when life begins for purposes of murder?
4. Identify and define the different types of murder.
5. What is malice aforethought?
6. What is the purpose of the felony murder rule?
7. List the typical felonies that will qualify a killing as first degree murder under the felony murder rule.
8. Describe the difference(s) between first and second degree murder.
9. List the elements of manslaughter.
10. What is the difference between voluntary and involuntary manslaughter?
11. Define the *heat of passion*.
12. What is a cooling-off period and when does it apply?
13. What is premeditation and why is it important?
14. When is someone considered dead under the law?
15. What is a depraved heart killing?

PORTFOLIO ASSIGNMENT

When judging obscenity, the trial court may instruct the jury to apply "community standards" without specifically defining the term. States are allowed to establish statewide standards for judging obscenity. Research the standards for your home state and write a memo discussing them to include in your portfolio.

Vocabulary Builders

Instructions
Use the key terms from this chapter to fill in the answers to the crossword puzzle.
NOTE: When the answer is more than one word, leave a blank space between words.

ACROSS
1. The crime of inducing or encouraging another to commit a crime.
6. An incipient crime; an act that generally leads to a crime.
9. The act or process of enticing or persuading another person to take a certain course of action.
11. By agreement, parties work together to create an illegal result, to achieve an unlawful end.
12. Affecting or obligating both parties.
13. A single conspiracy in which each person is responsible for a distinct act within the overall plan.

DOWN
2. Identifiable commission or omission, an intentional tort requirement.
3. A conspiracy in which a single member or group separately agrees with two or more other members or groups.
4. The doctrine that an agreement by two or more persons to commit a particular crime cannot be prosecuted as a conspiracy if the crime could not be committed except by the actual number of participants involved.
5. One-sided, relating to only one of two or more persons or things.
7. Abandonment of effort to commit a crime.
8. To actually try to commit a crime and have the actual ability to do so.
10. To cease an activity.

CASE IN POINT

STATE of West Virginia, Plaintiff Below, Appellee
v.
Michael DOONAN, Defendant Below, Appellant
640 S.E.2d 71
Supreme Court of Appeals of
West Virginia.
No. 33052.
Submitted: Nov. 1, 2006.
Decided: Dec. 1, 2006.

Background: Defendant was convicted in the Magistrate Court of driving under influence of alcohol (DUI). He appealed. The Circuit Court, Wood County, George W. Hill, J., affirmed. Defendant appealed.

Holdings: The Supreme Court of Appeals, Davis, C.J., held that:

1. magistrate court could not impose a duty of reciprocal discovery on defendant based on statute governing a prosecutor's duties to disclose certain evidence to a defendant upon request;
2. defendant had no duty to provide his expert-witness list to the state, and thus magistrate court could not exclude defense expert from testifying at trial as sanction for defendant's failure to provide list;
3. error in magistrate court's exclusion of defense expert's testimony was reversible error;
4. copy of printout of defendant's breath-test results was inad̲missible under rule governing admissi̲bl̲e̲ ̲o̲f̲ duplicates; and

requested to perform three different field sobriety tests: walk and turn, horizontal gaze nystagmus, and the one-legged stand. After Mr. Doonan failed all three tests, he was transported to the police station where his blood alcohol content was measured by breathalyzer at .134, which was over the legal limit.

Mr. Doonan was charged with first offense of driving under the influence pursuant to W. Va. Code § 17C-5-2 (2004) (Repl. Vol. 2004). On November 5, 2004, Mr. Doonan was found guilty by a magistrate court jury of first offense of driving under the influence, and was sentenced to serve forty-eight hours in the North Central Regional Jail. Mr. Doonan appealed his conviction to the circuit court, arguing it was improper to exclude his expert witness and that it was error to admit an illegible copy of his DUI printout. The circuit court recognized that some errors existed in the underlying court, but found that the errors were harmless and that there was sufficient evidence to uphold Mr. Doonan's conviction. This appeal then followed.

[Text omitted]

Portfolio Assignments

Ask students to use the skills mastered in each chapter to reflect on major legal issues and create documents that become part of the paralegal's portfolio of legal research. The Portfolio Assignments are useful both as reference tools and as samples of work product.

Vocabulary Builders

Provides crossword puzzle in each chapter that uses the key terms and definitions from that chapter to help students become more proficient with the legal terminology.

Case in Point

At the end of each chapter exposes students to real-world examples and issues through cases chosen to expand on key topics discussed in chapter.

Brief Contents

Table of Contents

APPENDIXES

A

B

Chapter 1

Sources of Criminal Law

CHAPTER OBJECTIVES

Upon completion of this chapter, you will be able to:

- Understand the origins of criminal law.

- Explain the differences between civil and criminal law.

- Define the term *crime* and the theories of punishment associated with it.

- Identify the classifications of crimes.

- Discuss jurisdiction in criminal law.

Criminal law is the area of law that is perhaps most familiar to the layperson. Television shows that are based in criminal law blanket the television networks. Salacious criminal trials such as those for O.J. Simpson and Michael Jackson are plastered across the news. Ordinary citizens are asked to serve on jury trials that deal with people being tried for committing crimes. With this exposure, people have become familiar with the basic aspects of criminal law. This chapter will seek to supplement the paralegal student's basic knowledge of criminal law and provide an overview of this important area of the law.

 A DAY IN THE LIFE OF A REAL PARALEGAL

Tony is a public defender who is working for the county. Sarah is Tony's paralegal. Tony does not know what he would do without Sarah's assistance She is invaluable to him not just for her expertise, but also because she works well with his style of practicing law. For example, Tony was just in trial in the county courthouse on a fairly well-publicized murder case. Tony was arguing a point of law that had recently been cited in the Supreme Court and Tony felt that he was making his point to the judge. He was caught up in the heat of his argument when the judge interrupted him to inquire if Tony had a copy of the case that he was arguing. Tony explained to the judge that he did not but that he could get one. The judge recessed the trial for lunch and told Tony to bring a copy of the case back with him after lunch. Tony did not panic. He knew that Sarah would be there for him. Tony called Sarah on his cell phone. Sarah knew the case that Tony was referring to as she had just helped him research it a couple of days before. Sarah asked Tony, "When do you need this by?" Tony told her 20 minutes and that she needed to bring a copy of the case to the courthouse. After uttering some expletives, Sarah said she would see him in a few minutes. Sarah proceeded to rapidly pull the case up on her computer and print it out. She made several copies just in case Tony needed them, got in her car, and raced to the courthouse. Sarah arrived just as the judge was calling the court into session. Tony was relieved. He handed the judge and the opposing party the case. The next day, when the judge made her ruling, she stated that she was basing her ruling on the precedent set by the case that Tony had been arguing. Thanks to Sarah's fast reaction to Tony's request, Tony was successful in court.

ORIGINS OF CRIMINAL LAW

common law
Judge-made law; the ruling in a judicial opinion.

crime
Any act done in violation of those duties that an individual owes to the community, and for the breach of which the law has provided that the offender shall make satisfaction to the public.

statutory law
Derived from the Constitution in statutes enacted by the legislative branch of state or federal government; primary source of law consisting of the body of legislative law.

Constitution
The organic and fundamental law of a nation or state, which may be written or unwritten, establishing the character and conception of its government, laying the basic principles to which its internal life is to be conformed, organizing the government, regulating functions of departments, and prescribing the extent to which a nation or state can exercise its powers.

Bill of Rights
Set forth the fundamental individual rights government and law function to preserve and protect; the first ten amendments to the Constitution of the United States.

case law
Published court opinions of federal and state appellate courts; judge-created law in deciding cases, set forth in court opinions.

Criminal law develops from the customs and traditions of people in a society. Those customs and traditions represent the behavior that is considered acceptable for that society. Each society develops its own norms of behavior based on the customs and traditions of its people. Over time, these customs and traditions became more formalized as rules, and from these widely recognized rules developed **common law**. A common law **crime** is one that was defined and enforced by the judicial system of a society when there were no statutes to define the crime.

In the United States, most criminal law principles can trace their origins back to English common law (except in the state of Louisiana, where many of the state laws were based on French or Spanish legal concepts as a large proportion of the settlers in Louisiana were from those two countries). The State of Louisiana practices Napoleonic codified law. The English colonists brought their common laws with them when they came to the Americas. After the American Revolution, the initial 13 states adopted some of the English common laws, but most of the states enacted statutes that defined criminal acts and established criminal procedures. The statutes enacted by state legislatures have their roots in common law and form the basis of state statutes. A murder is still a murder; a burglary is still a burglary. However, the state legislatures codified and added elements to the state statutes in order to modernize them to fit the public need in that state. Criminal statutes and codes that have been enacted by the legislatures are referred to as **statutory law**. The United States also has enacted criminal statutes and these statutes can be located under the U.S. Criminal Code. Therefore, statutory law exists both at the state and federal levels.

Since the enactment of statutes by the initial 13 states, there are essentially no common law crimes in the United States. Federal criminal law is governed entirely by statute. All states have statutes, ordinances, or regulations that prohibit some type of action and label it criminal. State statutes are the primary source of criminal law and are usually referred to as penal codes.

 RESEARCH THIS

The codification of criminal law has been present for thousands of centuries. One of the first known criminal codes was known as the Code of Hammurabi. Research the Code of Hammurabi. What areas of law are covered in the code? How are victims addressed under the Code?

Statutory law is not the only law that governs criminal law. Both the U.S. **Constitution** as well as state constitutions set forth basic liberties to which all citizens are entitled. For example, the Sixth Amendment of the **Bill of Rights** guarantees a person who has been accused of a crime the right to a speedy trial. These rights as they are enumerated in the U.S. Constitution are available to all citizens of the United States. State constitutions also exist and the rights stated in each state's constitution are available to citizens of that particular state.

Another important area of criminal law is that of judiciary opinions or **case law**. Case law is law that is made based on the decisions of the court, usually the appellate or supreme courts of a state or of the federal government. A substantial portion of law is case law. Court or judiciary opinions are interpretations by the court of the meaning of constitutional provisions or statutes as they pertain to a particular case

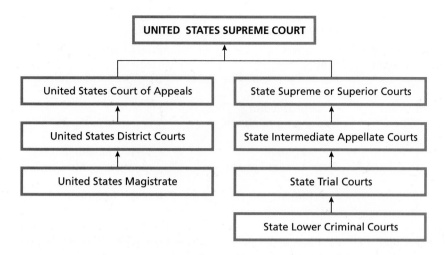

FIGURE 1.1
**Criminal Court
Structure**

**PRACTICE
TIP**

In 1962, the American Law Institute completed the Model Penal Code. The Model Penal Code was developed by a group of judges, lawyers, and scholars and was designed to codify as a single compilation the general criminal law of the United States. Since 1962, approximately two-thirds of the states have adopted criminal codes that reflect the guidelines set forth in the Model Penal Code. The Model Penal Code used now was last updated in 1981. It provides information on areas of criminal law and can be a great resource. However, the Model Penal Code is just that—a model. It is not to be cited as authority when writing legal documents or making legal arguments. It should be viewed as a reference and a guide.

being heard before them in court. Courts may be asked to interpret the meaning of the words in a code, the relationship between various codes as they pertain to the matter at hand, the legislative intent at the time the code was enacted, as well as whether or not a constitutional provision is violated by applying the code. The court will implement the doctrine of ***stare decisis*** when ruling on a particular matter. It will attempt to follow the decisions of higher courts that have ruled in similar matters. The doctrine of *stare decisis* advocates that accepting and applying established legal principles of cases that have been decided previously will help to provide security and certainty to the legal system. See Figure 1.1 for a Typical Criminal Law Structure.

Administrative law provides another source of criminal law. Administrative law is the body of law that regulates bureaucratic managerial procedures and is administered by the administrative agencies of the government. Administrative law defines the powers that are given to administrative agencies. This type of law will generally govern areas such as international trade, pollution, and taxation. For example, the Internal Revenue Service is an administrative agency that has been formed to govern the area of federal taxation. If you fail to pay your taxes, you have violated the administrative law as regulated by the IRS and you can be criminally prosecuted.

Court rules are used to provide standard procedures for handling the administration of cases as they proceed through the court system. They were developed to regulate processes in the court system that are not regulated by other types of law. Court rules regulate such items as how a case may be brought to court, the type of paperwork required during particular court processes as well as how a jury is selected. For most areas of court administration, a court rule exists to regulate it.

DIFFERENCES BETWEEN CRIMINAL AND CIVIL

Criminal law differs from civil law in many ways. The most important difference is that crimes involve acts that are considered public wrongs. Criminal acts violate the norms of socially acceptable behavior and, therefore, are considered to be acts against the public even if the act was committed against an individual. In civil law, a violation is considered a private wrong. A private wrong deals with a violation of relationships between people. In a criminal case, a jury must determine an accused's guilt or innocence. The jury determines if the accused is guilty of the crime **beyond a reasonable doubt** before rendering a verdict. The burden of proof is on the prosecutor to prove the guilt of the defendant. In a civil matter, a jury or judge may determine whether or not a defendant is liable for the **damages** or injuries sustained by the injured party.

stare decisis
From the Latin, "stand by the decision." The judicial process of adhering to prior case decisions.

FIGURE 1.2
Criminal and Civil Law Comparison

	Criminal	Civil
Type of violation	Public wrong	Private wrong
Category of responsibility	Guilt	Liability
Standard of proof	Beyond a reasonable doubt	By a preponderance of the evidence
Burden of proof	State/prosecutor	Plaintiff
Legal action initiation	Booking/arraignment, complaint	Filing of a lawsuit
Initiator	People/public	Private individual/entity
Resolution	Dismissal, judgment/ sentence	Judgment, settlement, dismissal
Remedy	Punishment	Money judgment

administrative law
The body of law governing administrative agencies, that is, those agencies created by Congress or state legislatures, such as the Social Security Administration.

court rules
Regulations with the force of law governing practice and procedure in the various courts.

beyond a reasonable doubt
The requirement for the level of proof in a criminal matter in order to convict or find the defendant guilty. It is a substantially higher and more-difficult-to-prove criminal matter standard.

damages
Money paid to compensate for loss or injury.

preponderance of the evidence
The weight or level of persuasion of evidence needed to find the defendant liable as alleged by the plaintiff in a civil matter.

arrest
The formal taking of a person, usually by a police officer, to answer criminal charges.

booking
Administrative step taken after an arrested person is brought to the police station that involves entry of the person's name, the crime for which the arrest was made, and other relevant facts on the police blotter.

arraignment
A court hearing where the information contained in an indictment is read to the defendant.

defendant
The party against whom a lawsuit is brought.

The jury will determine liability by a **preponderance of the evidence**. It is up to the plaintiff in a civil action to prove that the defendant is liable.

In order to end up in court, a criminal law action must be initiated by an **arrest**, **booking**, charging, and **arraignment** of the accused person. A civil law action is initiated by the filing of a lawsuit in the court. In criminal law, the **defendant** always has to show up in court. In a civil action, the defendant might never show up in court.

Criminal actions are brought against the accused by the People. For example, criminal actions could be brought by the People of the State of California or the People of the United States. The action is brought by the People as it represents a wrong against the public and the public is referred to as *the People*. This differs from civil actions that are brought by private individuals and entities against other private individuals or entities, for example, *John Smith v. Ted Anderson* or *Mildred McConogue v. Bright Corporation*.

The attorney who is prosecuting a criminal action is called a prosecutor, district attorney, or attorney general, or has some other similar title as a person who represents the public interest. In a civil action, the prosecuting attorney is called the attorney for the **plaintiff**.

The attorney for the defendant in a criminal action can be a private attorney or a public defender. The attorney for the defendant in a civil action is usually a private attorney and is referred to as the attorney for the defendant.

In criminal law, the resolution of the action ends with a **dismissal, conviction, sentencing,** or **plea bargain**. In civil law, the resolution of the action is by **judgment, settlement,** or dismissal.

In a criminal action, the defendant faces some type of punishment, be it jail time, community service, or probation. In a civil action, the defendant usually faces a money judgment. (See Figure 1.2.)

TORT VERSUS CRIME

A crime is not a tort. A crime is considered an offense against society as a whole. When a person is punished for committing a crime, he is punished for committing a wrong against society. For example, a person is being tried in state court for committing a murder. The prosecutor works for the state. The state represents the people or the public at large, not an individual. The interests of society are served when the offending person is punished for committing the crime. When a criminal case is being prosecuted, the rules of criminal procedure dictate how the case is to proceed. As stated previously, the burden of proof in a criminal case is on the prosecutor to prove the guilt of the defendant beyond a reasonable doubt. In a tort action, the burden of proof is the responsibility of the plaintiff and is by a preponderance of the evidence. The plaintiff must prove that the defendant is liable for their damage or injury.

A tort does have some similarities to crimes. For example, both are considered to be actions against societal utility or public policy. The intention of the perpetrator is

	Torts	Crimes
Purpose	To restore the victim back to whole/compensation	Punishment
Theory of offense	Offense to individual	Offense to society
Initiating party	The victim	The state
Verb/noun	Sue/suit	Try/trial
Category of responsibility	Liability	Guilt
Standard of proof	By a preponderance of evidence	Beyond a reasonable doubt
Procedural rules	Civil rules	Criminal rules
Domain of law	Civil	Criminal

FIGURE 1.3
Torts versus Crimes

plaintiff
The party initiating legal action.

dismissal
An order or judgment finally disposing of an action, suit, motion, or other without trial of the issues involved.

conviction
Results from a guilty finding by the jury in a criminal trial.

sentencing
The post-conviction stage of the criminal justice process in which the defendant is brought before the court for imposition of sentence.

plea bargain
The process whereby the accused and the prosecutor in a criminal case work out a mutually satisfactory disposition of the case subject to court approval.

judgment
The court's final decision regarding the rights and claims of the parties.

settlement
A negotiated termination of a case prior to a trial or jury verdict.

at the heart of an action for both crimes and torts. In a crime, the question is whether the intent was malicious. In a tort, the intent is looked at slightly differently to determine if it is blameworthy. (See Figure 1.3.)

DEFINING CRIME AND PUNISHMENT

Criminal law defines what constitutes a crime. Criminal law establishes what type of conduct is prohibited and what punishment may be imposed for violating its mandates. Criminal law establishes what degree of intent is required for criminal liability. In addition, criminal law sets out the defenses to criminal charges that may be asserted by the accused.

Crime is a broad term for violations of the law, punishable by the state, and codified by the legislatures. Crimes are typically distinguished by the following:

- A crime is an offense against society as a whole.
- Criminal defendants are prosecuted by the state, not by private parties.
- The penalties include fines, imprisonment, and, in some cases, death.
- Criminal law is primarily statutory law.
- A criminal act does not necessarily involve a specific victim.

It is possible for the same act to constitute both a crime and a civil action.

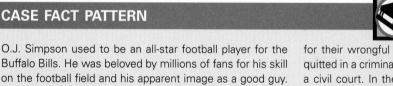

CASE FACT PATTERN

O.J. Simpson used to be an all-star football player for the Buffalo Bills. He was beloved by millions of fans for his skill on the football field and his apparent image as a good guy. After his professional football career had ended, O.J. became a sportscaster as well as a spokesperson for many companies. O.J. was married to Nicole Simpson, and together they had two children. O.J. and Nicole's marriage became stormy, and eventually they divorced. There were rumors of abusive behavior toward Nicole by O.J. One night, Nicole Simpson and her friend, Ron Goldman, were brutally murdered on the front steps of Nicole's home in Brentwood, California. After an infamous low-speed chase down the freeways of Southern California, O.J. Simpson turned himself in to the police and was arrested for the murders. What followed was one of the most widely publicized court trials in California history, consummating in the acquittal of O.J. Simpson for the murders. However, once Simpson was acquitted at the criminal trial, the families of Nicole Simpson and Ron Goldman sued O.J. Simpson in civil court for their wrongful deaths. After having been tried and acquitted in a criminal court, O.J. now faced similar charges in a civil court. In the criminal court, the jury could not find O.J. guilty beyond a reasonable doubt. Who could forget the famous line of Johnny Cochran, O.J.'s defense attorney, "If it doesn't fit, you must acquit," when referencing the fact that O.J.'s hand did not fit into the glove that was allegedly worn by the killer. In civil court, however, O.J.'s liability would be determined based on a different standard of proof: by a preponderance of the evidence. Under this standard, the jury had to determine if the evidence led them to conclude that it was more probable than not that O.J. committed the murders. O.J. was found liable by a preponderance of the evidence. The families of Nicole Simpson and Ron Goldman won a civil judgment against Simpson for millions of dollars for the wrongful deaths of Nicole and Ron. In the case of O.J., the same act led to both a crime and a civil action, but the two actions concluded very differently.

THEORIES AND JUSTIFICATIONS OF PUNISHMENT

deter
To turn aside, discourage, or prevent from acting.

The criminal law justice system uses punishment as a preventative tool. That is, it is hoped that the prospect of punishment (imprisonment, fines, even death) will **deter** criminal action. Several theories of punishment are used to penalize criminal behavior. Some of those theories are the following:

- Specific deterrence seeks to discourage individuals already convicted of crimes from committing future crimes. The arrest and conviction of an individual shows that individual that society has the capability to detect when a crime has been committed and is willing to punish those who commit crimes.

- General deterrence attempts to deter all members of society from engaging in criminal activity. A general deterrence punishment may deter persons other than the criminal from committing similar crimes because they would be in fear of incurring the same type of punishment.

incapacitation
Punishment by imprisonment, mutilation, or death.

- **Incapacitation**, also referred to as restraint, serves to prevent criminal conduct by restraining those who have committed crimes. Criminals are restrained in jail or prison or are sometimes executed. Criminals who are restrained are incapable of causing harm to the general public due to the restraint. This theory is often the rationale for long-term imprisonment of individuals who are believed to be beyond **rehabilitation**.

rehabilitation
Restoring a person to his or her former capacity.

- Rehabilitation is the theory that if society provides the opportunity, a criminal can be reformed into a person who, if returned to society, will conform his behavior to societal norms. The belief is that if the criminal is exposed to educational and vocational programs, treatment, counseling, and other measures, it is possible to alter the individual's behavior to conform to societal norms.

retribution
Punishment based on just deserts.

- **Retribution** is yet another method of punishing criminals. Punishment through the criminal justice system is society's method of avenging a wrong. The idea that one who commits a wrong must be punished has been handed down from ancient times. Therefore, punishing those who harm others has the effect of promoting social order by preventing undesirable conduct.

In the United States, more than one million people each year are arrested for crimes and enter the criminal justice system. Paralegals specializing in criminal law may work for prosecutors, public defenders, private law firms, or attorneys specializing in criminal defense.

CLASSIFICATION OF CRIMES

malum in se
An act that is prohibited because it is "evil in itself."

Crimes can be classified by the type of conduct that is involved. Crimes that are classified by conduct fall into one of two categories: **malum in se** or **malum prohibitum**.

Crimes that are considered malum in se are those crimes that are considered inherently evil. They are inherently evil either because they involve criminal intent as an element of the criminal action or because they involve a criminal action of **moral turpitude**. Examples of crimes that would be considered malum in se are murder, rape, robbery, burglary, arson, and larceny; they would be considered evils by society even if no law had been passed by the legislature making them prohibited.

malum prohibitum
An act that is prohibited by a rule of law.

moral turpitude
An act or behavior that gravely violates the sentiment or accepted standard of the community.

That a crime is considered malum prohibitum means that the conduct is prohibited, but not necessarily inherently evil. The action is wrong only because the law prohibits it. For example, it is against the law to fail to pay money into a parking meter, but the act is not inherently evil.

Crimes also can be categorized by the punishment that the accused faces if convicted of the crime. When crime based on punishment is categorized, the various crimes fall into the following classifications:

- Capital Felony—the penalty for a capital felony is death in states that have a death penalty statute or life in prison with or without the possibility of parole in states that do not have a death penalty statute.

- **Felony**—a serious crime that carries a penalty of imprisonment for more than one year in a state prison and/or the assessment of fines.

- Gross misdemeanor—crimes that are punishable by imprisonment for six months to one year in a state jail and/or a fine.

- **Misdemeanor**—a less serious crime for which the penalty includes imprisonment for a period of less than one year and/or a fine.

- Petty misdemeanor—also known as a violation or an infraction, usually not considered crimes and are punishable by fines. Petty offenses or **infractions** are the least serious kind of criminal or quasi-criminal wrong and include offenses such as running a stop sign or a building code violation.

JURISDICTION

Federal

Jurisdiction is the power of a court to exercise its authority over a person or the subject matter of a particular case. Jurisdiction over the subject matter refers to the authority that a court has to decide matters of that type. For example, tax courts have jurisdiction over cases that have the subject matter of taxes. If a court does not have jurisdiction, then it has no authority to act on the matter. Federal **jurisdiction** is limited to certain types of crimes. If a federal law defines a certain type of action as a crime, then it is a federal crime.

Generally, criminal jurisdiction exists in federal courts for crimes that occur outside the jurisdiction of a state, crimes involving interstate commerce or communications, crimes interfering with the operation of the federal government or its agents, and crimes directed at citizens or property located outside of the United States. The federal government has extensive power to enact criminal codes that govern conduct in the District of Columbia, the territories, and federal courthouses, national parks, and other areas controlled by the federal government. The federal government also has the power to criminalize conduct by U.S. citizens abroad such as for treason. The federal government's authority to criminalize conduct also extends to ships and airplanes. For example, after the September 11, 2001, terrorist attacks on the World Trade Center and the

felony
A crime punishable by more than a year in prison or death.

misdemeanor
A lesser crime punishable by less than a year in jail and/or a fine.

infraction
A violation of a statute for which the only sentence authorized is a fine and for which violation is expressly designated as an infraction.

jurisdiction
The power or authority of the court to hear a particular classification of case.

 EYE ON ETHICS

Ethics is a very important part of law. As a legal assistant, you are an extension of the attorney who is your supervisor. It is always important to conduct yourself in the most ethical manner possible. Although unethical conduct by a legal assistant does not necessarily result in punishment to the legal assistant, it can lead to disbarment or other disciplinary action of the supervising attorney. Always conduct yourself under the same codes of ethical conduct that

apply to the attorneys for whom you work. For example, it is unethical for a paralegal to discuss the facts or nature of the cases that they are working on. This is especially true in the area of criminal law. Why? Because information of potential crime(s) that a client may or may not have committed is private information and could prejudice the client's case. It is important to keep all information confidential.

Pentagon, the federal government began to place air marshals on airlines in order to arrest and prosecute persons who violate federal statutes while in the air.

State

Every state has an inherent authority to promote and protect the health, safety, and welfare of its citizens. Typically, the state in which the crime was committed assumes jurisdiction over the accused and prosecutes the accused within its court system. The following are instances in which a state can assume jurisdiction over an accused:

- The offense is committed wholly or partly within the state.
- The conduct outside the state constitutes an attempt or conspiracy to commit an offense within the state, plus the offense is inside the state.
- The conduct within the state constitutes an attempt, solicitation, or conspiracy to commit, in another jurisdiction, an offense under the laws of both the state and such other jurisdiction.
- An offense based on the omission of performance of a duty imposed by the law of a state is committed within the state, regardless of the location of the accused at the time of the omission of the act.

A DAY IN THE LIFE OF A REAL PARALEGAL

Paralegals who have knowledge of criminal law can find employment in a variety of capacities. Many work for private attorneys who are hired by their clients to represent them in criminal matters. District attorneys, prosecuting attorneys, and attorney general offices all hire paralegals to assist with legal work. A typical job duties description for a criminal paralegal might look like the following:

PRIMARY DUTIES AND RESPONSIBILITIES

- Provides assistance in interviewing and research for attorneys.
- Conducts interviews with witnesses to prepare them for testifying in court.
- Compiles list of witnesses and submits for subpoenas to ensure appropriate witnesses are present at next hearing.
- Contacts witnesses to ensure attendance in court.
- Attends court hearings to assist attorneys with research and witnesses.
- Assists in drafting pleadings to have appropriate orders and documents ready for hearing.
- Coordinates the scheduling of expert witnesses to ensure testimony of appropriate experts at hearing.
- Performs preliminary screening and review of criminal complaints to prepare criminal charges in cases.

SUPERVISORY RESPONSIBILITIES

This job has limited supervisory responsibilities. Provides work direction, training, and work oversight to law interns and clerical staff.

Criminal law developed from the customs and traditions of people in a society. The **Summary** customs and traditions represented the behavior that was considered acceptable for that society. Each society developed its own norms of behavior based on the customs and traditions of the people. Over time, these customs and traditions became more formalized rules and from these widely recognized rules developed common law. A common law crime is one that was created and enforced by the judicial system of a society when there were no statutes that defined the crime.

Criminal law differs from civil law in many ways. The most important distinction is that crimes involve acts that are considered public wrongs. Criminal acts violate the norms of socially acceptable behavior and, therefore, are considered to be acts against the public even if the act was committed against an individual. In civil law, a violation is considered a private wrong. A private wrong deals with a violation of relationships between people. In a criminal case, a jury must determine an accused's guilt or innocence. The jury determines if the accused is guilty of the crime "beyond a reasonable doubt" before rendering a verdict. In a civil matter, a jury or judge may determine whether or not a defendant is liable for the damages or injuries sustained by the injured party. The jury will determine liability by a "preponderance of the evidence."

Criminal law defines what constitutes a crime. Criminal law establishes what type of conduct is prohibited and what punishment may be imposed for violating its mandates. Criminal law establishes what degree of intent is required for criminal liability. In addition, criminal law sets out the defenses to criminal charges that may be asserted by the accused.

Specific deterrence seeks to discourage individuals already convicted of crimes from committing future crimes. The arrest and conviction of an individual show that individual that society has the capability to detect when a crime has been committed and is willing to punish those who commit crimes.

General deterrence attempts to deter all members of society from engaging in criminal activity. A general deterrence punishment may deter persons other than the criminal from committing similar crimes because they would be in fear of incurring the same type of punishment.

Incapacitation, also referred to as restraint, serves to prevent criminal conduct by restraining those who have committed crimes. Criminals are restrained in jail or prison or are sometimes executed. Criminals who are restrained are incapable of causing harm to the general public due to the restraint. This theory is often the rationale for long-term imprisonment of individuals who are believed to be beyond rehabilitation.

Rehabilitation is the theory that if society provides the opportunity, a criminal can be reformed into a person who, if returned to society, will conform her behavior to societal norms. The belief is that if the criminal is exposed to educational and vocational programs, treatment, counseling, and other measures, it is possible to alter the individual's behavior to conform to societal norms.

Retribution is yet another method of punishing criminals. Punishment through the criminal justice system is society's method of avenging a wrong. The idea that one who commits a wrong must be punished has been handed down from ancient times. Therefore, punishing those who harm others has the effect of promoting social order by preventing undesirable conduct.

Malum in se crimes are those crimes that are considered inherently evil either because they involve criminal intent as an element of the criminal action or because they involve a criminal action of moral turpitude. Examples of crimes that would be considered malum in se are murder, rape, robbery, burglary, arson, and larceny. They would be considered evils by society even if no law had been passed by the legislature making them prohibited.

Malum prohibitum crimes involve conduct that is prohibited, but not necessarily inherently evil. The action is wrong only because the law prohibits it. For example, it is against the law to fail to pay money into a parking meter, but the act is not inherently evil.

A capital felony is a crime for which the penalty is death in states that have a death penalty statute or life in prison without the possibility of parole in states that do not have a death penalty statute.

A felony is a serious crime that carries a penalty of imprisonment for more than one year in a state prison and/or the assessment of fines.

A gross misdemeanor is a crime that is punishable by imprisonment for six months to one year in a state jail and/or a fine.

A misdemeanor is a less serious crime for which the penalty includes imprisonment for a period of up to six months and/or a fine.

A petty misdemeanor, also known as a violation or an infraction, is not usually considered a crime and is punishable by fines. Petty offenses or infractions are the least serious kind of criminal or quasi-criminal wrong and include offenses such as a traffic ticket or building code violation.

Generally, criminal jurisdiction exists in federal courts for crimes that occur outside the jurisdiction of a state, crimes involving interstate commerce or communications, crimes interfering with the operation of the federal government or its agents, and crimes directed at citizens or property located outside of the United States. The federal government has extensive power to enact criminal codes that govern conduct in the District of Columbia, the territories, and federal courthouses, national parks, and other areas controlled by the federal government. The federal government also has the power to criminalize conduct by U.S. citizens abroad such as for treason. The federal government's authority to criminalize conduct also extends to ships and airplanes.

Every state has an inherent authority to promote and protect the health, safety, and welfare of its citizens. Typically, the state in which the crime was committed assumes jurisdiction over the accused and prosecutes the accused within its court system.

Key Terms

Administrative law	Incapacitation
Arraignment	Infraction
Arrest	Judgment
Beyond a reasonable doubt	Jurisdiction
Bill of Rights	Malum in se
Booking	Malum prohibitum
Case law	Misdemeanor
Common law	Moral turpitude
Constitution	Plaintiff
Conviction	Plea bargain
Court rules	Preponderance of the evidence
Crime	Rehabilitation
Damages	Retribution
Defendant	Sentencing
Deter	Settlement
Dismissal	*Stare decisis*
Felony	Statutory law

1. Where did common law criminal law first originate?
2. What is the function of criminal law in society?
3. List two types of crimes, not referenced in the text, that are malum prohibitum.
4. What is a crime?
5. What are the differences between a felony and a misdemeanor?
6. Define retribution and give an example.
7. What is the difference between general deterrence and specific deterrence?
8. What does the standard "beyond a reasonable doubt" mean? Provide an example.
9. How does the standard of proof of preponderance of the evidence differ from beyond a reasonable doubt?
10. List three job titles of attorneys who might prosecute a criminal case.

1. The Model Penal Code is not a source of law but a guide to criminal law. Locate the Model Penal Code. Research the definitions of a crime, murder, and sentencing in the Model Penal Code. Cite the sections of the Model Penal Code where you find those definitions.
2. You have learned how some actions can lead to both a criminal and a civil action against the defendant. Using whatever source available to you, locate another case that led to both a criminal prosecution and a civil action against the accused. Prepare an outline regarding the facts and findings of your case.
3. Locate the state statute in your state that imposes the strictest penalty for a criminal crime. Cite the statute and write a brief analysis of what it says.
4. Why is prosecuting the police officers in the Rodney King case in both federal and state court not double jeopardy? What U.S. constitutional amendment addresses the issue of double jeopardy?
5. Research three examples as to what may constitute a case belonging in federal court/jurisdiction rather than state jurisdiction.
6. Name three crimes that would belong to the classification of statutory criminals? What makes them statutory crimes?
7. Are criminals imprisoned for punishment or for rehabilitation? Explain your answer with supporting information.
8. What is malice aforethought? What is a layman's explanation for what malice means?

PORTFOLIO ASSIGNMENT

The punishment set forth for a given crime is different in each state. One of the most heinous of crimes is murder with special circumstances, meaning a grievous murder that carries the harshest penalty. Some states punish this type of criminal with life imprisonment without the possibility of parole. Some states are death penalty states and will put this type of criminal to death. Research your state. Is your state one that imposes capital punishment?

Vocabulary Builders

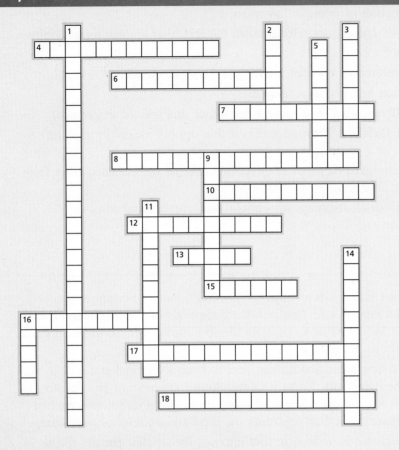

Instructions

Use the key terms from this chapter to fill in the answers to the crossword puzzle.

NOTE: When the answer is more than one word, leave a blank space between the words.

ACROSS

4. – the process whereby the accused and the prosecutor in a criminal case work out a mutually satisfactory disposition of the case subject to court approval.
6. a wrong in itself, an act or case involving illegality from the very nature of the transaction, upon principles of natural, moral, and public law.
7. an agreement by which parties having disputed matters between them reach or ascertain what is coming from one to another.
8. a wrong prohibited; an act which is not inherently immoral, but becomes so because its commission is expressly forbidden by positive law.
10. – procedure whereby the accused is brought before the court to plead to the criminal charge against him in the indictment or information.
12. the post-conviction stage of the criminal justice process in which the defendant is brought before the court for imposition of sentence.
13. a positive or negative act in violation of penal law.
15. a crime of a graver or more serious nature than those designated as misdemeanors.
16. the accused in a criminal case.
17. an act or behavior that gravely violates the sentiment or accepted standard of the community.
18. restoring a person to his or her former capacity.

DOWN

1. the facts proven, must by virtue of their probative force, establish guilt.
2. to deprive a person of his liberty by legal authority.
3. – administrative step taken after an arrested person is brought to the police station, which involves entry of the person's name, the crime for which the arrest was made, and other relevant facts on the police blotter.
5. the official and authentic decision of a court of justice upon the respective rights and claims of the parties to an action or suit therein litigated and submitted to its determination.
9. a person who brings an action
11. punishment based on just deserts
14. offenses lower than felonies and generally those punishable by fine, penalty, forfeiture or imprisonment otherwise than in penitentiary.
16. to turn aside, discourage, or prevent from acting.

GIDEON V. WAINWRIGHT, 372 U.S. 335 (1963)

GIDEON v. WAINWRIGHT, CORRECTIONS DIRECTOR.
CERTIORARI TO THE SUPREME COURT OF FLORIDA.
No. 155.
Argued January 15, 1963.
Decided March 18, 1963.

Charged in a Florida State Court with a noncapital felony, petitioner appeared without funds and without counsel and asked the Court to appoint counsel for him; but this was denied on the ground that the state law permitted appointment of counsel for indigent defendants in capital cases only. Petitioner conducted his own defense about as well as could be expected of a layman; but he was convicted and sentenced to imprisonment. Subsequently, he applied to the State Supreme Court for a writ of habeas corpus, on the ground that his conviction violated his rights under the Federal Constitution. The State Supreme Court denied all relief. Held: The right of an indigent defendant in a criminal trial to have the assistance of counsel is a fundamental right essential to a fair trial, and petitioner's trial and conviction without the assistance of counsel violated the Fourteenth Amendment. *Betts v. Brady*, 316 U.S. 455, overruled. Pp. 336–345.

Reversed and cause remanded.

MR. JUSTICE BLACK delivered the opinion of the Court.

Petitioner was charged in a Florida state court with having broken and entered a poolroom with intent to commit a misdemeanor. This offense is a felony under [372 U.S. 335, 337] Florida law. Appearing in court without funds and without a lawyer, petitioner asked the court to appoint counsel for him, whereupon the following colloquy took place:

> "The COURT: Mr. Gideon, I am sorry, but I cannot appoint Counsel to represent you in this case. Under the laws of the State of Florida, the only time the Court can appoint Counsel to represent a Defendant is when that person is charged with a capital offense. I am sorry, but I will have to deny your request to appoint Counsel to defend you in this case.
>
> "The DEFENDANT: The United States Supreme Court says I am entitled to be represented by Counsel."

Put to trial before a jury, Gideon conducted his defense about as well as could be expected from a layman. He made an opening statement to the jury, cross-examined the State's witnesses, presented witnesses in his own defense, declined to testify himself, and made a short argument "emphasizing his innocence to the charge contained in the Information filed in this case." The jury returned a verdict of guilty, and petitioner was sentenced to serve five years in the state prison. Later, petitioner filed in the Florida Supreme Court this habeas corpus petition attacking his conviction and sentence on the ground that the trial court's refusal to appoint counsel for him denied him rights "guaranteed by the Constitution and the Bill of Rights by the United States Government." Treating the petition for habeas corpus as properly before it, the State Supreme Court, "upon consideration thereof" but without an opinion, denied all relief. Since 1942, when *Betts v. Brady*, 316 U.S. 455, was decided by a divided [372 U.S. 335, 338] Court, the problem of a defendant's federal constitutional right to counsel in a state court has been a continuing source of controversy and litigation in both state and federal courts. To give this problem another review here, we granted certiorari. 370 U.S. 908. Since Gideon was proceeding in forma pauperis, we appointed counsel to represent him and requested both sides to discuss in their briefs and oral arguments the following: "Should this Court's holding in *Betts v. Brady*, 316 U.S. 455, be reconsidered?"

I.

The facts upon which Betts claimed that he had been unconstitutionally denied the right to have counsel appointed to assist him are strikingly like the facts upon which Gideon here bases his federal constitutional claim. Betts was indicated [sic] for robbery in a Maryland state court. On arraignment, he told the trial judge of his lack of funds to hire a lawyer and asked the court to appoint one for him. Betts was advised that it was not the practice in that county to appoint counsel for indigent defendants except in murder and rape cases. He then pleaded not guilty, had witnesses summoned, cross-examined the State's witnesses, examined his own, and chose not to testify himself. He was found guilty by the judge, sitting without a jury, and sentenced to eight years in prison. [372 U.S. 335, 339] Like Gideon, Betts sought release by habeas corpus, alleging that he had been denied the right to assistance of counsel in violation of the Fourteenth Amendment. Betts was denied any relief, and on review this Court affirmed. It was held that a refusal to appoint counsel for an indigent defendant charged with a felony did not necessarily violate the Due Process Clause of the Fourteenth Amendment, which for reasons given the Court deemed to be the only applicable federal constitutional provision. The Court said:

> "Asserted denial [of due process] is to be tested by an appraisal of the totality of facts in a given case. That which may, in one setting, constitute a denial of fundamental fairness, shocking to the universal sense of justice, may, in other circumstances, and in the light of other considerations, fall short of such denial." 316 U.S., at 462.

Treating due process as "a concept less rigid and more fluid than those envisaged in other specific and particular provisions of the Bill of Rights," the Court held that refusal to appoint counsel under the particular facts and circumstances in the Betts case was not so "offensive to the common and fundamental ideas of fairness" as to amount to a denial of due process. Since the facts and circumstances of the two cases are so nearly indistinguishable, we think the *Betts v. Brady* holding if left standing would require us to reject Gideon's claim that the Constitution guarantees him the assistance of counsel. Upon full reconsideration we conclude that *Betts v. Brady* should be overruled.

II.

The Sixth Amendment provides, "In all criminal prosecutions, the accused shall enjoy the right . . . to have the Assistance of Counsel for his defence." We have construed [372 U.S. 335, 340] this to mean that in federal courts counsel must be provided for defendants unable to employ counsel unless the right is competently and intelligently waived. Betts argued that this right is extended to indigent defendants in state courts by the Fourteenth Amendment. In response the Court stated that, while the Sixth Amendment laid down "no rule for the conduct of the States, the question recurs whether the constraint laid by the Amendment upon the national courts expresses a rule so fundamental and essential to a fair trial, and so, to due process of law, that it is made obligatory upon the States by the Fourteenth Amendment." 316 U.S., at 465. In order to decide whether the Sixth Amendment's guarantee of counsel is of this fundamental nature, the Court in *Betts* set out and considered "[r]elevant data on the subject . . . afforded by constitutional and statutory provisions subsisting in the colonies and the States prior to the inclusion of the Bill of Rights in the national Constitution, and in the constitutional, legislative, and judicial history of the States to the present date." 316 U.S., at 465. On the basis of this historical data the Court concluded that "appointment of counsel is not a fundamental right, essential to a fair trial." 316 U.S., at 471. It was for this reason the *Betts* Court refused to accept the contention that the Sixth Amendment's guarantee of counsel for indigent federal defendants was extended to or, in the words of that Court, "made obligatory upon the States by the Fourteenth Amendment." Plainly, had the Court concluded that appointment of counsel for an indigent criminal defendant was "a fundamental right, essential to a fair trial," it would have held that the Fourteenth Amendment requires appointment of counsel in a state court, just as the Sixth Amendment requires in a federal court. [372 U.S. 335, 341]

We think the Court in Betts had ample precedent for acknowledging that those guarantees of the Bill of Rights which are fundamental safeguards of liberty immune from federal abridgment are equally protected against state invasion by the Due Process Clause of the Fourteenth Amendment. This same principle was recognized, explained, and applied in *Powell v. Alabama*, 287 U.S. 45 (1932), a case upholding the right of counsel, where the Court held that despite sweeping language to the contrary in *Hurtado v. California*, 110 U.S. 516 (1884), the Fourteenth Amendment "embraced" those "'fundamental principles of liberty and justice which lie at the base of all our

civil and political institutions,'" even though they had been "specifically dealt with in another part of the federal Constitution." 287 U.S., at 67. In many cases other than *Powell* and *Betts*, this Court has looked to the fundamental nature of original Bill of Rights guarantees to decide whether the Fourteenth Amendment makes them obligatory on the States. Explicitly recognized to be of this "fundamental nature" and therefore made immune from state invasion by the Fourteenth, or some part of it, are the First Amendment's freedoms of speech, press, religion, assembly, association, and petition for redress of grievances. For the same reason, though not always in precisely the same terminology, the Court has made obligatory on the States the Fifth Amendment's command that [372 U.S. 335, 342] private property shall not be taken for public use without just compensation, the Fourth Amendment's prohibition of unreasonable searches and seizures, and the Eighth's ban on cruel and unusual punishment. On the other hand, this Court in *Palko v. Connecticut*, 302 U.S. 319 (1937), refused to hold that the Fourteenth Amendment made the double jeopardy provision of the Fifth Amendment obligatory on the States. In so refusing, however, the Court, speaking through Mr. Justice Cardozo, was careful to emphasize that "immunities that are valid as against the federal government by force of the specific pledges of particular amendments have been found to be implicit in the concept of ordered liberty, and thus, through the Fourteenth Amendment, become valid as against the states" and that guarantees "in their origin . . . effective against the federal government alone" had by prior cases "been taken over from the earlier articles of the federal bill of rights and brought within the Fourteenth Amendment by a process of absorption." 302 U.S., at 324–325, 326.

We accept *Betts v. Brady*'s assumption, based as it was on our prior cases, that a provision of the Bill of Rights which is "fundamental and essential to a fair trial" is made obligatory upon the States by the Fourteenth Amendment. We think the Court in Betts was wrong, however, in concluding that the Sixth Amendment's guarantee of counsel is not one of these fundamental rights. Ten years before *Betts v. Brady*, this Court, after full consideration of all the historical data examined in *Betts*, had unequivocally declared that "the right to the aid of [372 U. S. 335, 343] counsel is of this fundamental character." *Powell v. Alabama*, 287 U.S. 45, 68 (1932). While the Court at the close of its Powell opinion did by its language, as this Court frequently does, limit its holding to the particular facts and circumstances of that case, its conclusions about the fundamental nature of the right to counsel are unmistakable. Several years later, in 1936, the Court reemphasized what it had said about the fundamental nature of the right to counsel in this language:

> "We concluded that certain fundamental rights, safeguarded by the first eight amendments against federal action, were also safeguarded against state action by the due process of law clause of the Fourteenth Amendment, and among them the fundamental right of the accused to the aid of counsel in a criminal prosecution." *Grosjean v. American Press Co.*, 297 U.S. 233, 243–244 (1936).

And again in 1938 this Court said:

> "[The assistance of counsel] is one of the safeguards of the Sixth Amendment deemed necessary to insure

fundamental human rights of life and liberty. . . . The Sixth Amendment stands as a constant admonition that if the constitutional safeguards it provides be lost, justice will not 'still be done.'" *Johnson v. Zerbst*, 304 U.S. 458, 462 (1938). To the same effect, see *Avery v. Alabama*, 308 U.S. 444 (1940), and *Smith v. O'Grady*, 312 U.S. 329 (1941).

In light of these and many other prior decisions of this Court, it is not surprising that the *Betts* Court, when faced with the contention that "one charged with crime, who is unable to obtain counsel, must be furnished counsel by the State," conceded that "[e]xpressions in the opinions of this court lend color to the argument. . . ." 316 U.S., at 462–463. The fact is that in deciding as it did—that "appointment of counsel is not a fundamental right, [372 U.S. 335, 344] essential to a fair trial"—the Court in *Betts v. Brady* made an abrupt break with its own well-considered precedents. In returning to these old precedents, sounder we believe than the new, we but restore constitutional principles established to achieve a fair system of justice. Not only these precedents but also reason and reflection require us to recognize that in our adversary system of criminal justice, any person haled into court, who is too poor to hire a lawyer, cannot be assured a fair trial unless counsel is provided for him. This seems to us to be an obvious truth. Governments, both state and federal, quite properly spend vast sums of money to establish machinery to try defendants accused of crime. Lawyers to prosecute are everywhere deemed essential to protect the public's interest in an orderly society. Similarly, there are few defendants charged with crime, few indeed, who fail to hire the best lawyers they can get to prepare and present their defenses. That government hires lawyers to prosecute and defendants who have the money hire lawyers to defend are the strongest indications of the widespread belief that lawyers in criminal courts are necessities, not luxuries. The right of one charged with crime to counsel may not be deemed fundamental and essential to fair trials in some countries, but it is in ours. From the very beginning, our state and national constitutions and laws have laid great emphasis on procedural and substantive safeguards designed to assure fair trials before impartial tribunals in which every defendant stands equal before the law. This noble ideal cannot be realized if the poor man charged with crime has to face his accusers without a lawyer to assist him. A defendant's need for a lawyer is nowhere better stated than in the moving words of Mr. Justice Sutherland in *Powell v. Alabama*:

"The right to be heard would be, in many cases, of little avail if it did not comprehend the right to be [372 U.S. 335, 345] heard by counsel. Even the intelligent and educated layman has small and sometimes no skill in the science of law. If charged with crime, he is incapable, generally, of determining for himself whether the indictment is good or bad. He is unfamiliar with the rules of evidence. Left without the aid of counsel he may be put on trial without a proper charge, and convicted upon incompetent evidence, or evidence irrelevant to the issue or otherwise inadmissible. He lacks both the skill and knowledge adequately to prepare his defense, even though he have a perfect one. He requires the guiding hand of counsel at every step in the proceedings against him. Without it, though he be not guilty, he faces the danger of conviction because he does not know how to establish his innocence." 287 U.S., at 68–69.

The Court in *Betts v. Brady* departed from the sound wisdom upon which the Court's holding in *Powell v. Alabama* rested. Florida, supported by two other States, has asked that *Betts v. Brady* be left intact. Twenty-two States, as friends of the Court, argue that *Betts* was "an anachronism when handed down" and that it should now be overruled. We agree.

The judgment is reversed and the cause is remanded to the Supreme Court of Florida for further action not inconsistent with this opinion.

Reversed.

Source: Reprinted with the permission of Westlaw.

Chapter 2

Constitutional Requirements for Criminal Procedure

CHAPTER OBJECTIVES

Upon completion of this chapter, you will be able to:

- Identify the types of searches that can be conducted without a warrant.
- Discuss the difference between reasonable suspicion and probable cause as it relates to the Fourth Amendment.
- Recognize the Fifth Amendment *Miranda* requirement.
- Understand the Sixth Amendment right to counsel.
- Learn about the Eighth Amendment cruel and unusual punishment provision.

Many of the basic fundamental rights that we take for granted stem from the U.S. Constitution. Our founding fathers believed that many fundamental rights that were denied the citizens of Britain needed to be protected for those in the new nation. Rights such as the right to be represented by legal counsel and the right to have a speedy trial by jury are all engrained into the Constitution. Other rights such as the right to privacy have been thought to be guaranteed as one of the body of rights that are implied from the Constitution. This chapter will provide a brief examination of some of these basic rights that help to protect a person who has been accused of criminal activity.

Bill of Rights
Set forth the fundamental individual rights government and law function to preserve and protect; the first ten amendments to the Constitution of the United States.

Due Process Clause
Refers to two aspects of the law: procedural, in which a person is guaranteed fair procedures, and substantive, which protects a person's property from unfair governmental interference or taking.

THE CONSTITUTION

The first ten amendments to the U.S. Constitution are called the **Bill of Rights**. They concern rights that apply to a person who has been accused of criminal activity. These rights are designed to protect criminal defendants as they proceed through the process that people accused of crimes must go so that they have the opportunity to prove their innocence. Most of these rights are applicable to the states through what is known as the **Due Process Clause** of the Fourteenth Amendment. The following are some of the rights set forth by the Bill of Rights. These rights are binding on the states as well as the federal government:

- First Amendment: Free speech, freedom of the press, and freedom of assembly.
- Fourth Amendment: Prohibition against unreasonable searches and seizures, and the exclusionary rule.

Amendment	Protection
First Amendment	Freedom of religion
	Freedom of speech
	Freedom of the press
	Freedom of assembly
	Freedom of petition
Second Amendment	Right to keep and bear arms
	Right to maintain a militia
Third Amendment	Right to quartering soldiers during wartime
Fourth Amendment	Rights against unreasonable and unwarranted searches and seizures
	Conditions for issuing lawful search warrants by officials
	Right of individual security
	Probable cause for issuing of warrants
Fifth Amendment	Person cannot be held to answer for a serious crime unless by indictment by a Grand Jury except during wartime
	Double jeopardy
	Self-incrimination
	Assistance of counsel during interrogation
Sixth Amendment	Right to a speedy trial before a jury
	Right to receive information regarding accusations
	Right to face witnesses in court
	Right to present favorable witnesses
	Right to counsel during criminal procedures
Seventh Amendment	Right to jury trial for civil cases where the value in controversy exceeds $20
Eighth Amendment	No excessive fines
	No cruel or unusual punishments
	No excessive bail
Ninth Amendment	Guarantee of unspecified rights
Tenth Amendment	Powers reserved to states and people

FIGURE 2.1   **Bill of Rights and Its Protections**

- Fifth Amendment:
  - Privilege against compulsory **self-incrimination**.
  - Prohibition against double jeopardy.
- Sixth Amendment:
  - Right to a speedy trial.
  - Right to a public trial.
  - Right to a trial by jury.
  - Right to confront witnesses.
  - Right to compulsory process for obtaining witnesses.
  - Right to assistance of counsel in felony cases and in misdemeanor cases in which imprisonment is imposed.
- Eighth Amendment: Prohibition against cruel and unusual punishment.

  (See Figure 2.1.)

EXCLUSIONARY RULE

The **exclusionary rule** can be traced back to the Fourth Amendment. The rule is a remedy for violations of a defendant's Fourth, Fifth, and Sixth Amendment rights. The exclusionary rule is a judge-made doctrine that was a result of the 1914 Supreme

---

PRACTICE TIP

If you intend to become a paralegal working in the criminal law field, begin your networking with criminal attorneys and the criminal courts right away. Many attorneys will not hire inexperienced paralegals for the criminal field as the practice of criminal law involves the lives of victims and defendants and potentially major punishments. Because of this, many attorneys shy away from hiring paralegals who have just finished their paralegal training.

self-incrimination
Acts or declarations either as testimony at trial or prior to trial by which one implicates himself or herself in a crime.

exclusionary rule
Circumstances surrounding the seizure do not meet warrant requirements or exceptions; items seized deemed *fruit of the poisonous tree* are excluded from trial evidence.

Court's decision in the case of *Weeks v. United States,* 232 U.S. 383 (1914), where the Court held that evidence that had been obtained by federal officials in violation of a defendant's Fourth Amendment rights would not be admissible in federal criminal trials. In the case of *Mapp v. Ohio,* 367 U.S. 643 (1961), the Court held that the states were also bound by the exclusionary rule under the Fourteenth Amendment and could not use evidence obtained by an illegal search or seizure in criminal trials against the person whose rights are in jeopardy of being violated by the use of such evidence. Under the rule, illegally obtained evidence is inadmissible at trial, and all evidence obtained or derived from the use of that illegally obtained evidence also must be excluded (the "fruit of the poisonous tree").

fruit of the poisonous tree
Evidence tainted based on illegal seizure may not be used in a trial.

However, there are exceptions to the **fruit of the poisonous tree** doctrine. Some of the most noted exceptions are listed below:

- Evidence is obtained from a source that is independent of the original evidence that was obtained illegally.

- There is an intervening act of free will by the defendant (e.g., the defendant is illegally arrested but is released and later returns to confess to a crime).

- The evidence inevitably would have been discovered even if it had not been obtained illegally. For example, the prosecution can show that the police would have discovered the evidence anyway and it did not matter whether or not they acted unconstitutionally in obtaining it. However, Texas does not recognize this exception.

- The good faith exception is based on the principle that if a law enforcement officer was acting with a reasonable belief in good faith that his actions were legally justified, then the evidence would not be excluded based on any constitutional violation.

If illegal evidence is admitted at trial and the defendant is convicted, then the conviction can be overturned unless the prosecution can demonstrate beyond a reasonable doubt that the error that was committed by admitting the illegally obtained evidence was harmless and did not prejudice the defendant. A defendant is entitled to have the admissibility of evidence decided as a matter of law by a judge out of the hearing of the jury so that the evidence will not unduly prejudice the defendant's case. It is the job of the prosecution to establish the admissibility of any evidence by a **preponderance of the evidence**.

preponderance of the evidence
The weight or level of persuasion of evidence needed to find the defendant liable as alleged by the plaintiff in a civil matter.

The defendant has the right to testify at what is known as a **suppression hearing** in an effort to suppress any evidence that his counsel believes may not be legally admissible. The defendant can testify at the suppression hearing without the testimony being used against him at his trial on the issue of his guilt or innocence.

suppression hearing
A pretrial proceeding in criminal cases in which a defendant seeks to prevent the introduction of evidence alleged to have been seized illegally.

FIRST AMENDMENT

Most people are familiar with three of the basic rights contained in the First Amendment: the right to free speech, the right to freedom of religion, and the right to a free press. However, what areas are covered by the First Amendment continue to be controversial even today. For example, free speech is protected by the First Amendment; however, some exceptions do exist to this basic right. For example, if the speech involves obscenity, defamation, breach of the peace, incitement to commit a crime, fighting words, or sedition, it will not be protected by the First Amendment. Recently, First Amendment protection has been challenged again in the areas of hate crimes, disclosure of national security information, and cybercrimes on the Internet.

FOURTH AMENDMENT

The Fourth Amendment protects a person's right to be free from unreasonable governmental intrusion. Some of the basic rights that we take for granted such as the right to be free from searches and seizures from law enforcement without a **search warrant** that must be obtained with **probable cause** originate from the Fourth Amendment. The Fourth Amendment reads as follows:

> *The right of the people to be secure in their persons, houses, papers, and effects, against unreasonable searches and seizures, shall not be violated, and no Warrants shall issue, but upon probable cause, supported by Oath or affirmation, and particularly describing the place to be searched, and the persons or things to be seized.*

Various protections that have been built into the criminal process are based on this paragraph of the Fourth Amendment.

The Fourth Amendment prohibits unreasonable searches and seizures. It generally protects only against governmental conduct (i.e., police or public school officials) and not against searches by private persons such as private security guards unless they have been deputized as officers of the public police. In order to establish a Fourth Amendment right, a person must have a reasonable expectation of privacy with respect to the place that is the subject of the search or the item that is being seized. For example, in *Katz v. United States,* 389 U.S. 347 (1967), the defendant's telephone conversations were recorded by use of a listening device that was placed on the outside of a public telephone booth by law enforcement. The Court ruled that the reasonable expectation of privacy contained in the Fourth Amendment was meant to protect people and not places. The Court stated that when a person seeks to preserve his privacy even a public telephone booth is covered under the Fourth Amendment. The expectation of privacy must be reasonable and reasonable is determined by what society is willing to accept.

A person has **standing** to raise a Fourth Amendment claim if

- He is the owner of or has a right to possession of the place that is being searched;

- The place searched was his home; or

- He is an overnight guest of the owner of the place that is being searched.

A person does not have a reasonable expectation of privacy regarding items that are being held out to the public.

You have no reasonable expectation of privacy under the Fourth Amendment to the following:

- The sound of your voice.

- Your handwriting.

- Paint located on the outside of your vehicle.

- Account records held by a bank.

- The location of your vehicle on public roads or its arrival at a private residence.

- Areas outside your home and related buildings such as a barn, also known as **curtilage**.

- Garbage left for collection. Some jurisdictions indicate that garbage left for collection at the curb does not have a reasonable expectation of privacy; however, other jurisdictions require that the garbage must have made its way to a public dumping site before the reasonable expectation of privacy is extinguished.

- Land visible from a public place, even from a plane or helicopter.

- The smell of your luggage.

---

search warrant
Issued after presentation of an affidavit stating clearly the probable cause on which the request is based. In particular, it is an order in writing, issued by a justice or other magistrate, in the name of the state, and directed to a sheriff, constable, or other officer authorizing him to search for and seize any property that constitutes evidence of the commission of a crime, contraband, or the fruits of the crime.

probable cause
The totality of circumstances leads one to believe certain facts or circumstances exist; applies to arrests, searches, and seizures.

Standing
Legally sufficient reason and right to object.

Curtilage
Out buildings that are directly and intimately connected with the habitation and in proximity thereto and the land or grounds surrounding the dwelling that are necessary and convenient and habitually used for family purposes and carrying on domestic employment.

Some searches can be conducted without warrants being executed. These searches are sometimes referred to as Fourth Amendment exceptions. Some of the major warrantless searches are discussed below.

Arrest

Arrest
The formal taking of a person, usually by a police officer, to answer criminal charges.

An **arrest** is considered a seizure and, therefore, is covered under the Fourth Amendment. It is a seizure of a person who is, at least temporarily, denied his freedom. A person who is illegally seized may be facing criminal prosecution, so the legality surrounding an arrest is very important. Therefore, in order for an arrest to be considered valid, the arrest must comply with certain standards. A seizure arises when a reasonable person would believe that he is not free to leave and that his freedom is impaired.

At common law, a police officer is permitted to arrest a person without first obtaining an arrest warrant when

1. The police officer has reasonable belief that a felony has been committed and that this particular person committed it, or

2. A misdemeanor was committed in the police officer's presence.

Police do not need to secure an arrest warrant before arresting an individual in a public place, even if the police have time to get a warrant before making the arrest. However, they must have an arrest warrant to make a nonemergency arrest of an individual in her own home. All warrantless searches of homes are presumed to be unreasonable and law enforcement must obtain a warrant before searching a person's residence. Absent difficult circumstances, police executing an arrest warrant may not search for the subject of the warrant in the home of a third party without a search warrant for the third party's residence.

Investigatory Detentions

reasonable suspicion
Such suspicion that will justify an officer, for Fourth Amendment purposes, in stopping a defendant in a public place, as having knowledge sufficient to induce an ordinarily prudent and cautious man under the circumstances to believe that criminal activity is at hand.

detain
To restrain, arrest, check, delay, hinder, hold, keep, or retain in custody.

detention
The act of keeping back, restraining, or withholding, either accidentally or by design, a person or thing.

If law enforcement has a **reasonable suspicion** of criminal activity or the involvement of a person in a completed crime, and that suspicion is supported by clear facts that can be communicated and are not merely based on intuition, then they may **detain** a person for investigative purposes. The reasonable suspicion does not have to come from a person's personal knowledge. For example, it may arise from information contained in a report made to law enforcement. The **detention** of a person must be no longer than is necessary to conduct a limited investigation in order to verify the suspicion. If during the detention probable cause arises, the detention can become an arrest.

Reasonable suspicion is a standard that is less than probable cause. It provides the basis for a law enforcement officer to conduct a preliminary investigation. Factors that could be relevant in determining reasonable suspicion can include some of the following:

• Information contained in a police report.

• Appearance of a suspect.

• Actions of a suspect.

• Area in which the suspect is observed.

It is important to remember that if an investigatory detention cannot be justified by these factors, then any information or evidence obtained during the detention may not be admissible in court. The reasonable suspicion formulated by a law enforcement officer must be held to a standard that a reasonable law enforcement officer, in the same or similar position, would formulate the same suspicion of the person in question.

Stop and Frisk

As stated above, a law enforcement officer may stop a person without probable cause for arrest if he can demonstrate reasonable suspicion of criminal activity. If the officer reasonably believes that a person may be armed and immediately dangerous, then the law enforcement officer may conduct a **protective frisk**. An investigative detention or stop is not an arrest; therefore, an officer only needs to meet the standard of reasonable suspicion in order to have a justifiable stop. However, a frisk of the suspect **(stop and frisk)** will be justified only if the officer reasonably thinks that the suspect is in possession of a weapon.

The scope of a frisk of a person is generally limited to a pat-down search of the outer clothing to find concealed weapons. However, if the officer has specific information that a weapon is hidden in a particular area of the suspect's clothing, then a more extensive search may be justified.

protective frisk
A pat-down search of a suspect by police, designed to discover weapons for the purpose of ensuring the safety of the officer and others nearby.

stop and frisk
The situation where police officers who are suspicious of an individual run their hands lightly over the suspect's outer garments to determine if the person is carrying a concealed weapon.

RESEARCH THIS

Prior to 1968, law enforcement officers were unable to search someone without the issuance of a warrant. This all changed with the case of *Terry v. Ohio*, 392 U.S. 1 (1968). The *Terry* Court established the stop and frisk search. The *Terry* Court also developed the concept that there were different types of allowable searches with different degrees of intrusiveness into a person's expectation of privacy. To learn more about the development of detention searches, research the case of *Terry v. Ohio*, 392 U.S. 1 (1968).

Hot Pursuit, Transitory Evidence, and Other Emergencies

The law does not provide for a general "emergency" exception. However, law enforcement officers who are in hot pursuit of a fleeing felon may make a warrantless search and seizure and may even pursue the suspect into a private dwelling. Law enforcement may seize without a warrant evidence that is likely to disappear before a warrant can be obtained. Contaminated food or drugs, children in trouble, and burning fires may be situations that justify warrantless searches and seizures. For example, if a carjacker flees the car and runs into a nearby residence, due to the danger to the public as well as the police in "hot pursuit" of the suspect, the police may jump over fences or follow the suspect into the residence in order to apprehend him. Any evidence obtained on the suspect such as drugs can be seized without a warrant in this case.

Administrative Inspections and Searches

Inspectors must have a warrant for searches of private residences and commercial buildings, but the probable cause required to obtain a warrant is more lenient for administrative inspections than it is for other types of searches. A showing of a general and neutral enforcement plan will justify issuance of a warrant. Courts generally uphold searches of airline passengers prior to boarding. Also, a warrantless search is permitted by school officials who have reasonable grounds to believe that such a search is warranted. For example, school officials may search a child's locker if they believe that the child is harboring a dangerous item or drugs. In addition, a parolee's home is also an exception to the warrant requirement. Even though the person is not incarcerated, a **parolee** is still considered to be within the purview of the criminal justice system and therefore a warrant is not required to search a parolee's residence.

parolee
Ex-prisoner who has been released from jail, prison, or other confinement after having served part of a criminal sentence.

Border Searches

No warrant is necessary for border searches. Neither citizens nor noncitizens have any Fourth Amendment rights at the border to a country. The purpose of a border search is to protect citizens of the United States from illegal activities that can occur at the border such as smuggling, theft, and drug trafficking. Border searches assist in preserving national security; therefore, the expectation of privacy is reduced in favor of national security. This concept has become especially true in light of the September 11, 2001, terrorist attacks. Any person entering or reentering the United States is subject to a search. In fact, scrutiny of people coming into the United States has increased significantly due to these events. Roving patrols inside the U.S. border are allowed to stop a vehicle in order to question its occupants if an officer reasonably suspects that the vehicle may contain illegal aliens or contraband that is being smuggled across the border. Border officials may stop a vehicle at a fixed checkpoint inside the border for questioning of its occupants even without reasonable suspicion, but in order to conduct a search, they must have probable cause or consent of the occupants.

Automobile Stops

Police may not stop an automobile strictly for license and registration checks. They must have a reasonable belief that a violation has occurred or they must stop every car at a roadblock, or have some articulable neutral objective to justify the stopping (such as stopping every third car). Stopping automobiles for the purpose of checking the driver's sobriety has been deemed constitutional, as has the practice of establishing sobriety checkpoints.

When law enforcement has probable cause to believe that a vehicle contains evidence of a crime, and it is likely that the vehicle may become unavailable due to its mobility, they may search the whole car and any container inside the vehicle that might reasonably contain the item for which they had probable cause to search. If a warrantless search of a vehicle is valid, law enforcement is permitted to tow the vehicle to the station in order to search it at a later time.

Plain View

The police may make a warrantless seizure when they

- Are legitimately on the premises;
- Discover evidence, fruits, or instrumentalities of a crime;
- See such evidence in plain view; and
- Have probable cause to believe that the item is evidence, contraband, or a fruit or an instrumentality of crime.

Plain view is not considered to be a type of search. In order to constitute a search, there must be a reasonable expectation of privacy. However, if something is in plain view, out in the open, then there is no reasonable expectation of privacy, so no search has occurred. For example, if police officers are called to a residence on a domestic violence call and they observe lines of cocaine laid out on a table through a window, then the officers can use this evidence as the cocaine was in plain view through the window and no search was necessary to discover it.

Consent

A person can waive his constitutional rights and consent to a search. These warrantless searches are valid if the police have obtained a voluntary and intelligent consent given without the person being subject to duress. Whether or not a person has knowledge of the right to withhold consent is not required in order to establish voluntary and intelligent consent. The scope of the search may be limited by the scope of the consent.

Any person with an apparent right to use or occupy the property may consent to a search. Any evidence found on the premises may be used against the other owners or occupants. For example, if a roommate allows an apartment to be searched by law enforcement, any evidence obtained during the search can be used against all of the roommates of that same apartment. Also, if the officers have obtained a valid search warrant to search the premises for contraband, then that warrant enables the officers to detain occupants of the premises while conducting the search.

Search with a Warrant

Generally, the police must have a warrant to conduct a search unless it falls within one of the exceptions to the warrant requirement. A **warrant** must be based upon a showing of probable cause. Law enforcement officers must submit to a **magistrate** an affidavit that sets forth the circumstances necessary to facilitate the magistrate to make a determination that probable cause exists independent of the law enforcement officers' assumption.

An affidavit based on an informant's tip must meet what is known as the "totality of the circumstances" test. Under this test, the affidavit may be sufficient even though the reliability and credibility of the informer or the basis for such knowledge has not been verified or established.

A search warrant issued on the basis of an affidavit will be invalid if the defendant establishes all three of the following requirements:

1. A false statement was included in the affidavit by the **affiant**;
2. The affiant intentionally or recklessly included the false statement; and
3. The false statement was material to the finding of probable cause that led to the issuance of the warrant.

Evidence that is obtained by law enforcement in reasonable reliance on a warrant that appears valid on its face may be used by the prosecution even if it is ultimately found that the warrant was not supported by probable cause at the time it was issued by the magistrate.

A warrant is required to reasonably and accurately describe the place that is to be searched and the items that are to be seized. The magistrate who issues the warrant must be neutral, objective, and detached from the process. A warrant may be obtained to search premises belonging to people who are not suspects so long as probable cause exists that it would be reasonable to believe that evidence will be discovered on the premises that are the subject of the search.

Only law enforcement can execute a search warrant. The warrant must be executed without unreasonable delay. Police must knock and announce their purpose for entering the premises, except in the case of an emergency. Police may seize any contraband, evidence, or instrumentalities of a crime that they discover, whether or not such items were specified in the warrant.

A warrant that is based and issued on probable cause to search for contraband on premises also authorizes the police to be able to detain the occupants of the premises during the search. However, a search warrant does not authorize the police to search people located at the premises who were not specifically named in the warrant.

Wiretapping and Eavesdropping

Wiretapping as well as other types of electronic surveillance that potentially violate a person's reasonable expectation of privacy constitutes a search under the Fourth Amendment. A valid warrant authorizing a wiretap may be issued if

- There is showing of probable cause;
- The suspected people involved in the conversations to be overheard are named in the warrant;
- The warrant describes with specificity the conversations that will probably be overheard during the tapping;

warrant
Issued after presentation of an affidavit stating clearly the probable cause on which the request is based.

magistrate
A public civil officer, possessing such power—legislative, executive, or judicial—as the government appointing him may ordain.

affiant
The person who makes and subscribes an affidavit.

A DAY IN THE LIFE OF A REAL PARALEGAL

John, a new client, enters your firm. He has come to see you regarding a charge of burglary he has been arrested for and subsequently made bail. You have been working with this criminal law firm for two months and have learned a lot already. You ask John to have a seat and tell him the attorney will be with him shortly. In a frenzy, John blurts out, "I did the burglary and I am now going back to the store [in which the burglary happened] and kill the owner for turning me in!" With that, John runs out of the office. Diligent as you are, you tell the attorney immediately and you both call the police to report a potential violent act, even though he is your client.

- The wiretap is limited to a short period of time;
- The wiretap is terminated when the desired information has been obtained; and
- Return is made to the court, showing what conversations have been intercepted.

Confessions

The admissibility of a defendant's confession, or any other incriminating admission made by the defendant, must be analyzed under the Fourth, Fifth, Sixth, and Fourteenth Amendments as to the rights of the defendants and the possible use of those incriminating statements.

The Supreme Court itself has held that the Due Process Clause of the Fourteenth Amendment requires that self-incriminating statements be voluntarily given. In order to determine if the self-incriminating statement was made voluntarily, the totality of the circumstances must be examined.

Some official pressure must be present in order to determine that a statement was made involuntarily. For example, in *Brown v. Mississippi,* 297 U.S. 278 (1936), the Supreme Court held that a confession elicited from the defendant after he was tied to a tree and beaten until he confessed was inadmissible in court. The Court held that the confession that led to the conviction was extorted from the defendant in violation of his due process rights as required by the Fourteenth Amendment and reversed the lower court.

FIFTH AMENDMENT

double jeopardy
Being tried twice for the same act or acts.

The Fifth Amendment is important to protecting a person's rights when she is faced with being accused of a crime. The Fifth Amendment protects a person's right to be protected from **double jeopardy** and from being compelled to testify against herself. The Fifth Amendment reads as follows:

> *No person shall be held to answer for a capital, or otherwise infamous crime, unless on a presentment or indictment of a Grand Jury, except in cases arising in the land or naval forces, or in the Militia, when in actual service in time of War or public danger; nor shall any person be subject for the same offence to be twice put in jeopardy of life or limb, nor shall be compelled in any criminal case to be a witness against himself, nor be deprived of life, liberty, or property, without due process of law; nor shall private property be taken for public use without just compensation.*

Miranda Warnings

As stated above, the Fifth Amendment protects an accused person from having to testify against himself (hence the phrase "taking the Fifth"). In order for an admission or confession by the accused to be deemed admissible in court under the Fifth

FIGURE 2.2
Miranda **Rights and Demands**

Rights	Demands
• You have the right to remain silent and refuse to answer any questions.	• I will not talk to you or anyone about anything.
• Anything you say may be used against you in a court of law.	• I will not answer any questions or reply to any charges without my attorney present.
• You have the right to consult an attorney before speaking to the police and to have an attorney present during questioning now or in the future.	• I do not agree to perform any test, allow my property to be searched, or participate in any lineup.
• If you cannot afford an attorney, one will be appointed for you before questioning if you wish.	• I demand to have an attorney present before I speak to you.
• If you decide to answer questions now without an attorney present, you will still have the right to stop answering at any time until you talk to an attorney.	• I will not sign anything unless my attorney agrees I should do so.
• Knowing and understanding your rights as I have explained them to you, are you willing to answer my questions without an attorney present?	• I will not waive any of my constitutional rights.

Amendment privilege against self-incrimination, a person in **custody**, prior to questioning or **interrogation** by law enforcement, must be informed that

1. He has the right to remain silent.
2. Anything he says can and will be used against him in a court of law.
3. He has the right to the presence of an attorney.
4. If he cannot afford an attorney, one will be appointed for him if he so desires.

(See Figure 2.2.)

Despite the fact that the *Miranda* warnings mention a right to counsel, failure by law enforcement to give the warnings constitutes a violation of the defendant's Fifth Amendment right to be free from compelled self-incrimination. This right is different from a person's right to counsel that is contained in the Sixth Amendment. An accused does not have to be questioned without representation during the questioning. The Sixth Amendment provides for legal counsel throughout the entire legal proceeding.

If the accused indicates in any manner at any time prior to or during questioning by law enforcement that he wishes to remain silent and not answer any questions,

custody
The care and control of a thing or person.

interrogation
The process of questions propounded by police to a person arrested or suspected to seek solution of crime.

SURF'S UP

The court in *Miranda v. Arizona*, 384 U.S. 436 (1966), determined that a situation in which an accused person is being interrogated or questioned by law enforcement is inherently coercive in nature. Therefore, the famous *Miranda* court determined that an accused individual is entitled to have legal counsel present to advise the accused during questioning and interrogation. An accused person's *Miranda* rights are now an integral part of criminal procedure. To learn more about *Miranda* rights, visit some of the following Web sites:

- www.usgovinfo.about.com/od/rightsandfreedoms
- www.usgovinfo.about.com/cs/mirandarights
- www.publicdefender.cjis20.org/miranda.htm
- www.abanet.org
- www.expertlaw.com/library/criminal

EYE ON ETHICS

It is important that law enforcement officers read all accused persons their *Miranda* rights. If a person is not read his *Miranda* rights and he confesses or makes incriminating statements during his incarceration or detainment, those statements can be deemed to be inadmissible in court against him because the accused was not informed of his rights. If the accused is not informed of his rights, he cannot knowingly, intelligently, and voluntarily waive them. When representing an accused person in a criminal case, it is always important to ascertain if the accused was read his *Miranda* rights prior to any initial questioning conducted by law enforcement.

then interrogation or questioning must end. Similarly, if the accused requests legal counsel, then the questioning or interrogation must cease even as to issues that are unrelated to the questioning until the accused is given an attorney. A suspect may waive his *Miranda* rights, but the prosecution must prove that the waiver was given knowingly, voluntarily, and intelligently. A waiver will not be presumed from silence of the accused after warnings are given or from the fact that a confession was eventually obtained.

The Fifth Amendment right to counsel comes into effect only for the initial interrogation or questioning process. The Sixth Amendment right to counsel provides for legal counsel to represent the defendant for all legal proceedings, not just the initial interrogation. It is important to keep these differences separate as they are separate and distinct rights.

SIXTH AMENDMENT

The Sixth Amendment gives an accused person the right to a speedy jury trial as well as the right to be represented by legal counsel during the course of any legal proceedings brought against the accused. The Sixth Amendment reads as follows:

> *In all criminal prosecutions, the accused shall enjoy the right to a speedy and public trial, by an impartial jury of the State and district wherein the crime shall have been committed; which district shall have been previously ascertained by law, and to be informed of the nature and cause of the accusation; to be confronted with the witnesses against him; to have compulsory process for obtaining witnesses in his favor, and to have the assistance of counsel for his defence.*

The Sixth Amendment right to counsel prohibits the use of incriminating statements made by the person charged with a crime without the presence of his attorney. Every defendant has the right to be represented by a privately retained attorney or to have

CASE FACT PATTERN

Joey likes to party and oftentimes drinks too much. He has never been caught driving under the influence. He goes to a fraternity party at the college and proceeds to consume a number of alcoholic beverages. Though he is completely buzzed, Joey gets into his car and begins the drive home. While driving home, he is driving erratically, loses control of his car, and hits a parked vehicle. The police are called, and Joey is arrested and charged with driving under the influence. He is booked and brought to the court for an arraignment on the charges. He does not have money for an attorney. The court tells Joey that he has the right to legal counsel and that if he cannot afford an attorney, one will be appointed for him. Joey tells the court that he would like to have an attorney but that he cannot afford one. The court appoints a public defender named Stan to represent Joey.

legal counsel appointed for him by the state if he is **indigent**. A defendant has a right to defend himself if a judge decides that the defendant's waiver of his right to legal counsel is made with knowledge and intelligence. The defendant does not need to be found capable of representing himself effectively; it must only be found that his waiver was made with knowledge and intelligence. The Sixth Amendment grants to a defendant in a criminal prosecution the right to competent legal counsel during legal proceedings as well as the right to confront witnesses. The right to counsel under the Sixth Amendment attaches when the criminal proceedings have begun such as an arraignment or commencement of some other judicial proceeding. This right to counsel is different than that found under the Fifth Amendment. The Fifth Amendment right to counsel states that the defendant has the right to consult an attorney during interrogation or during a lineup, but without the criminal judicial proceedings having been commenced.

indigent
One who is needy and poor, or one who does not have sufficient property to furnish him a living or anyone able to support him or to whom he is entitled to look for support.

EIGHTH AMENDMENT

The Eighth Amendment prohibits a person from receiving excessive bail or cruel and unusual punishment in relation to crimes that he is accused of having committed. For example, the Eighth Amendment prohibits excessive bail. The purpose of bail is to ensure that the accused is present in court for criminal proceedings. The amount of bail will vary depending on the nature and character of the crime accused and the history of the defendant. Any amount set at a level higher than to achieve the objective of procuring the defendant's presence at trial will be deemed excessive and is reviewed on a case-by-case basis. For example, if Donna steals a loaf of bread from a local supermarket and the judge issues bail in the amount of $1 million for the offense, this bail would more than likely be deemed excessive.

The Eighth Amendment also states that no person should be subjected to cruel and unusual punishment. Areas that have gained scrutiny as of late are the constitutionality of the three-strikes law, whether or not the death penalty is cruel and unusual punishment, and whether prisoners held at times of war who are questioned or made to do embarrassing acts fall within the purview of the Eighth Amendment.

Summary

The first ten amendments to the U.S. Constitution are called the Bill of Rights. They concern rights that apply to a person who has been accused of criminal activity. These rights are designed to protect the process that people accused of crimes must go through so that they have an opportunity to prove their innocence. Most of these rights are applicable to the states through what is known as the Due Process Clause of the Fourteenth Amendment.

The exclusionary rule is contained in the Fourth Amendment. The rule is a remedy for violations of a defendant's Fourth, Fifth, and Sixth Amendment rights. Under the rule, illegally obtained evidence is inadmissible at trial and all evidence obtained or derived from the use of that illegally obtained evidence must also be excluded (the "fruit of the poisonous tree").

The Fourth Amendment prohibits unreasonable searches and seizures. The Fourth Amendment generally protects only against governmental conduct (i.e., police or public school officials) and not against searches by private persons such as private security guards unless they have been deputized as officers of the public police. In order to establish a Fourth Amendment right, a person must have a reasonable expectation of privacy with respect to the place that is the subject of the search or the item that is being seized.

An arrest is considered a seizure and is therefore covered under the Fourth Amendment. It is a seizure of a person who is, at least temporarily, denied his freedom. A person who is illegally seized may be facing criminal prosecution, so the legality surrounding an arrest is very important. Therefore, in order for an arrest to be considered valid, the arrest must comply with certain standards. A seizure arises when a reasonable person would believe that he is not free to leave and that his freedom is impaired.

If law enforcement has a reasonable suspicion of criminal activity or the involvement of a person in a completed crime, and that suspicion is supported by clear facts that can be communicated and are not merely based on intuition, then it may detain a person for investigative purposes. The reasonable suspicion does not have to come from a person's personal knowledge. The detention of a person must be no longer than is necessary to conduct a limited investigation in order to verify the suspicion. If during the detention probable cause arises, the detention can become an arrest.

As stated above, a law enforcement officer may stop a person without probable cause for arrest if she can demonstrate reasonable suspicion of criminal activity. If the officer reasonably believes that a person may be armed and immediately dangerous, then the law enforcement officer may conduct a protective frisk. An investigative detention or stop is not an arrest; therefore, an officer only needs to meet the standard of reasonable suspicion in order to have a justifiable stop. However, a frisk of the suspect will be justified only if the officer reasonably thinks that the suspect is in possession of a weapon.

Police may not stop an automobile strictly for license and registration checks. They must have a reasonable belief that a violation has occurred or they must stop every car at a roadblock, or have some articulable neutral objective to justify the stopping (for example, stopping every third car). Stopping automobiles for the purpose of checking the driver's sobriety has been deemed constitutional, as has the practice of establishing sobriety checkpoints.

A person can waive his constitutional rights and consent to a search. These warrantless searches are valid if the police have obtained a voluntary and intelligent consent given without the person being subject to duress. Whether or not a person has knowledge of the right to withhold consent is not required in order to establish voluntary and intelligent consent. The scope of the search may be limited by the scope of the consent.

Generally, the police must have a warrant to conduct a search unless it falls within one of the exceptions to the warrant requirement. A warrant must be based upon a showing of probable cause. Law enforcement officers must submit to a magistrate an affidavit that sets forth the circumstances necessary to facilitate the magistrate to make a determination that probable cause exists independent of the law enforcement officers' assumption.

The Sixth Amendment right to counsel prohibits the use of incriminating statements made by the person charged with a crime without the presence of his attorney. Every defendant has the right to be represented by a privately retained attorney or to have legal counsel appointed for him by the state if he is indigent. A defendant has a right to defend himself if a judge decides that the defendant's waiver of his right to legal counsel is made with knowledge and intelligence. The defendant does not need to be found capable of representing himself effectively; it must only be found that his waiver was made with knowledge and intelligence. The Sixth Amendment grants to a defendant in a criminal prosecution the right to competent legal counsel during legal proceedings as well as the right to confront witnesses.

The Fifth Amendment is important to protecting a person's rights when he is faced with being accused of a crime. The Fifth Amendment protects a person's right to be protected from double jeopardy and from being compelled to testify against himself.

Key Terms

Affiant
Arrest
Bill of Rights
Curtilage
Custody
Detain
Detention
Double jeopardy
Due Process Clause
Exclusionary rule
Fruit of the poisonous tree
Indigent
Interrogation
Magistrate
Parolee
Preponderance of the evidence
Probable cause
Protective frisk
Reasonable suspicion
Search warrant
Self-incrimination
Standing
Stop and frisk
Suppression hearing
Warrant

Review Questions

1. What is the difference between probable cause and reasonable suspicion?
2. What is the exclusionary rule?
3. What are three exceptions to the fruit of the poisonous tree doctrine? Give a fact pattern that might illustrate how each applies.
4. What standard is used to determine whether or not evidence will be admissible into the case?
5. What is a warrant?
6. List the requirements for a valid warrant?
7. List four areas in which an individual has no expectation of privacy and state why.
8. Why does an arrest fall under the Fourth Amendment?
9. List the items that are used to consider that a law enforcement officer has reasonable suspicion.
10. Why is there no expectation of privacy when crossing the U.S. border?
11. What elements are necessary for evidence to be considered in plain view?
12. List five times that law enforcement can conduct a warrantless search.
13. List the elements required for a valid wiretap. Explain why the elements are required and how they might be applicable to a cybercrime.
14. What is the difference between the Sixth Amendment right to counsel and the Fifth Amendment right to have legal representation?
15. What is double jeopardy?

Exercises

1. Sara and Daniel are using cocaine. They have cut lines of cocaine and have it on the living room table. The police are called to an apartment on the second floor for a domestic dispute call between a couple who are unrelated to Sara or Daniel. While walking back to their vehicle, the police pass by Sara and Daniel's window. They see the lines of cocaine on the table. The police pound on the door and announce themselves. They hear Sara and Daniel scurrying around, so they break down the door. They confiscate the cocaine and arrest Sara and Daniel. Will the cocaine be admitted into court as having been obtained legally or not? Explain your answer.

2. Robert is traveling on an airline to New York City. As he waits to go through security, two security officers with a dog walk up and down the line of people who are waiting to go through the security check. The dog stops at Robert and sniffs his carry-on bag. All of a sudden, the dog begins to howl and bark. The security guards ask Robert to step out of the line. Robert is angry. He is afraid that he is going to miss his flight and he has a very important business deal that he needs to attend to in New York. The security guards search Robert's carry-on bag and find nothing. They detain Robert for over an hour and he misses his flight. Was Robert's detention legal? Does Robert have any recourse against the security guards? Did Robert have a reasonable expectation of privacy?

3. Peter has been charged with murdering an elderly woman in her home. Peter is indicted and is waiting for his trial to begin. The police decide to place a paid informant who works for the police department in Peter's cell in order to elicit a confession. Harold is the paid informant. Harold tells Peter that he also is being incarcerated for murder. Harold continues to talk to Peter to get him to confess, but Peter does not. Finally, frustrated, Harold says to Peter, "You know we are going down unless we escape." Harold and Peter plan to escape and take actions toward that end. During the planning, Peter confesses to Harold. Is Peter's confession legally admissible at trial? Why or why not? Was Peter's Sixth Amendment right to legal counsel violated?

4. Police knock down your door with a search warrant that specifically lists unregistered firearms as searchable items. The police do not find any weapons but do find pornographic pictures and videos of children performing sexual acts. Can they confiscate those items even though not listed in the search warrant? Explain your answer.

5. Amendment Six speaks to affording the accused with the right to a *speedy trial.* Does our system follow through with that right or not? Explain your answer.

6. Why do you think the *Founding Fathers* included the right in the Fifth Amendment not to have to testify against yourself? Why was that important in the times in which they lived and now?

7. Look up and research the USA PATRIOT Act. In your opinion, does the act begin the decline of numerous individual rights as found in the Fourth, Fifth, and Sixth Amendments? Explain your answer fully.

8. Can a citizen make an arrest and, if so, would he/she be restricted like the police or a government agent would be by having to adhere to the Fourth, Fifth, and Sixth Amendments? Explain your answer fully.

 PORTFOLIO ASSIGNMENT

Visit the nearest correctional facility in your area. Arrange for a tour of the facility and have them show you the processing procedure that institution uses and write about your experience.

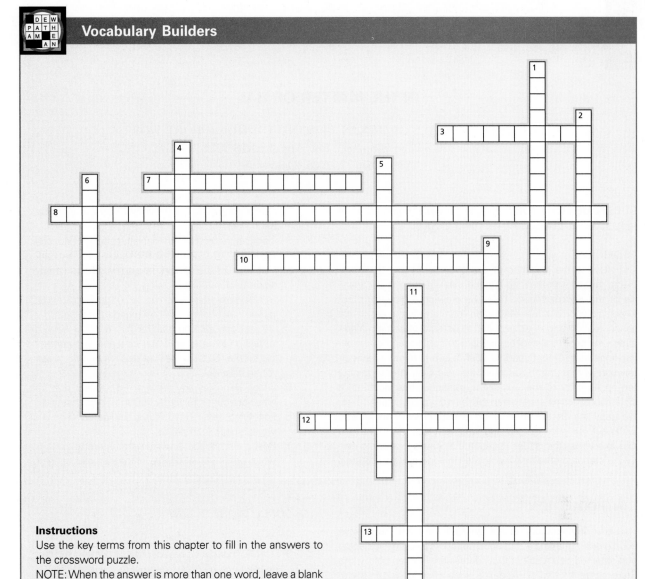

Instructions

Use the key terms from this chapter to fill in the answers to the crossword puzzle.

NOTE: When the answer is more than one word, leave a blank space between the words.

ACROSS

3. a public civil officer, possessing such power—legislative, executive, or judicial—as the government appointing him may ordain.

7. having a reasonable ground for belief in certain alleged facts.

8. evidence that is spawned by or directly derived from an illegal search or illegal interrogation is generally inadmissible against the defendant because of its original taint, though knowledge of facts gained independently of the original and tainted search is admissible.

10. under this rule evidence which is obtained by an unreasonable search and seizure is excluded from admissibility under the Fourth Amendment, and this rule has been held to be applicable to the States.

12. a pat-down search of a suspect by police, designed to discover weapons for the purpose of insuring the safety of the officer and others nearby.

13. an order in writing, issued by a justice or other magistrate, in the name of the state, directed to a sheriff, constable, or other officer, authorizing him to search for and seize any property that constitutes evidence of the commission of a crime, contraband, or the fruits of the crime.

DOWN

1. the process of questions propounded by police to person arrested or suspected to seek solution of crime.

2. acts or declarations either as testimony at trial or prior to trial by which one implicates himself in a crime.

4. the situation where police officers who are suspicious of an individual run their hands lightly over the suspect's outer garments to determine if the person is carrying a concealed weapon.

5. such suspicion which will justify an officer, for Fourth Amendment purposes, in stopping a defendant in a public place as having knowledge sufficient to induce an ordinarily prudent and cautious man under the circumstances to believe that criminal activity is at hand.

6. Fifth Amendment guarantee, enforceable against states through the Fourteenth Amendment, which protects against the second prosecution for the same offense after a person has received an acquittal or conviction, and against multiple punishments for the same offense.

9. the act of keeping back, restraining or withholding, either accidentally or by design, a person or thing.

11. a pretrial proceeding in criminal cases in which a defendant seeks to prevent the introduction of evidence alleged to have been seized illegally.

IN THE MATTER OF H.V.

COURT OF APPEALS OF TEXAS, SECOND DISTRICT, FORT WORTH
179 S.W.3d 746; 2005 Tex. App. LEXIS 9712
November 17, 2005, Delivered

SUBSEQUENT HISTORY: Petition for review granted by In re V., 2006 Tex. LEXIS 1191 (Tex., Dec. 1, 2006)

OPINION

Following the issuance of our original opinion, the State filed a motion for rehearing arguing that we erred in our analysis of the State's second issue by drawing a distinction between a custodial statement made voluntarily in the accidental absence of *Miranda* warnings and a custodial statement made after a suspect had invoked his right to counsel and questioning nonetheless continued (a post failure-to-honor-a-request-for-counsel statement). Because we hold that, in determining the applicability of the fruit-of-the-poisonous-tree doctrine, a distinction does exist between these two types of statements, we deny the State's motion for rehearing. We nonetheless withdraw our prior opinion and judgment and substitute this one to address the issues raised in the State's motion, to clarify the standard of review we applied in addressing the State's first issue, and to clarify certain facts.

I. INTRODUCTION

This is an interlocutory appeal by the State from the juvenile court's order granting a motion to suppress a confession and a gun obtained as a result of that confession. In three points, the State contends that (1) Appellee H.V.'s second written statement should not have been suppressed because H.V. did not make an unequivocal request for counsel, (2) there was no justification for suppression of the firearm as alleged "fruit" of H.V.'s second written statement, and (3) section 52.02 of the Texas Family Code did not provide a basis to suppress either H.V.'s second written statement or the fruit of that statement. We will affirm.

FINDINGS OF FACT

1. On September 12, 2003, Fort Worth Police officers attempted to secure a search warrant for the Respondent's residence. During that time, the Respondent and his father were advised not to re-enter the residence pending the search. Respondent was arrested after exiting his residence with a rug.
2. Respondent was placed in the back of a patrol car for approximately one hour. He was later taken out to remove his handcuffs. The Respondent was then placed back into the patrol car for approximately another thirty minutes before being transported to the Fort Worth Police Department to be interviewed by Detective Carroll. At no point while Respondent was in the patrol car was any attempt made by Fort Worth Police to contact Respondent's parents as required by Texas Family Code Section 52.02.
3. Upon arrival, Fort Worth Magistrate Judge Gabrielle Bendslev interviewed the Respondent, and advised him of the warning required by Texas Family Code Section 51.095.
4. *In response to questioning by Judge Bendslev regarding an attorney, the Respondent advised that he was only sixteen, that he did not know how to obtain an attorney, and that he wanted to contact his mother because he "wanted his mother to ask for an attorney."*
5. Judge Bendslev advised the Respondent that he was not entitled to contact his mother at that time.
6. Following this, Respondent indicated that he would speak with police.
7. Respondent made a written statement, Exhibit 4, which among other things, indicated the location of the firearm involved in the death of Daniel Oltmanns. The police were able to locate the weapon.

CONCLUSIONS OF LAW

. . .

3. *The Respondent's request to speak to his mother was an unambiguous request for counsel.*
4. *Because of the foregoing conclusions of law, and considering the totality of the circumstances, the statement made by Respondent, Exhibit 4, following his arrest was obtained improperly and is inadmissible in trial.*
5. The firearm recovered by the Fort Worth Police Department was only obtained as a result of improper questioning of Respondent, and therefore, is a "fruit of the poisonous tree" and is likewise inadmissible. [Emphasis added.]

II. INVOCATION OF RIGHT TO COUNSEL

In its first point, the State contends that the trial court erred by concluding that H.V.'s comments to Judge Bendslev constituted an unequivocal invocation of counsel. Specifically, the State argues that the trial court misapplied the law to the facts when it suppressed H.V.'s second written statement because its conclusion—that H.V. unambiguously invoked his right to counsel—is incorrect as a matter of law. H.V. responds that the trial court properly concluded that he made an unambiguous request for counsel, which should have ended the interview, when H.V. requested to speak to his mother so that she could ask for an attorney.

A. Law Regarding Unambiguous Request for Counsel

Prior to a custodial interrogation, a suspect must be advised that he has a right to consult with an attorney. *Miranda*, 384 U.S. at 467–68, 86 S. Ct. at 1624–25. Interrogation must cease immediately if the suspect states that he wants an attorney. *Id.* at 474, 86 S. Ct. at 1628; *see also Edwards v. Arizona*, 451 U.S. 477, 485, 101 S. Ct. 1880, 1885, 68 L. Ed. 2d 378 (1981); *McCarthy v. State*, 65 S.W.3d 47, 51 (Tex. Crim. App. 2001), *cert. denied*, 536 U.S. 972, 153 L. Ed. 2d 862, 122 S. Ct. 2693 (2002); *Dinkins v. State*, 894 S.W.2d 330, 350 (Tex. Crim. App.), *cert. denied*, 516 U.S. 832, 116 S. Ct. 106, 133 L. Ed. 2d 59 (1995). A suspect's invocation of his right to counsel must be "scrupulously honored." *See Michigan v. Mosley*, 423 U.S. 96, 103, 96 S. Ct. 321, 326, 46 L. Ed. 2d 313 (1975). A request for counsel must be unambiguous, meaning the suspect must "articulate his desire to have counsel present sufficiently clearly that a reasonable police officer in the circumstances would understand the statement to be a request for an attorney." *Davis v. United States*, 512 U.S. 452, 459, 114 S. Ct. 2350, 2355, 129 L. Ed. 2d 362 (1994). This standard, applied to adult suspects, also applies to juvenile suspects. *Fare v. Michael C.*, 442 U.S. 707, 725, 99 S. Ct. 2560, 2572, 61 L. Ed. 2d 197 (1979). A custodial statement made voluntarily after a suspect has invoked his right to counsel and questioning nonetheless continues renders the statement inadmissible in the State's case-in-chief, but the statement may be admissible for impeachment purposes. *See Harris*, 401 U.S. at 224–26, 91 S. Ct. at 644–46 (holding failure to warn suspect of his right to counsel rendered voluntary statement inadmissible in State's case-in-chief but statement was admissible for impeachment purposes); *Oregon v. Hass*, 420 U.S. 714, 722–24, 95 S. Ct. 1215, 1220–21, 43 L. Ed. 2d 570 (1975) (holding post failure-to-honor-request-for-counsel statement admissible for impeachment purposes); *Moran v. State*, 171 S.W.3d 382, 392–94 (Tex. App.—Austin 2005, no pet.) (Puryear, J. dissenting.) (same); *In re G.E.*, 879 A.2d 672, 676–80 (D.C. App. 2005) (regarding juvenile's statement).

When reviewing alleged invocations of the right to counsel, we typically look at the totality of the circumstances surrounding the interrogation, as well as the alleged invocation, in order to determine whether a suspect's statement can be construed as an actual invocation of his right to counsel. *Dinkins*, 894 S.W.2d at 351; *Lucas v. State*, 791 S.W.2d 35, 45–46 (Tex. Crim. App. 1989). The United States Supreme Court explained that the totality-of-the-circumstances approach allows the court the flexibility necessary to determine whether a juvenile has invoked his rights:

> There is no reason to assume that such courts—especially juvenile courts, with their special expertise in this area—will be unable to apply the totality-of-the-circumstances analysis so as to take into account those special concerns that are present when young persons, often with limited experience and education and with immature judgment, are involved. *Where the age and experience of a juvenile indicate that his request for his probation officer or his parents is, in fact, an invocation of his right to remain silent, the totality approach will allow the court the necessary flexibility to take this into account in making a waiver determination.* At the same time, that

approach refrains from imposing rigid restraints on police and courts in dealing with an experienced older juvenile with an extensive prior record who knowingly and intelligently waives his Fifth Amendment rights and voluntarily consents to interrogation.

Fare, 442 U.S. at 725–26, 99 S. Ct. at 2572 (emphasis added). This totality-of-the-circumstances test includes an evaluation of the juvenile's age, experience, education, background, and intelligence. *Id.* at 725, 99 S. Ct. at 2572; *In re R.D.*, 627 S.W.2d 803, 806–07 (Tex. App.—Tyler 1982, no writ).

B. Review of Trial Court's Totality-of-the-Circumstances Determination

The totality of the circumstances surrounding the interrogation reflects that H.V. was a sixteen-year-old junior in high school. H.V. is from Bosnia; he had lived in the United States fewer than six years when he was arrested. There is no evidence that H.V. had been in trouble before or had any prior juvenile record that would have familiarized him with the criminal justice system. H.V. was in custody for more than five hours before he made the statement, was handcuffed for one hour, and had no prior juvenile record. During the ten minutes that he received warnings from Judge Bendslev, he specifically asked to talk with his mother and said he wanted her to ask for an attorney. Judge Bendslev told him that he could not talk to his mother; if he did not want to talk to police, he would be returned to the juvenile facility, and she did not know what the timeframe was for H.V. to be able to speak to his mother. When Judge Bendslev tried to explain to H.V. that he himself could ask for an attorney, he said, "But I am only sixteen," clearly indicating that he did not understand how a sixteen-year-old person could ask for and go about contacting an attorney. Judge Bendslev did not testify that H.V. affirmatively indicated that he did not want an attorney. Nor did she indicate that H.V. affirmatively stated that he wanted to talk to police despite his right to an attorney. *Cf. Dewberry v. State*, 4 S.W.3d 735, 747 (Tex. Crim. App. 1999) (holding trial court properly denied motion to suppress confession when defendant was advised of right to counsel and responded by stating he had not "done anything wrong. I don't need a lawyer."), *cert. denied*, 529 U.S. 1131, 146 L. Ed. 2d 958 (2000). H.V. did not sign the "Warning to Child Offender" form, setting forth the *Miranda* warnings and signed by Judge Bendslev, in connection with his second written statement, and police chatted with H.V. for forty-five minutes to an hour before moving to the issue of the disappearance of Daniel Oltmanns.

The record demonstrates that H.V. articulated his desire to have counsel present sufficiently clearly that a reasonable magistrate judge in the circumstances would understand H.V.'s request to call his mother to be an unambiguous request for an attorney when such request was followed by his statement that he wanted his mother to ask for an attorney and his exclamation that he was only sixteen in response to Judge Bendslev's comment that he could ask for an attorney. *See Davis*, 512 U. S. at 459, 114 S. Ct. at 2355. This is not a situation in which the juvenile requested only to speak with his mother. *Compare R. D.*, 627 S.W.2d at 806–07 (applying totality-of-circumstances test to hold that in light of defendant's juvenile record and experience on probation, psychologist's report indicating defendant was functioning in average cognitive range, and lack of evidence juvenile was worn down by improper interrogation tactics or lengthy questions, juvenile's statement that "he wanted to talk to his mother" standing alone was not invocation of right to counsel). The undisputed evidence establishes that H.V. said, "I want to call my mother. I want her to ask for an attorney." When H.V. was told that he could ask for an attorney, he said, "But I am only sixteen." Consequently, this is more than a situation in which the defendant, with regard to hiring an attorney, equivocally says, "I want to talk to my mother *about whether to hire* an attorney"; this is a situation in which H.V. unequivocally indicated that he wanted an attorney—he wanted to call his mother; he wanted her to ask for an attorney. *Accord Loredo v. State*, 130 S.W.3d 275, 284 (Tex. App.—Houston [14th Dist.] 2004, pet. ref'd) (holding appellant's question of whether he could ask for a lawyer, followed by a police officer's comment that he could and that if he did the interrogation would cease, did not constitute an unambiguous invocation of the right to counsel when appellant thereafter continued to speak with the officer).

Moreover, the totality of the circumstances surrounding the interrogation supports the trial court's determination that H.V. invoked his right to counsel. *See Mayes v. State*, 8 S.W.3d 354, 361 (Tex. App.—Amarillo 1999, no pet.) (holding under totality of circumstances statement that "I have to get one for both of us" was unambiguous invocation of right to counsel). The facts at bar are the type of facts contemplated by the United States Supreme Court in *Fare*. 442 U.S. at 724–25, 99 S. Ct. at 2571–72. Here, H.V.'s age and lack of experience indicate that his request to call his mother, coupled with his statement that he wanted her to ask for an attorney and his exclamation that he was only sixteen, was in fact an invocation of his right to counsel, and the totality-of-the-circumstances approach allows the juvenile court the necessary flexibility to take this into account in determining whether a juvenile has invoked his Fifth Amendment rights. *See id.*

The cases relied upon by the State are distinguishable. The State cites *State v. Hyatt*, 355 N.C. 642, 566 S.E.2d 61 (N.C. 2002), *cert. denied*, 537 U.S. 1133, 154 L. Ed. 2d 823 (2003). But in *Hyatt*, evidence at the suppression hearing conclusively established that the defendant "whispered" to his father that he wanted his father to get an attorney for him. *Id.* at 70–71. In *Hyatt*, both officers testified that they did not hear the defendant ask his father to obtain an attorney, and the trial court made a specific finding of fact that "neither Agent Shook nor Detective Benjamin heard defendant's alleged invocation of his right to counsel." *Id.* Here, there is no question that Judge Bendslev heard H.V. state that he wanted to call his mother; he wanted her to ask for a lawyer, he was only sixteen.

The State also relies upon *Fare*. 442 U.S. at 719–20, 99 S. Ct. at 2569. But in *Fare*, the juvenile did not state that he wanted to call his mother because he wanted her to ask for a lawyer; the juvenile said he wanted to call his probation officer. *Id.* The United States Supreme Court held that the rule in *Miranda* is based on the critical position lawyers occupy in our legal system because of a lawyer's unique ability to protect the Fifth Amendment rights of a client undergoing custodial interrogation. *Id.* Because of a lawyer's special ability to help the client preserve his Fifth Amendment rights once the client becomes enmeshed in the adversary process, "the right to have counsel present at the interrogation is indispensable to the protection of the Fifth Amendment privilege." *Id.* (quoting *Miranda*, 384 U.S. at 469, 86 S. Ct. at 1625). Here, H.V. specifically indicated

that he wanted to talk to his mother; he wanted her to ask for a lawyer. Through this request, H.V. sought a lawyer's unique ability and assistance, not simply the assistance of his mother or a probation officer. The State also cites *Flamer v. Delaware*, 68 F.3d 710, 725 (3d Cir. 1995), *cert. denied*, 516 U.S. 1088, 116 S. Ct. 807, 133 L. Ed. 2d 754 (1996). *Flamer* involved a twenty-five-year-old adult suspect. *Id.* at 719. At his arraignment hearing, Flamer asked permission to call his mother "to inquire about bail and possible representation by counsel." *Id.* at 725. The Third Circuit held that "a request for an attorney at arraignment is, in itself, insufficient to invoke the Fifth Amendment right to counsel at subsequent custodial interrogation." *Id.* at 726. Here, H.V. did not request an attorney at arraignment; he indicated that he wanted his mother to ask for an attorney prior to custodial interrogation.

Because the trial court is the sole judge of the credibility of the witnesses and the weight of their testimony, we hold that the trial court's findings and conclusions are supported by the record. *Ross*, 32 S.W.3d at 855. Viewing the totality of the circumstances, we hold that the trial court did not abuse its discretion in suppressing H.V.'s second written statement when it properly determined that H.V.'s request to talk to his mother because he wanted her to hire an attorney was a request for counsel. *Compare R.D.*, 627 S.W.2d at 805–07 (applying totality of the circumstances and holding that bare request to talk to mother, without more, was not request for counsel). We overrule the State's first point.

III. SUPPRESSION OF WEAPON

In his second statement, which the trial court suppressed, H.V. explained that he "threw the gun in the gutter close to [his] house." At the suppression hearing, Detective Carroll indicated that, as a result of H.V.'s second statement, police located the gun. During Detective Carroll's questioning, he said that H.V. told him that he took the gun and placed it in a sewer near his house, that H.V. drew a diagram of the gun's location, and that police found the gun.

In its second point, the State argues that even if H.V.'s second written statement is suppressed, the trial court erred by suppressing the gun as the alleged "fruit" of H.V.'s second written statement. H.V. responds that the violation of his Fifth Amendment right to counsel mandates the suppression of not only his second statement but also the derivative evidence obtained from that statement.

Once an accused in custody has requested the assistance of an attorney, officers must terminate all interrogation until counsel is made available or the accused voluntarily reinitiates communication. *See Minnick v. Mississippi*, 498 U.S. 146, 153, 111 S. Ct. 486, 491, 112 L. Ed. 2d 489 (1990); *Edwards*, 451 U.S. at 484–85, 101 S. Ct. at 1885; *Cross v. State*, 144 S.W.3d 521, 526 (Tex. Crim. App. 2004). An accused's request for an attorney is per se an invocation of his Fifth Amendment rights, requiring that all interrogation cease. *Edwards*, 451 U.S. at 485, 101 S. Ct. at 1885; *Fare*, 442 U.S. at 719, 99 S. Ct. at 2569; *Rhode Island v. Innis*, 446 U.S. 291, 298, 100 S. Ct. 1682, 1688, 64 L. Ed. 2d 297 (1980). The presence of counsel insures the process of police interrogation conforms to the dictates of the Fifth Amendment privilege by insuring that an accused's statements made in a government-established atmosphere are not the product of compulsion. *Miranda*, 384 U.S. at 466, 86 S. Ct.

at 1623; *see also Fare*, 442 U.S. at 719, 99 S. Ct. at 2569. Any statement taken after a person invokes his Fifth Amendment privilege "cannot be other than the product of compulsion, subtle or otherwise." *Fare*, 442 U.S. at 717, 99 S. Ct. at 2568 (quoting *Miranda*, 384 U.S. at 473–74, 86 S. Ct. at 1627–28).

Here, the trial court found that H.V. invoked his right to counsel. Deferring, as we must, to the historical facts found by the trial court and not challenged by the State, we have held that the trial court did not abuse its discretion by concluding that H.V. invoked his Fifth Amendment right to counsel. Consequently, all interrogation should have ceased. *Edwards*, 451 U.S. at 485, 101 S. Ct. at 1885; *Fare*, 442 U.S. at 719, 99 S. Ct. at 2569; *Innis*, 446 U.S. at 298, 100 S. Ct. at 1688. H.V.'s subsequent statement, "cannot be other than the product of compulsion, subtle or otherwise." *Fare*, 442 U.S. at 717, 99 S. Ct. at 2568 (quoting *Miranda*, 384 U.S. at 473–74, 86 S. Ct. at 1627–28). The magistrate's failure to honor H.V.'s invocation of his right to counsel, placing him instead directly into a custodial interrogation without counsel, operated to overcome H.V.'s free choice in producing a statement. *See Miranda*, 384 U.S. at 474, 86 S. Ct. 1628. The remaining question is whether our holding—that H.V.'s statement disclosing the location of the gun was taken in violation of his invoked right to the presence of counsel during custodial interrogation—mandates suppression of the gun as determined by the trial court.

The State points out, and we agree, that the "fruit of the poisonous tree" doctrine articulated in *Wong Sun* does not apply to a mere failure to provide *Miranda* warnings to a suspect prior to custodial interrogation when the suspect makes a voluntary statement: while the statement must be suppressed, other evidence subsequently obtained as a result of that accidentally unwarned statement, that is the "fruit" of the statement, need not be suppressed. *United States v. Patane*, 542 U.S. 630, 639, 124 S. Ct. 2620, 2628, 159 L. Ed. 2d 667 (2004) (holding accidental failure to give suspect *Miranda* warnings did not require suppression of physical fruits of suspect's unwarned but voluntary statement); *Oregon v. Elstad*, 470 U.S. 298, 307, 105 S. Ct. 1285, 1292, 84 L. Ed. 2d 222 (1985) (holding accidentally unwarned statements may be used to impeach defendant's testimony at trial); *see also Michigan v. Tucker*, 417 U.S. 433, 452, 94 S. Ct. 2357, 2368, 41 L. Ed. 2d 182 (1974); *Baker v. State*, 956 S.W.2d 19, 22 (Tex. Crim. App. 1997); *accord Marsh v. State*, 115 S.W.3d 709, 715 (Tex. App.—Austin 2003, no pet.) (involving allegation of post-arrest interrogation before receiving *Miranda* warnings); *Montemayor v. State*, 55 S.W.3d 78, 90 (Tex. App.—Austin 2001, pet. ref'd) (same). Here, however, H.V.'s second statement was not simply an unwarned statement; H.V. invoked his right to counsel before he made his second statement.

The State argues in its motion for rehearing that no distinction exists between fruit from an accidentally unwarned statement, like in *Patane*, and fruit from a post failure-to-honor-a-request-for-counsel statement, like H.V.'s here. The Supreme Court of the United States has not explicitly addressed the issue of whether fruits derivative of a voluntary, post failure-to-honor-a-request-for-counsel statement are admissible in the State's case-in-chief, but numerous state and federal courts have, and they are split on the issue. *See Patterson v. United States*, 485 U.S. 922, 922, 108 S. Ct. 1093, 1094, 99 L. Ed. 2d 255 (1988) (White and Brennan, JJ., dissenting from denial of certiorari) (recognizing that the United States Supreme Court had "expressly left open the question of the admissibility of physical

evidence obtained as a result of an interrogation conducted contrary to the rules set forth in *Miranda*" and recognizing the split among the lower courts). Because, as discussed below, in *Elstad* the Supreme Court recognized a distinction between the admissibility of fruit from a custodial statement voluntarily made in the accidental absence of *Miranda* warnings—which does not involve a constitutional violation—and fruit from a violation of an accused's constitutional rights, and because the Supreme Court in *Dickerson v. United States* and in *Missouri v. Siebert* affirmed that *Miranda* set forth a constitutionally based rule, we hold that such a distinction does exist and that fruits derivative of a voluntary, post failure-to-honor-a-request-for-counsel statement are inadmissible in the State's case-in-chief. *See also Harris*, 544 N.W.2d at 553 (holding "there is a critical difference between a mere defect in the administration of *Miranda* warnings 'without more' and police-initiated interrogation conducted after a suspect unambiguously invokes the right to have counsel present during questioning); Mark S. Bransdorfer, Note, *Miranda Right-to-Counsel Violations and the Fruit of the Poisonous Tree Doctrine*, 62 IND. L.J. 1061, 1061, 1097 (1987) (explaining why *Wong Sun's* fruit-of-the-poisonous-tree doctrine should apply to "second generation derivative evidence after an *Edwards* violation").

We begin by examining the fruit-of-the-poisonous-tree doctrine. Only evidence uncovered as a result of police infringement of a constitutional right is "fruit of the poisonous tree" because the constitutional infringement creates a "poisonous tree," and the evidence discovered as a result of the constitutional violation is the "fruit" of that violation. *Wong Sun*, 371 U.S. at 485–86, 83 S. Ct. at 416 (the purpose of fruit of poisonous tree doctrine is to "deter police from violations of constitutional and statutory protections"). There is no constitutional right, however, to receive *Miranda* warnings; that is, there is no constitutional right to be warned of your constitutional rights. *New York v. Quarles*, 467 U.S. 649, 654, 104 S. Ct. 2626, 2630, 81 L. Ed. 2d 550 (1984) (quoting *Tucker*, 417 U.S. at 444, 94 S. Ct. at 2364) (recognizing that "the prophylactic *Miranda* warnings therefore are 'not themselves rights protected by the Constitution but [are] instead measures to insure that the right against compulsory self-incrimination [is] protected'"). Thus, because the accidental failure to give *Miranda* warnings does not infringe upon an accused's constitutional rights, an accidental failure to warn does not create a "poisonous tree." *See, e.g., Patane*, 542 U.S. at 637, 124 S. Ct. at 2626 (holding "mere failures to warn" do not violate the Constitution); *Elstad*, 470 U.S. at 304, 105 S. Ct. at 1290 (holding accidental failure to warn does not require suppression of second warned statement); *Tucker*, 417 U.S. 433, 452, 94 S. Ct. 2357, 2368, 41 L. Ed. 2d 182 (same). In the absence of a "poisonous tree," physical "fruit" from a voluntary, accidentally unwarned statement need not be suppressed. *See Patane*, 542 U.S. at 636–37, 124 S. Ct. at 2626; *Elstad*, 470 U.S. at 304, 105 S. Ct. at 1290.

We consequently come to the question of whether a suspect's in-custody invocation of the right to counsel—that he has just been advised he possesses—constitutes the invocation of a constitutional right. If a suspect's invocation of his right to counsel constitutes the invocation of a constitutional right, the fruit-of-the-poisonous-tree doctrine is applicable. *Accord id.* at 470 U.S. at 304, 105 S. Ct. at 1290. If a suspect has no constitutional right to counsel during custodial interrogation, then the fruit-of-the-poisonous-tree doctrine is inapplicable, and the State's position is correct. *Accord Patane*, 542 U.S. at 636, 124 S. Ct. at 2625–26. Support for the proposition that the right to counsel during custodial interrogation is a Fifth Amendment constitutional right is found in numerous Supreme Court cases dealing with the right to counsel in the Fifth Amendment context.

As discussed in connection with the State's first point, the Supreme Court has repeatedly emphasized the importance of the right to counsel during custodial interrogation:

> The rule in *Miranda* . . . was based on this Court's perception that the lawyer occupies a critical position in our legal system because of his unique ability to protect the Fifth Amendment rights of a client undergoing custodial interrogation. Because of this special ability of the lawyer to help the client preserve his Fifth Amendment rights once the client becomes enmeshed in the adversary process, the Court found that *'the right to have counsel present at the interrogation is indispensable to the protection of the Fifth Amendment privilege under the system' established by the Court.*

Fare, 442 U.S. at 719, 99 S. Ct. at 2568–69 (emphasis added); *see also Edwards*, 451 U.S. at 484, 101 S. Ct. at 1884–85 (citing *North Carolina v. Butler*, 441 U.S. 369, 372–76, 99 S. Ct. 1755, 1757–59, 60 L. Ed. 2d 286 (1979)) (safeguarding invoked right to counsel by imposing restrictions on subsequent waiver of that right).

Additional support for the constitutional nature of the right to counsel during custodial interrogation is found in *Dickerson*. 530 U.S. at 440, 120 S. Ct. at 2334. In *Dickerson*, the United States Supreme Court affirmed that the *Miranda* "system established by the Court," presumably including the right to counsel during custodial interrogation, is founded upon the Fifth Amendment. *Id.* at 440, 120 S. Ct. at 2334 nn. 5, 6 (holding *Miranda* is "constitutionally based" and string citing multiple Supreme Court opinions). Because the *Miranda* rules are constitutionally based, the *Dickerson* Court declared unconstitutional a statute that required courts to gauge a confession's admissibility based solely on its voluntariness, without regard to compliance with *Miranda. Id.* at 440, 120 S. Ct. at 2334. The *Dickerson* Court held, "In sum, we conclude that *Miranda* announced a constitutional rule that Congress may not supersede legislatively." *Id.* at 444, 120 S. Ct. at 2336. We have no doubt that *Dickerson* prohibits a legislature from not only a wholesale abandonment of *Miranda's* constitutional rule but also from a piecemeal abandonment of *Miranda's* constitutional rule, such as a legislative elimination of a suspect's right to counsel during custodial interrogation. *Accord Edwards*, 451 U.S. at 482, 101 S. Ct. at 1883 (stating that "an accused has a Fifth and Fourteenth Amendment right to have counsel present during custodial interrogation"). Accordingly, because pursuant to *Dickerson* it would appear that a legislature is without authority to eliminate an accused's right to counsel during custodial interrogation, that right appears to be part and parcel of *Miranda's* Fifth Amendment constitutional rule.

Finally, still more support for the proposition that the right to counsel during custodial interrogation is a Fifth Amendment constitutional right is found in the Supreme Court's recent decision in *Missouri v. Seibert*. In *Seibert*, the Supreme Court addressed the admissibility of a statement when the *Miranda* warnings that were given were rendered totally ineffective.

542 U.S. at 604, 124 S. Ct. at 2605. Likewise, the "indispensable" right to counsel during custodial interrogation cannot function effectively as *Miranda* requires if the police are free to ignore an accused's invocation of his right to counsel in hopes of obtaining physical evidence that will be admissible against the accused. Counsel cannot exercise his unique ability to protect the Fifth Amendment rights of a client undergoing custodial interrogation if the custodial interrogation is completed in his absence. . . .

Regarding minimizing the seriousness of police misconduct and breeding contempt for the law, Professor Yale Kamisar has written:

> Consider, for example, a situation where the suspect has invoked his right to counsel, but the police continue to question him in order to retrieve the murder weapon or some other nontestimonial evidence. In this set of circumstances[,] the police have nothing to lose by rejecting the request for counsel (they will lose any statement the suspect might make, but they would have lost any statement anyway if they had honored the suspect's request for counsel and immediately ceased all questioning) and something to gain (the use of physical evidence that the inadmissible statement might turn up).

Knapp, 700 N.W.2d at 918–19 (quoting Yale Kamisar, *Postscript: Another Look at Patane and Seibert, the 2004 Miranda "Poisoned Fruit" Cases*, 2 OHIO ST. J. CRIM. L. 97, 105 (2004)).

To nonetheless hold that, if interrogation does not cease, fruits from the post invocation-of-the-right-to-counsel statement are admissible would impermissibly erode *Miranda's* concrete constitutional guidelines and drain all substance from the purported right to counsel during custodial interrogation. For these reasons, we hold that the right to counsel during custodial interrogation is a constitutional, Fifth Amendment right.

As we have held, and the trial court found, H.V. invoked his right to counsel when he was informed of that right by Judge Bendslev. Nonetheless, Judge Bendslev turned H.V. over to police for interrogation and, from shortly after 7:30 p.m. until 10:35 p.m., police interrogated H.V. in the absence of counsel. After more than two hours of custodial interrogation, Detective Carroll began typing H.V.'s statement. The custodial interrogation of H.V. despite H.V.'s invocation of his right to counsel infringed upon H.V.'s constitutional Fifth Amendment right to counsel. *See Edwards*, 451 U.S. at 481–82, 101 S. Ct. at 1883–84 (recognizing that Fifth Amendment right to counsel attaches during custodial interrogation). After H.V. incriminated himself in his second statement and therein disclosed the location of the gun, police concluded their interrogation and H.V.'s Fifth Amendment right to have counsel present during that completed interrogation was forever lost. This constitutional violation of H.V.'s Fifth Amendment right to counsel created a "poisonous tree." The evidence discovered as a result of this constitutional violation—the gun—is the "fruit" of that violation and must be suppressed, at least in the State's case-in-chief. *See Hass*, 420 U.S. at 722–24, 95 S. Ct. at 1220–21; *Wong Sun*, 371 U.S. at 485–86, 83 S. Ct. at 416.

We realize that we are to maintain the "closest possible fit . . . between the Self-Incrimination Clause and any judge-made rule designed to protect it." *Patane*, 542 U.S. at 643, 124 S. Ct.

at 2629–30. Here, the "fit" between H.V.'s invocation of his Fifth Amendment right to counsel and the trial court's suppression of the gun—the judge-made ruling—is a proper, close "fit." The Fifth Amendment right to counsel is protected only by an exclusionary rule that requires suppression of the physical fruits located as a result of information provided in a post failure-to-honor-a-request-for-counsel statement; otherwise, the Fifth Amendment right to counsel would truly exist only when interrogators decided to honor a suspect's request for counsel. For these reasons, we hold that the trial court did not abuse its discretion by granting H.V.'s motion to suppress the gun located by police as a result of his second statement. *Accord* TEX. FAM. CODE ANN. § 54.03(e) (Vernon Supp. 2005) (stating that evidence illegally seized or obtained is inadmissible in an adjudication hearing).

Nor was evidence introduced at the suppression hearing that the gun would have been, or was, discovered by means sufficiently distinguishable to be purged of the violation of H.V.'s Fifth Amendment privilege. *Compare Thornton v. State*, 145 S.W.3d 228, 233–34 (Tex. Crim. App. 2004) (holding sufficient attenuating factors existed dissipating taint of illegal arrest from derivative evidence obtained as a result of arrest). We overrule the State's second point.

IV. CONCLUSION

Having overruled all of the State's points, we affirm the trial court's order suppressing H.V.'s second written statement and the gun obtained as a result of that statement.

[Footnotes omitted]

Source: 179 S.W.3d 746; 2005 Tex. App. LEXIS 9712. Printed with permission from LexisNexis.

Chapter 3

Elements of the Criminal Act

CHAPTER OBJECTIVES

Upon completion of this chapter, you will be able to:

- Discuss actus reus of a crime.

- Explain the mens rea requirement.

- Understand the importance of proving each element of a particular law.

- Understand concurrence.

- Identify causation and presumption.

Every crime has four basic elements: the physical act, the defendant's state of mind, the physical act and the requisite state of mind coming together to form the crime, and the resulting harm. A defendant cannot be found guilty of a crime unless he commits a physical act (actus reus) with the intent necessary to carry it out (mens rea). Understanding the basic elements of the crime and the relationship among these elements is essential to a study in criminal law and these elements will be explained in more detail in the following paragraphs.

---

elements of the crime
Those constituent parts of a crime that must be proved by the prosecution to sustain a conviction.

actus reus
The guilty act.

mens rea
"A guilty mind"; criminal intent in committing the act.

concurrence
A meeting or coming together of a guilty act and a guilty mind.

causation
Intentional act resulted in harm or injury to the complaining plaintiff.

ELEMENTS OF A CRIME

In order to convict a person of a crime, the prosecutor must prove the **elements of the crime** beyond a reasonable doubt. Each crime consists of four basic elements. These elements are

- **Actus reus**—a guilty act.
- **Mens rea**—a guilty mind.
- **Concurrence**—a guilty act and guilty mind that exist at the same time.
- **Causation**—a harmful result.

Each element of the crime relates to a general principle of criminal liability. Almost all crimes require a physical act by the criminal and some form of intent. In other words, an accused cannot be found guilty of a crime unless he committed a wrongful act with the required mental state.

A DAY IN THE LIFE OF A REAL PARALEGAL

Rhonda, with rose-colored glasses, has been working at the district attorney's office as a criminal paralegal for two months, working vigorously on [Case #23] trying to convict an alleged rapist. Many months have gone by and Rhonda was looking forward to celebrating as she thought her office did a great job in prosecuting Case #23. When the trial was over, the defendant was found innocent and walked out of the court a free man. His acquittal was due to the fact that Rhonda's office failed to prove all elements of the crime in order to convict. It is important to remember not to include your emotions in your professionalism when prosecuting and defending clients.

RESEARCH THIS

Research your state law. How does the state statute define a crime in your jurisdiction? What are the elements of a crime as prescribed by your state law?

ACTUS REUS

For a finding of criminal liability, a defendant must have either performed a voluntary physical act or failed to act when she was under a legal duty to act. The physical act is defined as having performed a bodily movement. A thought is not considered a physical act. Therefore, thinking bad thoughts does not by itself constitute a physical act or lead to criminal liability.

The Model Penal Code of the American Law Institute provides that a person is not guilty of an offense unless his liability is based on conduct that includes a voluntary act or the omission to perform an act of which he is physically capable. For example, as in tort situations of omission, people who fail to prevent injury are generally not criminally liable, but some defendants may have a *duty* to act. Such a duty may result due to a statute, a contract, or a special relationship that exists between the parties. (See Figure 3.1.)

Certain acts are not considered "voluntary" under the Model Penal Code and generally will not form the basis of a conviction. Such acts include a reflex or convulsion, a bodily movement during unconsciousness or sleep, conduct during hypnosis or resulting from hypnotic suggestion, and bodily movements that are not products of the effort or determination of the actor.

Section 2.01.

(1) A person is not guilty of an offense unless his liability is based on conduct that includes a voluntary act or the omission to perform an act of which he is physically capable.

(2) The following are not voluntary acts within the meaning of this section:
  (a) a reflex or convulsion;
  (b) a bodily movement during unconsciousness or sleep;
  (c) conduct during hypnosis or resulting from hypnotic suggestion;
  (d) a bodily movement that otherwise isn't a product of the effort or determination of the actor, either conscious or habitual.

(3) Liability for the commission of an offense may not be based on an omission unaccompanied by action unless
  (a) the omission is expressly made sufficient by the law defining the offense; or
  (b) a duty to perform the omitted act is otherwise imposed by law . . .

(4) Possession is an act, within the meaning of this Section, if the possessor knowingly procured or received the thing possessed or was aware of his control thereof for a sufficient period to have been able to terminate his possession.

FIGURE 3.1
Model Penal Code, Section 2.01
The Model Penal Code of the American Law Institute states the following concerning the physical action necessary for a crime.
Source: Copyright 1985 by the "Model Penal Code, American Law Institute. Reprinted with permission"

A DAY IN THE LIFE OF A REAL PARALEGAL

You have been thinking about your weekend trip for months, you are so looking forward to getting away and relaxing. Life at the firm has been getting crazy; you are putting in more hours each week. A nice weekend away is just what the doctor ordered. As you pack up your belongings to head out Friday afternoon for the planned weekend, your boss, one of the partners, asks you to stay that night and to be at work Saturday morning as a very big case has been moved up on the court docket. It's an exciting yet busy profession!

Liability for an offense may not be based on an omission unless that omission is expressed sufficiently by the law defining the offense, or a duty to perform the omitted act exists. For example, Dana, an off-duty lifeguard, was having a picnic on the beach with some friends when she spotted a drowning child. Dana knew she could help, but she had just gotten her hair done and didn't want to ruin it. Paul, who was also picnicking, attempted to help the child but, being a poor swimmer, failed to do so and the child drowned. In this situation, Dana had no duty to act, despite having the ability to help. Had she been on duty, a duty would have existed and her failure to assist the child would have resulted in liability.

Possession is considered an act within the meaning of section 2.01 of the MPC if the possessor knowingly procured or received the thing possessed or was aware of his control of the thing.

An act involves physical behavior by the defendant. The mental process of the crime is not part of the act. Only the physical act that gives rise to the crime is considered the actus reus. The actus reus is known at the evil act of the defendant. The actus reus of a crime causes a social harm that constitutes the crime. The actus reus of a crime is important because it enables society to make **inferences** regarding the defendant's state of mind based on his actions. However, in order for the actions of the defendant to qualify as the actus reus of a crime, the defendant must have committed voluntary actions.

inference
A conclusion reached by considering other facts and deducing a logical consequence.

Voluntary Act

Voluntary acts are necessary in order for the defendant's actions to be considered a criminal act. A voluntary act is an act that is done with a conscious exercise of free will. It includes muscular contractions that are willed by the defendant. The law will not punish an involuntary act such as a reflexive movement or spasm. Likewise, criminal liability will not attach for acts performed while a defendant is unconscious or sleepwalking. Therefore, in order for a defendant to be blameworthy, he must have committed a voluntary act.

A voluntary act is different from mere thoughts. The defendant must go beyond thinking about the crime and must commit some overt physical act toward the commission of the crime. The voluntary action necessary for the commission of a crime varies from crime to crime. Since a voluntary actus reus is an element of a crime, the burden of proof falls on the prosecutor to prove that the defendant's act was of her own volition.

Involuntary Act

The Model Penal Code at section 2.01(2) lists some types of acts that should be considered involuntary:

- A reflex or convulsion.
- Unconsciousness or sleep.
- Hypnosis.
- Other acts that are involuntary if they are "a bodily movement that otherwise is not a product of the effort or determination of the actor, either conscious or habitual."

Perhaps the clearest example of an involuntary act is one that is a reflex or is convulsive. A person who commits an alleged criminal act as the result of a reflex or convulsion will not be guilty of committing a crime because his act was done involuntarily. For example, Doug is an epileptic and periodically suffers epileptic attacks. While shopping in the local mall, Doug suffers an attack. In the midst of his attack, Doug's arms are flailing uncontrollably. People rush to his side to assist him, including Sally, who is a cashier at one of the nearby stores. As Doug is flailing, his arm strikes Sally in the face, breaking her nose. Since Doug's act was involuntary and he had no control over his muscular contractions, Doug will not be deemed to have committed a criminal act. However, if Doug had been told by his doctor to take medication to control his seizures and he neglected to do so, he may then be criminally liable for his failure to take the medication.

If a person commits an act while being unconscious, then the act will not rise to the level of criminal liability because the act will be considered to be involuntary as it does not involve the will of the defendant. Not all jurisdictions accept the assertion made by the Model Penal Code that a person under hypnosis acts involuntarily. Some jurisdictions consider that a person would not commit an act under hypnosis that he would not commit had he not been under hypnosis.

Omission to Act

Generally speaking, under common law, a defendant does not have a duty to act in order to prevent harm to another person. However, there are exceptions to the rule. If a defendant fails to act when she has a legal duty to do so, then she may be found criminally liable. The defendant must have a legal duty to act, not a moral duty. A moral duty in and of itself may not be sufficient for criminal liability to attach. Legal duties to act are generated by three methods:

- Statutes
- Contracts
- Special relationships

The legislature may decide that, in certain circumstances, a person must act or suffer legal consequences; therefore, a statute is created specifying the legal duty surrounding the act. For example, every April 15th, the Internal Revenue Service requires by law that individuals file income tax returns. Failure to act, or, in other words, failure to file an income tax return, imposes criminal liability.

A legal duty to act can arise via a contract. The contract does not necessarily need to be between the defendant and the victim. For example, the City may employ Ben as a lifeguard for the local pool. Ben's hiring in the position of a lifeguard is a contract whereby Ben has a legal duty to save people from drowning. For performing this legal duty to act, Ben receives payment. If Ben fails to save a drowning person in the City pool, Ben can be criminally prosecuted.

If a special relationship exists between the defendant and the victim, then that relationship may give rise to a duty on the part of the defendant to act. For example, a parent has a special relationship to his children. On the basis of the parental relationship, a parent is legally obligated to provide for the necessities of his children. If a parent fails to provide substances or medical care to his children, he can be held criminally liable for abusing the child. Other special relationships exist between doctors and their patients, employers and their employees, and carriers and their passengers, to name a few.

Other situations exist where a defendant may have a legal duty to act. If the defendant places a victim in danger due to her own actions, then the defendant will have a legal duty to act. If Beverly accidentally starts a fire in her apartment building and fails to call the fire department, she may be found criminally liable for failing to act under the circumstance. Another instance in which a legal duty to act occurs is when a person voluntarily renders assistance to another person who was already in danger. The person rendering assistance has the duty to continue to provide aid to the victim, particularly if discontinuing assistance would leave the victim in a worse position than if the defendant had not acted at all.

MENS REA

A prosecutor needs more than a criminal act in order to prosecute a potential defendant for a crime. The pulse of society is that a person should not be punished for a crime if the harm was caused innocently. In order for a defendant to be considered blameworthy, he must have possessed the requisite culpable state of mind. *Mens rea* is the term used to refer to a defendant's criminal intent or guilty mind. It is the defendant's intent to commit a crime. Normally, the mens rea is described in the statutes using the following terms: *malice aforethought; premeditated; fraudulent intent; willful, wanton, and reckless with disregard for human life.* Mens rea should not be confused with *motive*. **Motive** is the wish of the defendant that induces the defendant to intend to commit a criminal act. However, motive is not considered an element of any crime. A prosecutor does not need to prove motive to prove criminal intent. However, sometimes motive can be used to help establish the existence of a mens rea.

motive
Something such as willful desire that causes an individual to act.

Mens rea can be categorized into four distinct categories: general intent, specific intent, constructive intent, and transferred intent.

For a defendant to possess a *general intent,* the only state of mind that the defendant must have is the desire to commit the act that served as the actus reus for the crime. General intent is usually sufficient to fulfill the mens rea requirement for most crimes. The prosecution must demonstrate that the defendant committed the act that constituted the crime and knew that such act was wrong. Typically, if the prosecution can prove that the defendant committed the actus reus of the crime, criminal intent is presumed. General intent crimes do not contain a specific mens rea element other than that which relates to committing the actus reus. For example, battery is considered to be a general intent crime. In a general intent crime, the only necessary element is the intentional application of force upon another. The defendant only has to have the intent to apply force to another person. No specific mental state is stated in the crime.

Specific intent crimes specify that the defendant must have both the desire to commit the actus reus and the desire to do something further. The defendant must desire to bring about a specific result. Specific intent crimes require proof that the defendant had to possess a certain mental state or knowledge in addition to committing the act. A defendant must possess what is known as *scienter*. **Scienter** means the amount of knowledge that a defendant has that makes him culpable for his criminal acts.

scienter
A degree of knowledge that makes a person legally responsible for his or her act or omission.

A specific intent crime is one in which the characterization of the crime includes that the defendant must have intent to achieve some consequence that goes beyond the conduct that constituted the crime, or the defendant must possess an awareness of the statutory circumstances surrounding his actions. An example of a specific intent crime murder. A defendant must not only have committed the killing but must possess the mens rea of **malice aforethought**. This requisite mental state for common-law murder involves either (1) the intent to kill, (2) the intent to inflict grievous bodily harm, (3) extremely reckless indifference to the value of human life, or (4) the intent to commit a dangerous felony. Intent to kill is often proved by circumstantial evidence such as the defendant's words or a deadly weapon. For example, the day before the victim was found dead, the defendant argued with the victim and yelled, "I'll see you dead if it is the last thing I do!" The defendant's words imply malice and would help prove the mens rea element.

malice aforethought
The prior intention to kill the victim or anyone else if likely to occur as a result of the defendant's actions or omissions.

Constructive intent refers to the state of mind possessed by someone who does not intend any harm to occur but should have known that his actions would result in a high probability that harm would befall someone. For example, Mike and Joe are street racing on a local residential street at high speeds in the rain. Mike and Joe do not intend to harm anyone by their actions; however, speeding on a residential street in the rain possesses a high probability that someone will be harmed. Mike, Joe, or both could have an accident. They could strike a pedestrian. They could lose control over their vehicle and strike another vehicle or plow through a nearby home. Should some harm occur to someone as a result of Mike's or Joe's actions, constructive intent would be inferred upon them based on their dangerous actions.

Transferred intent refers to an incident in which the defendant intends to harm a particular person but instead harms someone else. The law transfers the defendant's state of mind regarding the intention toward one victim to the one who is actually harmed. The classic example of transferred intent is a situation in which the defendant intends to shoot a specific individual but by mistake or accidentally shoots and kills another person. The intent toward the intended victim will be transferred to the actual victim for the sake of prosecution of the defendant.

The Model Penal Code is a proposed criminal code drafted by the American Law Institute and is used as the basis for criminal-law revision by many states; it is not imposed on a mandatory basis. Its authors established four states of mind that rise to the level of criminal culpability with respect to the definition of each offense. The mental states are

- Purposely
- Knowingly
- Recklessly
- Negligently

The Model Penal Code at section 2.02 sets forth the minimum requirements of culpability and states that a person is not guilty of an offense unless he acted purposely, knowingly, recklessly, or negligently. A person acts *purposely* when the element involves the nature of his conduct or is a result of it, the person consciously chooses to engage in the conduct that is likely to cause a criminal result, and, if the element involves attendant circumstances, the purposeful actor is aware of the existence of those circumstances and either believes or hopes such circumstances exist.

An actor acts *knowingly* with respect to an element of an offense if the element involves the nature of his conduct or the attendant circumstances, he is aware of the nature of his conduct, and, if the element is a result of his conduct, the actor was aware of the likelihood that his conduct would cause such a result.

An actor is *reckless* with respect to a material element when he consciously disregards a substantial and unjustifiable risk that the material element exists or will result from his conduct. On the other hand, an actor is *negligent* with respect to a material element when he should be aware of a substantial or unjustifiable risk that the material element exists or will result.

The Model Code uses the term *purposely* to denote a defendant's state of mind in which he is aware of the circumstances whereby harm may occur to someone as a result of his action. Purposely refers to awareness by the defendant as to the circumstances of the criminal activity or the attendant circumstances. The defendant must have a specific intent to commit the criminal activity or harm.

A defendant acts knowingly when he is aware that he is causing harm to the victim. He may not have acted purposely, but at the time of the act, he knew that he was causing harm.

A defendant acts recklessly when he does not necessarily know that his actions are in fact causing harm, but he should realize that his actions are creating a high degree

CASE FACT PATTERN

Benjamin owns an antique store downtown. One day, a young man comes into his store with several pieces of antique jewelry that he would like to sell to Benjamin. Benjamin recognizes the pieces as jewelry that had been stolen a couple of years ago in a series of home invasion robberies that had been televised on the news. Benjamin knows that he can sell the pieces for a pretty penny as that type of jewelry is fairly rare and in vogue. Benjamin offers the man $1,000 for four pieces that he knows are worth ten times that much. The man accepts the deal, takes the money, and leaves the jewelry with Benjamin. Benjamin exhibits the jewelry with other antique jewelry that he has for sale in one of his display cabinets. Approximately one month later, Martha comes into Benjamin's store. She recognizes the pieces as those that have been stolen from her house the year before. She calls the police. Benjamin hides the stolen pieces before the police arrive. The police question Benjamin and nervously he denies having the pieces in his possession. The police obtain a search warrant based on the statements made by Martha and conduct a search of Benjamin's store. They locate the pieces and arrest Benjamin. Benjamin is charged with knowingly accepting stolen property.

of risk for harm. The street racing example presented above demonstrates defendants who are acting recklessly.

A defendant will possess a negligent state of mind if he should have known, even if he did not know, that his actions created a risk of harm to the victim. The defendants in the street racing example also could have been found to have acted with a negligent state of mind as they should have known that traveling at a high rate of speed down a residential street creates a risk of harm.

strict liability
Liability that is based on the breach of an absolute duty rather than negligence or intent.

Lastly, at the very bottom of the intent ladder is strict liability. **Strict liability** results in the imposition of criminal liability for an action that causes a criminal result, even if traditional mens rea is not present. For example, Miles bought fireworks in State X believing they were lawful in his home, State Y. Miles took the fireworks home. He did not know that State Y had outlawed such fireworks. Miles may still be convicted under State Y's law since possession of the fireworks would probably be a strict liability crime.

CONCURRENCE

Actus reas and mens rea must occur at the same time. The two elements must occur together in order to have a crime. One without the other probably does not constitute a crime. *Concurrence* refers to the point in time where the actus reus and mens rea come together to form the crime.

Concurrence does not exist if, at the time of the defendant's act, he did not possess the required mental states for criminal culpability. A defendant may have formed the culpable mental state after he has acted or had abandoned the requisite mental state prior to committing the act. For example, an argument can be made that concurrence does not occur if a defendant is involuntarily intoxicated and then commits a criminal act because the defendant did not possess the requisite mens rea at the time of

EYE ON ETHICS

Every person charged with a crime is entitled to a defense. Even if the client tells his attorney that he is guilty, the attorney is under the obligation to present the client's case in the best possible light under the circumstances. An attorney should not bias a client's defense based on her own opinions. If the attorney has accepted the case, she must defend her client adequately. As a legal assistant, you are to work diligently on your attorney's client's behalf, regardless of your own personal feelings concerning his guilt or innocence.

SURF'S UP

To learn more about actus reus and mens rea, visit some of the following Web sites:

- www.crimblawg.com/mens_rea
- www.lycos.com/info/mens-rea.html
- www.lawteacher.net/CrimePages/ Crime02.html.

the act. If a series of acts by the defendant constitute the harmful act and if the mens rea can be established for any one of the acts, then concurrence between mind and act will be considered established.

CAUSATION

Actual cause may be satisfied by either of two tests: the "but for" test and the substantial factor test. For example, in a homicide case, the "but for" would be satisfied if the victim would not have died absent the defendant's act. If there are multiple causes or other parties involved in a homicide, the courts also will find causation on the part of the defendant if the defendant's act was a substantial factor causing the victim's death.

Proximate or legal cause exists only when the defendant is held legally responsible for a crime. The critical issue is whether other involved parties or forces will be considered superseding causes. Proximate cause is a complex legal doctrine. For example, at common law, if the victim died more than one year and one day after the defendant's act, the courts would hold that the act was not actually the proximate cause. However, most states have either eliminated this rule or extended the period within which the defendant can be held legally accountable. Additionally, where the actions of both a defendant and a third party work together to cause a criminal result, the causation question may vary depending on whether the defendant's act was the direct or indirect cause.

PRACTICE TIP

Be careful not to interchange words like *liable* for *guilty*, *sue* for *prosecute*, *state* for *person*, *assault* for *battery*, and so forth. Law is a language of words and it is vital to maintain the definitions to such to keep things clear and as accurate as possible.

Summary

In order to convict a person of a crime, the prosecutor must prove the elements of the crime beyond a reasonable doubt. Each crime consists of four basic elements: actus reus—a guilty act; mens rea—a guilty mind; concurrence—a guilty act and guilty mind that exist at the same time; and causation—a harmful result.

An act involves physical behavior by the defendant. The mental process of the crime is not part of the act. Only the physical act that gives rise to the crime is considered the actus reus. The actus reus is known as the evil act of the defendant. The actus reus of a crime causes a social harm that constitutes the crime. The actus reus of a crime is important because it enables society to make inferences regarding the defendant's state of mind based on her actions. However, in order for the actions of the defendant to qualify as the actus reus of a crime, the defendant must have committed voluntary actions.

Voluntary acts are necessary in order for the defendant's actions to be considered a criminal act. A voluntary act is an act that is done with a conscious exercise of free will. It includes muscular contractions that are willed by the defendant. The law will not punish an involuntary act such as a reflexive movement or spasm. Likewise, criminal liability will not attach for acts performed while a defendant is unconscious or sleepwalking. Therefore, in order for a defendant to be blameworthy, she must have committed a voluntary act.

Generally speaking, under common law, a defendant does not have a duty to act in order to prevent harm to another person. However, there are exceptions to the rule. If a defendant fails to act when he has a legal duty to do so, then he may be found criminally liable. The defendant must have a legal duty to act, not a moral duty. A moral duty in and of itself may not be sufficient for criminal liability to attach. Legal duties to act are generated by three methods: statutes, contracts, and special relationships.

A prosecutor needs more than a criminal act in order to prosecute a potential defendant for a crime. The pulse of society is that a person should not be punished for a crime if the harm was caused innocently. In order for a defendant to be considered blameworthy, she must have possessed the requisite culpable state of mind. Mens rea is the term used to refer to a defendant's criminal intent or guilty mind. It is the defendant's intent to commit a crime. Normally the mens rea is described in the statutes using the following terms: *malice aforethought; premeditated; fraudulent intent; willful, wanton, and reckless with disregard for human life.* Mens rea should not be confused with motive. Motive is the wish of the defendant that induces the defendant to intend to commit a criminal act. However, motive is not considered an element of any crime. A prosecutor does not need to prove motive to prove mens rea. However, sometimes motive can be used to help establish the existence of a mens rea.

Mens rea can be categorized into four distinct categories: general intent, specific intent, constructive intent, and transferred intent.

The authors of the Model Penal Code established four states of mind that rise to the level of criminal culpability with respect to the definition of each offense. These mental states are purposely, knowingly, recklessly, and negligently.

Actus reus and mens rea must occur at the same time—together—in order to have a crime. One without the other probably does not constitute a crime. Concurrence refers to the point in time when the actus reus and mens rea come together to form the crime.

Key Terms

Actus reus	Malice aforethought
Causation	Mens rea
Concurrence	Motive
Elements of the crime	Scienter
Inference	Strict liability

Review Questions

1. List the elements of a crime.
2. What is actus reus and why is it important to criminal law?
3. Why is concurrence important and what happens when it does not occur?
4. What is scienter?
5. What is the difference between a legal and a moral duty?
6. Define *mens rea*.
7. Why is the failure to act when you have a legal duty to do so punishable under criminal law?
8. Why does a defendant's criminal act have to be voluntary?
9. What is a general intent crime?
10. What is transferred intent? Give an example.
11. What is the difference between the mens rea elements of purposely and knowingly?
12. What is the difference between the mens rea elements of recklessly and negligently?

1. Paris and Brittney were both canvassing the parking lot of a local mall at Christmas time looking for a parking space. As someone pulled his car out of a space, both Paris and Brittney tried to maneuver their vehicles into the spot, each blocking the other from doing so. After each woman yelled at the other regarding who was entitled to park in the spot, Paris got out of her car and pulled a switchblade out of her purse. Intending only to scare Brittney, Paris touched the blade to Brittney's throat. However, Brittney reacted by turning her head in the opposite direction and the blade sliced her throat, causing a severe injury. Paris did not intend to injury Brittney, only scare her. The law in the jurisdiction in which the incident occurred states that assault is a crime that requires "general intent." May Paris properly be found guilty of assault, and, if so, why?

2. Miranda was visiting the crowded community swimming pool. She is a strong swimmer and was a member of the high school swim team years ago. While Miranda was at the pool, a little girl who had been playing along the side of the pool slipped and fell into the pool. The little girl could not swim. Miranda could have easily jumped into the pool and saved the little girl but did not. The little girl drowned. If Miranda is charged with criminal homicide in the death of the little girl, the court should find her
   a. Guilty, because she could have saved the little girl without any risk to herself.
   b. Guilty, if she knew that she was the only person present who was aware of the little girl's plight and who was able to rescue her.
   c. Not guilty, unless she was related to the little girl.
   d. Not guilty, because she had no duty to aid the little girl.

3. Maria has been stalked by a co-worker who claims that he is in love with her. Fearful, Maria purchases a handgun to carry in her purse. One night, as Maria walks home from work, she is certain that she is being followed. Maria turns around to see the stalker walking behind her. Maria fires the gun at the stalker, missing the stalker and striking a man who was walking down the street behind him. Will Maria be found guilty of attempted murder for shooting the victim?

4. Jimmy gets caught speeding by the police. He first cries "Entrapment" because the police officer was hiding underneath an overpass on the highway. Why is it not entrapment and what classification of crime does speeding fall into?

5. Why does the law differentiate between criminal negligence and higher-penalty crimes that have intent?

6. Why is "ignorance of the law" no excuse when getting caught in the act of a crime?

7. Susie sleepwalks. She is unconscious when she falls victim to it and has no idea she is awake and walking. One night while sleepwalking, she enters the garage, takes a rifle off the wall, returns to the house, walks into her bedroom, and shoots and kills her husband. What are the issues here regarding her killing of her husband? Any defenses on Susie's part?

8. Research what percentage of felons are incarcerated throughout the country because of simple possession of a controlled substance. What are some of the things the statistics can tell you?

 PORTFOLIO ASSIGNMENT

Research how many criminal defense law firms there are in your county. What do the statistics and information tell you? Is the information found reflective of our culture?

Vocabulary Builders

Instructions

Use the key terms from this chapter to fill in the answers to the crossword puzzle.

NOTE: When the answer is more than one word, leave a blank space between the words.

ACROSS

3. something that produces an effect or result.
5. a wrongful deed that renders the actor criminally liable if combined with mens rea.
8. a meeting or coming together of a guilty act and a guilty mind.
10. those constituent parts of a crime that must be proved by the prosecution to sustain a conviction.

DOWN

1. something such as willful desire that causes an individual to act.
2. liability that is based on the breach of an absolute duty rather than negligence or intent.
4. the requisite mental state for common-law murder; involves either (1) the intent to kill, (2) the intent to inflict grievous bodily harm, (3) extremely reckless indifference to the value of human life; or (4) the intent to commit a dangerous felony.
6. a guilty or wrongful purpose.
7. a conclusion reached by considering other facts and deducing a logical consequence.
9. a degree of knowledge that makes a person legally responsible for his or her act or omission.

FRANCOIS HOLLOWAY, *aka* ABDU ALI, PETITIONER
v. UNITED STATES
on writ of certiorari to the United States Court of
Appeals for the Second Circuit
No. 97-7164.
March 2, 1999

[Text omitted]

Justice Stevens delivered the opinion of the Court.

Carjacking "with the intent to cause death or serious bodily harm" is a federal crime. The question presented in this case is whether that phrase requires the Government to prove that the defendant had an unconditional intent to kill or harm in all events, or whether it merely requires proof of an intent to kill or harm if necessary to effect a carjacking. Most of the judges who have considered the question have concluded, as do we, that Congress intended to criminalize the more typical carjacking carried out by means of a deliberate threat of violence, rather than just the rare case in which the defendant has an unconditional intent to use violence regardless of how the driver responds to his threat.

I

A jury found petitioner guilty on three counts of carjacking, as well as several other offenses related to stealing cars. In each of the carjackings, petitioner and an armed accomplice identified a car that they wanted and followed it until it was parked. The accomplice then approached the driver, produced a gun, and threatened to shoot unless the driver handed over the car keys. The accomplice testified that the plan was to steal the cars without harming the victims, but that he would have used his gun if any of the drivers had given him a "hard time." When one victim hesitated, petitioner punched him in the face but there was no other actual violence.

The District Judge instructed the jury that the Government was required to prove beyond a reasonable doubt that the taking of a motor vehicle was committed with the intent "to cause death or serious bodily harm to the person from whom the car was taken." App. 29. After explaining that merely using a gun to frighten a victim was not sufficient to prove such intent, he added the following statement over the defendant's objection:

> "In some cases, intent is conditional. That is, a defendant may intend to engage in certain conduct only if a certain event occurs.
>
> "In this case, the government contends that the defendant intended to cause death or serious bodily harm if the alleged victims had refused to turn over their cars. If you find beyond a reasonable doubt that the defendant had such an intent, the government has satisfied this element of the offense. . . ."

In his postverdict motion for a new trial, petitioner contended that this instruction was inconsistent with the text of the statute. The District Judge denied the motion, stating that there "is no question that the conduct at issue in this case is precisely what Congress and the general public would describe

as carjacking, and that Congress intended to prohibit it in § 2119." 921 F. Supp. 155, 156 (EDNY 1996). He noted that the statute as originally enacted in 1992 contained no intent element but covered all carjackings committed by a person "possessing a firearm." A 1994 amendment had omitted the firearm limitation, thus broadening the coverage of the statute to encompass the use of other weapons, and also had inserted the intent requirement at issue in this case. The judge thought that an "odd result" would flow from a construction of the amendment that "would no longer prohibit the very crime it was enacted to address except in those unusual circumstances when carjackers also intended to commit another crime—murder or a serious assault." *Id.*, at 159. Moreover, the judge determined that even though the issue of conditional intent has not been discussed very often, at least in the federal courts, it was a concept that scholars and state courts had long recognized.

Over a dissent that accused the majority of "a clear judicial usurpation of congressional authority," *United States* v. *Arnold*, 126 F. 3d 82, 92 (CA2 1997) (opinion of Miner, J.), the Court of Appeals affirmed. The majority was satisfied that "the inclusion of a conditional intent to harm within the definition of specific intent to harm" was not only "a well-established principle of common law," but also, and "most importantly," comported "with a reasonable interpretation of the legislative purpose of the statute." *Id.*, at 88. The alternative interpretation, which would cover "only those carjackings in which the carjacker's sole and unconditional purpose at the time he committed the carjacking was to kill or maim the victim," the court concluded, was clearly at odds with the intent of the statute's drafters.

To resolve an apparent conflict with a decision of the Ninth Circuit, *United States* v. *Randolph*, 93 F. 3d 656 (1996), we granted certiorari. 523 U. S. ___ (1998).

II

Writing for the Court in *United States* v. *Turkette,* 452 U. S. 576, 593 (1981), Justice White reminded us that the language of the statutes that Congress enacts provides "the most reliable evidence of its intent." For that reason, we typically begin the task of statutory construction by focusing on the words that the drafters have chosen. In interpreting the statute at issue, "[w]e consider not only the bare meaning" of the critical word or phrase "but also its placement and purpose in the statutory scheme." *Bailey* v. *United States*, 516 U. S. 137, 145 (1995).

The specific issue in this case is what sort of evil motive Congress intended to describe when it used the words "with the intent to cause death or serious bodily harm" in the 1994 amendment to the carjacking statute. More precisely, the question is whether a person who points a gun at a driver, having decided to pull the trigger if the driver does not comply with a demand for the car keys, possesses the intent, at that moment, to seriously harm the driver. In our view, the answer to that question does not depend on whether the driver immediately hands over the keys or what the offender decides to do after he gains control over the car. At the relevant moment, the offender plainly does have the forbidden intent.

The opinions that have addressed this issue accurately point out that a carjacker's intent to harm his victim may be either "conditional" or "unconditional." The statutory phrase at issue theoretically might describe (1) the former, (2) the latter, or (3) both species of intent. Petitioner argues that the "plain text" of the statute "unequivocally" describes only the latter: that the defendant must possess a specific and unconditional intent to kill or harm in order to complete the proscribed offense. To that end, he insists that Congress would have had to insert the words "if necessary" into the disputed text in order to include the conditional species of intent within the scope of the statute. See Reply Brief for Petitioner 2. Because Congress did not include those words, petitioner contends that we must assume that Congress meant to provide a federal penalty for only those carjackings in which the offender actually attempted to harm or kill the driver (or at least intended to do so whether or not the driver resisted).

We believe, however, that a commonsense reading of the carjacking statute counsels that Congress intended to criminalize a broader scope of conduct than attempts to assault or kill in the course of automobile robberies. As we have repeatedly stated, "'the meaning of statutory language, plain or not, depends on context.'" Brown v. Gardner, 513 U. S. 115, 118 (1994) (quoting King v. St. Vincent's Hospital, 502 U. S. 215, 221 (1991)). When petitioner's argument is considered in the context of the statute, it becomes apparent that his proffered construction of the intent element overlooks the significance of the placement of that element in the statute. The carjacking statute essentially is aimed at providing a federal penalty for a particular type of robbery. The statute's *mens rea* component thus modifies the act of "tak[ing]" the motor vehicle. It directs the factfinder's attention to the defendant's state of mind at the precise moment he demanded or took control over the car "by force and violence or by intimidation." If the defendant has the proscribed state of mind at that moment, the statute's scienter element is satisfied.

Petitioner's reading of the intent element, in contrast, would improperly transform the *mens rea* element from a modifier into an additional *actus reus* component of the carjacking statute; it would alter the statute into one that focuses on attempting to harm or kill a person in the course of the robbery of a motor vehicle. Indeed, if we accepted petitioner's view of the statute's intent element, even Congress' insertion of the qualifying words "if necessary," by themselves, would not have solved the deficiency that he believes exists in the statute. The inclusion of those words after the intent phrase would have excluded the unconditional species of intent—the intent to harm or kill even if not necessary to complete a carjacking. Accordingly, if Congress had used words such as "if necessary" to describe the conditional species of intent, it would also have needed to add something like "or even if not necessary" in order to cover both species of intent to harm. Given the fact that the actual text does not mention either species separately—and thus does not expressly exclude either—that text is most naturally read to encompass the *mens rea* of both conditional and unconditional intent, and *not* to limit the statute's reach to crimes involving the additional *actus reus* of an attempt to kill or harm.

Two considerations strongly support the conclusion that a natural reading of the text is fully consistent with a congressional decision to cover both species of intent. First, the statute as a whole reflects an intent to authorize federal prosecutions as a significant deterrent to a type of criminal activity that was a matter of national concern. Because that purpose is better served by construing the statute to cover both the conditional and the unconditional species of wrongful intent, the entire statute is consistent with a normal interpretation of the specific language that Congress chose. See John Hancock Mut. Life Ins. Co. v. Harris Trust and Sav. Bank, 510 U. S. 86, 94–95 (1993) (statutory language should be interpreted consonant with "the provisions of the whole law, and . . . its object and policy" (internal quotation marks omitted)). Indeed, petitioner's interpretation would exclude from the coverage of the statute most of the conduct that Congress obviously intended to prohibit.

Second, it is reasonable to presume that Congress was familiar with the cases and the scholarly writing that have recognized that the "specific intent" to commit a wrongful act may be conditional. See Cannon v. University of Chicago, 441 U. S. 677, 696–698 (1979). The facts of the leading case on the point are strikingly similar to the facts of this case. In People v. Connors, 253 Ill. 266, 97 N. E. 643 (1912), the Illinois Supreme Court affirmed the conviction of a union organizer who had pointed a gun at a worker and threatened to kill him forthwith if he did not take off his overalls and quit work. The Court held that the jury had been properly instructed that the "specific intent to kill" could be found even though that intent was "coupled with a condition" that the defendant would not fire if the victim complied with his demand. That holding has been repeatedly cited with approval by other courts and by scholars. Moreover, it reflects the views endorsed by the authors of the Model Criminal Code. The core principle that emerges from these sources is that a defendant may not negate a proscribed intent by requiring the victim to comply with a condition the defendant has no right to impose; "[a]n intent to kill, in the alternative, is nevertheless an intent to kill."

This interpretation of the statute's specific intent element does not, as petitioner suggests, render superfluous the statutes "by force and violence or by intimidation" element. While an empty threat, or intimidating bluff, would be sufficient to satisfy the latter element, such conduct, standing on its own, is not enough to satisfy § 2119's specific intent element. In a carjacking case in which the driver surrendered or otherwise lost control over his car without the defendant attempting to inflict, or actually inflicting, serious bodily harm, Congress' inclusion of the intent element requires the Government to prove beyond a reasonable doubt that the defendant would have at least attempted to seriously harm or kill the driver if that action had been necessary to complete the taking of the car.

In short, we disagree with petitioner's reading of the text of the Act and think it unreasonable to assume that Congress intended to enact such a truncated version of an important criminal statute. The intent requirement of § 2119 is satisfied when the Government proves that at the moment the defendant demanded or took control over the driver's automobile the defendant possessed the intent to seriously harm or kill the driver if necessary to steal the car (or, alternatively, if unnecessary to steal the car). Accordingly, we affirm the judgment of the Court of Appeals.

It is so ordered.

[Footnotes and Dissenting Opinion omitted]

Source: Francois Holloway, aka Abdu Ali v. United States, 1999 U.S. LEXIS 1708; 526 U. S. 1 (1999). Reprinted with the permission of LexisNexis.

Chapter 4

Homicide

CHAPTER OBJECTIVES

Upon completion of this chapter, you will be able to:

• Identify the elements of each type of homicide.

• Explain the different types of murder.

• Discuss the felony-murder rule.

• Understand the differences between the two types of manslaughter.

Most people are familiar with the term *homicide* as it has been readily used for decades in numerous television shows that deal with law enforcement, murder mysteries, or the legal industry. Social intrigue with crimes involving homicides permeates history from Jack the Ripper to the Black Dahlia, from Charles Manson to O.J. Simpson. However, the term *homicide* is a generic term, and the criminal killing of another human being can be classified by type and degree when it comes to legal terminology. This chapter examines the laws that involve homicide.

TYPES OF HOMICIDES

Homicide is a broad term that refers to the killing of one human being by another. Any unlawful killing of one person by another will fall under the term *homicide*. Common law has recognized three types of homicide: justifiable, excusable, and criminal.

A *justifiable* homicide is a killing of one human being by another in which the killing is sanctioned or excused by the law. For example, when a person is executed on death row, the executioner is excused from criminal punishment because the killing of the death row inmate is sanctioned by law. Other examples of justifiable homicide are killings done by the police using deadly force or during times of war. A homicide is not criminal in and of itself. A justifiable homicide is still a homicide, but it is not considered criminal because the person doing the killing does not possess any evil intent and the killing is permitted under the law.

Excusable homicides occur accidentally or while the killer is insane. For example, suppose a person runs out in front of an automobile so that the driver has no time to avoid hitting the person. This type of killing would be considered an excusable homicide.

A homicide that is not justifiable or excusable is considered *criminal*. A criminal homicide is one that involves unlawful conduct and evil intent by the killer.

In addition to the categories of homicides listed above, criminal homicides have been further categorized into three levels: murder, voluntary manslaughter, and involuntary manslaughter. The distinguishing factor among the types of murder has to do with the

homicide
The killing of a human being by the act or omission of another.

mens rea of each crime. As each of the different levels of homicide is described in this chapter, you will see how the mens rea of the crime determines what level of homicide has been committed. It is also important to note that no human body need be found to convict someone of murder or manslaughter; however, some jurisdictions do abide by the *corpus delecti* rule. **Corpus delicti** is the material substance or the physical evidence of a crime such as a the body of the murdered person. The *corpus delecti* rule is a doctrine that prohibits a prosecutor from proving the *corpus delicti* based solely on a defendant's extrajudicial statements; however, the prosecution must establish the *corpus delicti* with corroborating evidence to secure a conviction. Circumstantial evidence can be used.

corpus delicti
[Latin "body of the crime"] The fact of the transgression or the physical evidence of a crime such as the body of a murder victim.

MURDER

Murder is the most serious criminal act that can be committed by someone. Society punishes murder harshly. Some states permit capital punishment or the death penalty as punishment for murder in some circumstances. The elements of murder are

murder
The killing of a human being with intent.

- The unlawful killing
- Of one human being
- By another human being
- With **malice aforethought**.

First, in order to have the actus reus of the crime of murder, there must be a death of a human being. The death must have occurred by the defendant's actions or by the defendant's failure to act when he had a duty to do so. The Model Penal Code at section 210.2 states that a murder has taken place when

malice
aforethought
The prior intention to kill the victim or anyone else if likely to occur as a result of the defendant's actions or omissions.

1. *the defendant causes the death of another human being, and*
2. a. *it is committed purposely or knowingly, or*
   b. *it is committed recklessly under circumstances manifesting extreme indifference to the value of human life. Such recklessness is presumed if the defendant is an actor or an accomplice in the attempt or commission or flight after commission of the crimes of robbery, rape, deviate sexual intercourse by force or fear, arson, burglary, kidnapping, or felonious escape.*

The elements of the crime state that there must be a killing of another human being. It is presumed that this human being is alive. However, an issue arises as to when life actually occurs. It is uniformly accepted that once a baby is born, it is considered a human being, but at what point during its development is it considered alive? Is a fetus considered a live human being for the purposes of murder? The issue of whether a fetus is considered a human being is a matter of public policy that has been left up to the legislature to resolve. As such, each state has laws that vary on the subject. Some states have laws that specifically delineate that the killing of a person or fetus constitutes the actus reus of a homicide. Other states have specific fetal death statutes that define when life begins for the purposes of the law. However, most states have been reluctant to consider a fetus a human being for the purposes of murder. While the death may fall under one of the other levels or categories of homicide, it is often not considered a murder to kill an unborn fetus.

Laci Peterson, a young wife who was eight months pregnant, disappeared on December 24, 2002. A nationwide search followed. Four months later, her body and the body of her unborn son were found and her husband, Scott, was subsequently charged with two counts of murder. In *The People of the State of California v. Scott Peterson,* the jury convicted Peterson of first degree murder with special circumstances for killing his wife and second degree murder for killing his unborn son.

Just as it must be determined when life begins for purposes of the law, so it must be determined when life ends. One cannot murder a person who is already dead. With the

RESEARCH THIS

The California Supreme Court has wrestled with the issue of when life begins in various cases. Two cases that involve this issue are *Keeler v. Superior Court*, 470 P.2d 617 (Cal. 1970), and *People v. Davis*, 872 P.2d 591 (Cal. 1994). Research both cases. How did the courts rule in each of these cases? When is a fetus considered a human being according to both courts?

ability of modern medicine to keep a person's body alive without brain function, a condition known as being **brain dead**, the traditional definition of death (when the person stops breathing and the heart stops pumping) has become obscured. Is a person who is declared brain dead considered alive if being kept alive by machines? In an effort to resolve this issue, the National Conference of Commissioners on Uniform State Laws developed a model code known as the Uniform Brain Death Act (American Law Institute 1985 [2:1], at 10–11). Model Penal Code, copyright 1985 by the American Law Institute. Reprinted with permission. The Uniform Brain Death Act states that an individual is considered to be dead if he has suffered irreversible termination of all brain functions that include those in the brain stem. This act has not been adopted in all jurisdictions. The determination of when life ends has become a public policy question that has been left to the legislatures of each of the various jurisdictions to determine.

The element that delineates murder from homicide is the mens rea. In the case of murder, the mens rea is malice aforethought. Malice aforethought can be either express or implied and refers to a particularly evil or heinous state of mind. Malice aforethought goes beyond the defendant's having premeditated thoughts about killing the victim or that the defendant meant for the victim to be killed. It goes strictly to the heinousness of the crime.

Malice aforethought includes the following states of mind:

1. Intent to kill the victim. This is the most common state of mind that is found in murder. One person deliberately, purposefully, and without legal justification takes the life of another person. This is sometimes referred to as killing a person in cold blood.

2. Intent to seriously harm the victim. The defendant seriously harms the victim without intending to kill him. However, the victim dies as a result of the injuries inflicted by the defendant. The likelihood that a person would die as a result of the seriousness of the injuries sustained by him is high; therefore, the defendant is considered to have possessed malice aforethought.

3. **Felony murder rule**. In the commission of a dangerous felony (e.g., burglary, robbery, rape, or arson), there is almost always the likelihood that someone could get killed. Therefore, a defendant is considered to have malice aforethought if he commits a dangerous felony and someone is killed. For example, if the security guard is killed during the commission of a bank robbery, then the defendant will be charged with murder.

brain death
When the body shows no response to external stimuli, no spontaneous movements, no breathing, no reflexes, and a flat reading on a machine that measures the brain's electrical activity.

felony murder rule
The doctrine holding that any death resulting from the commission or attempted commission of a dangerous felony is murder.

EYE ON ETHICS

It is important to know the laws of your jurisdiction. For example, a doctor who harvests an organ from an organ donor before the law determines that the donor is dead could be prosecuted for murder. When dealing with issues of criminal homicide, the laws of each jurisdiction should be examined carefully to determine the extent to which the law determines when life begins and ends.

depraved heart murder
A murder resulting from an act so reckless and careless of the safety of others that it demonstrates the perpetrator's complete lack of regard for human life.

4. **Depraved heart murder**. The defendant does something that has a high risk of death or serious injury with a disregard for the consequences. That is, the defendant acts in a manner that creates a situation in which there is a high degree of risk that someone could die; however, it stops short of a substantial certainty that a death will occur. For example, a defendant shoots into a crowd or shoots a gun up into the air without regard for the consequences. There is a high degree of risk that someone could be killed although it is not certain.

5. Killing a police officer while resisting arrest. The killing of a police officer while resisting arrest, even if the defendant did not mean to kill the officer or even to hurt him, will be considered murder with malice aforethought. The killing of a police officer is always seen as a grave event and dealt with harshly.

premeditation
Conscious consideration and planning that precedes some act.

Murder is designated into degrees based on amount of planning and **premeditation** involved in the killing. Most states have at least two degrees of murder, but some states have more. The degree of punishment will be determined by the degree of murder. Typically, a murder in the first degree will carry the most severe punishment. The difference between the degrees of murder is typically centered on the defendant's intent in committing the crime or the manner in which the crime is carried out. The severity of the punishment for the crime is linked to the degree of murder.

First Degree Murder

Most states recognize a class of murder known as first degree murder. First degree murder is usually a premeditated or planned murder. A premeditated murder is when the defendant had time to plan and reflect on his actions and formed the intent to kill. A murder is found to be in the first degree when it is committed under the following circumstances:

• Murder that was willful, deliberate, and premeditated.

• Murder by poison, torture, explosives, or ambush.

• Felony murder.

SURF'S UP

To learn more about murder and the various degrees of murder, the following Web sites can be helpful:

- www.courttv.com

- www.findarticles.com
- www.prisonsfoundation.org
- www.emory.edu

No specific set time has been determined to be the formula for premeditation. The modern view is that a reasonable period of time must exist in which deliberation and planning have occurred. In determining if a murder was premeditated, three elements have been used: (1) there is evidence of planning activity prior to the murder; (2) there is usually evidence of a motive; and (3) the killing was done in such a manner that it must have been committed by a preconceived idea.

Murders that were committed by someone who was lying in wait for the victim, by torture, or by poison are generally classified as murders in the first degree. The rationale behind this designation is that some planning must have occurred in order to commit a murder in this manner. In addition, murders that occur as a result of the commission of a felony are also usually considered murder in the first degree. Some states use the term *capital punishment* for crimes that may merit death. As of 2006, 38 states as well as the federal government have laws allowing capital punishment in certain circumstances.

Second Degree Murder

Murders that are not premeditated, justified, or excused are generally designated as second degree murder. Some of the types of murder that would be considered second degree murder are

- Murder in which the suspect intended to kill the victim, but the killing was not premeditated.
- Murder in which the suspect intended to cause the victim serious bodily harm but did not intend to kill the victim.
- A depraved heart killing.
- A killing that occurred during the course of a felony that is not a felony under the felony murder rule (typically, those felonies that are not rape, robbery, arson, or burglary).

FELONY MURDER

The intent to commit a felony that is unrelated to the homicide that occurred during its commission is found to be sufficient to meet the mens rea requirement for murder under the felony murder rule. The unintentional death will be considered a murder. Felony murder does not require that the defendant possess intent to kill or intent to inflict serious bodily injury. The specific intent to commit the felony is considered intent to commit the killing.

The felony murder rule is limited in most jurisdictions to certain felonies that are considered inherently dangerous. The felonies are usually rape, kidnapping, robbery, arson, and burglary. Those felonies that are committed **malum in se** are normally the felonies to which the felony murder rule applies. A causal relationship must exist between the felony and the death of the victim. It is not enough that the death occurs at the same time that the felony is being committed. The felony must have given rise in some manner to the death. That is, the felony must be the proximate cause of the death.

malum in se
An act that is prohibited because it is "evil in itself."

Dwight hangs out with a notorious gang, the Creeps, in the inner city. He wants to be accepted as a full member of the Creeps. The Creeps have determined that in order to be a full-fledged member of the gang, the person must commit a bank robbery. Dwight and five other gang members plan to hold up the United City Bank right before closing on a Friday. The girlfriend of one of the gang member works at the bank and provides the prospective robbers with a drawing of the inside of the bank. She tells them of the procedures in place for handling robbery situations. Armed with inside information and AKs-47 assault weapons, the five gang members and Dwight go into the bank at 4:50 on Friday afternoon.

Dwight is the person who is supposed to watch the door for the cops. As they enter the bank, there are several customers in line waiting for the tellers. The other gang members scream at them all to get on the floor, proceed to the tellers, and have them begin to place their money into bags. Everything is going according to plan until an elderly gentleman who had been standing in line waiting for a teller begins to have severe chest pains. The man begins screaming that he is having a heart attack. The gang members grab their loot and flee the bank. The elderly man dies of a heart attack as a result of the stress of the robbery. Dwight and the other gang members are identified by the images captured on the surveillance cameras located in the bank. All gang members are charged with the bank robbery as well as the murder of the elderly man. When Dwight inquires of his attorney as to why he has been charged with murder because they did not kill anyone, the attorney informs Dwight that he has been charged with murder under the felony murder rule that states that a death as a result of a dangerous felony will result in the death being charged to the perpetrators as a murder in the first degree.

The purpose of developing the felony murder rule was to (1) deter people from committing felonies that could lead to death, (2) reduce violent crime by inducing prospective felons to act more cautiously for fear of being prosecuted for murder should the felony lead to a death, and (3) punish people who intentionally commit these types of felonies that have a high degree of risk of death.

MANSLAUGHTER

manslaughter
The unlawful killing of a human being without premeditation.

Manslaughter covers homicides that are not considered to be heinous enough to be murder but still are blameworthy and need to be punished. The general elements of manslaughter are considered to be

- Unlawful killing of a human being
- By another human being
- But without malice aforethought.

The Model Penal Code under section 210.3 defines manslaughter as

1. *The unlawful killing of another human being*
2. a. *committed in a reckless manner, or*
   b. *committed under the influence of extreme mental or emotional disturbance for which there is a reasonable explanation or excuse.*

Manslaughter is classified into two types: voluntary and involuntary.

voluntary manslaughter
An act of murder reduced to manslaughter because of extenuating circumstances such as adequate provocation or diminished capacity.

mitigating circumstance
A fact or situation that does not justify or excuse a wrongful act or offense but that reduces the degree of culpability and thus may reduce the damages in a civil case or the punishment in a criminal case.

heat of passion
Rage, terror, or furious hatred suddenly aroused by some immediate provocation.

Voluntary Manslaughter

Voluntary manslaughter is an intentional killing without malice aforethought. A death has occurred, but there are usually **mitigating circumstances** such as **heat of passion** that do not qualify the crime as a murder. Generally, extreme mental or emotional disturbance that has a reasonable explanation can cause a death to be designated as manslaughter. For example, Bob comes home from a business trip to find his wife of seven years in bed with his best friend. Bob becomes so outraged that he picks up a candlestick and strikes his wife with it. She is killed by the blow. Due to the severe emotional distress that Bob experienced as result of finding his wife in bed with his best friend, the killing is designated as voluntary manslaughter instead of murder. Voluntary manslaughter also can occur when the death of the victim resulted from the defendant's criminal negligence rather than any intent to kill.

The facts that typically involve a killing that qualifies as voluntary manslaughter are

- The defendant acts as a result of provocation whereby a reasonable person may lose his self-control;
- The defendant acts under the heat of passion;
- The time that lapsed between the provocation and the killing is not a sufficient period of time for the defendant to cool off and regain his self-control; and
- The defendant had not cooled off when the killing occurred.

Voluntary manslaughter is usually considered the second most serious homicide next to murder. The killing, even though it was intended, is usually not of the same factual circumstances that would normally classify it as a murder. The killing is downgraded to manslaughter if adequate provocation of the defendant can be determined.

Involuntary Manslaughter

The Model Penal Code includes a provision, less serious that manslaughter, imposing homicide liability for killings committed negligently. **Involuntary manslaughter** is based on criminal negligence by the defendant. Many states have adopted negligent homicide statutes. What constitutes negligent homicide in most jurisdictions would have been considered involuntary manslaughter at common law. If the defendant's conduct is determined to be grossly negligent so that he accidentally kills another human being, then the defendant will be guilty of involuntary manslaughter. The defendant does not need to possess a depraved or evil mind when the killing was committed. Criminal negligence must be determined by a **totality of the circumstances** of the incident. For example, if the defendant was engaged in an inherently dangerous activity in which a person is accidentally killed, the courts will probably find the defendant guilty of involuntary manslaughter. For example, in many jurisdictions, young adults engage in street racing, which is the racing of two or more vehicles at excessive speeds down local streets. Due to the fact that the activity is inherently dangerous, most jurisdictions are implementing laws against such activity. Therefore, if a death occurs as a direct result of a street race, the street racers would probably be prosecuted for involuntary manslaughter.

A death that occurs as a result of an unlawful act that does not constitute a felony such as a misdemeanor or infraction and was the result of the defendant's negligence would be classified as involuntary manslaughter. **Vehicular homicide** is one example. For example, Jeff is driving his truck and talking to his friends. Jeff is not paying particular attention to the road; as a result, he runs a stop sign and broadsides a small, compact car. A baby in the backseat is killed in the collision. The death of the baby would be involuntary manslaughter as it is a result of the negligent conduct of Jeff in violating a traffic ordinance. *Misdemeanor manslaughter* is a term used in some jurisdictions to refer to an unintentional homicide that occurs during the commission of a misdemeanor such as a traffic violation.

SUICIDE

Suicide was historically treated as a criminal homicide, but over time that has changed. The act is not modernly viewed as a legal wrong. However, the United States has long held **assisted suicide** as a criminal act. People who assist others in killing themselves can be charged with murder, manslaughter, and other offenses. Most states

involuntary manslaughter Homicide in which there is no intention to kill or do grievous bodily harm but that is committed with criminal negligence or during the commission of a crime not included within the felony murder rule.

totality of the circumstances A legal standard that requires focus on the entire situation and not on one specific factor.

vehicular homicide The killing of another person by one's unlawful or negligent operation of a motor vehicle.

PRACTICE TIP

Generally, "driving under the influence," aka DUI, or "driving while intoxicated," aka DWI, and killing someone in the process is considered an involuntary form of manslaughter. Drag racing cars, resulting in a death occurring, *as mentioned*, would be another example.

assisted suicide The intentional act of providing a person with the medical means or the medical knowledge to commit suicide.

introduced legislation prohibiting assisted suicide in the 1990s after Dr. Jack Kevorkian and others caused national debate on the issue by assisting terminally ill patients end their lives.

Summary

Homicide is a broad term that refers to the killing of one human being by another. Any unlawful killing of one person by another will fall under the term *homicide*. The common law has traditionally recognized three types of homicide: justifiable, excusable, and criminal.

Murder is considered the most serious criminal act that can be committed by someone. Thus, society punishes murder harshly. In some states, the punishment for murder is capital punishment, or taking the life of the killer. The elements of murder are (1) the unlawful killing (2) of one human being (3) by another human being (4) with malice aforethought.

The element that differentiates murder from other types of homicide is the mens rea. The mens rea required for murder is often malice aforethought. Malice aforethought can be either express or implied. It refers to a particularly evil or heinous state of mind and it goes beyond the defendant's having premeditated thought about killing the victim or having meant for the victim to be killed. Malice aforethought goes strictly to the heinousness of the crime.

Murder is categorized by degrees based on amount of planning and premeditation involved in the killing. Most states have at least two degrees of murder, but some states may have more. The degree of punishment will be determined by the degree of murder. Typically, a murder in the first degree will carry the most severe punishment. The difference between the degrees of murder is typically centered on the defendant's intent in committing the crime or the manner in which the crime is carried out and the severity of the punishment for such a crime.

Most states recognize a class of murder known as first degree murder. First degree murder is usually a premeditated or planned murder. A premeditated murder is one that the defendant had time to plan and for which he reflected on his actions and formed the intent to kill. A murder is found to be in the first degree when it is committed under the following circumstances: (1) murder that was willful, deliberate, and premeditated; (2) murder by poison, torture, explosives, or ambush; and (3) felony murder.

Murders that are not premeditated, justified, or excused are generally designated as second degree murder. Some of the types of murder that would be considered second degree murder are (1) murder in which the suspect intended to kill the victim, but the killing was not premeditated; (2) murder in which the suspect intended to cause the victim serious bodily harm but did not intend to kill the victim; (3) a depraved heart killing; and (4) a killing that occurred during the course of a felony that is not covered by the felony murder rule (typically those felonies that are not rape, robbery, arson, or burglary).

The intent to commit a felony that is unrelated to the homicide that occurred during its commission is found to be sufficient to meet the mens rea requirement for murder under the felony murder rule. The unintentional death will be considered a murder. Felony murder does not require that the defendant possess intent to kill or intent to inflict serious bodily injury. The specific intent to commit the felony is considered intent to commit the killing.

The felony murder rule is limited in most jurisdictions to certain felonies that are considered inherently dangerous. The felonies are usually rape, kidnapping, robbery, arson, and burglary. Those felonies that are committed malum in se are normally the felonies to which the felony murder rule applies. A causal relationship must exist between the felony and the death of the victim. It is not enough that the death occurs at the same time that the felony is being committed. The felony must have given rise in some manner to the death and must be the proximate cause of the death.

Manslaughter covers homicides that are not considered to be heinous enough to be murder but still are blameworthy and need to be punished. The general elements of manslaughter are considered to be (1) unlawful killing of a human being (2) by another human being (3) but without malice aforethought.

Voluntary manslaughter is an intentional killing without malice aforethought. A death has occurred, but there are usually mitigating circumstances such as heat of passion that do not qualify the crime as a murder. Generally, extreme mental or emotional disturbance that has a reasonable explanation can cause a death to be designated as manslaughter.

Involuntary manslaughter is based on criminal negligence by the defendant. If the defendant's conduct is determined to be grossly negligent so that he accidentally kills another human being, then the defendant will be guilty of involuntary manslaughter. The defendant did not need to possess a depraved or evil mind when the killing took place to be guilty of involuntary manslaughter. The existence of criminal negligence is determined by a totality of the circumstances of the incident.

Key Terms

Assisted suicide
Brain death
Corpus delicti
Depraved heart murder
Felony murder rule
Heat of passion
Homicide
Involuntary manslaughter
Malice aforethought

Malum in se
Manslaughter
Mitigating circumstance
Murder
Premeditation
Totality of the circumstances
Vehicular homicide
Voluntary manslaughter

Review Questions

1. What is the definition of a homicide?
2. List the differences between justifiable and excusable homicide.
3. Why is it difficult to determine when life begins for purposes of murder?
4. Identify and define the different types of murder.
5. What is malice aforethought?
6. What is the purpose of the felony murder rule?
7. List the typical felonies that will qualify a killing as first degree murder under the felony murder rule.
8. Describe the difference(s) between first and second degree murder.
9. List the elements of manslaughter.
10. What is the difference between voluntary and involuntary manslaughter?
11. Define the *heat of passion.*
12. What is a cooling-off period and when does it apply?
13. What is premeditation and why is it important?
14. When is someone considered dead under the law?
15. What is a depraved heart killing?

Exercises

1. Bob was walking down the street and saw a couple walking ahead of him. He decided to rob the two people. Bob pointed a gun at the couple and attempted to rob them. All of a sudden, to Bob's surprise, the female pulled a gun out of her purse and pointed it at Bob in an effort to thwart the robbery. Bob fired his gun at the female and she returned fire. She aimed at Bob but missed and accidentally shot and killed an elderly woman who was walking on the opposite side of the street. Bob is arrested. What will he be charged with?

2. Derek was a professional baseball player who was scheduled to play in the series championship on Sunday. On Friday, after wagering heavily on the game, Tim decided to attack Derek with a baseball bat. Tim's intention was to inflict injuries on Derek severe enough to keep Derek from playing in the game. As a result of the beating, Derek is taken to the hospital. While he is there, Derek has an allergic reaction to medication given to him for his injuries and he dies. If Tim is charged with the murder of Derek, he should be found
   a. Not guilty because Derek's allergic reaction to the drug was an intervening cause of death.
   b. Not guilty, if Derek's death was proximately caused by the medical facility's negligence.
   c. Guilty, only if Derek's death was proximately caused by Tim's attack.
   d. Guilty, unless the medical facility's conduct is found to be reckless or grossly negligent.

3. Anthony belongs to an inner-city gang. The gang is out celebrating New Year's Eve when they shoot their guns up into the air. The bullets from Anthony's gun rain down on a house four blocks over, penetrating the roof. The bullets strike a nine-year-old girl in the head, killing her instantly. If it is determined that the bullets from Anthony's gun killed the girl, what will he be charged with and why?

4. Patrick goes to a party with his friends at the local college. While at the party, Patrick drinks heavily and becomes intoxicated. Patrick decides that he has had enough and should go home. Patrick gets into his vehicle and attempts to drive home. While on his way home, Patrick strikes a man in a crosswalk and kills him. What form of homicide will Patrick be charged with and why?

5. Bob comes home and hears noise up in a bedroom on the second floor of the house. He ascends the staircase and discovers his wife in bed with another man having sex. He stands and looks amazed and then proceeds downstairs and out into the garage to retrieve a handgun. He then stops and pauses and proceeds to go back into the house, up the stairs, and into the bedroom where he shoots his wife and the man in bed with her; both die of the wounds shortly thereafter. What will Bob be charged with and why?

6. Ted and Mike had been drag racing each other down a relatively deserted highway for most of their teenage and young adult lives. On a recent Saturday night, both men decided, for old time's sake, to race one more time. A crowd of people showed up to watch the race and many were drinking on top of it. At the start of the race, both men burned rubber as they sped off down the dark road with bystanders watching closely. As the race came toward its end, Ted's car sped out of control into the crowd, killing three people, two of whom were children. Who will be charged with a homicide and with which homicide will he or they be charged and why?

7. Terri hated her ex-husband's new wife. Terri had been known to get drunk in the past and on numerous occasions has been known to mutter that she would "kill my *ex-husband's new wife*" if it was the last thing she would do on this

planet. One Saturday afternoon, Terri got wind of the fact that her ex-husband and his new wife were going to be at the Central Park Little League Stadium to see her ex-husband's child *with Terri* play in his first Little League game. Terri arrived drunk and began waving a gun indiscriminately toward the crowd, yelling at both her ex-husband and his new wife. Before you knew it, three people, including Terri's ex-husband, were dead. His new wife survived. The other two people that were killed were a stadium worker and a hot dog salesperson. Terri was the shooter in all three shootings. What crime(s) will she be charged with and why?

8. Four people were shot and killed while the killers were robbing a bank in your town or city. Does your state statute encompass the language from the Model Penal Code for homicide?

PORTFOLIO ASSIGNMENT

Research your county of venue for the following information:

- List all of the types of homicides that have occurred in your county of venue for calendar year 2006.

- Which form of homicide had the highest occurrence of frequency per the population of the county?

Instructions
Use the key terms from this chapter to fill in the answers to the crossword puzzle.
NOTE: When the answer is more than one word, leave a blank space between the words.

ACROSS
6. an act of murder reduced to manslaughter because of extenuating circumstances such as adequate provocation or diminished capacity.
7. the unjustifiable, inexcusable, and intentional killing of a human being without deliberation, premeditation, and malice.
8. the killing of a human being by the act or omission of another.
10. the unlawful killing of a human being by another with malice aforethought, either express or implied.
11. a predetermination to commit an act without legal justification or excuse.
12. [Latin "body of the crime"] the fact of the transgression or the physical evidence of a crime such as the body of a murder victim.
13. rage, terror, or furious hatred suddenly aroused by some immediate provocation.
14. the doctrine holding that any death resulting from the commission or attempted commission of a dangerous felony is murder.

DOWN
1. the killing of another person by one's unlawful or negligent operation of a motor vehicle.
2. a fact or situation that does not justify or excuse a wrongful act or offense but that reduces the degree of culpability and thus may reduce the damages in a civil case or the punishment in a criminal case.
3. homicide in which there is no intention to kill or do grievous bodily harm, but that is committed with criminal negligence or during the commission of a crime not included within the felony-murder rule.
4. a murder resulting from an act so reckless and careless of the safety of others that it demonstrates the perpetrator's complete lack of regard for human life.
5. when the body shows no response to external stimuli, no spontaneous movements, no breathing, no reflexes, and a flat reading on a machine that measures the brain's electrical activity.
9. conscious consideration and planning that precedes some act.

JOSEPH ROBERT FLETCHER, Appellant, v. STATE OF FLORIDA, Appellee.

Case No. 5D01-2069

DISTRICT COURT OF APPEAL OF FLORIDA, FIFTH DISTRICT

828 So. 2d 460; 2002 Fla. App. LEXIS 15161; 27 Fla. L. Weekly D 2292

October 18, 2002, Opinion Filed

SUBSEQUENT HISTORY:

Released for Publication November 1, 2002.

PRIOR HISTORY:

Appeal from the Circuit Court for St. Johns County, John M. Alexander, Judge.

DISPOSITION:

Reversed and remanded.

CASE SUMMARY:

PROCEDURAL POSTURE:

The Circuit Court for St. Johns County, Florida, convicted defendant of murder. Defendant appealed.

OVERVIEW:

After all the evidence and closing arguments, the trial court began instructing the jury on the elements of second degree murder and the lesser included crime of manslaughter. However, the trial court failed to read the definitions of justifiable or excusable homicide. The State argued that defense counsel failed to object to the trial court's failure to read the definitions of justifiable or excusable homicide. The appellate court held that the trial court committed fundamental, reversible error in failing to read the instructions on justifiable and excusable homicide. Defense counsel's failure to object did not constitute an affirmative waiver of this error.

OUTCOME:

The judgment of the trial court was reversed and the case was remanded.

JUDGES: PLEUS, J. COBB and PALMER, JJ., concur.

OPINION:

PLEUS, Judge.

This is a good example of a case in which an inadvertent oversight in reading the standard jury instructions can result in the reversal of a murder conviction. This court has jurisdiction pursuant to Florida Rule of Appellate Procedure 9.140.

After all the evidence and closing arguments, the trial court began instructing the jury on the elements of second degree murder and the lesser included crime of manslaughter. The court then stated:

> However, the defendant cannot be guilty of manslaughter if the killing was either justifiable or excusable homicide, **as I have previously explained those terms. I will explain that in a minute. I've got it a little bit backwards, but I will explain that.**

(Emphasis added). The record shows, however, that the court failed to read the definitions of justifiable or excusable homicide, as contained in Florida Standard Jury Instruction, "Introduction to Homicide." Although Fletcher failed to object to the trial court's failure to give instructions on justifiable and excusable homicide, the state concedes that such error has been found to constitute fundamental error, and can be raised for the first time on appeal. *See, e.g., Black v. State*, 695 So. 2d 459 (Fla. 1st DCA 1997); *Blandon v. State*, 657 So. 2d 1198 (Fla. 5th DCA 1995).

It is well-established that trial courts are required to read the instructions on justifiable and excusable homicide in all murder and manslaughter cases. *Hall v. State*, 677 So. 2d 1353 (Fla. 5th DCA 1996); *Blandon*, 657 So. 2d at 1198 citing *State v. Smith*, 573 So. 2d 306 (Fla. 1990)). Failure to read these instructions constitutes fundamental error, even if there is no basis in fact for the charge. *Blandon*, 657 So. 2d at 1199. An exception to this rule occurs when defense counsel requests or affirmatively agrees to the omission or alteration of a jury instruction. *See, e.g., Armstrong v. State*, 579 So. 2d 734 (Fla. 1991); *Hall; Blandon*. For this exception to apply, defense counsel must be aware of the omission, alteration or incomplete instruction, and affirmatively agree to it. *Black*, 695 So. 2d at 460. In the instant case, the trial court failed to give these instructions, and there is no evidence in the record showing that defense counsel was aware of and affirmatively agreed to these omissions.

The state acknowledges our holding in *Ortiz v. State*, 682 So. 2d 217 (Fla. 5th DCA 1996), that "the mere failure to object to the omission of a justifiable homicide charge . . . does not constitute an affirmative waiver." However, it attempts to argue, without supporting case law, that Fletcher affirmatively waived this fundamental error by repeatedly failing to object to the erroneous instructions as the trial court instructed and re-instructed the jury a total of three times. This argument lacks merit.

The state's argument that defense counsel failed to object three different times is not entirely accurate. The trial judge re-read the instruction on justifiable use of deadly force one time and read the definitions of aggravated assault and aggravated battery one time. Both of these instructions related to the self defense instructions, not to the crimes charged. Since the judge only instructed the jury on the crimes charged one time, he only failed to read the instructions on justifiable and excusable homicide one time. Thus, at best, defense counsel failed to object to these incomplete instructions one time, not three.

In summary, the trial court committed fundamental, reversible error in failing to read the instructions on justifiable and excusable homicide. Defense counsel's failure to object did not constitute an affirmative waiver of this error. Accordingly, we reverse and remand for a new trial. We take this opportunity to remind trial courts of the importance of giving the full instruction on excusable and justifiable homicide in every murder and manslaughter case unless clearly and affirmatively waived by the defendant. In light of our decision to reverse, we need not address Fletcher's other arguments.

REVERSED AND REMANDED FOR A NEW TRIAL.

COBB and PALMER, JJ., concur.

[Footnote omitted.]

Source: 2002 Fla. App. LEXIS 15161. Reprinted with the permission of LexisNexis.

Chapter 5

Crimes against the Person

CHAPTER OBJECTIVES

Upon completion of this chapter, you will be able to:

- Explain assault.

- Identify the elements of battery.

- Discuss kidnapping and false imprisonment.

- Understand the concept of mayhem.

- Recognize the various sex crimes.

The most serious crime against a person is murder; however, there are other crimes that are less serious in which one human being causes injury to another. These types of crimes involve **bodily injury**, restraints on freedom, and sexual offenses. This chapter will examine the various types of crimes against a person that do not involve a homicide.

bodily injury
Physical damage to a person's body.

BATTERY

A **battery** is an unjustified touching of another human being without the victim's consent. The elements that are required for a battery to occur are

- The deliberate harmful or offensive touching

- Of another person

- Without his/her consent.

The actus reus of the crime is the actual touching of the victim. Under common law, a battery requires an intentional mens rea. However, intent is no longer a required element. Many states have adopted the mental states of reckless and criminal negligence as well.

The touching of the victim does not have to cause injury. For example, John is talking to Mary, whom he just met. He finds her attractive, so as they are walking to class, John places his hand on Mary's buttocks. Mary is offended by John's touching as it is inappropriate and makes her feel uncomfortable since they just met each other. In the case of John and Mary, John offensively touched Mary but did not cause injury. The touching does not have to be applied directly by the defendant. For instance, if the defendant causes his/her dog to attack another person, then a battery has occurred without the defendant actually physically committing the touching of the victim him/herself.

battery
An intentional and unwanted harmful or offensive contact with the person of another; the actual intentional touching of someone with intent to cause harm, no matter how slight the harm.

A DAY IN THE LIFE OF A REAL PARALEGAL

Paralegals provide support and coordination of support during criminal litigation efforts and help prosecutors prepare a case for trial. This special category of paralegal has special skills regarding the support, assistance, and coordination of victims and witnesses. Such role requires the paralegal to have strong interpersonal communication skills. Job responsibilities include the ability to interview both friendly and hostile witnesses, the ability to contact and establish and maintain a rapport with victims and witnesses, and the ability to adequately prepare witnesses to testify.

aggravated battery
A criminal battery accompanied by circumstances that make it more severe such as the use of a deadly weapon or the fact that the battery resulted in serious bodily harm.

serious bodily injury
Serious physical impairment of the human body; especially, bodily injury that creates a substantial risk of death or that causes serious, permanent disfigurement or protracted loss or impairment.

deadly weapon
Any firearm or other device, instrument, material, or substance that, from the manner in which it is used or is intended to be used, is calculated or likely to produce death.

assault
Intentional voluntary movement that creates fear or apprehension of an immediate unwanted touching; the threat or attempt to cause a touching, whether successful or not, provided the victim is aware of the danger.

Battery is classified into degrees. A simple offensive touching such as occurred between John and Mary would be considered a misdemeanor in most states. However, a more serious battery, called an **aggravated battery**, usually is classified as a felony and carries a more severe punishment.

In many jurisdictions, a battery is considered aggravated when it involves one of the following:

- A battery is committed by the defendant with the intent to create **serious bodily injury** to the victim.
- A **deadly weapon** is used in the battery even if serious bodily injury does not occur to the victim.
- The battery is committed with the defendant's possessing intent to kill or rape or some other felonious state of mind.
- The victim of the battery is a child, woman, or police officer.

Consent may be a defense to battery so long as the contact with the victim is not considered unlawful. For example, people participating in a football game imply consent to be touched during the course of the game even if it may cause injury to them. In contrast, a person cannot legally consent to being shot with a handgun. However, other defenses such as self-defense or defense of others could be asserted in a case involving a battery.

ASSAULT

Assault and battery are oftentimes confused as being the same crime; however, they are very separate crimes that can occur together in the same incident or independently of each other. It is possible to have a battery without an assault and vice versa. The elements that constitute an assault are

- Imminent apprehension or fear
- Of a harmful or offensive touching
- Of another person
- Without his/her consent.

Assault and battery are not the same thing. The assault is the apprehension or awareness that a harmful or offensive touching is about to occur; a battery is the actual touching. Assaults typically fall into one of two categories: attempted battery or threatened battery. In an attempted battery, the defendant has the specific intent to commit the battery, takes substantial steps toward its commission, but fails to complete the crime. A threatened battery is an intentional scaring of the victim that a battery is about to occur. For example, pointing a gun at someone with the intent to scare the person that he/she might be shot constitutes an assault.

Battery	Assault
1. Intentful touching	1. Imminent apprehension or fear
2. Of another human being	2. On part of victim
3. Without consent	3. Of a harmful or offensive touching
4. Does not have to result in injury	4. Without consent
5. Victim does not have to be consciously aware of touching	5. Victim must be consciously aware of apprehension or fear

FIGURE 5.1
Differences between Battery and Assault

In an assault, the crime centers on the fact that the victim must be aware that a harmful or offensive touching may occur or is threatened. If a person walks up behind another person holding a baseball bat above his/her head as if he/she were going to strike the apparent victim, but the victim does not see the person, no assault will have occurred because the fear and apprehension of the physical contact has not occurred. If the person strikes the victim from behind, a battery has occurred but without an assault as the victim did possess the fear or apprehension necessary for an assault.

Most assaults are considered misdemeanors unless they are committed with the intent to commit a violent felony such as murder, rape, or robbery or they involve a deadly weapon. When an assault elevates above a misdemeanor, it is known as a felonious assault or aggravated assault. An assault against a police officer usually is considered an **aggravated assault**. Assault with a deadly weapon would be an example of an aggravated assault. It is important to remember that while assault is threatening to use force, battery requires the actual use of force. Assault is classified on the actor's intent, the extent of the injury to the victim, or the use of a deadly weapon. (See Figure 5.1.)

MAYHEM

At common law, **mayhem** was the dismemberment or disablement of a body part. The crime was later expanded to include disfigurement or maiming. The elements of mayhem are

• The deliberate act

• Of maiming, dismembering, disabling, or disfiguring

• A body part of a person

• For the purpose of intending to harm or causing permanent disfigurement.

For example, Jill and Joyce were to compete in a local beauty competition. The competition was fierce and they exchanged heated words prior to the competition. Jill was fearful that Joyce was prettier than she was and would win the competition. One day, while Joyce was shopping in a nearby mall, Jill walked up to Joyce and, with the intent to disfigure her, threw acid on Joyce's face. The acid burned Joyce's face, causing permanent scarring. Jill is guilty of mayhem. Today, most states have included or consider the crime of mayhem as a form of aggravated assault.

STALKING

Stalking is a serious and, at times, a life-threatening crime. It is a series of actions that makes a person fear for his or her safety. A stalking victim may be followed, harassed, telephoned, or watched; receive unwanted mail; or be subject to other frightening actions. The exact legal definition varies from state to state, but all states have enacted laws against stalking and the Federal Interstate Stalking Law was enacted in 1996.

aggravated assault
Criminal assault accompanied with circumstances that make it more severe such as the intent to commit another crime or the intent to cause serious bodily injury.

mayhem
The maiming, dismembering, disabling, or disfigurement of the body part of another with the intent to harm or cause permanent injury.

PRACTICE TIP

The Federal Interstate Stalking Law makes it a federal crime to cross a state line with the intent to injure or harass another. Criminal stalking laws by state can be found at www.ncvc.org/src/.

stalking
The act or offense of following or loitering near another with the purpose of annoying or harassing that person or committing a further crime.

KIDNAPPING

kidnapping
The unlawful confinement, removal, or hiding of a person against his/her will for the purpose of holding the person to obtain a ransom, to serve as a hostage, to facilitate the commission of a felony, to inflict harm or terrorize the victim, or to interfere with the performance of a governmental or political function.

Kidnapping involves the taking away of a person's freedom by some type of confinement as well as moving or hiding the victim. One of the most infamous kidnapping cases of all time was the 1932 kidnapping of the son of aviator Charles Lindbergh. Lindbergh's son was later found dead. Prior to the Lindbergh kidnapping, the crime of kidnapping was not a serious offense. In fact, in the State of New Jersey, where the crime occurred, kidnapping was classified as a misdemeanor. Due to the notoriety surrounding the Lindbergh kidnapping, many kidnapping statutes were enacted, making kidnapping a serious felony. Congress passed the Lindbergh Act in 1932. It was intended to enable federal authorities to step in and pursue kidnappers once they have crossed a state border with their victim. Several states have implemented their own similar versions of the act to cover acts of kidnapping that do not involve crossing a state line.

The elements of a kidnapping are

- The seizing,
- The confining or restraining, and
- The unlawful moving of the person
- By force or threat of force
- Against his/her will.

asportation
The act of carrying away or removing property or a person.

The actus reus of kidnapping is the seizing and carrying away of or concealment of the victim. The term **asportation** is also sometimes used to refer to the seizing and carrying away of the victim. The mens rea is the intent to confine, hold, or conceal the victim. Kidnapping requires the defendant to act without the authority of the law. Therefore, if the defendant believes that the taking of the person is authorized by law, then a kidnapping may not have occurred.

Like assault and battery, kidnapping also is divided into two degrees: simple and aggravated. In order for a kidnapping to rise to the level of aggravated, it usually involves an act such as the following:

- Kidnapping for ransom.
- Sexual invasions.
- Child stealing.
- Holding someone hostage.
- Robbing or murdering the victim.
- Blackmailing.
- Terrorizing or injuring the victim.
- Political reasons.

In some jurisdictions, the penalty for aggravated kidnapping has been elevated to life imprisonment or death.

parental kidnapping
The kidnapping of a child by one parent in violation of the other parent's custody or visitation rights.

The majority of all child abductions in the United States are **parental kidnappings**. If a parent kidnaps his or her child and moves to another state, it becomes a federal issue. If the parent takes the kidnapped child to a foreign country, the Hague Convention of Civil Aspects of International Child Abduction generally applies. The majority of states have signed the federal Uniform Child Custody Jurisdiction Enforcement Act making it a felony to kidnap one's own child. In states that have not adopted the UCCJEA, parental kidnapping is generally a misdemeanor. The general purpose of the UCCJEA is to prevent parental abductors from getting custody orders outside the child's home state.

SURF'S UP

Elizabeth Smart was kidnapped from her bedroom on June 5, 2002, by a man who had broken into her family's home. Fortunately, the story had a happier ending than that of the Lindbergh kidnapping; Elizabeth was found alive March 12, 2003, with her kidnapper, Brian Mitchell, who had formerly worked at the Smart home. Thousands of children go missing every year from kidnapping. One valuable mechanism in the recovery of abducted children is the Amber Alert. When activated, the Amber Alert assists law enforcement by providing access to information from a network of thousands. Signs posted on freeways that identify the license plate and vehicle description of any vehicle involved in such a reported abduction is one example of a step that may be taken. By posting such information, law enforcement can utilize the public on a vast scale to help in its search and relocation of kidnapped children. In addition to Amber Alerts, numerous Web sites have been created so that the public can post and track tips for kidnapped and missing children. The details on the child and pictures of the child as well as details regarding the abduction are posted to the Web site. One such Web site is www.missingkids.com. This Web site solicits the public's help in locating missing children. In addition, an "800" number has been established to receive all tips from the public in an effort to locate the child. To learn more about the Amber Alert System, go to www.codeamber.org.

Another threat to children is from sexual predators. Since the death in New Jersey of seven-year-old Megan Kanka, who was raped and killed by a known child molester who had moved across the street from the family's home without their knowledge, many states have implemented what has been called Megan's law. This law provides for Internet access and public notices when known sex offenders move into a particular neighborhood. The sex offender is required by law to register as a sex offender with law enforcement and the information concerning the whereabouts of the convicted child molester is placed on the Internet so that people seeking to protect their children from such threats can locate that type of information. To examine such a state Web site, visit California's Web site at www.meganslaw.ca.gov.

FALSE IMPRISONMENT

False imprisonment is a lesser form of a crime that involves taking away the victim's freedom of movement. The crime of false imprisonment is usually a lesser and included offense of a kidnapping. The elements required for false imprisonment are

* The unlawful confinement
* Of a person
* Without his/her consent.

false imprisonment
Any deprivation of a person's freedom of movement without that person's consent and against his or her will, whether done by actual violence or threats.

The key difference between false imprisonment and kidnapping is the element of moving or concealing the victim. False imprisonment only constitutes a confinement.

The actus reus of false imprisonment is the confinement of the victim. False imprisonment is a specific intent crime. The defendant must intend to confine the victim. The prosecutor must prove that the defendant was aware that his/her action of confining the victim was unlawful in order to obtain a conviction of false imprisonment. The motive for the confinement is irrelevant to the crime. (See Figure 5.2.)

Under the Model Penal Code, the crime of false imprisonment can rise to the level of aggravated false imprisonment. The Model Penal Code calls this "felonious restraint." The Model Penal Code explains this difference in section 212.2:[1]

A person commits a felony of the third degree if he knowingly:
a. restrains another unlawfully in circumstances exposing him to risk of serious bodily injury; or
b. holds another in a condition of involuntary servitude.

Kidnapping	False Imprisonment
1. The seizing, confining, restraining, and unlawful moving	1. Unlawful confinement
2. Of a human being	2. Of a human being
3. By force or threat of force	3. Without his/her consent
4. Against the victim's will	

FIGURE 5.2
Differences between Kidnapping and False Imprisonment

[1] Model Penal Code, copyright 1985 by The American Law Institute. Reprinted with permission.

HATE CRIMES

hate crime
A crime motivated by the victim's race, color, ethnicity, religion, or national origin.

Hate crimes differ from other crimes in that the perpetrator is driven by bias. Hate crimes are criminal acts committed against a person because of his or her race, religion, sexual orientation, disability, ethnicity, gender, or age. American citizens have basic civil rights. The law provides protection when those rights are violated. Hate crime laws punish acts, not beliefs. The constitutionality of hate crime laws has been addressed in both *R.A.V. v. City of St. Paul,* 505 U.S. 377 (1992) and *Wisconsin v. Mitchell,* 508 U.S. 47 (1993). In both cases, the court concluded that a criminal statute may consider bias motivation when that motivation is tied directly to a defendant's criminal conduct.

SEXUAL OFFENSES

Many people who deal with sex crimes consider them to be crimes of violence and aggression rather than being crimes involving sexual drive or association. Sex crimes are serious even if no physical injury occurs as they violate a person's intimacy and typically cause emotional injury. Sex crimes can be difficult because of the embarrassment and emotional distress suffered by most victims. However, in recent times, the judicial system has become much more sensitive to sex crime victims.

Rape

rape
Unlawful sexual intercourse with a person without consent.

Rape is one of the oldest sex crimes recognized by law. Over the years, the laws have changed so as to protect the victim. For example, under common law and up until the 1970s and 1980s, a woman's past sexual conduct could be presented as evidence. Recent statutes have changed that element, recognizing that a person's past sexual history is not relevant to the rape and have banned the introduction of such evidence against the victim.

The elements of rape are

- Unlawful sexual penetration
- Committed by use of force, fear, or trick.

The crime of rape does not always mean forced sexual intercourse that leads to emission of ejaculatory fluids. For example, penetration of the female's sex organ by the male is sufficient. The penetration does not have to involve vaginal penetration to satisfy the requirement.

Generally, any forced sexual penetration, no matter how slight, may be considered rape. Rape also can occur when an artifice is used for penetration; it does not have to be the male sexual organ.

The actus reus of a rape also includes the force or fear that is used to achieve the penetration. Different types of force satisfy this element of rape. Brute force can be used to overcome the victim and force submission. The threat of harm can be used to force the victim to submit or face apparently dire consequences. And the last situation is that the victim can be tricked into submission through the use of alcohol, drugs, or apparent authority over a minor. Actual force is not necessary to satisfy the

CASE FACT PATTERN

Peter was arrested and charged with raping a coed named Margaret on campus. At the trial, Peter testified that he had only put his fingers between the folds of skin over Margaret's vagina but had not inserted his fingers into the vagina. Do Peter's actions qualify as rape?

requirement. The threat or fear of harm is sufficient. If the rape is committed while the defendant brandishes a weapon, then the force element is satisfied. If consent is obtained through fraudulent circumstances such as tricking a minor, then the force requirement is satisfied.

The Model Penal Code defines the crime of rape as follows:[2]

> *A male who has sexual intercourse with a female not his wife is guilty of rape if:*
> a. *he compels her to submit by force or threat of imminent death, serious bodily injury, extreme pain, or kidnapping to be inflicted on anyone; or*
> b. *he has substantially impaired her power to appraise or control her conduct by administering or employing without her knowledge drugs, intoxicants, or other means for the purpose of preventing resistance; or*
> c. *the female is unconscious; or*
> d. *the female is less than 10 years old.*

Rape in the only crime discussed in the Model Penal Code that is not gender neutral.

In order for a rape to have occurred, the sexual penetration must have taken place without the consent of the victim. Nonconsent by the victim is an element that must be proved by the prosecution, and consent is a defense that a defendant can assert in the defense of a rape charge. In fact, consent is almost always asserted as a defense in a rape case. Consent can be demonstrated by the actions of the victim; words are not necessary. Consent is often argued when a defendant is charged with date rape. A rape is considered date rape when it is committed by a person who is escorting the victim. Similarly, acquaintance rape is used to refer to a rape committed by someone known to the victim. The modern trend is to require actual consent of the woman despite the historical view that a husband could not be found guilty of raping his wife.

Historically, laws pertaining to rape were written in a way that made them inapplicable to spousal rape on some sort of standing implied consent theory. In 1993, spousal rape became a crime in all 50 states. However, in many states, including Texas, there are still some exemptions given to husbands from rape prosecutions.

If the rape consists of sexual penetration of a minor, then the element of force is presumed by law due to the fact that the child is not of majority. This type of rape is referred to as **statutory rape**. In a statutory rape case, the law has determined that minors are incapable of consenting; therefore, the consent or nonconsent of the minor child is neither an element of nor a defense to the crime of statutory rape. Statutory rape is sometimes considered a **strict liability** crime.

Rape can elevate to aggravated rape due to the circumstances. Some of the circumstances that elevate rape into aggravated rape include

- The victim suffers serious bodily harm.
- The rape occurs in connection with another crime.
- A deadly weapon is used or brandished during the rape.
- The rapist has accomplices.

Professional basketball star Kobe Bryant made national news when he was accused of raping a hotel employee whom he had invited into his hotel suite while in Colorado. As the hearings began, it was clear that Bryant's defense team would attack the victim's credibility, making rape shield laws a subject of national debate. Rape shield laws are designed to protect a rape victim from having past sexual history used to attack the credibility of testimony. In the Bryant case, the trial judge ruled that the alleged victim's sexual activity in the days just prior to being examined by police

statutory rape
The sexual intercourse with a female who is under a certain age (usually 14 to 18, depending on the state). The minor child is considered legally incapable of consenting.

strict liability
Liability that is based on the breach of an absolute duty rather than negligence or intent.

---

[2] Model Penal Code, copyright 1985 by the American Law Institute. Reprinted with permission.

would be admissible. Prosecutors hoped that the Colorado Supreme Court would reverse the ruling, but the charges against Bryant were dropped after the victim told prosecutors she did not want to testify.

Sodomy

sodomy
Oral or anal copulation between humans.

Sodomy is a crime that in some states is still punishable between consenting adults, no matter if they are heterosexual or homosexual. The elements of sodomy are

- Unlawful sexual penetration of the mouth or anus of one person
- By the penis of another
- By use of force or fear.

The force or fear that is required to overcome the victim's resistance is still an element of the crime, just as it is in rape. Consent is a defense to the crime of sodomy. Prior to 2003, four states still had laws banning private consensual sex between adults of the same sex. However, in 2003 the U.S. Supreme Court struck down the Texas anti-sodomy law as it pertained to consenting adults. Today, no state can criminalize sodomy among consenting adults.

The sexual penetration necessary for the crime of sodomy is penetration of the anal cavity of another human being. Whether the victim is male or female is of no relevance. The crime is complete with any penetration of the anal cavity, although penal penetration is the most common form.

Summary

While homicide is perhaps the most notorious crime, other crimes against the person exist and are very serious in nature. A battery is an unjustified touching of another human being without the victim's consent. The elements that are required for a battery to occur are the deliberate harmful or offensive touching of another person without his/her consent. The actus reus of the crime is the actual touching of the victim. Under common law, a battery requires an intentional mens rea. However, intent is no longer a required element. Many states have adopted the mental states of reckless and criminal negligence as well.

In many jurisdictions, a battery is considered aggravated when it involves one of the following: (1) it is committed by the defendant with the intent to create serious bodily injury to the victim; (2) a deadly weapon is used; (3) the intent to kill or rape, or some other felonious state of mind is present; or (4) the victim is a child, woman, or police officer.

Assault and battery are often confused as being the same crime; however, they are very separate crimes that can occur together in the same incident or independently of each other. It is possible to have a battery without an assault and vice versa. An assault is the imminent apprehension or fear of a harmful or offensive touching of another person without his/her consent.

In an assault, the victim must be aware that a harmful or offensive touching may occur or is threatened. If a person walks up behind another person holding a baseball bat above his/her head as if he/she were going to strike the apparent victim, but the victim does not see the person, no assault will have occurred because the fear and apprehension of the physical contact has not occurred. If the person strikes the victim from behind, a battery has occurred but not an assault because the victim did possess the fear or apprehension necessary for an assault.

The elements of a kidnapping are the seizing of a person, the confining or restraining of the person, and the unlawful moving of the victim by force or threat of force against his/her will. The actus reus of kidnapping is the seizing and carrying away of or concealment of the victim. The mens rea is the intent to confine, hold, or conceal the victim. Kidnapping requires the defendant to act without the authority of the law. Therefore, if the defendant believes that the taking of the person is authorized by law, then a kidnapping may not have occurred. The majority of child abductions are actually parental kidnappings.

False imprisonment is a lesser form of a crime that involves taking away the freedom of movement of the victim. The crime of false imprisonment is usually a lesser and included offense of a kidnapping. The elements required for false imprisonment are the unlawful confinement of a person without his/her consent.

At common law, mayhem was the dismemberment or disablement of a body part. The crime was later expanded to include disfigurement or maiming. The elements of mayhem are the deliberate act of maiming, dismembering, disabling, or disfiguring a body part of a person for the purpose of intending to harm or causing permanent disfigurement.

Rape is the unlawful sexual penetration committed by use of force, fear, or trick. Rape does not require sexual intercourse that leads to emission of ejaculatory fluids. For the purposes of rape, penetration of the female's sex organ by the male is sufficient. The penetration does not have to involve vaginal penetration to satisfy the requirement.

If the rape consists of sexual penetration of a minor, then the element of force is presumed by law due to the fact that the child is not of majority. This type of rape is referred to as statutory rape. In a statutory rape case, the law has determined that minors are incapable of consenting; therefore, the consent or nonconsent of the minor child is neither an element of nor a defense to the crime of statutory rape. Statutory rape is sometimes considered a strict liability crime.

The elements of sodomy are unlawful oral or anal sexual penetration of one person by the penis of another by use of force or fear. Sodomy between consenting adults is no longer a punishable crime.

Key Terms

Aggravated assault
Aggravated battery
Asportation
Assault
Battery
Bodily injury
Deadly weapon
False imprisonment
Hate crime

Kidnapping
Mayhem
Parental kidnapping
Rape
Serious bodily injury
Sodomy
Stalking
Statutory rape
Strict liability

Review Questions

1. List four situations that can elevate rape to aggravated rape.
2. Why is statutory rape considered a strict liability crime?
3. What are the elements of battery?
4. Explain the difference(s) between assault and battery.
5. What is the difference between attempted battery and threatened battery?
6. By whom are the majority of children kidnapped?
7. What is sodomy?
8. Why is it essential that the victim be aware during an assault?
9. When is consent not a defense to a rape?
10. What is false imprisonment? Give an example.
11. What is the difference between false imprisonment and kidnapping?
12. What is mayhem and why is it sometimes included in the crime of aggravated battery?
13. What situations will elevate a battery from simple to aggravated?
14. Is penetration necessary for a rape? Why or why not?
15. Give three examples of a battery and three examples of an assault.

Exercises

1. Tom likes to play practical jokes on his fraternity brothers, particularly on Neil. One day, as Neil came up the walkway of the fraternity house, Tom, who was waiting on the balcony, dropped a balloon filled with urine as Neil passed under him. The balloon broke as it hit Neil in the head, covering Neil in urine. Neil was not hurt, but he was appalled by the event. What crime, if any, has Tom committed?

2. Marty and Tina had been husband and wife but have been separated for over a year. Although the two were in the midst of the divorce, they were not officially divorced. Tina had been maintaining a separate residence from Marty for the entire year. One night, Marty forced his way into Tina's apartment. Marty grabbed Tina and told her to be quiet or that he would kill her. Marty proceeded to engage in sexual intercourse with Tina. What crime, if any, has Marty committed and why?

3. Mikey and Tony had been drinking. The two men were boasting about how tough they are. Mikey tensed up his stomach and invited Tony to hit him as hard as he could to prove his physical toughness. Mikey was apprehensive, but, after some encouragement by Mikey, Tony hit Mikey as hard as he could. Mike collapsed on the floor, seriously injured by the blow he sustained from Tony. Has Tony committed a crime? Why or why not?

4. Little Granny Moses, all 74 pounds of her on her 4′3″ stature, loved to attend professional wrestling matches. On a Saturday night, approximately two weeks ago, Little Granny Moses attended the "Super, Duper World-Wide Drag 'Em Down Wrestling Match" being held at Madison Ridge Garden. "Hulk, the Giant" was to wrestle in the main event. Hulk was 7′2″ tall and weighed 350 pounds, all muscle. When Hulk came out to wrestle in the main match, he proceeded to walk around the outside of the ring taunting the audience. Sitting in her first-row seat, Little Granny Moses shot up out of her chair, ran over to the Hulk, stopped short, looked up at him, and said, "I'm gonna kick your butt, buddy," as she waved her clinched fist at him. In a split second, Hulk ran out of the arena crying and thrashing his arms, claiming he was frightened of Granny and could not return to the match. Has a crime been committed? Which one, if any? Is there a defense to the crime, if committed?

5. What are the differences between the elements found in the crimes of false imprisonment and kidnapping? What are the similarities? Are they really the same crime? If they are similar, why are the penalties for kidnapping usually more extreme?

6. Little Sammy the Snake was known for committing insurance scams by purposely walking into moving vehicles in order to collect for an injury, whether real or imagined. One day, Sammy, like always, stepped into a moving vehicle. This time, Sammy misjudged how fast the vehicle was moving and, as a result, suffered life-threatening injuries to his internal organs. He was admitted to emergency surgery where Doctor "First Time" was on duty. Sammy was unconscious. They wheeled Sammy in and the doctor began to operate on Sammy to save his life. Unbeknownst to Sammy, this was the doctor's first surgery. Sammy had never met the doctor and never consented to allow this doctor to operate on him. Was a crime committed by the doctor? Why or why not?

7. Provide three examples of where an assault has been committed without committing a battery in the same action. Provide three additional examples of where a battery has been committed but not an assault in the same action.

8. Can men be sexually assaulted? If not, explain why.

PORTFOLIO ASSIGNMENT

Gather five friends and/or acquaintances into a room with classroom desks and chairs. Make sure that the individuals you ask to take part in this assignment are not part of this class and are not paralegal students. Together, come up with five different scenarios of what may constitute the elements of the crime of false imprisonment. Use the items left in the room—desks, chairs, and so on—to aid you in your assignment. The elements of the crime must be present and provable. Ask yourself the following questions when completing this assignment:

- Does it matter if the victim knows he/she is being falsely imprisoned?

- Can props, items, mazes, puzzles, furniture, walls, doors, closed windows, and other daily fixtures of life play a part in the false imprisonment?

- Is it easy to falsely imprison someone based on the elements of the crime?

Vocabulary Builders

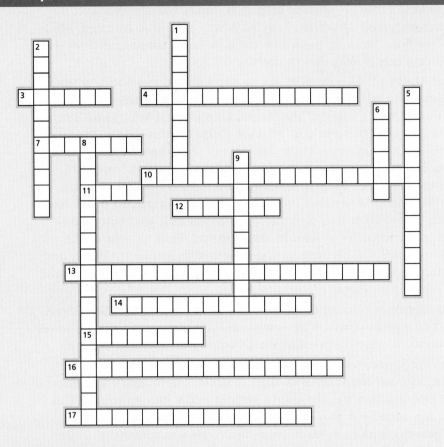

Instructions
Use the key terms from this chapter to fill in the answers to the crossword puzzle.
NOTE: When the answer is more than one word, leave a blank space between words.

ACROSS

3. oral or anal copulation between humans.
4. the sexual intercourse with a female who is under a certain age (usually 14 to 18, depending on the state). The minor child is considered legally incapable of consenting.
7. intentional voluntary movement that creates fear or apprehension of an immediate unwanted touching; the threat or attempt to cause a touching, whether successful or not, provided the victim is aware of the danger.
10. a criminal battery accompanied by circumstances that make it more severe such as the use of a deadly weapon or the fact that the battery resulted in serious bodily harm.
11. unlawful sexual intercourse with a person without consent.
12. an intentional and unwanted harmful or offensive contact with the person of another; the actual intentional touching of someone with intent to cause harm, no matter how slight the harm.
13. serious physical impairment of the human body; especially, bodily injury that creates a substantial risk of death or that causes serious, permanent disfigurement or protracted loss or impairment.
14. any firearm or other device, instrument, material, or substance that, from the manner in which it is used or is intended to be used, is calculated or likely to produce death.

15. the act or offense of following or loitering near another with the purpose of annoying or harassing that person or committing a further crime.
16. any deprivation of a person's freedom of movement without that person's consent and against his or her will, whether done by actual violence or threats.
17. liability that is based on the breach of an absolute duty rather than negligence or intent.

DOWN

1. the unlawful confinement, removal, or hiding of a person against his/her will for the purpose of holding the person to obtain a ransom, to serve as a hostage, to facilitate the commission of a felony, to inflict harm or terrorize the victim, or to interfere with the performance of a governmental or political function.
2. the act of carrying away or removing property or a person.
5. physical damage to a person's body.
6. the maiming, dismembering, disabling, or disfigurement of the body part of another with the intent to harm or cause permanent injury.
8. criminal assault accompanied with circumstances that make it more severe such as the intent to commit another crime or the intent to cause serious bodily injury.
9. a crime motivated by the victim's race, color, ethnicity, religion, or national origin.

STEVEN ARMSTRONG, APPELLANT v. STATE OF MISSISSIPPI, APPELLEE
COURT OF APPEALS OF MISSISSIPPI
828 So. 2d 239; 2002 Miss. App. LEXIS 523
September 24, 2002, Decided

PRIOR HISTORY:

COURT FROM WHICH APPEALED: JACKSON COUNTY CIR-CUIT COURT ROBERT. DATE OF TRIAL COURT JUDGMENT: 11/22/2000

TRIAL JUDGE: HON. JAMES W. BACKSTROM

TRIAL COURT DISPOSITION: AGGRAVATED ASSAULT HA-BITUAL OFFENDER SENTENCED TO SERVE 15 YEARS IN THE CUSTODY OF MDOC.

DISPOSITION:

AFFIRMED.

CASE SUMMARY

Procedural Posture:

Defendant was convicted in the Circuit Court of Jackson County (Mississippi) on a charge of aggravated assault. After a sentencing hearing, he was found to be a habitual offender and sentenced to serve a term of 15 years without parole in the custody of the Mississippi Department of Corrections. Defendant appealed after his motion for a judgment notwithstanding the verdict, or in the alternative, a new trial which was denied by the court.

Overview:

Defendant struck the victim with a wooden stake two times after they got in an argument. Evidence at trial indicated that the victim did not take any hostile action toward defendant before he was struck. Defendant argued that he struck the victim as he thought the victim was going to go after a "skill" saw. Defendant claimed an instruction under Miss. Code Ann. § 97-3-7(1)(b) (Rev. 2000) should have been provided. The court held that since § 97-3-7(1)(b) was based [on] the negligent use of a deadly weapon, the instruction would have been improper here. The court also noted that defendant did not request such an instruction at trial, and it was not the court's obligation to offer it sua sponte. The appellate court held that it was not an error for the court not to re-type the **assault** instruction that was given, and the instruction was not improper simply because it did not follow the exact language of the statute. Finally, the court held that there was sufficient evidence to find that defendant was the same individual who had been convicted of two felonies in Michigan, as the birth date and the fingerprints were the same.

Outcome:

The conviction and the sentence were affirmed.

JUDGES: BRANTLEY, J., McMILLIN, C. J., KING AND SOUTHWICK, P. JJ., BRIDGES, THOMAS, LEE, IRVING, MYERS AND CHANDLER, JJ., CONCUR.

OPINION BY: BRANTLEY
NATURE OF THE CASE: CRIMINAL FELONY

Steven Armstrong was convicted in the Circuit Court of Jackson County on a charge of aggravated assault. After a sentencing hearing, he was found to be an habitual offender and sentenced to serve a term of fifteen years without parole in the custody of the Mississippi Department of Corrections. He then filed a motion for a judgment notwithstanding the verdict, or in the alternative, a new trial which was denied by the court. Armstrong appeals asserting the following assignments of error:

I. WHETHER THE TRIAL COURT ERRED IN AMENDING JURY INSTRUCTION D-8.
II. WHETHER THE TRIAL COURT ERRED IN FINDING THAT THE EVIDENCE PRESENTED WAS SUFFICIENT TO ESTABLISH ARMSTRONG'S HABITUAL OFFENDER STA-TUS PURSUANT TO MISS. CODE ANN. SECTION 99-19-83 (REV. 2000).

Finding no error, we affirm.

FACTS

On May 10, 1999, Bonnie Pace, sixty-one years of age, was in charge of a worksite for setting forms for pouring concrete. Steven Armstrong was employed on the worksite to cut the wooden stakes used to hold the concrete forms in place. Pace and Armstrong had an argument about what length the stakes should be. After this exchange, Armstrong intentionally struck Pace twice with a wooden stake which resulted in Pace's hospitalization for about a week. Although it is clear that Armstrong intentionally struck Pace, the testimony was in dispute as to why it happened.

At trial, the State called Pace and he testified that, at the conclusion of the exchange, he instructed Armstrong to follow his directions and turned to work on other matters. At this time, Pace was struck without warning on the side of his head by Armstrong. Armstrong then struck Pace again, but Pace was able to partially deflect the second blow with his arm. The State further showed that Pace was making no hostile demonstration toward Armstrong, and that he did not have a tool or any other object in his hands when Armstrong struck him. This testimony was corroborated by other workmen on the site at that time.

Alternatively, Armstrong alleged that he struck Pace in self-defense. He alleges that after the argument ensued, Pace "pushed-turned" him and turned away in the direction of a "Skill" saw. He claimed that he thought Pace was drunk and was going to reach for the saw and attack him. Therefore, according to this perception, he hit Pace with one of the stakes in self-defense. The evidence showed that a saw was in the area. No challenge is brought on this appeal concerning the sufficiency or the weight of the evidence concerning Armstrong's guilt.

ANALYSIS

I. Whether the Trial Court Erred in Amending Jury Instruction D-8.

Armstrong presented a theory of self-defense. In the event the jury did not believe his argument of self-defense, he wanted the jury to determine whether the board or stake used to assault Pace constituted a deadly weapon for purposes of aggravated assault. Therefore, he represented to the court that if the jury found that the board was *not* a deadly weapon, then they should consider whether he attempted to cause or did purposefully, knowingly or recklessly cause bodily injury for the purposes of simple assault.

Based on his argument and on Miss. Code Ann. § 97-3-7(1)(a), Armstrong submitted the following lesser offense instruction, D-8, on the crime of simple assault:

> If you find that the State has failed to prove any one or more of the essential elements of the crime of aggravated assault, you will then proceed with your deliberations to decide whether the State has proved beyond a reasonable doubt all of the elements of the crime of simple assault.
> If you find from the evidence in this case beyond a reasonable doubt that Steven Armstrong on or about May 10, 1999, did purposefully, knowingly, or recklessly cause bodily injury to Bonnie Pace, [not with a deadly weapon, or] not in his necessary self-defense, then you shall find Steven Armstrong guilty of simple assault.

Miss. Code Ann. § 97-3-7(1)(a) (Rev. 2000) provides that "(1) [a] person is guilty of simple assault if he (a) attempts to cause or purposely, knowingly or recklessly causes bodily injury to another."

Alternatively, the State prosecuted Armstrong for aggravated assault based on Miss. Code Ann. § 97-3-7(2)(b) (Rev. 2000). Section 97-3-7(2)(b) provides that "[a] person is guilty of aggravated assault if he (b) attempts to cause or purposely or knowingly causes bodily injury to another with a deadly weapon or other means likely to produce death or serious bodily harm. . . ." Specifically, the indictment alleged that Armstrong "did unlawfully, feloniously, willfully, and purposefully cause bodily injury to Bonnie Pace with a deadly weapon, a wooden board." Therefore, the State requested that the simple assault instruction, D-8, include the words "not with a deadly weapon, or," which are underlined and set out within the brackets above. The State requested the insertion in order to avoid possible confusion between the applicable form of simple assault, which was advanced by Armstrong, and aggravated assault, which was advanced by the State. The addition served to clarify and distinguish the applicable two forms of assault for the jury by explicitly setting forth the essential difference of whether bodily injury, if any, was caused by the use of a deadly weapon.

The State also requested the addition in order to be consistent with another instruction, S-2. Instruction S-2 defined simple assault and aggravated assault in accordance with the evidence presented in the case. Instruction S-2 also included the added language in an attempt to clarify and distinguish the available lesser offense of simple assault from the given definition of aggravated assault on the basis of whether a deadly weapon was used to cause the bodily injury.

The trial court granted the instruction for simple assault because of the possibility that the jury might find that the wooden stake was not a deadly weapon, an essential and required element for a conviction of aggravated assault. The trial judge also admitted the addition with the instruction. Armstrong makes several arguments in this assignment of error. First he asserts that it was an error to allow the additional language because it incorrectly apprized the jury of the various forms of simple assault and denied him the right to present to the jury an instruction in support of his various theories of defense. He states that the additional language in the instruction limited the jury to only consider the simple assault verdict if there was a finding that the stake was not a deadly weapon. He states that this is incorrect because a verdict of simple assault is also available even when a deadly weapon is used according to Miss. Code Ann. § 97-3-7(1)(b). Section 97-3-7(1)(b) provides that an accused may be found guilty of simple assault if he negligently used a deadly weapon to cause bodily harm. In the present case, Armstrong asserts that such an instruction based on § 97-3-7(1)(b) was applicable because he was negligent in his assessment that Pace was about to obtain the saw and hit him. He argues that where an accused has negligently concluded that another is presenting or is about to present a risk of imminent serious bodily injury, a negligent simple assault instruction should be given. Therefore, he argues that the additional language effectively denied the jury the opportunity to consider this other form of simple assault.

To warrant the lesser-included offense instruction, a defendant must point to some evidence in the record from which a jury could reasonably find him not guilty of the crime with which he was charged and at the same time find him guilty of the lesser-included offense. *Toliver v. State,* 600 So. 2d 186, 192 (Miss. 1992). Upon review, the instruction given did not inform the jury of the form of simple assault based on the negligent use of a deadly weapon. However, Armstrong clearly proceeded at trial under Miss. Code Ann. Section 97-3-7(1)(a) for an instruction of simple assault based on a finding that the wooden stake was not a deadly weapon and *never presented a theory of defense based on negligence as provided in Section 97-3-7(1)(b)*. As stated, Section 97-3-7(1)(b) provides that the lesser verdict of simple assault is available if the jury finds that the bodily injury was caused by the negligent use of a deadly weapon. Therefore, in light of *Toliver,* a jury could not have reasonably found him guilty of the lesser-included offense of simple assault based on the negligent use of a deadly weapon because no such evidence was ever presented before them.

In addition, Armstrong's argument based on the statute is misplaced. Miss. Code Ann. § 97-3-7(1)(b) (Rev. 2000), provides that a person is guilty of simple assault if he negligently causes bodily injury to another with a deadly weapon. The allegation that Armstrong might have been mistaken in his perception does not establish that his subsequent act of assaulting Pace was negligent. The intentional striking of Pace necessarily excluded any theory of a negligent striking. That Armstrong might have erred in his assessment of what Pace was doing does not potentially establish a negligent act because, regardless of what he believed and the reasonableness of what he believed, he did, in fact, intend to strike Pace. Pace was not negligently struck with the board or the stake; he was intentionally struck. Negligence for purposes of this form of simple assault does not have reference to an accused's state of mind.

It has reference to his action. *Nobles v. State*, 464 So. 2d 1151, 1154 (Miss. 1985). Therefore, an instruction based on the negligent use of a deadly weapon would have been improper to grant because there was never any evidence presented to warrant a negligent simple assault instruction under Miss. Code Ann. § 97-3-7(1)(b) (Rev. 2000). *See Murphy v. State*, 566 So. 2d 1201, 1206 (Miss. 1990); *Goodnite v. State*, 799 So. 2d 64, 69 (¶24) (Miss. 2001); *Alley v. Praschak Mach. Co.*, 366 So. 2d 661, 665 (Miss. 1979).

Furthermore, he never requested or submitted an instruction for the lesser verdict of simple assault based on the negligent use of a deadly weapon as provided in Section 97-3-7(1)(b). Also, no argument was made by Armstrong when instruction D-8 was being considered that any theory of negligence would be cut off by the modification. Consequently, his claim is barred. *Billiot v. State*, 454 So. 2d 445, 462 (Miss. 1984) (failure to request instruction and failure to object to lack of instruction works waiver of issue on appeal); *Oates v. State*, 421 So. 2d 1025, 1030 (Miss. 1982) (objections to instructions not made in trial court are waived on appeal).

Armstrong further argues that it was the duty of the trial court to inform the jury of the form or element of simple assault that applies to the finding that a deadly weapon was used in a negligent manner to cause bodily injury as provided in Miss. Code Ann. § 97-3-7(1)(b). A defendant is entitled to have jury instructions given which present his theory of the case. *Heidel v. State*, 587 So. 2d 835, 842 (Miss. 1991). However, this entitlement is limited to instructions that have a foundation in the evidence. *Id.* In addition, the trial court has no duty to instruct a jury where no request has been made for such instruction. *Ballenger v. State*, 667 So. 2d 1242, 1252 (Miss. 1995). In the present case, the trial court provided instructions on the defendant's theory of self-defense and granted an instruction on the lesser charge of simple assault applicable to this case. As stated earlier, there was also no request for the instruction and such an instruction was not supported by the evidence.

In Armstrong's second argument in this assignment of error, he contends that the trial court erred by inserting language that was not in the statute. Armstrong cites no authority for the notion implicit in his argument that to include language not found in a statute is error, and we have found none ourselves. On the other hand, while it is certainly true that a trial court does not likely commit error in an instruction of law when it follows the language of a statute, *Lenox v. State*, 727 So. 2d 753, 759 (¶37) (Miss. Ct. App. 1998), there is no authority of which we are aware to the effect that instructions must be restricted to the particular words of the statute in question. The lower court enjoys considerable discretion regarding the form and substance of jury instructions. *Rester v. Lott*, 566 So. 2d 1266, 1269 (Miss. 1990). The dispositive question is whether the jury was fully and correctly instructed on the principle of law involved.

If the instructions given provide correct statements of the law and are supported by the evidence, there is no prejudice to the defendant. *Johnson v. State*, 792 So. 2d 253, 258 (¶16) (Miss. 2001). If the instructions fairly announce the law of the case and create no injustice, no reversible error will be found. *Fielder v. Magnolia Beverage Co.*, 757 So. 2d 925, 929 (¶10) (Miss. 1999). We find that the instruction was correct as a matter of law and relevant to the facts and evidence presented in this case. The court's modification to the simple assault instruction clarified for the jury the distinction between the forms of simple and aggravated assault involved in the case at bar, distinctly whether bodily injury, if any, was caused by the use of a deadly weapon. The additional language does inform the jury correctly and adequately on the simple assault claim advanced by Armstrong, as well as clarifies and avoids confusion between the forms of aggravated assault and simple assault applicable to this case. Therefore, the trial court did not err by inserting the language not contained in the statute.

Armstrong next claims in this assignment of error that by not having the instruction re-typed, the trial court drew unnecessary attention to the additional language, "not with a deadly weapon." Therefore, he further claims that this obliterated any consideration it had of the lesser offense once it found that the board in evidence in this case was a deadly weapon. Cases are legion in which a trial court has corrected or modified instructions by hand. Armstrong has cited no authority in support of this argument. There is no requirement that an instruction be re-typed that we are aware of. In addition, this Court will not review any issues where the party has failed to cite relevant authority. *Williams v. State*, 708 So. 2d 1358, 1360–61 (¶12) (Miss. 1998). In any event, the trial court instructed the jurors that they were not to place any significance to the way or manner instructions were given to them. We find that this was sufficient to cure any prejudicial effect that Armstrong claims.

Armstrong's final argument in this assignment of error is that the board that was placed into evidence was a different size than the board that he used to strike Pace. The work crew was using 4x4 boards and splitting them into 2x4 boards to make the stakes. A 4x4 board was introduced into evidence, but the testimony showed that Pace was struck with a 2x2 board. We find no prejudice because the 4x4 board introduced into evidence simply showed what the men were using and the testimony clearly showed that these were split. There was no confusion, given the testimony. The State was not attempting to prove that Armstrong had used some instrumentality in the attack that he did not in fact use. Therefore, this assignment of error is without merit.

II. Whether the Trial Court Erred in Finding that the Evidence Presented was Sufficient to Establish Armstrong's Habitual Offender Status Pursuant to Miss. Code Ann. Section 99-19-83 (Rev. 2000).

The trial court found that Armstrong was an habitual offender based on evidence presented by the State that he had been convicted of two felonies in the State of Michigan. Armstrong argues that the evidence was insufficient to prove that he was the same Steven Armstrong who was convicted of the crimes in Michigan. This Court disagrees.

Where a trial judge makes a factual finding supported by the record, we will not overturn that finding of fact unless it is clearly erroneous. *West v. State*, 463 So. 2d 1048, 1056 (Miss. 1985). In the present case, the lower court's factual findings were supported by substantial, credible evidence in the record that the appellant was the same person that was convicted in Michigan.

The record reflects that the State's proof was legally sufficient to demonstrate that Steven Armstrong in the present case and the Steven Armstrong who was twice convicted in the State of Michigan are one and the same. First, the State presented and entered into evidence from the State of Michigan certified copies of two prior convictions of Steven Armstrong resulting in sentences of more than one year. The documents further provided identification information of the convicted Steven Armstrong such as date of birth and an assigned state number. Next, the record also reflects the testimony of two persons, the case officer and an accepted qualified expert in fingerprinting.

The case officer of the Ocean Springs Police Department testified as to the information in their investigative file obtained for the case from Armstrong at the time of arrest. He stated that the file contained information such as Armstrong's date of birth, fingerprints, social security number, physical description (gender, race, height, weight, scars), and a photograph. He further stated that he conducted a National Crime Information Center (NCIC) check on Armstrong to see if he had a prior criminal history or was wanted in another state. After his request, he received a NCIC report which included information regarding Steven Armstrong such as his date of birth, social security number, physical information, a numerical fingerprint description code, and listed that he had been convicted of two separate felonies in the State of Michigan and a Michigan identification number. The officer stated that the information provided in the NCIC report matched the information obtained from Armstrong at the time of arrest, particularly as to his date of birth, social security number, and physical description, including sex, race, height, weight, and a scar on the left leg. The NCIC report and a photocopy of Armstrong's fingerprints obtained at the time of arrest from the Ocean Springs Police Department were admitted into evidence.

The record also reveals that the second witness, accepted by the court as a qualified expert in the field of fingerprint examination, testified concerning his comparison of the appellant's fingerprints obtained at the time of arrest and the numerical description regarding the fingerprints provided in the NCIC report of the Steven Armstrong convicted in Michigan. He concluded that "given this comparison and the other identifying data from the NCIC report, he was ninety-nine percent certain that the appellant was one and the same person as the individual described in the NCIC report." On cross-examination, the officer also testified that in his years of experience in law enforcement he has found NCIC reports to be accurate and reliable.

Upon further review, we also note that the date of birth provided in the certified documents from Michigan was identical to the date of birth in the Mississippi investigative file and the Michigan identification number provided in the documents was the same as the number on the NCIC report. In addition, there was no evidence offered against the State's evidence.

Armstrong next claims that the NCIC report was improperly admitted because it was "inadmissible hearsay," unreliable and not subject to the "business record exception" under M.R.E. 803(6). However, this claim is without merit because the Mississippi Supreme Court stated in *Randall v.*
State "that Rule 101 and 1101(b)(3) [provide] that the Rules of Evidence do not apply to sentence hearings." *Randall v. State*, 806 So. 2d 185, 231–32 (¶131) (Miss. 2001). Mississippi Rule of Evidence 101 states that the rules apply to all proceedings except those stated in Rule 1101(b)(3). M.R.E. 1101(b)(3) states that the rules of evidence are inapplicable to proceedings in sentencing.

Although this Court in *Harveston v. State*, 798 So. 2d 638, 640–41 (¶7) (Miss. Ct. App. 2001), subsequent to the holding in *Randall*, stated that an NCIC report offered by a local investigating officer was inadmissible hearsay, and not able to satisfy the business record rule exception of M.R.E. 803(6) because an issue of trustworthiness arises when one organization seeks to introduce records in its possession that were actually prepared by another. Unlike in the present case and distinguished from the exceptions set forth in M.R.E. 1101(b)(3), in *Harveston* the report was offered not during the sentencing proceeding, but in the trial phase of a burglary prosecution to prove an essential element, ownership of a stolen vehicle. Therefore, because of this distinction, our holding in the present case, which is consistent with *Randall* and the Rules of Evidence, is not in conflict with *Harveston*.

Armstrong's last claim in this assignment of error is that the State failed to prove that he served separate terms of at least one year each on his prior convictions. "An essential ingredient [element] of this section [99-19-83] is that the defendant shall have served at least one year under each sentence." *Ellis v. State*, 485 So. 2d 1062 (Miss. 1986).

The certified copies of the two prior convictions stated that Armstrong was to serve minimum two year sentences on each conviction. According to the certified documents from Michigan, Armstrong's first sentence to serve a minimum of two years began on May 25, 1988, and while in prison, he assaulted an employee and was convicted on June 26, 1989, and sentenced to serve another minimum term of two years. This is all that is required of the State. *See Nathan v. State*, 552 So. 2d 99, 106 (Miss. 1989). Thus, this assignment of error is without merit.

THE JUDGMENT OF THE JACKSON COUNTY CIRCUIT COURT OF CONVICTION OF AGGRAVATED ASSAULT AND SENTENCE OF FIFTEEN YEARS AS AN HABITUAL OFFENDER IN THE CUSTODY OF THE MISSISSIPPI DEPARTMENT OF CORRECTIONS IS AFFIRMED. ALL COSTS ARE ASSESSED TO JACKSON COUNTY.

McMILLIN, C.J., KING AND SOUTHWICK, P.JJ., BRIDGES, THOMAS, LEE, IRVING, MYERS AND CHANDLER, JJ., CONCUR.

[Footnotes omitted]

Source: Reprinted with the permission of LexisNexis.

Chapter 6

Crimes Involving Property

CHAPTER OBJECTIVES

Upon completion of this chapter, you will be able to:

- Identify and distinguish among the different types of theft crimes.

- Explain the specific offenses related to the taking of property.

- Discuss the differences between robbery, larceny, and extortion.

- Understand some property cybercrimes.

Crimes involving property are different than crimes against habitation. Crimes involving property have to do with **personal property**, not **real property**. Crimes against habitation usually deal with crimes that involve real property. **Theft** is a word that is often associated with crimes involving property. However, this term is basically a generic categorization of separate and distinct property crimes. This chapter will discuss and explain the different types of property crimes.

personal property
Movable or intangible thing not attached to real property.

real property
Land and all property permanently attached to it, such as buildings.

theft
The taking of property without the owner's consent.

LARCENY

Larceny was a felony in common law. Its roots date back to English law. Larceny is a crime that deals with the **possession** of property, not necessarily with ownership. It involves the taking of another's personal property. The elements of larceny are

- The unlawful taking
- And carrying away of
- Another's personal property
- With the intent to permanently deprive the **owner** of the property.

There are two types of larceny:

1. Grand larceny—usually the taking of something valued at approximately $500.00 or more, a felony.

2. Petit larceny—usually the taking of something valued at less than $500.00, a misdemeanor.

In order for a larceny to have occurred, there first has to be a trespassory taking of the property. A **trespassory taking** is where the thief essentially trespasses on the possession of the property of someone else. For example, a person picks the pocket of a bystander, taking his wallet. The act of picking the wallet out of the pocket is the trespassory taking. The taking does not have to be for a long period of time; it

larceny
The common law crime of taking property of another without permission.

possession
Having or holding property in one's power; controlling something to the exclusion of others.

owner
One who has the right to possess, use, and convey something.

trespassory taking
The act of seizing an article from the possession of the rightful owner.

simply has to be for as long a period as is required to take control and possession of the property. However, if the defendant who took the property is already in rightful possession of the property at the time that he takes it, then he cannot be guilty of larceny as he already had rightful possession. Also, if the owner of the property gives his consent to the taking of the property, then no larceny has occurred because the taking was not wrongful or unlawful.

asportation
The act of carrying away or removing property or a person.

Once the property has been unlawfully taken, an **asportation**, or carrying away, must occur. The carrying away need only be slight. Moving someone else's property from the place at which it was located by even a few inches is sufficient to constitute an asportation. All that is required is that the property be moved at all from the exact place from which it was taken. A larceny cannot occur without the carrying away of the property after it is unlawfully taken.

tangible property
Personal property that can be held or touched such as furniture or jewelry.

intangible property
Personal property that has no physical presence but is represented by a certificate or some other instrument such as stocks or trademarks.

trade secret
Property that is protected from misappropriation such as formulas, patterns, and compilations of information.

The property taken must be personal property. The crime of larceny was created to protect someone's right to possession of his/her personal property. Common law larceny was limited to **tangible property** such as books, cars, purses, money, and other items that can be touched and felt. Modern law includes **intangible property** such as stocks, bonds, and **trade secrets**. In addition, the personal property must belong to someone other than the taker. Therefore, if one member of a partnership takes the property of the partnership, then it would not be considered larceny because each partner in a partnership has equal right to possession of any property owned by the partnership.

The mens rea for the crime of larceny is the intent to permanently deprive the owner of his/her property. Larceny is a crime of intent. Generally, the defendant must demonstrate that he/she intended to permanently deprive the owner of his/her property. An intent to temporarily take the property or borrow it is not sufficient. Property that has been lost, abandoned, or mislaid is treated differently. Someone who comes into the control of such property knowing that it is lost or mislaid commits larceny if he/she does not take reasonable steps to return the property to its rightful owner. For example, if a package is delivered to you by mistake and you know that it belongs to someone else, but you keep the property and fail to take steps to return it to the person to whom it was originally intended, you have committed larceny. Abandoned property is not the subject of larceny.

EMBEZZLEMENT

embezzlement
The fraudulent appropriation of property by one lawfully entrusted with its possession.

conversion
An overt act to deprive the owner of possession of personal property with no intention of returning the property, thereby causing injury or harm.

Embezzlement is the unlawful **conversion** of someone else's property. The elements are

- The wrongful taking
- Of property
- That someone else has entrusted to you
- And converting it.

The difference between larceny and embezzlement is that with embezzlement, the defendant begins with lawful possession of the property and then it turns into an unlawful possession. With larceny, the possession is unlawful from the beginning. The mens rea for the crime of embezzlement is the intent to fraudulently deprive the owner of his/her property once the defendant had been lawfully given possession of it. The defendant also must convert the property so as to deprive the owner of a significant part of the property's usefulness.

Like larceny, embezzlement can occur only with property that belongs to someone else, so if the defendant has any right to lawful possession, then no crime has occurred.

Perhaps the classic example of embezzlement is when a business manager for a movie star or rock star is entrusted with the star's money and then misappropriates the money for purposes of his/her own. (See Figure 6.1.)

FIGURE 6.1
Differences between Larceny and Embezzlement

Larceny	Embezzlement
1. Trespassory taking and carrying away of the property of another.	1. Property must be in embezzler's lawful possession when he misappropriates it.
2. Requires only a taking and an asportation.	2. Requires a conversion.
3. Moving the property a short distance is enough.	3. The mere act of moving the property a short distance is not enough.
4. Requires an intent to steal which must occur simultaneously with the act of taking.	4. Without consent

SURF'S UP

Embezzlement crimes usually occur in a situation in which a person is entrusted with the possession of property for another. For example, on January 15, 2007, in St. Louis, Missouri, Angela Smiley, who was the owner of American Payroll Service, was convicted of embezzling over $600,000 of her clients' money that was intended to pay quarterly FICA and federal withholding taxes. Ms. Smiley had access to the funds of her clients, who entrusted her to pay their federal payroll obligations. Ms. Smiley was given lawful possession of the property and misappropriated it for her own use. There are numerous resources available on the Internet to learn more about embezzlement and how to safeguard against it. For more information, visit the following Web sites:

- www.criminal.findlaw.com/crimes/a-z/embezzlement.html
- www.answers.com/topic/embezzlement
- www.onlinelawyersource.com/criminal_law/embezzlement.html
- www.embezzlementnews.com/.

EYE ON ETHICS

A person who is placed in a position of trust is known as a fiduciary. Relationships that are based on trust are known as **fiduciary** relationships. Some examples of fiduciary relationships are doctor/patient, lawyer/client, psychiatrist/patient, and trustee/beneficiary. A person who is placed in a fiduciary position is held to a higher standard of care than a normal person. Sometimes, an attorney is named as the trustee for a trust. In this fiduciary position, the attorney must act in the best interest of the beneficiaries of the trust since he/she is in control of the property owned by the trust for the benefit of the beneficiaries. It is very important that an attorney acting as a trustee maintain detailed accounts of the activity of the trust and keep all trust monies separate and apart from the attorney's accounts. **Commingling** the accounts would give the impression of impropriety and could result in an allegation of embezzlement.

fiduciary
One who owes to another the duties of good faith, trust, confidence, and candor.

commingling
A term for mixing a client's funds with the attorney's personal funds without permission; an ethical violation.

false pretenses
False representations of material past or present facts, known by the wrongdoer to be false, made with the intent to defraud a victim into passing title in property to the wrongdoer.

title
The legal link between a person who owns property and the property itself; legal evidence of a person's ownership rights.

FALSE PRETENSES

False pretense is defined as the acquisition of **title** or possession of property from a victim by fraud or misrepresentation of a material past or present fact. The crime of false pretenses requires

- Obtaining title to property
- By making a false representation about a material fact
- With the intent to permanently deprive the owner of possession of the property.

The act of knowingly making a misrepresentation constitutes the mens rea for this crime. In order to establish a crime of false pretenses, the prosecution must demonstrate that the misrepresentation was false and the defendant knew of its falsity. Additionally, the defendant must intend to defraud the victim of his/her property. Opinion and **puffing** are not considered misrepresentation as they do not misrepresent the material facts but are used for enhancement. Although there is some flexibility involved in puffing goods, a seller may never mispresent the product or say that the product has attributes it does not actually possess.

puffing
The use of an exaggerated opinion—as opposed to a false statement—with the intent to sell a good or service.

It is essential that the victim of the false pretenses must actually be deceived by the misrepresentation and rely on that misrepresentation, and, as a result of the misrepresentation, the victim grants title of the property to the defendant. If the defendant simply makes a false promise or statement or gives an opinion, that is not sufficient to constitute the actus reus for false pretenses.

Title to the property must pass between the parties in order to establish false pretenses. Simply making a misrepresentation to someone but with no title to property being transferred does not constitute false pretenses. False pretense has a similarity to larceny as the taking must be wrongful; however, it is also similar to embezzlement in that title is given to the perpetrator. The owner of the property is induced to transfer title on reliance of the misrepresentation by the defendant. For example, Cindy entered Macy's intending to buy her twin sister, Mindy, a new pair of shoes. Cindy, who had only $35 in her possession, found a pair of shoes for $50 that Mindy would like. Realizing she did not have enough money to pay for the shoes, she ripped off the $50 sticker from the shoebox. When no one was looking, she took a $30 sticker off another box and placed it on the box containing the $50 pair of shoes. She then bought the $50 shoes for $30 and walked out of the store. Cindy has committed theft by false pretenses.

LARCENY BY TRICK

larceny by trick
Larceny in which the taker misleads the rightful possessor, by a misrepresentation of fact, into giving up possession of the property in question.

Larceny by trick is a form of larceny where the defendant obtains possession of the personal property of another by means of a representation or promise that he or she knows is not true at the time he or she takes possession. In larceny by trick, the defendant's fraud is used to cause the victim to give possession, not title. (See Figure 6.2.)

FIGURE 6.2
Differences between False Pretenses and Larceny by Trick

False Pretenses	Larceny by Trick
1. Wrongdoer makes false representation of a past or present fact	1. Wrongdoer obtains personal property of another
2. Wrongdoer knows it's a false representation	2. By means of a misrepresentation or false promise.
3. Wrongdoer has intent to defraud	3. Wrongdoer's fraudulent act causes victim to relinquish possession
4. Victim relinquishes title to property	

A DAY IN THE LIFE OF A REAL PARALEGAL

Students need to remember that there is a difference between having possession and having title. This distinction is the primary difference between larceny by trick and false pretenses. The crime of false pretenses requires that the defendant, by his or her misrepresentations of the truth, obtain title. If the defendant obtains possession without title by means of his or her misrepresentations, the crime committed is larceny by trick. When a driver drove off without paying for the gasoline an attendant put in his car, the court in *Hufstetler v. State*, 37 Ala. App. 71 (1953), held that the defendant was guilty of larceny by trick because he got possession but not title of the gasoline through the fraudulent taking.

CASE FACT PATTERN

Steve had just gotten into a fight with Tony, who was a local gang member from down the street. Worried that the gang was going to immediately pursue him, Steve knew that he had to get away. Brandishing a knife, Steve ran to the corner where a gas station was located. At one of the gas pumps, Penny was pumping gas into her brand-new Cadillac Escalade. Steve ran up to Penny and grabbed her by the wrist. He pulled out the knife and forced Penny into the car, telling her to drive. Penny was scared to death. Once the vehicle had traveled approximately five miles from the scene, Steve reached across Penny, opened the driver's side door, and pushed her out of the moving vehicle. Steve moved into the driver's seat and proceeded to steal Penny's car.

People in the neighborhood had seen Penny being pushed out of her car. They went to her aid, calling both the police and the paramedics. Penny sustained a broken arm along with cuts and contusions, but none of her injuries were life-threatening. Steve was arrested later that day driving Penny's vehicle. He was taken into custody and charged with robbery. Steve had taken Penny's vehicle from her presence by threat of force with the intent to deprive her of her property. Later, Steve was convicted of robbery and was sentenced to 10 years in the state prison under state law.

ROBBERY

Robbery is sometimes considered an aggravated form of larceny. Robbery contains all the elements of larceny plus two more. Those additional elements are the taking by force from a victim's person or presence. The elements of robbery are

- The use of force or fear of force
- Or the threat of immediate force
- To take money or property
- From a person or his/her presence.

The Model Penal Code at section 222.1 defines robbery as follows:

> A person is guilty of robbery, if, in the course of committing a theft, he:
> a. inflicts serious bodily injury upon another; or
> b. threatens another with or purposely puts him in fear of immediate serious bodily injury; or
> c. commits or threatens immediately to commit any felony of the first or second degree.
> An act shall be deemed "in the course of committing a theft" if it occurs in an attempt to commit theft or in flight after the attempt or commission.[1]

The forced used to satisfy the elements is no greater than any effort used to take and carry away the property. Remember, the significance of a taking in a robbery is that the property is taken from a person or the presence of a person; therefore, the threat of force can be used to accomplish the act without necessarily using any more force than is necessary to actually take the property. Imitation, fear, or threat of force is sufficient to satisfy the element of force for robbery.

The value of the property taken is insignificant in a robbery. Any value and any property taken from someone will satisfy a robbery. A main difference between robbery and larceny is that the theft in a robbery occurs directly from the person or in the person's presence while a larceny can occur outside of a person's presence. With the additional elements of force or threat of force as well as the taking having occurred from the person or in the person's presence, robbery is sometimes considered aggravated. **Aggravated robbery**, sometimes referred to as armed robbery, carries a higher punishment than simple robbery.

A crime similar to robbery that is becoming more prevalent in the United States is **carjacking**. It involves stealing a motor vehicle while the vehicle is occupied. Usually, the carjacker is armed and the driver is forced out of the car at gunpoint.

robbery
The direct taking of property from another through force or threat.

aggravated robbery
Robbery committed by a person who either carries a dangerous weapon or inflicts bodily harm on someone during the robbery.

carjacking
The crime of stealing a motor vehicle while the vehicle is occupied.

---

[1] Model Penal Code, copyright 1985 by the American Law Institute. Reprinted with permission.

RECEIVING STOLEN PROPERTY

The elements of the crime of receiving stolen property are

- Intentionally receiving, retaining, concealing, transferring, or disposing of
- The property of another
- That has been stolen.

receiving stolen property
The crime of acquiring or controlling property known to have been stolen by another person.

Receiving stolen property is a specific-intent crime. A person must gain control over the property knowing that the property was stolen and intend to permanently deprive the owner of the property. Stolen property is property that is acquired as a result of a theft, robbery, burglary, or other theft crime. A person cannot be guilty of receiving and stealing the same property. The person has done either one or the other. However, if someone receives stolen property with the purpose of returning it to its rightful owner, then he/she has not committed the crime of receiving stolen property because the requisite mens rea is not present.

FORGERY

forgery
The process of making or adapting objects or documents with the intention to deceive.

signatory
A party that signs a document, becoming a party to an agreement.

Forgery is considered a felony typically because of the value the forged instrument represents and the fact that it has breached the confidence in the credibility of a legal document. A forgery exists when a document is falsified. The falsification must relate to the genuineness of the document such as purporting that a person's signature is that of someone else other than the actual **signatory**. The elements of forgery are

- The making
- Or altering
- Of a writing
- That has some legal significance.

It is not necessary for the document to be circulated or to cause someone to transfer possession or title to property. The fact that a document with legal significance is altered is enough to establish forgery. The mens rea of the crime of forgery is the specific intent to defraud with the forged document, usually for the purposes of acquiring some property.

uttering
The crime of presenting a false or worthless document with the intent to harm or defraud.

The passing or circulating of a forged document with the intent to defraud is called **uttering**. The person who is passing the document may not be the person who committed the forgery. If one person forges a document and then circulates the document with the intent to defraud, then that person is guilty of two separate crimes: forgery and uttering. In order to be guilty of uttering, the person must know that the document that he/she is passing has been forged.

counterfeiting
Forging, copying, or imitating without a right to do so and with the purpose of deceiving or defrauding.

Counterfeiting is a type of forgery that involves the manufacture of false money for gain. For example, the manufacture of fake paper money would be considered counterfeiting, as would the manufacture of fake food stamps.

A DAY IN THE LIFE OF A REAL PARALEGAL

All jurisdictions have enacted what is commonly known as "bad check" legislation to handle situations when either no account exists or a check is written on insufficient funds with the intent to defraud. The giving of such a check is considered an implied representation of sufficient funds without postdating or some other means of notification of inadequate credit by the party writing the check.

EXTORTION

Extortion is also referred to as blackmail. It is the only property crime that involves general intent. Extortion is distinguished from other theft crimes as it involves the threat of future harm. The element of time is the distinguishing factor. Where a robbery involves the threat of immediate harm, extortion is the threat of future harm. The victim and defendant need not ever confront one another for this crime to occur. Extortion can be accomplished over the telephone, by mail, or by e-mail. The victim's cooperation in the crime is also not necessary to establish extortion.

The elements of extortion are

- Forcing another
- To hand over property
- By threatening future violence, threatening to expose secrets, or taking or withholding some type of official action.
- Event is to happen at some time in the future.

The Model Penal Code defines extortion in section 223.4 as follows:

> *A person is guilty of theft if he purposely obtains property of another by threatening to:*
> 1. *inflict bodily injury on anyone or commit any other criminal offense; or*
> 2. *accuse anyone of a criminal offense; or*
> 3. *expose any secret tending to subject any person to hatred, contempt or ridicule, or to impair his credit or business repute; or*
> 4. *take or withhold action as an official, or cause an official to take or withhold action; or*
> 5. *bring about or continue a strike, boycott or other collective unofficial action, if the property is not demanded or received for the benefit of the group in whose interest the actor purports to act; or*
> 6. *testify or provide information or withhold testimony or information with respect to another's legal claim or defense; or*
> 7. *inflict any other harm which would not benefit the actor.*
> *It is an affirmative defense to prosecution based on paragraphs (2), (3) or (4) that the property obtained by threat of accusation, exposure, lawsuit or other invocation of official action was honestly claimed as restitution or indemnification for harm done in the circumstances to which such accusation, exposure, lawsuit or other official action relates, or as compensation for property or lawful services.[2]*

In extortion, the threatened harm may be to someone other than the possessor of the property and it does not have to be a threat of physical violence. For example, suppose a politician's wife had posed for nude photographs years before they were married. An extortionist may threaten to reveal those photographs to the public if he is not paid a large sum of money.

CYBERCRIMES

Computer crimes have opened a whole new area for property crimes. Oftentimes, these crimes involve intangible property and the victim may not have any idea that a theft actually occurred until a significant amount of time has passed since the crime was committed. Information stored on computers has become the target of many thieves. For example, a thief may hack into a computer system and steal a person's name, Social Security number, and date of birth and use that information to steal someone's identity. Armed with this information, the criminal can open credit card accounts in the victim's name, charge items, and ruin the victim's credit rating. This type of theft is known as identity theft and it is growing in its frequency and popularity as technology grows.

extortion
The obtaining of property from another induced by wrongful use of actual or threatened force, violence, or fear, or under color of official right.

PRACTICE TIP

Credit card fraud occurs when a defendant, intending to defraud the owner, obtains title to personal property through use of a stolen or an unauthorized credit card. Check fraud occurs when a defendant, intending to defraud the owner, obtains title to personal property through the use of stolen checks or a check drawn on an account without sufficient funds.

---

[2] Model Penal Code, copyright 1985 by the American Law Institute. Reprinted with permission.

RESEARCH THIS

In recent times, both federal and state laws have had to be enacted to make the stealing of information or victimizing of people by use of technology a crime in the eyes of the law. For example, in 2004, the CAN-SPAM Act (18 U.S.C.A. § 1037) was enacted in order to address commercial e-mail transmissions that were made by people with the intent to deceive their victim. In 1999, the State of Virginia made it illegal to flood a person's e-mail account with unwanted e-mails, known as spam. Research your state and determine what anti-spam or other cybercrime laws have been enacted to protect people from this new and dangerous threat to their property.

A DAY IN THE LIFE OF A REAL PARALEGAL

A good paralegal must be aware of both the common law and the law embodied within the Model Penal Code. The Model Penal Code has included the following theft offenses within section 223.1. In summary, there are 8 common law violations grouped under this section including theft by: an unlawful taking, deception, extortion/blackmailing, theft of property lost or delivered by mistake, receiving of stolen property, theft of services, theft by not making the required placement of funds received and the unauthorized use of cars, trucks.

Computers also are being used as a tool in the commission of cybercrimes. A victim's identity can be stolen, access to information can be obtained from computer systems, and money can be transferred, all from the comfort of the criminal's home via a computer. Computers also can be considered incidental to a crime. For example, a drug dealer's list of customers, an embezzler's accounts of monies received from his/her crime as well as evidence used to blackmail a victim may be found located on the criminal's computer.

Other types of property crimes that involve technology are the stealing of a person's PIN number to access his/her bank account and withdraw funds illegally as well as accessing a person's cell phone number in order to make calls using the victim's telephone number. It is inevitable that with the increased capabilities in the rapidly growing technology fields, other property crimes will come to light that have not yet been seen.

Summary

Although the Model Penal Code has consolidated most common law crimes against property into a general theft category, it is still important for a paralegal to be able to distinguish the various theft offenses. Larceny was a felony in common law. Its roots date back to English law. Larceny is a crime that deals with possession of property, not necessarily ownership. It involves the taking of another's personal property. The elements of larceny are the unlawful taking and carrying away of another's personal property with the intent to permanently deprive the owner of the property.

Once the property has been unlawfully taken, an asportation must occur. This act of carrying away need only be slight. Moving someone else's property from the place where it was located by even a few inches is sufficient to constitute an asportation. All that is required is that the property be moved at all from the exact place from which it was taken. A larceny cannot occur without the carrying away of the property after it is unlawfully taken.

Embezzlement is the unlawful conversion of someone else's property. The elements are the wrongful conversion of property of another by one who is already in lawful possession.

The crime of false pretenses is defined as the acquisition of title or possession of property from a victim by fraud or misrepresentation of a material past or present fact.

Therefore, the elements for a crime of false pretenses are obtaining title to property by making a false representation about a material fact with the intent to permanently deprive the owner of possession of the property.

Robbery is sometimes considered an aggravated form of larceny. Robbery contains all the elements of larceny plus two more. Those additional elements are the taking by force from a victim's person or presence. The elements of robbery are the use of force or fear of force or the threat of immediate force to take money or property from a victim's person or presence.

Aggravated robbery occurs when a robbery is commited by a person who either has a dangerous weapon or inflicts bodily harm on someone during the robbery.

Receiving stolen property is a specific-intent crime. A person must gain control over the property knowing that the property was stolen and intend to permanently deprive the owner of the property. Stolen property is property that is acquired as a result of a theft, robbery, burglary, or other theft crime. A person cannot be guilty of receiving and stealing the same property. He or she has to have done either one or the other. However, if someone receives stolen property with the purpose of returning it to its rightful owner, then he or she has not committed the crime of receiving stolen property because the requisite mens rea is not present.

A forgery exists when a document is falsified. The falsification must relate to the genuineness of the document such as purporting that a person's signature is that of someone else other than the actual signatory. The elements of forgery are the making or altering of a writing that has some legal significance. Counterfeiting is a type of forgery.

The passing or circulating of a forged document with the intent to defraud is called uttering. The person who is passing the document may not be the person who committed the forgery. If one person forges a document and then also circulates the document with the intent to defraud, then he/she is guilty of two separate crimes: forgery and uttering. In order to be guilty of uttering, the person must know that the document he/she is passing has been forged.

Extortion is also referred to as blackmail. It is the only property crime that involves general intent. Extortion is distinguished from other theft crimes as it involves the threat of future harm. The element of time is the distinguishing factor. Where a robbery involves the threat of immediate harm, extortion is the threat of future harm. The victim and defendant need not ever confront one another for this crime to occur. Extortion can be accomplished over the telephone, by mail, or by e-mail. The victim's cooperation in the crime is also not necessary to establish extortion.

Modern technology has opened the door to a whole new group of property crimes known as cybercrimes. One example is the growing crime of identify theft.

Key Terms

Aggravated robbery	Owner
Asportation	Personal property
Carjacking	Possession
Commingling	Puffing
Conversion	Real property
Counterfeiting	Receiving stolen property
Embezzlement	Robbery
Extortion	Signatory
False pretenses	Tangible property
Fiduciary	Theft
Forgery	Title
Intangible property	Trade secret
Larceny	Trespassory taking
Larceny by trick	Uttering

Review Questions

1. What does it mean to asportate something?
2. Give three examples of tangible property and three examples of intangible property.
3. List the elements of larceny.
4. Why is robbery considered an aggravated form of larceny? What elements of the two crimes are the same? What elements are different? Give an example of the difference.
5. In what ways are computers now involved in property crimes?
6. What types of threats can be used in a crime of extortion?
7. List the elements of false pretenses and provide an example of the type of crime that would be considered false pretenses.
8. Is passing counterfeit money considered uttering? Why or why not?
9. What is the difference between forgery and uttering?
10. Explain the differences between larceny, embezzlement, false pretenses, and robbery.
11. Can someone be convicted of larceny of real property? Why or why not?
12. Why is receiving stolen property a crime? What are the actus reas and the mens rea for this crime?
13. List the elements for embezzlement.
14. What does it mean to convert someone else's property? Give an example.
15. What is a trade secret?

Exercises

1. On David's birthday, his friend Justin gave him a new MP3 player as a gift. The following day, when David opened the box and began using the MP3 player, he noticed that there was no warranty document with it. David telephoned Justin and asked Justin for the missing warranty documentation. Justin replied, "I can't give it to you because the MP3 player was stolen." David kept the MP3 player and continued to use it. David is guilty of
   a. Receiving stolen property only.
   b. Larceny only.
   c. Receiving stolen property and larceny.
   d. No crime.
2. After looking at a car that Martha had advertised for sale, Bernie agreed to purchase the car for $20,000. Bernie gave Martha $5,000 in cash, promising to bring the balance and to pick up the vehicle the following week. In fact, Martha was a thief who had no intention of selling the vehicle. She had been collecting cash down payments from buyers all over the state for the sale of the same vehicle. As soon as Bernie left, Martha ran off with the $5,000. One month later, Martha was arrested and charged with embezzlement and larceny. She can be convicted of
   a. Embezzlement only.
   b. Larceny only.
   c. Embezzlement and larceny.
   d. Neither embezzlement nor larceny.
3. Donna was walking down a crowded city street one day wearing her brand new pearl necklace, which was worth about $500.00. Ellen came by on a moped, grabbed Donna's necklace, and yanked it off her neck. Ellen sped off before Donna could react to the theft. Several hours later, Ellen was caught and charged with robbery. May Ellen be properly convicted of robbery? Why or why not? Give a specific and detailed analysis.

4. Melanie leaves the grocery store carrying a bag of groceries and her purse. A man comes up behind her and says, "I have a gun and, if you do not give me your purse, I will kill you." Melanie is scared and gives the man her purse. Is the man guilty of larceny, robbery, or both? Explain your answer.

5. Donald drives into the gas station and tells the attendant to fill the tank. The attendant pumps nine gallons of gas into Donald's vehicle, filling the gas tank. Donald then drives off without paying for the gas. Of what crime against possession is Donald guilty?

6. Ollie, the office manager of a law firm, goes into the office after hours and fraudulently converts $300 from the petty cash fund. Is Ollie guilty of larceny or embezzlement? Explain your answer.

7. Jimmy, the janitor of a law firm, breaks into the petty cash drawer and takes $300. Is Jimmy guilty of larceny or embezzlement? Explain your answer.

8. Anna and Hannah, co-workers, were having lunch at a small café. Unbeknownst to Anna, when she left the table to take a phone call, her purse fell open on the floor. Hannah saw the purse fall open. She saw a loose $20 bill. She grabbed it and quickly put it in her pocket. Before Anna returned to the table, Hannah had a change of heart and decided to put the money back in Anna's purse. Is Hannah guilty of a theft crime? If so, which one?

 PORTFOLIO ASSIGNMENT

Research the steps it would take you to regain your identity after someone else stole it and used your identity, name, and account numbers of credit cards and bank accounts.

Vocabulary Builders

Vocabulary Builders

Instructions

Use the key terms from this chapter to fill in the answers to the crossword puzzle.

NOTE: When the answer is more than one word, leave a blank space between words.

ACROSS

2. personal property that has no physical presence but is represented by a certificate or some other instrument such as stocks or trademarks.

5. larceny in which the taker misleads the rightful possessor, by a misrepresentation of fact, into giving up possession of the property in question.

7. the direct taking of property from another through force or threat.

11. false representations of material past or present facts, known by the wrongdoer to be false, made with the intent to defraud a victim into passing title in property to the wrongdoer.

13. the process of making or adapting objects or documents with the intention to deceive.

14. one who owes to another the duties of good faith, trust, confidence, and candor.

16. personal property that can be held or touched such as furniture or jewelry.

18. felonious stealing, taking and carrying, leading, riding, or driving away another's personal property with the intent to convert it or to deprive the owner thereof.

20. a term for mixing a client's funds with the attorney's personal funds without permission; an ethical violation.

22. the obtaining of property from another induced by wrongful use of actual or threatened force, violence, or fear, or under color of official right.

23. the removal of things from one place to another.

24. the crime of acquiring or controlling property known to have been stolen by another person.

DOWN

1. the fraudulent appropriation of property by one lawfully entrusted with its possession.

3. property that is protected from misappropriation such as formulas, patterns, and compilations of information.

4. a party that signs a document, becoming a party to an agreement

6. the act of seizing an article from the possession of the rightful owner.

8. the legal link between a person who owns property and the property itself; legal evidence of a person's ownership rights.

9. robbery committed by a person who either carries a dangerous weapon or inflicts bodily harm on someone during the robbery.

10. an overt act to deprive the owner of possession of personal property with no intention of returning the property, thereby causing injury or harm.

12. the use of an exaggerated opinion—as opposed to a false statements—with the intent to sell a good or service.

15. the crime of presenting a false or worthless document with the intent to harm or defraud.

17. having or holding property in one's power; controlling something to the exclusion of others.

19. forging, copying, or imitating without a right to do so and with the purpose of deceiving or defrauding.

21. the crime of stealing a motor vehicle while the vehicle is occupied.

25. one who has the right to possess, use, and convey something.

UNITED STATES of America, Plaintiff-Appellee,

v.

Alfred SMITH, Defendant-Appellant.

No. 03-4650.

United States Court of Appeals,

Fourth Circuit.

Argued: Feb. 27, 2004.

Decided: June 24, 2004.

BACKGROUND:

Defendant was convicted in the United States District Court for the Eastern District of Virginia, Henry Coke Morgan, Jr., J., for embezzling, stealing, purloining, and converting to his own use funds belonging to the Social Security Administration.

HOLDINGS:

The Court of Appeals held that:

(1) indictment properly aggregated charged conduct into one count, and

(2) indictment could be charged in conjunctive as continuing offense.

Affirmed.

OPINION

PER CURIAM:

Appellant, Alfred Smith, appeals his conviction for embezzling, stealing, ***563** purloining and converting to his own use funds belonging to the Social Security Administration ("SSA") in violation of 18 U.S.C. § 641. Smith asserts that the indictment against him was unconstitutionally duplicitous, i.e., that it joined two or more distinct and separate offenses in one single count. *United States v. Burns*, 990 F.2d 1426, 1438 (4th Cir. 1993). When an indictment impermissibly joins separate offenses that occurred at different times, prosecution of the earlier acts may be barred by the statute of limitations. *United States v. Beard*, 713 F. Supp. 285 (S.D. Ind. 1989).

The district court held that aggregation of Smith's individual offenses was proper because each was part of a single scheme or plan. For the reasons that follow, we affirm.

I.

On January 24, 2003, a Grand Jury returned a one-count indictment against Smith, charging:

> Estelle Smith died on February 4, 1994. The defendant, ALFRED SMITH did not report the death of Estelle Smith to the Social Security Administration and continued on a monthly basis to receive Estelle Smith's monthly Social Security benefits until February 3, 1998. Beginning in or about March 1994, and continuing until in or about February 1998, in the Eastern

> District of Virginia and elsewhere, the defendant ALFRED SMITH, did knowingly, intentionally and willfully embezzle, steal, purloin and convert to his own use, on a recurring basis, a record, voucher, money and thing of value belonging to the Social Security Administration, to wit: Social Security Administration benefits issued to Estelle Smith, totaling approximately $26,336.00.

> (In violation of Title 18, United States Code, Section 641).

Section 641 provides that theft of property with a value in excess of $1,000 is a felony punishable by a maximum term of imprisonment of ten years. If the property has a value of less than $1,000, the violation is a misdemeanor with a term of imprisonment not to exceed one year. 18 U.S.C. § 641 (2004).

From March 1994 through February 1998, 48 payments were electronically deposited into Smith's joint account with his mother; each deposit was between $525 and $583. In all, Smith received approximately $26,336 after his mother's death.

Smith wrote checks and withdrew funds from the account. When interviewed by SSA agents, Smith admitted writing numerous checks on the account and acknowledged that he knew it was wrong for him to receive the benefit payments after his mother's death.

II.

The purpose of a statute of limitations is to limit exposure to criminal prosecution following an illegal act. *Toussie v. United States*, 397 U.S. 112, 114, 90 S. Ct. 858, 25 L. Ed. 2d 156 (1970). A statute of limitations protects individuals from having to defend against charges "when the basic facts may have become obscured by the passage of time," and minimizes "the danger of official punishment because of acts in the far-distant past." *Id.* at 114–15, 90 S. Ct. 858.

Statutes of limitations should not be extended "'except as otherwise expressly provided by law.'" *Id.* at 115, 90 S. Ct. 858 (quoting 18 U.S.C. § 3282). Normally, the statute of limitations will begin to run when a single criminal act is complete. *Id.* Criminal acts over an extended period, however, may be treated as ***564** a "continuing offense" for limitations purposes when a criminal statute explicitly compels that result, or if "the nature of the crime involved is such that Congress must assuredly have intended that it be treated as a continuing one." *Id.*

But we must first decide whether Smith's charged conduct was properly aggregated into a single count. In determining whether a series of takings are properly aggregated, the court must examine the intent of the actor at the first taking. *United States v. Billingslea*, 603 F.2d 515, 520 (5th Cir. 1979). If the actor formulated "a plan or scheme or [set] up a mechanism which, when put into operation, [would] result in the taking or diversion of sums of money on a recurring basis," the crime may be charged in a single count. *Id.*

Smith's failure to report his mother's death evidences the intent to establish a mechanism for the automatic and continuous receipt of funds for an indefinite period. Smith's criminal conduct was patterned and methodical. Therefore, the indictment properly aggregated his charged conduct into one count.

The indictment charges the acts of its single count in the conjunctive. *See* J.A. 46–47 (alleging that Smith "did knowingly . . . embezzle, steal, purloin, *and* convert to his own use" the funds at issue) (emphasis added). But given that section 641 lists those acts disjunctively, the government, of course, only was required to prove that Smith's conduct satisfied one of those acts to convict on that count. *See United States v. Brandon*, 298 F.3d 307, 314 (4th Cir. 2002). The indictment, therefore, would be sufficient if embezzlement, a distinguishable act, can be charged as a continuing offense.

We think that it can; the nature of embezzlement is such that Congress must have intended that, in some circumstances, it be treated in section 641 as a continuing offense. The term "embezzle" includes "the fraudulent appropriation of property"—*e.g.*, "the deliberate taking or retaining of the . . . property of another with the intent to deprive the owner of its use or benefit"—"by a person . . . into whose hands it has lawfully come. It differs from larceny in the fact that the original taking of the property was lawful, or with the consent of the owner." Kevin F. O'Malley *et al.*, *Federal Jury Practice and Instructions*, §§ 16.01, 16.03 (2000 & Supp. 2003) (quoting from and elaborating on "the classic, almost standard, definition of 'embezzlement' . . . given by the Supreme Court in" *Moore v. United States*, 160 U.S. 268, 269–70, 16 S. Ct. 294, 40 L. Ed. 422 (1895)).

Although many state embezzlement statutes require that the embezzled property be acquired through some relationship of trust, it is not a universal requirement. *See* 3 Wayne R. LaFave, *Substantive Criminal Law* § 19.6 (2d ed. 2003) (noting that while, "in general, [embezzlement] may be defined as: (1) the fraudulent (2) conversion of (3) the property (4) of another (5) by one who is already in lawful possession of it," "*some* statutes limit the scope of embezzlement by requiring that the property be 'entrusted' . . . to the embezzler") (emphasis added). We do not think that section 641 imposes this requirement, a conclusion that is amply supported by a leading Supreme Court case on the scope of embezzlement under federal law, as well as by the interpretations made by other circuits of section 641 in particular. *See, e.g.*, Paul C. Jorgensen, *Embezzlement*, 24 Am. Crim. L. Rev. 513, 514 (1987) ("A defendant accused of violating Section 641's embezzlement provisions initially must have lawfully acquired the property at issue, *although he need not have received it through holding a position* ***565** *of trust or fiduciary relation.*") (emphasis added) (citations omitted).

Indeed, the classic definition of "embezzlement" set forth in *Moore v. United States*, 160 U.S. 268, 269–270, 16 S. Ct. 294, 40 L. Ed. 422 (1895) implicitly suggests that lawful possession need not be acquired through a relationship of trust. The *Moore* Court, interpreting a precursor to section 641, defined embezzlement under that statute to be "the fraudulent appropriation of property *by a person to whom such property has been intrusted, or into whose hands it has lawfully come.*" 160 U.S. at 270, 16 S. Ct. 294 (emphasis added).

If the distinction made by this phrasing were not enough, the reasoning set forth in *Moore* firmly supports the conclusion that a fiduciary relationship is not an essential element of embezzlement. *Moore* involved a challenge to an indictment for embezzlement under the Act of March 3, 1875 ("the 1875 Act") based, in part, on the ground that while the indictment named the defendant as a post office employee, it did not allege that the embezzled government monies "came into the possession of the defendant by virtue of his employment." *Id.* at 270, 16 S. Ct. 294. In assessing the requirements for embezzlement under the 1875 Act, the Court discussed several earlier state and English cases that made the existence of a fiduciary or other employment relationship a necessary element of embezzlement. *Id.* at 270–73, 16 S. Ct. 294.

The *Moore* Court explained that "[t]he ordinary form of an indictment for larceny" simply would require a sufficiently specific "allegation that the defendant stole, took, and carried away certain specified goods belonging to the person named," without regard to a particular relationship between the thief and the victim. *Id.* at 273, 16 S. Ct. 294. Notably, the prohibitions of the 1875 Act "applie[d] to 'any person,' and use[d] the words 'embezzle, steal, or purloin' in the same connection, and as applicable to the same persons and to the same property." *Id.* In contrast, "[t]he cases reported from the English courts and from the courts of the several states have usually arisen under statutes limiting the offense to certain officers, clerks, agents, or servants of individuals or corporations." *Id.* at 272, 16 S. Ct. 294; *see also* LaFave, *supra*, § 19.6 (noting the distinction between the specificity of embezzlement statutes historically and the "modern view" which "is to make it embezzlement . . . fraudulently to convert another's property in one's possession," avoiding "the danger of omitting someone who ought to be included" from the list of persons covered by an embezzlement statute). The Court concluded that cases interpreting the requirements for embezzlement under more specific statutes "are not wholly applicable to a statute [such as the 1875 Act] which extends to *every* person, regardless of his employment." 160 U.S. at 272, 16 S. Ct. 294 (emphasis added). Rather, the *Moore* court, although eventually holding the indictment defective on a different ground, went only so far as to say that, as to the necessary relationship for an embezzlement indictment under the 1875 Act, "the rules of good pleading would suggest, even if they did not absolutely require, that the indictment should set forth *the manner or capacity in which the defendant became possessed of the property.*" *Id.* at 274, 16 S. Ct. 294 (emphasis added).

An indictment alleging embezzlement under the current form of that statute, *i.e.*, under section 641, requires no more. Section 641 is indistinguishable from the 1875 Act in all relevant respects; its strictures cover "*whoever* embezzles, steals, purloins, or knowingly converts to his use or the use of another" property of the government. ***566** (Emphasis added). Moreover, other circuits have similarly interpreted embezzlement under section 641 in light of *Moore*, and held that lawful possession need not be acquired through any particular relationship.

See United States v. Miller, 520 F.2d 1208, 1211 (9th Cir. 1975) ("Section 641 is not limited to persons who come into possession of property by virtue of a particular fiduciary relationship, but rather applies to all persons, regardless of their employment."); *United States v. Davila*, 693 F.2d 1006, 1007 (10th Cir. 1982) (citing *Miller* and adding that "[u]nder [*Moore's*] definition [of embezzlement], lawful original possession is enough to support the crime of embezzlement [under section 641]; it is not necessary to prove a breach of fiduciary duty."); but *see*, *e.g.*, *Colella v. United States*, 360 F.2d 792, 799 (1st Cir. 1966) (interpreting embezzlement in 29 U.S.C. § 501(c) and concluding that the term "carries with it the concept of a breach of fiduciary relationship").

Our opinion in *United States v. Stockton*, 788 F.2d 210 (4th Cir. 1986), which dealt not with section 641 but with 29 U.S.C. § 501(c), does not require a contrary result. Admittedly, the *Stockton* court did say that the extent of "embezzlement" in federal statutes "should be viewed as roughly identical to the scope of the offense as generally interpreted under state law." *Id.* at 215. More importantly, however, after enunciating that general principle, the court went into detail as to what that actually meant as to the requirements of embezzlement in section 641. The *Stockton* court first explained that at the core of embezzlement is the act of conversion, which, of course, requires no relationship of trust. *Id.* at 216. The court then stated that

> [t]he crime of embezzlement builds on the concept of conversion, *but adds two further elements*. First, the embezzled property must have been in the lawful possession of the defendant at the time of its appropriation. Second, embezzlement requires knowledge that the appropriation is contrary to the wishes of the owner of the property.

Id. at 216–217 (emphasis added). Notably, the court did not enunciate any requirement that a defendant's lawful possession be acquired through a relationship of trust, despite our recognition only a page earlier that prosecuting conversions made after gaining lawful possession through some fiduciary capacity was a motivating force for the creation of many embezzlement statutes.

The fact remains that Congress has seen fit to enact numerous statutes criminalizing various forms of embezzlement, and all indications are that where Congress has thought a particular capacity or relationship to be a necessary element of embezzlement in a given circumstance, it has specified as much in the statute. *See*, *e.g.*, 18 U.S.C. § 656 (2000) (criminalizing embezzlement of a bank's funds by "[w]hoever, being an officer, director, agent or employee of, or connected in any capacity with [such] bank"); 18 U.S.C. § 666(a)(1)(A) (2000) (proscribing embezzlement by "agent[s] of an organization, or of a State, local, or Indian tribal government" of those organization's or government's funds when those entities receive federal grants); 29 U.S.C. § 501(c) (2000) (proscribing embezzlement of the property "of a labor organization of which [a person] is an officer"). But where, as in section 641, a federal embezzlement statute applies, by its express terms, to *all* persons; does not specify any manner or capacity in which an act of embezzlement must be carried out; and lists embezzlement with other acts that apply to the same persons and property but that, even traditionally, do not require the defendant to have any particular relationship with the property's ***567** owner, we

should not read a relationship of trust into the definition of embezzlement under that statute. This is especially true when precedent indicates that the prohibited acts in section 641 were not meant to be so narrowly read. *See*, *e.g.*, *United States v. Morison*, 844 F.2d 1057, 1077 (4th Cir. 1988) ("Manifestly, as the Court in *Morissette* said[,] [section 641] was not intended simply to cover 'larceny' and 'embezzlement' as those terms were understood at common law but was also to apply to 'acts which shade into those crimes but which, most strictly considered, might not be found to fit their fixed definitions.'") (quoting *Morissette v. United States*, 342 U.S. 246, 268 n. 28, 72 S. Ct. 240, 96 L. Ed. 288 (1952)).

Accordingly, we believe that if an indictment for embezzlement under section 641 alleges the manner or capacity in which the defendant came into lawful possession of the property that he willfully converted, it is adequate in this respect. The instant indictment satisfies this standard, and is sufficient to fairly inform Smith of the conduct for which he was being charged with embezzlement, among other acts, pursuant to section 641, and to support a claim of double jeopardy in a future prosecution on the same basis.

As a joint owner of the checking account, Smith had legal control over the funds therein, including the ability to withdraw the full amount of such funds. *See* Va. Code Ann. § 6.1-125.9 (Michie 1999). As such, when the government voluntarily placed these funds into the account, they came into his lawful control, *i.e.*, his lawful possession. But that he had lawful possession of the funds—the issue disputed by Smith in his reply memorandum below—did not give him the right to appropriate them for his own purposes. Thus, it was his lack of legal entitlement to *own* the funds that renders his misappropriation of them after their deposit embezzlement.

Smith's lawful right to control the funds after their initial deposit in his account distinguishes his possession from that which follows a common-law larceny, in that Smith's possession did not require a "trespass in the taking"; rather, the government voluntarily, though incorrectly, continued to deposit his mother's Social Security benefits into their jointly owned checking account after her death. *See* LaFave, *supra*, §§ 19.2, 19.6 (explaining this distinction between larceny and embezzlement); *Moore*, 160 U.S. at 269–70, 16 S. Ct. 294 ("[Embezzlement] differs from larceny in the fact that [with embezzlement] the original taking of the property was lawful, or with the consent of the owner . . . ."). In the present case, however, the indictment can be fairly construed to aver a charge of embezzlement that could be proven, without surprise to Smith, by evidence showing that Smith, having legal possession of the funds as they were initially deposited into his account, then, after realizing that his continued possession was improper, willfully retained the funds for his own use, and maintained that recurring, automatic scheme of embezzlement during the charged period.

Embezzlement is the type of crime that, to avoid detection, often occurs over some time and in relatively small, but recurring, amounts. *See*, *e.g.*, *MacEwen v. State*, 194 Md. 492, 71 A.2d 464, 468–69 (1950) ("While embezzlement is sustained by the diversion of a single sum of money at a particular time, in many cases it runs for a long period of time and consists of converting different sums of money on many dates to the use of the thief."). At least in those cases where the defendant created a recurring, automatic scheme of embezzlement under section 641 by conversion of funds voluntarily placed in the

*568 defendant's possession by the government, and maintained that scheme without need for affirmative acts linked to any particular receipt of funds—cases in which there is a strong "temporal relationship between the [completion of the] offense and culpability," *United States v. Blizzard*, 27 F.3d 100, 103 (4th Cir. 1994)—we think that Congress must have intended that such be considered a continuing offense for purposes of the statute of limitations.

And, of course, that is precisely what Smith has done, a conclusion that is supported by our analysis under *Billingslea*. Accordingly, we believe that the specific conduct at issue here is more properly characterized as a continuing offense rather than a series of separate acts. The facts found by the district court were sufficient to prove that he set into place and maintained an automatically recurring scheme whereby funds were electronically deposited in his account and retained for his own use without need for any specific action on his part, a scheme which continued from his mother's death until payments were terminated in February of 1998.

This is not to say that all conduct constituting embezzlement may necessarily be treated as a continuing offense as opposed to merely "a series of acts that occur over a period of time"; indeed, it may well be that different embezzlement conduct must be differently characterized in this regard. Nor do we lightly dismiss the dissent's citation to cases from other circuits that might require a different conclusion as to the application of the "continuing offense" doctrine. We are satisfied, however, that in addition to being properly aggregated into a single count, the particular kind of embezzlement that occurred in this case is correctly considered, under *Toussie*, to be a continuing offense.

Smith's embezzlement scheme concluded on February 3, 1998. The Grand Jury returned an indictment against him on January 24, 2003, within five years of the final deposit of social security funds. Smith's indictment, therefore, was timely.

For the reasons discussed above, we conclude that Smith's conduct constituted a single continuous scheme to embezzle government funds and was of a nature that Congress must have intended that it be treated as a continuing offense. Accordingly, the judgment of the district court is

AFFIRMED.

[Dissenting opinion omitted]

Source: U.S. v. Smith, 373 F.3d 561. Reprinted with permission from Westlaw.

Chapter 7

Crimes against Habitation

CHAPTER OBJECTIVES

Upon completion of this chapter, you will be able to:

- Identify the elements of burglary.
- Explain the concept of criminal trespass.
- Discuss the elements of arson.
- Understand malicious mischief.

habitation
Place of abode; dwelling place; residence.

Crimes against **habitation**, sometimes referred to as structure crimes, are not the same thing as crimes against property. Crimes against habitation deal with crimes against someone's home, not someone's house. A house is property, but a home is a person's living space and provides a sense of security. Laws regarding crimes against habitation are designed to protect people from invasion, intrusion, damage, or destruction of their home or environment as well as prevent such acts from impeding on their sense of security. This chapter examines crimes against someone's home.

BURGLARY

burglary
Breaking and entering into a structure for the purpose of committing a crime.

breaking
In the law of burglary, the act of entering a building without permission.

dwelling
A house or other structure that is used or intended for use as a residence.

Burglary has been a crime for centuries. Under common law, the elements of burglary are

- The trespassory **breaking**
- And entering
- Of the **dwelling** of another
- At night
- With the intent to commit a crime.

Most modern burglary statutes now make it a crime to enter any structure, in the day or night, with the intent to commit a crime. It is important to understand the elements of common law burglary because they provide the foundation upon which modern burglary statutes have been built. For example, common law burglary had to be done at night (between sunset and sunrise), but modern laws have largely removed this element. Some jurisdictions have retained the "at night" aspect of burglary, not as an essential prima facie element, but rather as a factor relevant when determining the degree or severity of the crime in question. Similarly, whether or not a deadly weapon is used during the commission of a burglary is also a relevant factor.

Breaking does not necessarily mean causing damage, but it does typically require some use of force to create an opening. Breaking refers to any act that causes some part of the structure that is being entered to move, for example, a turning of a door knob, the pushing open of a door, or the opening of an unlocked window. The main consideration of a breaking is that an opening into the structure must be created by the defendant. Modern statutes have relaxed the "breaking" element to include even the smallest enlargement of an already existent opening. Though, in *People v. Williams,* 29 A.D.2d 780(NY 2nd Dept. Ct. App. 1968), it was held that during a prosecution for burglary, it was error to instruct the jury that an entry through an already wide open window was a "breaking" when no further opening of the window in question occurred. Some jurisdictions have eliminated the breaking element altogether.

After the breaking has occurred, there must be some type of an entry by the defendant. The most common scenario is when the defendant's person enters the structure; however, if some type of tool or instrument is used to enter and to commit the target felony, it also will qualify as an entry. Additionally, the defendant need not enter the structure with his/her entire body. For example, pushing his/her hands through an open window or door is sufficient. Entry occurs when the defendant breaks the plane of the opening into the structure with a portion of his/her body. The entry into the structure must be unauthorized and without consent of the occupants or owner. In addition, if an individual has consent to be inside one portion of a structure but then enters a portion of the building that is restricted or not open to the public and proceeds to steal something, then the entry requirement of burglary also will be satisfied. In *State v. Pappen,* 193 Neb. 80, 225 N.W.2d 416 (1975), the court held that when an entry has been limited to a specific place, time, or purpose, then burglary may be committed if the entry is outside the specific limitations. For example, Scott enters a public library. While the librarian is busy helping some children, Scott goes into a restricted part of the library and steals some computer software. Scott has committed burglary even though the crime took place in a building that was open to the public. Burglary also may occur if the entry in question is achieved by fraud. This is sometimes referred to as a constructive breaking. For example, Frankie rings Donna's doorbell at her home. Donna walks to the door and asks, "Who's there?" Frankie lies about his identity and tells Donna that he is from Federal Express and has a package for her. Donna opens the door. Frankie then shoves Donna to the floor, enters her home, and steals her purse. Frankie's actions would fulfill the breaking requirement for burglary since he entered by use of fraud. It is important to remember, however, that a defendant cannot be guilty of burglarizing his or her own home. Entry into one's own dwelling, even if done with felonious intent, invades no right of habitation and thus is not considered burglary. For example, an individual who enters an apartment he or she shares with a roommate with the purpose of stealing his or her roommate's television when that television is located within the common living space cannot be convicted of burglary. However, if the television was located in the roommate's bedroom and the individual opened the roommate's closed bedroom door to get access to it, then a burglary may have occurred.

Burglary statutes are designed to protect the dwelling house of an individual. At common law, only a house used as a home where people slept met this definition, although the dwelling could be unoccupied at the time of entry. Modern burglary statutes apply to most any structure whether a dwelling or not. For example, in *State v. Burston,* 693 So. 2d 600 (Fla. 2d Dist. Ct. App. 1997), a carport from which a lawn mower was stolen was held to be part of the curtilage of a dwelling and thus the defendant who entered the carport with the intent to steal the lawn mower was held to be guilty of burglary. In *State v. Bennett,* 565 So. 2d 803 (Fla. 2d Dist. Ct. App. 1990) , an unsold mobile home on a dealer's lot that was "designed" to be an occupied structure was considered a "dwelling" within the meaning of the relevant burglary statute. Additionally, in *People v. Dail,* 139 Ill. App. 3d 941 (Ill. 3d Dist. Ct. App. 1985), a defendant was held to have committed burglary when he opened the hood of a car, reached inside, and removed the car's battery.

Additionally, because burglary statutes are designed to protect occupants of structures, they may not offer protection to the owner of the structure. For example, Rachel rents an apartment from David. One weekend when Rachel is out of town, someone breaks into the apartment and steals her television. Rachel has been burglarized, but David has not. The owners and occupants of a dwelling are not necessarily the same individuals. As discussed previously, a person cannot be guilty of burglarizing his or her own residence because the entry would not be trespassory. However, landlords can burglarize their tenants. In *State v. Schneider,* 36 Wash. App. 237, 673 P.2d 200 (1983), it was held that the owner of a residential property could be found guilty of burglarizing that same property that was leased to a tenant.

Burglary is a specific-intent crime. The intent to commit a crime must have been formulated prior to entering into the structure. For example, if Henry was hiking through the forest and a storm hit, forcing him to seek shelter in Martin's cabin, no burglary would have taken place because Henry lacked the requisite intent to commit a crime prior to entering the structure. Generally, burglary requires that the breaking and entering be accompanied by the intent to commit a felony; however, the law of some jurisdictions maintains that the intent to commit any crime, even a misdemeanor, is adequate. Typically, a burglary is associated with the crime of theft, but in many states the intent to commit any crime will satisfy this element. It is not necessary or required that the crime must have been completed in order for a burglary to have occurred.

There is no merger with regard to the crime of burglary. A defendant who either commits, or attempts to commit, the intended or target crime can be convicted of both burglary and the target crime. Also, the crime of burglary is complete as soon as the defendant succeeds or even when he or she continues with efforts to complete the target crime.

The Model Penal Code at section 221.1 defines burglary as follows:

> 1. Burglary Defined. *A person is guilty of burglary if he enters a building or occupied structure, or separately secured or occupied portion thereof, with the purpose to commit a crime therein, unless the premises are at the time open to the public or the actor is licensed or privileged to enter. It is an affirmative defense to prosecution for burglary that the building or structure was abandoned.*

PRACTICE TIP

Because burglary is a specific-intent crime, the typical criminal defenses apply. If the defendant lacked the requisite intent, that defendant will not be guilty. For instance, voluntary intoxication and unreasonable mistake may negate the requisite specific-intent elements needed to establish a burglary.

 RESEARCH THIS

In modern burglary statutes, some jurisdictions have divided burglary into degrees, with first degree usually being the most grievous of the degrees. However, other jurisdictions have categorized burglary as simple burglary and aggravated burglary. Oftentimes, the grading of a burglary is dependent upon the nature and potential danger to the victim of the structure. Research your jurisdiction and determine if burglary is divided into degrees. How are the degrees delineated? If burglary is not categorized into degrees, does it bear the designations of simple and aggravated burglary? What constitutes an aggravated burglary?

CRIMINAL TRESPASS

criminal trespass
The offense committed by one who, without license or privilege to do so, enters or surreptitiously remains in any building or occupied structure.

Criminal trespass is a less serious offense than burglary. The significant factor of criminal trespass is the unwanted presence of the defendant in a structure. Criminal trespass involves the entering or remaining on a property without permission. The trespass does not have to occur in an occupied building. The property must be marked in some manner so that the defendant knew that he/she should not remain. Criminal trespass can occur to a building, land, and even to computer systems through unauthorized access to electronic media. The presence needs to be unauthorized.

In a criminal trespass, the defendant does not have to possess intent to commit a crime. The Model Penal Code at section 223.5 defines criminal trespass as follows:

1. Buildings and Occupied Structures. *A person commits an offense if, knowing he is not licensed or privileged to do so, he enters or surreptitiously remains in any building or occupied structure, or separately secured or occupied portion thereof. An offense under this subsection is a misdemeanor if it is committed in a dwelling at night. Otherwise, it is a petty misdemeanor.*

2. Defiant Trespasser. *A person commits an offense if, knowing that he is not licensed or privileged to do so, he enters or remains in any place to which notice against trespass is given by:*

   actual communication to the actor; or

   posting in a manner prescribed by law or reasonably likely to come to the attention of intruders; or

   fencing or other enclosure manifestly designed to exclude intruders. An offense under this subsection constitutes a petty misdemeanor if the offender defies an order to leave personally communicated to him by the owner of the premises or other authorized person. Otherwise, it is a violation.

3. Defenses. *It is an affirmative defense to prosecution under this section that:*

   a building or occupied structure involved in an offense under Subsection (1) was abandoned; or the premises were at the time open to members of the public and the actor complied with all lawful conditions imposed on access to or remaining in the premises; or the actor reasonably believed that the owner of the premises, or other person empowered to license access thereto, would have licensed him to enter or remain.

Some states will have varying degrees of criminal trespass that are categorized depending on the circumstances involved. Some jurisdictions require not only a lack of consent, but also a lack of notice before an individual can be found guilty of trespassing. For example, if a sign stating "No Trespassing" was posted and an individual ignored it, entering the property without consent, then that individual has committed criminal trespass. The element of "notice" varies from jurisdiction to jurisdiction. Additionally, many law enforcement agencies are reluctant to prosecute trespassers criminally, preferring the individuals who trespass are instead pursued in a civil action.

ARSON

Arson is a crime that dates back to ancient times. Arson involves the setting of a fire that reaches a structure and burns it. It is a general-intent crime. At common law, arson was a felony and was addressed and punished in a manner similar to murder. The guilty party was not held to have merely violated property rights. The essence of the crime was the harm to man's habitation. The horror of seeing one's own home in flames and the large risk to humans were both factors when considering how to classify the crime and how to punish the wrongdoer. During the reign of Edward the First in England, those found guilty of arson were executed. The elements of common law arson are

- The malicious
- Burning
- Of a dwelling or structure
- Of another.

As with burglary, some modern statutes have relaxed some of these common law elements.

Because setting fire to a structure is dangerous, malicious intent will be inferred from the dangerous activity caused by the defendant. The intent to start a fire, even if no structure is burned, is enough to satisfy the malicious-intent requirement for the crime of arson. Malice can be proven by either an intent to burn or extreme and wanton recklessness.

arson
At common law, arson had four requisites. First, there must be some actual burning (though this requirement did not include destruction of the building or even of any substantial part of the building). Second, the burning must be malicious (negligence is not sufficient). Third, the object burned must be a dwelling house. Fourth and finally, the house burned must be the habitation of another.

Negligence, however, will not satisfy the necessary intent needed for arson. Because arson has been found to involve such an extreme degree of risk to human life, the perpetrator is held to have a state of mind referred to as malice aforethought. Because of this state of mind, if a death is caused by the act of arson, it will be considered a homicide whether or not there was any intent to kill by the wrongdoer.

The amount of burning that occurs is immaterial to the crime of arson. No matter how slight the burning, arson has occurred as long as there has been some burning or charring of the structure. However, a mere blackening of a structure from smoke will generally not qualify as a "burning." The structure does not have to burn to the ground to complete the crime. The majority of states have expanded the definition of arson to include almost any structure so long as what was damaged is considered part of the dwelling such as a fixture. However, the burning of a person's personal property such as furniture does not satisfy the element of burning for arson unless there is fire damage to the structure the personal property is located within. The manner in which the defendant starts the fire is also immaterial to the crime. Explosions also are thought to constitute a burning.

Under common law, the element of a dwelling of another was established to protect an occupant from someone setting fire to his/her home. However, modern statutes have expanded the definition to include vehicles as well as structures. With the modern occurrence of a structure owner intentionally setting fire to his/her own dwelling or structure in order to collect insurance money, many states also have expanded their arson statutes to address this trend. In *State v. Durant*, 674 P.2d 638 (Utah 1983), it was held that an owner of property who caused a person to burn his home for reasons other than to fraudulently collect on an insurance police also could be convicted of arson. Other statutory crimes have been put into force to prohibit such acts as well. Many modern arson statutes also have added specific provisions regarding the use of explosive devices.

Common law arson requires that the structure must be occupied to be considered a "dwelling." For example, a structure that is not occupied for an extensive period of time would not constitute a dwelling. Modern arson statutes may address the crime of maliciously burning buildings besides dwellings such as places of business.

Arson, like many other crimes, is subject to a grading system under the Model Penal Code. Normally, the grades are called degrees. The Model Penal Code at section 220.1 defines and grades arson into degrees as follows:

1. Arson. *A person is guilty of arson, a felony of the second degree, if he starts a fire or causes an explosion with the purpose of:*

   destroying a building or occupied structure of another; or

   destroying or damaging any property, whether his own or another's, to collect insurance for such loss. It shall be an affirmative defense to prosecution under this paragraph that the actor's conduct did not recklessly endanger any building or occupied structure of another or place any other person in danger of death or bodily injury.

2. Reckless Burning or Exploding. *A person commits a felony of the third degree if he purposely starts a fire or causes an explosion, whether on his own property or another's, and thereby recklessly:*

   places another person in danger of death or bodily injury; or

   places a building or occupied structure of another in danger of damage or destruction.

A DAY IN THE LIFE OF A REAL PARALEGAL

One of the most famous cases of arson was in response to the DuPont Plaza Hotel fire on New Year's Eve of 1986. Hotel employees had been in the middle of a heated labor dispute and intended to set some small fires to scare tourists away from the hotel. The small fire quickly burned out of control and spread through the hotel and adjoining casino. In the end, 97 people lost their lives. Three employees were eventually convicted of arson.

CASE FACT PATTERN

Timothy gets a thrill from starting fires. He loves to watch them burn. He has set numerous fires during his life just to watch them burn. Timothy lives in Southern California, which is an area that has been prone to violent wildfires that spread rapidly because of the Santa Ana winds that blow through the area from time to time. Parts of Southern California have been devastated by wildfires in the past, and these fires have caused significant damage and injuries.

Timothy has set wildfires before just for the thrill. One day, the Santa Ana winds began blowing heavily through the Riverside County area of Southern California. Some of the gusts clocked speeds of 80 mph. Timothy was thrilled with the weather conditions. He knew that if he set a fire today, it would spread rapidly due to the winds. The thought of the fire burning made his heart pound with excitement.

Armed with an incendiary device as well as gasoline, Timothy drove up into the Esperanza Canyon area of the county near the desert. The area was heavily vegetated with dry brush as the area had not received much rainfall the previous year. Timothy drove to a somewhat desolate area and started the fire. As he watched it burn, he felt the thrill of the destruction.

The winds whipped the fire up rapidly. Fueled by dry brush and high dry winds, the fire spread through thousands of acres. Firefighters made various stands against the fire, only to retreat as it advanced fiercely and rapidly. Five firefighters drove rapidly to a house to try to save it from destruction. On the way, the fire overtook them and they died. The fire charred over 40,200 acres, or 63 square miles, before it was finally contained and extinguished. Arson investigators were brought in to make a determination as to the cause of the fire. It was determined that the fire was caused by arson and Timothy had been seen by witnesses fleeing the scene.

After a thorough investigation by arson investigators as well as the FBI and local police, Timothy was arrested and charged with arson as well as felony murder due to the fact that the firefighters lost their lives as a result of Timothy's actions.

3. *Failure to Control or Report Dangerous Fire. A person who knows that a fire is endangering life or a substantial amount of property of another and fails to take reasonable measures to put out or control the fire, when he can do so without substantial risk to himself, or to give a prompt fire alarm, commits a misdemeanor if:*

> *he knows that he is under an official, contractual, or other legal duty to prevent or combat the fire; or*

> *the fire was started, albeit lawfully, by him or with his assent, or on property in his custody or control.*

EYE ON ETHICS

People who investigate arson are held in a position of trust. Arson investigators need to be unbiased and are in a position to protect the public. Ethics is vital in any criminal investigation. Numerous fire departments throughout the country have codes of ethics to follow, as do certain private entities. As an example, the International Association of Arson Investigators (IAAI) has a code of ethics it follows. In brief, the IAAI ethical code sets forth the following points:

- Arson investigation is an honorable position;
- My behavior, privately and publicly, should inspire confidence of the community at large;
- Never shall I depend on my position of trust for any personal advantage, including profit;
- My fellow investigators shall be held to the same standards set for me;

- I will never betray any confidences nor hinder any investigation;
- I shall always educate myself on the latest aspects of my profession;
- I will never align myself with anyone whose goals are dishonest and biased;
- I shall never make any claims of knowledge or qualifications that I do not have;
- If any positive or negative publicity should befall me, I shall share that publicity with my fellow investigators;
- I shall always maintain loyalty to my organization, and fellow investigators; and
- The truth has the utmost importance and is more important to be sure the innocent are protected than to convict the guilty.

For more information about the IAAI, please see their Web site at www.firearson.com.

4. *Definitions. "Occupied structure" means any structure, vehicle, or place adapted for over-night accommodation of persons, or for carrying on business therein, whether or not a person is actually present. Property is that of another, for purposes of this section, if anyone other than the actor has a possessory or proprietary interest therein. If a building or structure is divided into separately occupied units, any unit not occupied by the actor in an occupied structure of another.*[1]

MALICIOUS MISCHIEF

malicious mischief
The act of willfully damaging or destroying the personal property of another; sometimes referred to as criminal mischief.

vandalism
Such willful or malicious acts are intended to damage or destroy property.

Malicious mischief, also known as **vandalism** or hooliganism, is the destroying or damaging of someone's property. The word *vandalism* originates from the word *vandal*, an ethnic slur used to reference the Vandals who invaded ancient Rome. The elements of malicious mischief are

- Knowingly
- Destroying or damaging the property
- Of another.

Criminal mischief is another name for malicious mischief. The Model Penal Code at section 220.3 defines criminal mischief as follows:

1. *Offense Defined. A person is guilty of criminal mischief if he:*
   a. *damages tangible property of another purposely, recklessly, or by negligence in the employment of fire, explosives, or other dangerous means; or*
   b. *purposely or recklessly tampers with tangible property of another so as to endanger person or property; or*
   c. *purposely or recklessly causes another to suffer pecuniary loss by deception or threat.*

2. *Grading. Criminal mischief is a felony of the third degree if the actor purposely causes pecuniary loss in excess of $5,000, or a substantial interruption or impairment of public communication, transportation, supply of water, gas or power, or other public service. It is a misdemeanor if the actor purposely causes pecuniary loss in excess of $100, or a petty misdemeanor if he purposely or recklessly causes pecuniary loss in excess of $25. Otherwise criminal mischief is a violation.*[2]

Malicious mischief is generally a misdemeanor, but, as indicated by the Model Penal Code, if the property damage is substantial, the crime can be designated as a felony. Malicious mischief is punished more severely when it is committed extensively or violently and is intended to intimidate or express feelings of extreme hatred. The property that is damaged does not have to be completely destroyed for the elements of the crime to be satisfied. However, the damage to the property must generally impair the property's utility or materially diminish the property value. For example, harming a family pet can constitute damage to property under the crime of malicious mischief. Other examples of malicious mischief or vandalism might include breaking the headlights on a car or throwing eggs at the side of a house. See Figure 7.1 for additional examples of malicious mischief.

If the criminal activity is conducted by a juvenile, the parents of that juvenile could be held financially responsible for the damages caused by their child.

FIGURE 7.1
Examples of Malicious Mischief

- Examples of malicious mischief include but are not limited to
- Harming an animal.
- Stealing street signs.
- Spraying graffiti onto walls and overpasses.
- Damaging a cemetery.
- Shooting out street lights.
- Throwing firecrackers or stink bombs.

[1] Model Penal Code, copyright 1985 by the American Law Institute. Reprinted with permission.
[2] Model Penal Code, copyright 1985 by the American Law Institute. Reprinted with permission.

SURF'S UP

Malicious mischief is a crime in many states. In the State of Washington, malicious mischief is defined into degrees. Under section 9A.48.090, the Washington Code defines malicious mischief in the third degree as

(1) A person is guilty of malicious mischief in the third degree if he or she:
(a) Knowingly and maliciously causes physical damage to the property of another, under circumstances not amounting to malicious mischief in the first or second degree; or
(b) Writes, paints, or draws any inscription, figure, or mark of any type on any public or private building or other structure or any real or personal property owned by any other person unless the person has obtained the express permission of the owner or operator of the property, under circumstances not amounting to malicious mischief in the first or second degree.

(2) (a) Malicious mischief in the third degree under subsection (1)(a) of this section is a gross misdemeanor if the damage to the property is in an amount exceeding fifty dollars.
(b) Malicious mischief in the third degree under subsection (1)(a) of this section is a misdemeanor if the damage to the property is fifty dollars or less.
(c) Malicious mischief in the third degree under subsection (1)(b) of this section is a gross misdemeanor.

To read more about state laws concerning malicious mischief, visit the following Web sites:

- www.witkin.com
- www.boalt.org

A DAY IN THE LIFE OF A REAL PARALEGAL

Paralegals often perform the important task of legal research. When working on a criminal case, they often will be required to find information concerning a party's past criminal record. The Internet has made this task much simpler. There are many good Web sites where a paralegal can quickly and efficiently search and locate public records online, including criminal records. One good example is www.Webinvestigator.com.

Summary

Crimes against habitation are not the same thing as crimes against property. Crimes against habitation deal with crimes against someone's home, not someone's house. A house is property, but a home is a person's living space and provides a sense of security. Laws regarding crimes against habitation are designed to protect people from invasion, intrusion, damage, or destruction of their home or environment as well as preventing such acts from impeding on their sense of security.

Burglary has been a crime for centuries. Under common law, the elements of burglary are the breaking and entering of the dwelling of another at night with the intent to commit a crime. Modern burglary statutes now make it a crime to enter any structure, in the day or night, with the intent to commit a crime.

Criminal trespass is a less serious offense than burglary. The significant factor of criminal trespass is the unwanted presence of the defendant in a structure. Criminal trespass involves the entering or remaining on a property without permission. The trespass does not have to occur in an occupied building. The property must be marked in some manner so that the defendant knew that he should not remain. Criminal trespass can occur to a building, to land, and even to computer systems through unauthorized access to electronic media. The presence needs to be unauthorized.

Arson is a crime that dates back to ancient times. Arson involves the setting of a fire that reaches a structure and burns it. Arson is a general-intent crime. The elements of arson are the malicious burning of the dwelling or structure of another.

Malicious mischief, also known as vandalism, is destroying or damaging someone's property. The elements of malicious mischief are knowingly destroying or damaging the property of another.

Key Terms

Arson
Breaking
Burglary
Criminal trespass

Dwelling
Habitation
Malicious mischief
Vandalism

Review Questions

1. Identify the elements of burglary.
2. What is the difference between burglary and robbery?
3. What rights are the laws regarding crimes against habitation designed to protect?
4. What are the elements of a criminal trespass?
5. Discuss the differences between criminal trespass and burglary. Give examples of each type of crime.
6. Describe how the crime of criminal trespass applies to computer hackers.
7. What does a criminal have to do in order to satisfy the element of entering for a burglary? Give an example of the minimum act by a criminal that will satisfy the element of an entry.
8. List the elements of arson.
9. How is malice determined in the crime of arson?
10. Does a building have to burn down to satisfy the crime of arson? Why or why not?
11. Under modern law, what type of structures can satisfy the elements for crimes against habitation?
12. List the elements of malicious mischief.
13. Explain how malicious mischief can be considered a crime against habitation.
14. List five activities that can be considered malicious mischief.
15. Describe the mens rea requirement for arson. What is different about the mens rea required for arson than for other crimes against habitation.

Exercises

1. Jason and Martha had been dating for two years. After two years, Martha broke off the relationship. Jason was devastated. He was still in love with Martha. His love became an obsession. Martha would not see Jason or take his telephone calls. Jason was determined to see Martha. The next night, while Martha was sleeping, Jason opened a downstairs window in her apartment, climbed through the window, and went up the stairs to Martha's bedroom. He opened the door, went inside the room, and stood beside Martha's bed. Jason's only intent was to stand beside Martha's bed and gaze at her lovely face. While Jason was gazing at Martha, she woke up and discovered Jason in her room. Terrified with Jason's presence in her room, she called the police. The police arrested Jason and charged him with burglary. Can Jason be convicted of burglary? Explain your answer.

2. Monty's store was not performing very well and he was losing a substantial amount of money. He had made a large investment in inventory of some unique doorknockers, thinking that they were going to be the next great item in the home improvement market. However, the doorknocker product was a dismal failure. Facing substantial debt, Monty decided to set fire to the warehouse in which

the doorknockers were located and destroy them. If Monty could collect insurance money on the doorknockers, then he could break even and save his business. One night, Monty set a fire outside the warehouse. Soon the entire warehouse was consumed with flames and everything in it was destroyed. Using the elements of the crimes listed in this chapter, write a comprehensive and detailed analysis of what crime(s) Monty is guilty of committing.

3. Tony loves the museum. He loves to look at the artwork and the sculptures. One day, Tony decides to go the museum. He spends hours there browsing the beautiful pieces of artwork. All of a sudden, Tony hears the intercom announcing that the museum is closing and that everyone should make their way to the front exit and exit the building. Tony does not want to leave. He loves it in the museum. Tony decides that he is going to stay in the museum. He hides in one of the restaurants and waits for the museum to close to the public. Once everyone is gone, Tony remains in the museum. What crime has Tony committed, if any, and why?

4. Uncle Ed was hiking through the woods when a storm suddenly hit. He broke into Mike and Maggie's vacation cabin for shelter. After the storm passed, he left the cabin and continued hiking through the words. Has Uncle Ed committed burglary? Why or why not?

5. Nick, a homeless man, breaks into a bakery one night and steals a dozen donuts. If the jurisdiction abides by the common law requirements for burglary, has Nick committed burglary? Why or why not?

6. Discuss whether or not it is possible for a landlord to burglarize his or her tenant.

7. Marcy had been dating Jason for six months when he left her for Mandy. One night, after drinking a substantial amount of alcohol at Tom's Tavern, Marcy started talking to her cousin Cathy, who had recently gotten divorced. The two women talked about how much they would like to take revenge upon the men who had broken their hearts. Marcy's walk home led her directly past Jason's house. His newspaper, delivered earlier in the day, still lay in front of his door. Marcy walked to the newspaper, picked it up, and lit it on fire with her cigarette lighter. She then threw it in some dry bushes near the house and ran off. The fire slightly charred the exterior of the house but didn't cause any damage to the interior. If Marcy is prosecuted for common law arson, what is the likely result?

8. Research the word *vandalism*. What did the word come from and what did it represent?

PORTFOLIO ASSIGNMENT

Research and discover why the original common law definition of *burglary* included the breaking and entering *at night* of another's dwelling with the intent to commit a felony. Why was "at night" part of the elements?

Vocabulary Builders

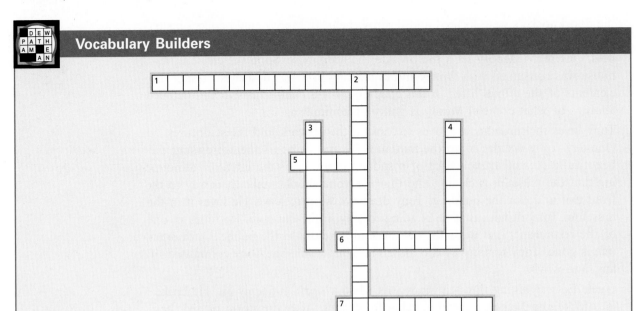

Instructions

Use the key terms from this chapter to fill in the answers to the crossword puzzle.

NOTE: When the answer is more than one word, leave a blank space between words.

ACROSS

1. the act of willfully damaging or destroying the personal property of another; sometimes referred to as criminal mischief.
5. at common law, the malicious burning of someone else's dwelling house; under modern law, the intentional and wrongful burning of someone else's property or one's own property so as to fraudulently collect insurance.
6. in the law of burglary, the act of entering a building without permission.
7. place of abode; dwelling place; residence
8. such willful or malicious acts are intended to damage or destroy property.

DOWN

2. the offense committed by one who, without license or privilege to do so, enters or surreptitiously remains in any building or occupied structure.
3. the common law offense of breaking and entering another's dwelling at night with the intent to commit a felony; the modern offense of breaking and entering any building at any time of day with the intent to commit a felony.
4. a house or other structure that is used or intended for use as a residence.

PORTILLO-CANDIDO V. U.S.

Douglas Ulisses PORTILLO-CANDIDO, Petitioner

v.

UNITED STATES OF AMERICA, Respondent.
—F. Supp. 2d—, 2005 WL 3262549
United States District Court,
S.D. Texas, Houston Division.
Nov. 30, 2005.

ORDER

HITTNER, J.

Pending before the Court is the Motion Under 28 U.S.C. § 2255 to Vacate, Set Aside or Correct Sentence by a Person in Federal Custody (Civil Document No. 1, Criminal Document No. 34) filed by Douglas Ulisses Portillo-Candido. Having considered the motion, submissions, and applicable law, the Court determines Douglas Ulisses Portillo-Candido's motion should be denied.

BACKGROUND

On February 12, 2003, Defendant Douglas Ulisses Portillo-Candido ("Portillo-Candido") was indicted for illegal re-entry after deportation, in violation of 8 U.S.C. § 1326(a) and (b)(2). On April 29, 2003, Portillo-Candido appeared with counsel and entered a plea of guilty with no plea agreement. On July 23, 2003, the Court sentenced Portillo-Candido to 69 months confinement, to be followed by a three-year term of supervised release. The Court increased Portillo-Candido's guideline range 16 levels pursuant to the United States Sentencing Guidelines ("Sentencing Guidelines") § 2L1.2(b)(1)(A)(ii) because Portillo-Candido had been deported following a 1994 Texas conviction for a crime of violence, namely burglary of a habitation with intent to commit theft.

Portillo-Candido appealed the sentence and the United States Court of Appeals for the Fifth Circuit affirmed the judgment of this Court. On October 29, 2004, the United States Supreme Court denied Portillo-Candido's petition for a writ of certiorari. On May 19, 2005, Portillo-Candido filed the instant motion.

In his § 2255 motion, Portillo-Candido alleges two grounds for relief. Portillo-Candido first claims ineffective assistance of counsel, alleging his attorney failed to make an investigation into the 16-level enhancement based on his 1994 Texas conviction. Portillo-Candido next argues the Court improperly increased his sentence based on the 1994 Texas conviction because he alleges burglary of a habitation is not a crime of violence.

LAW & ANALYSIS

Burglary of a Habitation as a Crime of Violence

Portillo-Candido alleges the Court committed error in enhancing his sentence based on illegal re-entry after deportation following a crime of violence, namely burglary of a habitation with intent to commit theft. Portillo-Candido also alleges ineffective assistance of counsel because his attorney did not investigate his sentence enhancement for a violent crime. The Sentencing Guidelines provide for a 16-level increase in a base level offense if the defendant was previously deported after a conviction for an aggravated felony. U.S.S.G. § 2L1.2(b)(1)(A)(ii). An aggravated felony is "any crime of violence for which the term of imprisonment imposed (regardless of any suspension of such imprisonment) is at least five years." 18 U.S.C. § 16 (2000). A conviction qualifies as a crime of violence in one of two ways. It qualifies if either the conviction is an offense listed as a crime of violence under the Sentencing Guidelines, or the conviction "has as an element the use, attempted use, or threatened use of physical force against the person of another." U.S.S.G. § 2L1.2, cmt. n. 1(B)(iii). Burglary of a dwelling is listed as a crime of violence in the definitions that accompany the Sentencing Guidelines. *Id.*

The success of both Portillo-Candido's arguments turns on whether the definition of the Texas state crime of burglary of a habitation is construed the same way as burglary of a dwelling or is otherwise interpreted as a crime of violence for purposes of the Sentencing Guidelines. Therefore, the Court will address this threshold issue before analyzing Portillo-Candido's substantive claims.

At sentencing, Portillo-Candido received a 16-level enhancement to his guideline range because he had been previously deported following a crime of violence, namely a conviction for burglary of a habitation under the Texas Penal Code. The Texas Penal Code defines habitation as:

> "Habitation" means a structure or vehicle that is adapted for the overnight accommodation of persons, and includes:
> (A) each separately secured or occupied portion of the structure or vehicle; and
> (B) each structure appurtenant to or connected with the structure or vehicle.

TEX. PENAL CODE § 30.01(1) (Vernon 2003). The Fifth Circuit has held that burglary of a habitation, as defined by the Texas Penal Code, is a crime of violence within the career offender provisions of the Sentencing Guidelines. *See United States v. Cruz,* 882 F.2d 922 (5th Cir. 1989) (holding that burglary of a habitation is a "crime of violence" within the meaning of sentence enhancement for career offenders); *United States v. Flores,* 875 F.2d 1110 (5th Cir. 1989) (holding that burglaries of residences constituted "crimes of violence"). Moreover, the Fifth Circuit recognizes that burglary of a habitation in violation of the Texas Penal Code constitutes a "crime of violence" under the immigration provisions of the Sentencing Guidelines. *See United States v. Guadardo,* 40 F.3d 102, 104 (5th Cir. 1994) (holding burglary of a habitation is a "crime of violence" within the meaning of sentence enhancement for illegal presence in the United States after deportation). "[B]urglary of a habitation under the Texas Penal Code is always a crime of violence . . . , thus obviating the need for a district court to consider the factual context of such a conviction." *Id.* Thus, the Court determines that the law in this circuit is well established and holds that a Texas crime of burglary of a habitation is a crime of violence.

"At the time of sentencing in *Cruz* and *Flores,* U.S.S.G. § 4B1.2 stated that the term 'crime of violence' as used in this provision is defined under 18 U.S.C. § 16. Likewise, the term 'crime of violence' as used in U.S.S.G. § 2L1.1 is defined under 18 U.S.C. § 16." *Guadardo,* 40 F.3d at 104.

In his § 2255 motion, Portillo-Candido relies heavily on the unpublished Fifth Circuit opinion in *United States v. Rodriguez,* 93 F. App'x 663 (5th Cir. 2004). In *Rodriguez,* the Fifth Circuit held that a district court improperly used a defendant's two prior New Jersey burglary convictions to enhance his federal sentence for illegal reentry. *Id.* at 664–65. The Fifth Circuit, in analyzing the two underlying New Jersey state burglary convictions, determined the district court should not have enhanced the sentence because it was unclear whether either of the convictions involved "burglary of a dwelling." *Id.* The record for one of the convictions did not indicate whether or not a dwelling was involved. The other burglary conviction resulted from Rodriguez's unlawful entry into a structure with the intent to commit an offense therein. *Id.* at 665. The definition of "structure" under New Jersey law includes "*any* building, room, ship, vessel, car, vehicle or airplane, and also means any place adapted for overnight accommodation of persons, or for carrying on business therein, whether or not a person is actually present." N.J. STAT. ANN.. § 2C:18-1 (1997). Thus, the language in the New Jersey statute encompasses a broader range of conduct than the Sentencing Guidelines definition of burglary of a dwelling. *Compare* N.J. STAT. ANN.. § 2C:18-1 *with* U.S.S.G. § 2L1.2. Accordingly, the court determined Rodriguez's New Jersey convictions could not, based on the record, be considered crimes of violence for enhancement purposes. *Rodriguez,* 93 F. App'x at 665.

Portillo-Candido relies on *Rodriguez* to supports [sic] his position that his conviction was improperly deemed a crime of violence. Specifically, Portillo-Candido provides:

> The defendant (sic) receive an enhancement for prior offense of burglary to habitation of 16 levels because according to the probation officer in the P.S.I. was a crime of violence, but in a decision from the Court of Appeals in [*Rodriguez*] said that burglary to a dwelling is not a crime of violence. The patitioner (sic) review the word dwelling in the black law dictionary and the definition is the same as a habitation . . .

Portillo-Candido, ostensibly misreading *Rodriguez,* appears to aver that *Rodriguez* holds that burglary of a dwelling is not a crime of violence. Thus, he compares "dwelling" to "habitation" in Black's Law Dictionary, which similarly defines both terms, and reaches the conclusion that his conviction for burglary of a habitation under Texas law should be interpreted the same way as burglary of a dwelling, which he argues is not a crime of violence. Indeed, the Black's Law Dictionary definitions clearly show "dwelling" and "habitation" are synonyms and both describe a place used as a residence. However, Portillo-Candido's argument fails because *Rodriguez* does not hold that burglary of a dwelling is not a crime of violence. As discussed above, the Fifth Circuit merely held that it was unable to determine that either of the Defendant's burglary convictions involved burglary of a dwelling. *See Rodriguez,* 93 F. App'x at 665. Accordingly, Portillo-Candido's reliance on *Rodriguez* is misplaced in the instant context.

Black's Law Dictionary defines a dwelling as "[t]he house or other structure in which a person or persons live; a residence; abode; habitation; the apartment or building, or group of buildings, occupied by a family as a place of residence. Structure used as place of habitation." Black's Law Dictionary 454 (5th ed. 1979). Habitation is defined as a "place of abode; dwelling place; residence." Black's Law Dictionary 640 (5th ed.1979).

In sum, the Fifth Circuit has held that the Texas crime of burglary of a habitation qualifies as a crime of violence under the Sentencing Guidelines. Further, *Rodriguez* is distinguishable from the case at bar. Therefore, Portillo-Candido's argument that the Court improperly determined that burglary of a habitation is a "crime of violence" under the Sentencing Guidelines fails.

A. Misapplication of the Guidelines Argument

Based on his argument that burglary of a habitation is not a crime of violence, Portillo-Candido alleges he received an improper enhancement of his guideline range. The Court will uphold a sentence under the guidelines unless it violates the law, is incorrectly applied, or is an unreasonable departure from the guideline range. *United States v. Anderson,* 5 F.3d 795, 798 (5th Cir. 1993). Portillo-Candido received a base offense level of 8 for illegal re-entry after deportation. He then received a 16-level enhancement because he was previously deported following a conviction for a crime of violence, namely burglary of a habitation with intent to commit theft. Because the Court properly determined burglary of a habitation is a crime of violence, the 16-level enhancement did not violate the law, result in an improper application of the guideline range, or result in an unreasonable departure from the guideline range. Therefore, Portillo-Candido did not receive an improper enhancement of his guideline range.

B. Ineffective Assistance of Counsel Claim

Like his argument that the Court misapplied the Sentencing Guidelines, Portillo-Candido's ineffective assistance of counsel argument is predicated upon his argument that burglary of a habitation is not a crime of violence. The right to counsel means the right to the effective assistance of counsel. *McMann v. Richardson,* 397 U.S. 759, 771 n. 14, 90 S. Ct. 1441, 25 L. Ed. 2d 763 (1970). Ineffective assistance of counsel claims are not typically resolved on direct appeal because such claims raise an issue of constitutional magnitude. *United States v. Pierce,* 959 F.3d 1297, 1301 (5th Cir. 1992). "Judicial scrutiny of counsel's performance must be highly deferential." *Id.* at 689. The defendant must overcome the presumption that counsel's actions were effective. *See Michel v. Louisiana*, 350 U.S. 91, 101, 76 S. Ct. 158, 100 L. Ed. 83 (1955); *United States v. Payne*, 99 F.3d 1273, 1282 (5th Cir. 1996). A judge does not evaluate effectiveness based on hindsight, but instead evaluates the conduct from counsel's perspective. *Strickland*, 466 U.S. at 669. There is no one way to provide effective assistance in each case. *Id.* at 689.

Courts analyze an ineffective assistance of counsel claim in a § 2255 motion under the *Strickland* test. *Strickland*, 466 U.S. at 687–88; *United States v. Willis*, 273 F.3d 592, 598 (5th Cir. 2001). Under the *Strickland* test, the defendant "must show that his counsel's performance was both deficient and prejudicial." *Willis*, 273 F.3d at 598. To show deficiency, the defendant must prove counsel's performance was objectively unreasonable. *Strickland*, 466 U.S. at 688; *Hernandez v. Johnson*, 213 F.3d 243, 249 (5th Cir. 2000). To demonstrate prejudice, the defendant must also show the deficient performance led to an unfair and unreliable sentence. *United States v. Dovilina*, 262 F.3d 472, 474–75 (5th Cir. 2001). A court need not address both prongs of the *Strickland* test if the defendant makes an insufficient showing on either one. *Carter v. Johnson*, 131 F.3d 452, 263 (5th Cir. 1997).

The standard for effective assistance is reasonable conduct under prevailing professional norms. *Strickland*, 466 U.S. at 669. "[C]ounsel has a duty to make reasonable investigations or to make a reasonable decision that makes particular investigations unnecessary." *Id.* at 691. "A defendant who alleges a failure to investigate on the part of his counsel must allege with specificity what the investigation would have revealed and how it would have altered the outcome of the trial." *United States v. Green*, 882 F.2d 999, 1003 (5th Cir. 1989).

Here, as previously discussed, burglary of a habitation constitutes a crime of violence. Thus, any attempt to raise the issue at sentencing would have been futile. Counsel is not required to make futile claims or objections. *See Carter*, 131 F.3d at 464 (1997). Further, unsubstantiated allegations will not surmount the presumption counsel performed adequately. Therefore, with nothing more than unsubstantiated allegations that counsel acted deficiently, Portillo-Candido fails to establish his counsel acted deficiently by not investigating whether burglary of a habitation was a crime of violence. *See Sayre v. Anderson*, 238 F.3d 631, 636 (5th Cir. 2001).

Although the Court finds no deficiency in Counsel's performance, the Court will examine the second prong of the *Strickland* test. "The defendant must show that there is a reasonable probability that, but for counsel's unprofessional errors, the result of the proceeding would have been different." *Ramirez v. Dretke*, 398 F.3d 691, 698 (5th Cir. 2005). The defendant must affirmatively prove prejudice; a mere possibility is not enough to satisfy petitioner's burden. *Kunkle v. Dretke*, 352 F.3d 980, 991 (5th Cir. 2003). Portillo-Candido fails to demonstrate deficiency of counsel or prejudice, and therefore cannot satisfy either of the two prongs of the *Strickland* test.

CONCLUSION

Portillo-Candido's claim that the Court improperly enhanced his guideline contradicts Fifth Circuit precedent, which recognizes burglary of a habitation is a crime of violence. Portillo-Candido also fails to show deficiency of counsel. Given the foregoing, the Court hereby

ORDERS that Douglas Ulisses Portillo-Candido's Motion Under 28 U.S.C. § 2255 to Vacate, Set Aside or Correct Sentence by a Person in Federal Custody (Civil Document No. 1, Criminal Document No. 34) is DENIED.

Source: 2005 WL 3262549 (S.D. Tex. 2005). Reprinted with permission from Westlaw.

Chapter 8

Complicity

CHAPTER OBJECTIVES

Upon completion of this chapter, you will be able to:

- Identify the elements of the crime of complicity.
- Explain guilt of the principal.
- Discuss the role of the accomplice.
- Understand accessory before the fact.
- Understand accessory after the fact.

Criminal law seeks to punish defendants for their criminal acts as well as their criminal state of mind. However, there are instances in which a person can be guilty for the criminal acts of another. When one is **complicit**, he or she is criminally liable, even though he or she did not personally commit the criminal act. This chapter examines when a person can be criminally liable for the crimes of another.

complicity
A state of being an accomplice; participation in guilt.

principal in the first degree
The criminal actor; the one who actually commits the crime, either by his/her own hand, by an inanimate agency, or by an innocent human agent.

aid and abet
Help, assist, or facilitate the commission of a crime; promote the accomplishment thereof; help in advancing or bringing it about; or encourage, counsel, or incite as to its commission.

principal in the second degree
The one who is present at the commission of a criminal offense and aids, counsels, commands, or encourages the principal in the first degree in the commission of that offense.

PARTIES TO CRIME

Under common law, there were four distinct ways in which a person could be a party to a felony:

- Principal in the first degree.
- Principal in the second degree.
- Accessory before the fact.
- Accessory after the fact.

A **principal in the first degree** is the person who personally performed the criminal act. Every completed crime has at least one principal in the first degree. Suppose Josh and Tony plan to shoot Bill. Josh is the one who actually pulls the trigger and shoots Bill. Josh would be considered the principal in the first degree.

The person who is present during the crime and **aids and abets** in its commission but does not personally commit the criminal act is known as a **principal in the second degree**. A principal in the second degree either helps, advises, commands, or encourages the principal in the first degree. In the example above, Tony would be considered a principal in the second degree because he did not actually pull the trigger in the shooting. However, Tony also could have been a principal in the second degree if he was not actually at the shooting but acted as a lookout while Josh committed the crime. A person who is in the vicinity of the crime and aids in its commission is considered to be constructively present at the crime; this will be enough to establish him/her as a principal in the second degree.

An **accessory before the fact** is similar to a principal in the second degree. He/she does not commit the actual crime and he/she aids and abets the criminal. However, unlike the principal in the second degree, the accessory before the fact is not actually present at the crime, nor is he/she constructively present. An accessory before the fact can be involved in the crime by helping in the planning, purchasing the weapon, or offering some slight assistance such as finding out some type of information. The accessory before the fact completes his/her participation prior to the actual commission of the crime. An accessory before the fact is sometimes, but not always, considered a conspirator. For example, Bonnie gives Clyde a gun that she knows Clyde intends to use in a bank robbery. She also helps Clyde case the bank in order to decide what time of day to commit the robbery. Clyde robs the bank, but Bonnie is not physically present during the robbery. Bonnie is still an accessory before the fact.

An **accessory after the fact** is also someone who does not actually participate in the crime. However, this person offers assistance to the perpetrator of the crime after it has been committed. The type of assistance that is typically provided is to enable the perpetrator to evade arrest for the crime. An example of an accessory after the fact is when someone hides the criminal so that law enforcement cannot find him/her or offers him/her safe passage out of the jurisdiction in order to assist the criminal in evading arrest. In *People v. Nguyen,* 21 Cal. App. 4th 518, 26 Cal. Rptr. 2d 323 (1993), the court held that an accessory after the fact must lend assistance to the principal after the commission of the offense with the intent of assisting the principal to elude capture, trial, or punishment. Both an accessory before the fact and an accessory after the fact must have knowledge that a crime is about to be or has been committed to be charged as an accessory. Mens rea is required to establish criminal liability for accessories even if it is not required to establish the criminal liability of the principal to a crime. For example, in a strict liability crime, a principal may not have had any mens rea and yet still be guilty. However, if the principal had an accessory, that accessory must have had the requisite mens rea to be held criminally liable. In *People v. Howard,* 1 Cal. 4th 1132, 5 Cal. Rptr. 2d 268 (1992), a principal's girlfriend who counted some stolen money, hid evidence, and helped her boyfriend dispose of stolen credit cards was held to be an accessory after the fact. In this case, the accessory's knowledge was made obvious by her actions. (See Figure 8.1 for a comparison of the different levels of accomplices.)

In some jurisdictions, a person cannot be charged as an accessory to a crime unless a crime has actually taken place. Additionally, some jurisdictions do not allow a person to be charged as an accessory to a crime committed by a spouse.

accessory before the fact
One who orders, counsels, encourages, or otherwise aids and abets another to commit a felony and who is not present at the commission of the offense.

accessory after the fact
A person who, knowing a felony to have been committed by another, receives, relieves, comforts, or assists the felon in order to enable him/her to escape from punishment, or the like.

Party	Criminal Act
Principal in the first degree	The person who personally performed the criminal act
Principal in the second degree	A person present at the commission of a crime who either helps, advises, commands, or encourages the principal in the first degree
Accessory before the fact	A person not present at the commission of a crime but who aids and abets the principal in the first degree prior to the commission of the actual crime
Accessory after the fact	A person not present at the commission of a crime but who offers assistance to the perpetrator of the crime after it has been committed

FIGURE 8.1
Comparison of the Different Levels of Accomplices in a Criminal Act

Party	Criminal Act
Principal	The person who actually commits the crime
Accomplice	A person who aids, counsels, or encourages the principal before, during, or after the crime
Accessory	A person who assists the principal in some manner knowing he/she is about commit to or has already committed a felony

accomplice
One who knowingly, voluntarily, and with common intent unites with the principal offender in the commission of a crime.

Under modern laws, all parties to a crime can be found guilty of the criminal offense. The designations of principals and accessories have given way to three designations: principal, **accomplice**, and accessory. The principal is the person who actually commits the crime. An accomplice is the person who aids, counsels, or encourages the principal before, during, or after the crime. The accessory assists the principal in some manner knowing that he/she is about to commit or has already committed a felony. It is important to be aware that the Model Penal Code and the jurisdictions that follow the Code do not actually use the terms *principal* and *accessory* to refer to criminal actors. The terms *person* and *actor* are used in their place but are parallel in their use. (See Figure 8.2.)

ACCOMPLICE

Any person who assists before or during the commission of a crime, even if he/she did not actually commit the crime, is sometimes referred to as an accomplice. The term *accomplice,* however, is not a formal legal term in all states. Several states consider the term to be legal slang. In jurisdictions that do recognize accomplice liability, the crime is very serious because the accomplice is tried for the same crime as the principal; however, accomplice liability only holds for acts of a principal in the first degree that are reasonably foreseeable. The U.S. Supreme Court has held that an accomplice cannot be executed for the capital crimes of a principal in the first degree when those capital crimes were not foreseeable. However, generally, an accomplice will have the same degree of guilt as the person he or she is assisting and also generally will face the same criminal penalty. Therefore, in the example above using Josh and Tony, if Josh is convicted of murdering Bill, then Tony will face the same charge.

The Model Penal Code defines an accomplice in section 2.06:

> 3. A person is an accomplice when she:
>   a. with the purpose of promoting or facilitating the commission of the crime,
>   (i) solicits another person to commit it, or
>   (ii) aids or agrees or attempts to aid such person in planning or committing it, or
>   (iii) having a legal duty to prevent the offense, fails to take reasonable efforts to do so, or
>   b. her conduct is expressly declared by law to establish her complicity.[1]

It is not enough for a person to be present at a crime in order to establish accomplice liability. The person must perform an actus reus for accomplice liability to attach. The actus reus for accomplice liability is that the person must aid, abet, encourage, or assist the perpetrator in some manner toward the commission of the crime. Since encouragement is one method by which accomplice liability can attach, the use of only words of encouragement could lead a person to be criminally liable for the crime as an accomplice.

The accomplice must intentionally aid or encourage the perpetrator of the criminal activity. Some jurisdictions require that the accomplice also must possess the mental

---

[1] Model Penal Code, copyright 1985 by the American Law Institute. Reprinted with permission.

state necessary for the crime that is committed by the perpetrator. When intentionally offering aid, the defendant must intend to commit the act that he/she is aiding and encouraging and the defendant must intend that his/her actions will help bring about the criminal activity of the perpetrator. For example, Martin wants to commit a bank robbery. Martin asks Ellen to purchase an AK47 for him. Ellen asks Martin why he needs the gun. Martin tells Ellen that he is going to rob a bank. Ellen gets the AK47 for Martin. Ellen knows that Martin intends to rob a bank, she aided by getting the AK47 for Martin, and she knew that her actions were likely to bring about a bank robbery by Martin. The actions of the accomplice must have the purpose of bringing about the crime such as Ellen's actions did in the example above.

There are times when the accomplice possesses the intent for a particular crime and aids the perpetrator in that crime, but the perpetrator commits a more heinous crime. Suppose that the perpetrator commits a murder as opposed to a bank robbery. The accomplice can be convicted of the more heinous crime even though he/she had no intent to aid or encourage that crime. In the above example, if Martin commits a murder, Ellen may be liable for that murder as an accomplice. It also is possible that the accomplice can be liable for a lesser crime and not be held responsible for the more heinous crime of the perpetrator because he/she did not possess the requisite mens rea for the more heinous crime.

Knowledge by a person that aiding and encouraging the perpetrator will lead the perpetrator to commit a particular crime, but the person does not intend for the crime to occur, typically will not subject that person to accomplice liability.

RESEARCH THIS

One of the most important and influential judges in American legal history was Judge Learned Hand. Many important judicial decisions in this country's history were ruled upon and written by Judge Hand. One of the best-known cases on accomplice liability is the case of *U.S. v. Peoni*, 100 F.2d 401 (2d Cir. 1938). In this case, Judge Hand's opinion expressed that knowledge without criminal intent is not sufficient for accomplice liability. Research the case of *U.S. v. Peoni* and determine why Judge Hand ruled in this manner.

If the defendant assists and encourages the perpetrator to commit a particular offense, but the perpetrator commits that crime as well as others, the defendant may be held accountable for the additional crimes under the theory of accomplice liability. The court will look to see if the additional crimes were probable or foreseeable. If the additional criminal acts were not probable or foreseeable, then the potential accomplice may not be liable for the perpetrator's additional crimes. For example, suppose Carson encouraged his friend Dick to beat up William in a fistfight. Unbeknownst to Carson, Dick had concealed a knife. During the fistfight, Dick takes out his knife and kills William. If William's death was not probable and foreseeable as a result of the criminal act, Carson will not be held liable as an accomplice to the murder. In *Carter v. Commonwealth,* 232 Va. 122 (1986), a defendant was held criminally responsible as an accomplice for shooting the victim of a robbery where the defendant was aware that a co-robber had a gun and the co-robber and the defendant had the common intent to use force against the victim to achieve the robbery. In this situation, the shooting was both a probable and a foreseeable consequence of the criminal act of robbery. At trial, the jury must be convinced beyond a reasonable doubt that the criminal act was a natural and probable consequence of the intended criminal act. The Model Penal Code states that an accomplice is only liable for the acts of a primary when the accomplice "acts with the kind of culpability, if any, with respect to that result that is sufficient for the commission of that offense."

At common law it used to be that the principal needed to be convicted before the accomplice could be convicted. Under modern law, this is not necessarily the case. There are times when the principal is not convicted of the crime, but the accomplice is. One situation in which this can occur is when the crime is committed, but the perpetrator is never caught. The accomplice can still be convicted for his/her part in aiding and encouraging the crime. In *United States v. Standefer*, 610 F.2d 1076 (3d Cir. 1979) (en banc), the court held that "neither fairness nor justice argue for allowing these aiders and abettors to escape responsibility for their criminal activity merely because their respective principals have escaped punishment." In *United States v. Campa*, 679 F.2d 1006 (1st Cir. 1982), the court held that that the principal need not even be identified to convict a defendant as an accomplice to the crime. However, an accomplice generally cannot be convicted of a criminal act under accomplice liability if the perpetrator did not possess the required mens rea for the crime.

An accomplice may change his/her mind and decide not to aid or encourage the perpetrator in their criminal act. He/she may decide to withdraw his/her assistance. In order for a person to avoid accomplice liability, it is not enough to simply have a change of heart and stop the aid or encouragement. The accomplice must clearly repudiate his/her aid and encouragement to the perpetrator. Sometimes a verbal withdrawal is sufficient. Other times, an act by the accomplice to rectify the situation is required. For instance, if the accomplice has furnished the perpetrator with weapons, then the accomplice must get the weapons back in order to withdraw his/her aid. Withdrawal also can be effectuated by warning law enforcement of the perpetrator's intent to commit the crime or by taking efforts to stop the perpetration of the crime. For example, the accomplice may warn an intended murder victim that he/she is in danger. However, it is not a requirement that the crime be stopped in order for an accomplice to withdraw.

ACCESSORY AFTER THE FACT

An accessory after the fact is a person who knowingly gives assistance to the perpetrator for the intention of helping the perpetrator avoid being apprehended by law enforcement. The elements for accessory are

* The accessory personally aided the person who committed the crime.
* The accessory knew that the crime was committed.
* The aid was given for the purpose of assisting the perpetrator in avoiding apprehension by authorities.
* The accessory did not actually commit the crime.

The Model Penal Code at section 242.3 deals with accessory as follows:

> 3. A person is an accessory if he, with the purpose to hinder the arrest or other legal process against a person:
> a. harbors or conceals the other, or
> b. provides aid or other means of avoiding arrest, or
> c. conceals or destroys evidence or other information, or
> d. warns the other party, or
> e. supplies false information to a police officer.[2]

In order for a person to be found criminally liable as an accessory, a crime has to have been committed. It is not enough that the accessory believes that a crime has been committed. The crime must actually have been committed. The accessory also must possess knowledge of the essential elements of the crime that was committed. The accessory also must personally have given the assistance to the perpetrator. Usually, the crime of accessory after the fact is a lesser crime than the one that was actually committed by the perpetrator.

PRACTICE TIP

Mario is the leader of a drug cartel. He has been pursued hotly by one particular drug enforcement officer who has dogged him repeatedly. Mario decides that he is going to kill the drug enforcement officer in order to be able to continue his drug operation without interference. One day, Mario ambushes the drug enforcement officer in broad daylight on a street corner where he is standing, shooting him repeatedly until he dies.

Mario makes his escape. In an attempt to avoid apprehension, Mario goes to the house of his girlfriend, Lucille. Mario tells Lucille what happened and asks her to hide him. Mario goes upstairs in Lucille's house to take a shower. While Mario is taking a shower, Lucille sees a news bulletin reporting the murder.

Lucille tells Mario that she knows how to get him out of the country. Lucille drives Mario to the border and arranges for a friend of hers to take Mario safely across the border in order to avoid apprehension. A month later, Mario is apprehended in Mexico and extradited back to the United States. Lucille is arrested as an accessory after the fact.

Remember, it's important to understand that most jurisdictions follow the modern interpretation of *principal, accomplice,* and *accessory after the fact.* Compared to the common law interpretation, *principal* and *accessory after the fact* remained the same. The modern interpretation combines the old common law parties of *principal in the second degree* and *accessory before the fact* into one modern element, that of *accomplice.*

SURF'S UP

In order to learn more about complicity, visit the following Web sites:

* www.judiciary.state.n.j.us/criminal
* www.law.cornell.edu
* www.kentlaw.edu
* www.lawspirit.com
* www.freedictionary.com
* www.answers.com
* www.quizlaw.com.

A DAY IN THE LIFE OF A REAL PARALEGAL

A paralegal must be aware that the law of every jurisdiction is not identical. For example, there is a split of authority as to whether or not a lesser mental state will be sufficient for accomplice liability. The majority of jurisdictions hold that an accomplice must intend that his/her acts have the effect of assisting or encouraging another. Other jurisdictions hold that mere knowledge that one is aiding a crime is enough for accomplice liability.

A DAY IN THE LIFE OF A REAL PARALEGAL

The law firm that Sarah joined this past year, as a criminal paralegal, has many clients that have been accused, in the past, of participating in crimes like extortion, murder, drug and gun running, and assault. Her firm was very successful many years ago in defending their clients and still has successes today but fewer than in the past. Sarah was given the job of researching the federal RICO statutes and cases that have been brought under those codes in the prosecuting of certain organized crime figures. Sarah's findings show that since the advent of RICO, the prosecution of organized crime figures has become more successful due to the codifying of complicity as found in those statutes. It's important to read RICO and understand the ramifications for defendants accused of complicity in RICO-like crimes.

CONSPIRACY

conspiracy
By agreement, parties work together to create an illegal result, to achieve an unlawful end.

The common law crime of **conspiracy** requires an agreement, between two or more persons, with the intent to commit a crime. Because conspiracy is a specific-intent crime, a successful prosecution must show both the agreement as well as the intent to commit the elements of a criminal offense. The element of "agreement" necessary to prove a criminal conspiracy may be proven by conduct. Conspirators are not required to evidence such agreement by spoken or written words. Modern statutes usually require that conspirators intend to commit a crime to be found guilty of conspiracy. At common law, a conspiracy only occurred after the parties *agreed* to commit a crime. If a crime is committed, it must be both in furtherance of the conspiracy and a reasonably foreseeable result of the conspiracy; then all conspirators may be liable for the crime regardless of which conspirator committed it. In *United States v. Brasco,* 516 F.2d 816 (2d Cir. 1975), it was held that a co-conspirator is bound by the acts done in the furtherance of a conspiracy whether or not he or she performed or was even aware of those acts.

Additionally, under the common law theory, husband and wife could not be found guilty of conspiracy if no third person was involved because husband and wife were viewed as one person. Under modern law, this theory has largely been disregarded and courts have held that a married couple in fact can be co-conspirators.

Summary

A principal in the first degree is the person who personally performs the criminal act. Every completed crime has at least one principal in the first degree.

The person who is present during the crime and aids and abets in its commission but does not personally commit the criminal act is known as a principal in the second degree.

An accessory before the fact is similar to a principal in the second degree. He/she does not commit the actual crime and he/she aids and abets the criminal. However, unlike the principal in the second degree, the accessory before the fact is not actually present at the crime, nor is he/she constructively present. An accessory before the fact can be involved in the crime by helping in the planning, purchasing the weapon, or offering some slight assistance such as finding out some type of information. The accessory before the fact completes his/her participation prior to the actual commission of the crime.

An accessory after the fact is also someone who does not actually participate in the crime. However, this person offers assistance to the perpetrator of the crime after it has been committed. The type of assistance that is typically provided is to enable the perpetrator to evade arrest for the crime.

Any person who assists before or during the commission of a crime, even if he/she did not actually commit the crime, will be prosecuted as an accomplice. Accomplice liability is very serious because the accomplice is tried for the same crime as the principal.

An accessory after the fact is a person who knowingly gives assistance to the perpetrator with the intention of helping the perpetrator avoid being apprehended by law enforcement. The elements for accessory are (1) the accessory personally aided the person who committed the crime, (2) the accessory knew that the crime was committed, (3) the aid was given for the purpose of assisting the perpetrator in avoiding apprehension by authorities, and (4) the accessory did not actually commit the crime.

The common law crime of conspiracy requires an agreement between two or more persons, with the intent to achieve an unlawful purpose. Modern laws tend to require that at least one of the conspirators commit some act in furtherance of the conspiracy.

Key Terms

Aid and abet
Complicity
Conspiracy
Accessory after the fact

Accessory before the fact
Accomplice
Principal in the first degree
Principal in the second degree

Review Questions

1. What is the reasoning behind complicity?
2. What is a principal in the first degree?
3. What is the difference between an accessory before the fact and an accomplice?
4. List six ways in which a person can aid and abet a perpetrator in a crime.
5. Give an example of a situation involving a principal in the second degree.
6. What is the difference between accomplice and accessory liability?
7. List four elements of accessory liability.
8. What constitutes a criminal act under accomplice liability?
9. When are words enough to be liable for accomplice liability?
10. Explain how an accomplice can withdraw from a situation so that he/she may avoid accomplice liability.
11. Explain the mens rea requirement for accessory after the fact.
12. List four ways in which an accessory after the fact can assist a perpetrator.
13. When can an accomplice be convicted of a lesser crime than the perpetrator?
14. What type of situation might occur that would enable an accomplice to avoid liability even though the perpetrator actually committed the crime?
15. How does the modern view of conspiracy differ from the common law view?

Exercises

1. Joan is persuaded by her friends to assist in the robbery of a local liquor store on a nearby corner. Joan accompanies her friends to the liquor store with the intent to rob the store. However, once in the neighborhood, Joan gets scared that

someone in the neighborhood might recognize her so she flees the scene prior to the crime's occurring. Is Joan guilty of a crime? If so, what is the crime? Explain your answer in detail.

2. Dan was an accomplished burglar, but he had not committed a burglary in six months. Fred, the fence to whom Dan sold most of his merchandise, was upset as one of his supply lines had become inactive. One day, Fred told Dan, "I think that your next hit should be on Spencer's house. I understand that he is going to be gone on vacation for two weeks and his wife has a lot of valuable jewelry." Dan took Fred's advice and burglarized Spencer's house, taking all of his wife's jewelry. Dan was arrested the next day based on an eye witness account to the crime. Can Fred be convicted of burglarizing Spencer's home? Give the reason for your answer.

3. Melissa and Brenda are college students who are desperate for money. One night, Melissa suggests that they hold up the local market. Brenda is afraid to commit the robbery. Melissa tells Brenda that she will commit the crime if Brenda waits in the getaway car with the engine running so that they can make a getaway after the robbery is completed. The next day, the two drive to a gun store and purchase a gun. About a week later, Brenda drives Melissa to the store that has been identified as their target. Melissa goes into the store, points the gun at the cashier, and makes the cashier give her all the money that is in her cash register. With the money in hand, Melissa runs out of the store. When Brenda sees Melissa running at her, she becomes scared and drives away. Brenda is guilty of
   a. Conspiracy only.
   b. Robbery only.
   c. Conspiracy and robbery.
   d. Either conspiracy or robbery, but not both.

4. Max helps Freddie with a plan to steal a car from Al's Autos. While committing the larceny, Max finds a homeless man sleeping in a car. He throws the man out of the car and then proceeds to kick him several times. Would Freddie be liable as an accomplice for battery? Why or why not?

5. Maggie knew that her sister Mindy despised Jessica. Maggie was concerned about what Mindy might do to Jessica but didn't say anything because she didn't want Mindy to get into trouble. One day Mindy sees Jessica crossing the street; she quickly accelerates and her car strikes Jessica. Jessica suffers serious bodily harm and later slips into a coma and dies from her injuries. Mindy is arrested for murder. Is Maggie liable for Jessica's death as an accomplice? Why or why not?

6. Tommy was an 18-year-old gang member who lived in Los Angeles. One day Tommy was walking down the street and saw Vince, who was a member of a rival gang. Tommy assaulted Vince, pushing him to the ground. Tommy struck Vince in the face, telling Vince that if he showed up on his turf again, the punishment would be much worse. Suddenly Nico, a member of Tommy's gang, appeared and asked Tommy what was going on. Nico then told Tommy that Vince shouldn't get away with being on their turf. Tommy then pulled out a knife and stabbed Vince, fatally wounding him. What crime is Nico guilty of and why?

 PORTFOLIO ASSIGNMENT

Research your state's statute on criminal *complicity* and see what the elements are for complicity crimes in your jurisdiction. How close do they follow the modern interpretation of principal, accomplice, and accessory after the fact?

Vocabulary Builders

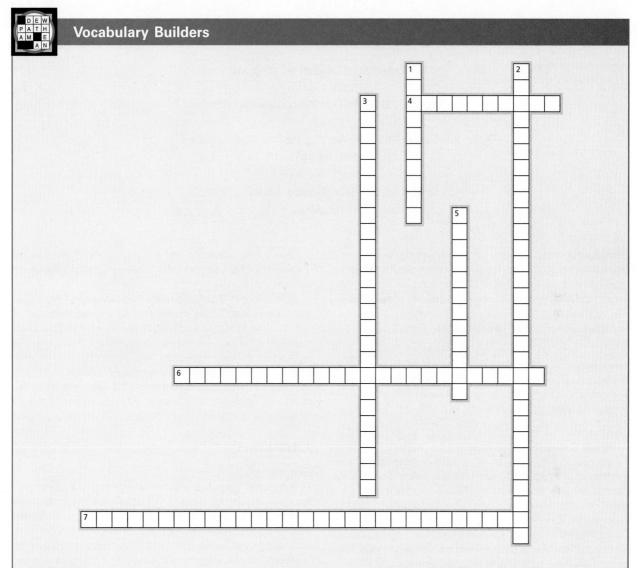

Instructions
Use the key terms from this chapter to fill in the answers to the crossword puzzle.
NOTE: When the answer is more than one word, leave a blank space between words.

ACROSS
4. a state of being an accomplice; participation in guilt.
6. a person who, knowing a felony to have been committed by another, receives, relieves, comforts, or assists the felon in order to enable him/her to escape from punishment, or the like.
7. the criminial actor; the one who actually commits the crime, either by his/her own hand, by an inanimate agency, or by an innocent human agent.

DOWN
1. one who knowingly, voluntarily, and with common intent unites with the principal offender in the commission of a crime.
3. the one who is present at the commission of a criminal offense and aids, counsels, commands, or encourages the principal in the first degree in the commision of that offense.
4. one who orders, counsels, encourages, or otherwise aids and abets another to commit a felony and who is not present at the commission of the offense.
5. help, assist, or facilitate the commission of a crime; promote the accomplishment thereof; help in advancing or bringing it about; or encourage, counsel, or incite as to its commission.

United States Court of Appeals,
Sixth Circuit.
Kelvin THOMPSON Petitioner-Appellant,

v.

Khelleh KONTEH, Warden Respondent-Appellee.
No. 04-3631.
March 14, 2006.
Rehearing En Banc Denied June 22, 2006.
170 Fed. Appx. 945

Background: After his state court aggravated murder conviction was upheld on direct appeal, petitioner sought federal habeas relief. The United States District Court for the Northern District of Ohio denied petition, and certificate of appeal ability was granted.

Holdings: The Court of Appeals, Rose, District Judge, held that:

1. jury instruction on complicity did not amount to instruction of conspiracy that permitted conviction for aggravated murder without proof of required mental state, and
2. jury instructions required unanimity.

Affirmed.

ROSE, District Judge.

On February 4, 1994, an Ohio state jury convicted Kelvin Thompson of aggravated murder with a firearm specification. Thompson was sentenced to life imprisonment plus three years of consecutive incarceration. Following unsuccessful appeals to the Ohio Court of Appeals and the Ohio Supreme Court, Thompson sought a writ of habeas corpus in federal district court. The district court denied the petition in its entirety and did not issue a certificate of appeal ability.

Thompson then sought a certificate of appeal ability from this Court. This Court granted a certificate of appeal ability only on the issue of whether Thompson was denied the effective assistance of trial counsel. For the following reasons, we affirm the district court and deny Thompson's petition for a writ of habeas corpus.

I. BACKGROUND

In 1993, Thompson, Wilbert Houston, and Lance Carter were indicted on one count of Aggravated Murder for the murder of Junius Chaney. They each pled not guilty and proceeded to trial together. Carter pled guilty midway through the trial and testified against Thompson and Houston. Thompson was found guilty and sentenced to life in prison for aggravated murder and to three years on a firearm specification.

Evidence was presented at trial that Houston shot Chaney with a shotgun provided by Thompson. Evidence was also presented that Thompson, who was on probation for drug trafficking and was concerned about drug trafficking in the area, was heard to say, "I'm goin' mess around and kill me a nigger tonight."

Thompson's conviction and sentence were affirmed by the Ohio Court of Appeals. The Ohio Supreme Court did not accept the case for review.

In this appeal, Thompson raises two arguments. He argues that the jury instructions are unconstitutional because they allowed him to be convicted of aggravated murder without proof that he had the requisite culpable mental state. Thompson also argues that the jury instructions are unconstitutional because the jury was not properly instructed to agree unanimously upon one theory in order to convict, and two theories were presented to the jury. According to Thompson, instructions regarding both conspiracy and aggravated murder were presented to the jury.

II. ANALYSIS

[Text omitted]

Thompson raises two arguments regarding the jury instructions. He argues that the jury instructions are unconstitutional because they allowed him to be convicted of aggravated murder without proof that he had the requisite culpable mental state. According to Thompson, the court did not require proof of the necessary mental state because the jury instructions allowed him to be convicted of conspiracy which does not require proof of the mental state that is required for aggravated murder.

Thompson also argues that the jury instructions are unconstitutional because the jury was not properly instructed to agree unanimously upon one theory in order to convict and two theories were presented to the jury. According to Thompson, instructions regarding both conspiracy and aggravated murder were presented to the jury.

In this case, then, we must examine the challenged jury instructions and determine if the government was required to prove every element of aggravated murder, the charge of which Thompson was found guilty. We must also determine if there is a reasonable likelihood that the jury applied the jury instructions in a way that did not require the government to prove every element of the offense with which Thompson was charged and found guilty.

The jury instructions that are relevant to the issues here are as follows:

[Text omitted]

> Complicity. Now you have heard testimony from Lance Carter, another person who pled guilty to this crime, who was said to have been an accomplice.

The testimony of an accomplice does not become inadmissible because of his complicity, moral turpitude or self interest, but the admitted or claimed complicity of a witness may correct his credibility and make his testimony subject to grave suspicion and required that it be weighed with great caution.

It is for you as jurors in light of all the facts presented to you from the witness stand to evaluate such testimony and determine its quality and worth or its lack of quality.

An accomplice is one who purposely knowingly assists and joins another person in the commission of a crime.

Now aider and abetter. The defendant, Mr. Thompson, is charged as an aider and abetter under the complicity statute. Aiding and abetting is when two or more persons have a common person[sic] to commit a crime and when one does one part and the other performs the other part.

As to aider and better[sic], only the mere fact that a person is present when a criminal act is committed does not make him an aider and abetter, unless he does some substantial overt act in furtherance of the crime charged in the indictment.

Now aid. Aid means to help, assist or strengthen.

Abet means to encourage, counsel, incite or assist.

Overt act. Overt act means any conduct when it is of such character as to manifest a purpose on the part of the actor that the crime charged be committed.

Purpose. A person acts purposely when it is his specific intent to cause a certain result. Purpose is a decision of the mind to do an act with a conscious objective of producing a specific result. To do an act purposely is to do it intentionally and not accidentally. Purpose and intent mean the same thing. The purpose which a person does an act is known only to himself unless he expresses it to others or indicates it by his conduct. . . .

A person who purposely aids and abets or assists another person in the commission of a crime is just as guilty as if he personally performed every act constituting the crime.

Complicity. Complicity in law means that a person purposely either solicited or procured another to commit such criminal offense and/or purposely aided and abetted another or others in the commission of such criminal offense and/or conspired with another to commit an offense.

Solicit means to seek, to ask, to influence, to invite, to attempt, to lead on, to bring pressure to bear.

Procured. Procure means to get, obtain, adduce, bring about, motivate.

Aided and abetted. These terms have been previously defined and the same definitions apply.

Substantial overt act. A person cannot be convicted of a criminal act by conspiring to commit such crime unless a substantial overt act in furtherance of the conspiracy is proved to have been done by him and that such act was performed subsequent to, after that[sic], the defendant's entrance into the conspiracy.

An overt act is substantial when it is of such character as to manifest a purpose on the part of the actor that the object of the conspiracy would be completed. Depending upon your factual findings the law on aider and abetter may be applicable to the crime charged.

If you determine that the defendant acted in concert with others, then you shall refer to this instruction on aiding and abetting as I reviewed the elements of the crime charged.

[Text omitted]

Having set forth the relevant jury instructions, the analysis turns to Thompson's arguments. Thompson first argues that the jury instructions allowed him to be convicted for entering into a conspiracy and for aggravated murder and that the jury was not required to unanimously agree to one or the other. However, the jury was not instructed on a conspiracy charge. The jury was instructed on the charge of complicity.

Thompson also argues that the jury was instructed that he could be convicted of complicity if he "conspired with another to commit an offense" and that this is a charge of conspiracy. However, it is not. The instruction given specifically refers to being convicted of complicity and is taken from the Ohio Jury Instructions regarding complicity.

Therefore, the jury was not, as Thompson argues, given instructions on both conspiracy and aggravated murder. Only an instruction on complicity was given and there are not varying forms of complicity as argued by Thompson.

Under Ohio law, a court may instruct the jury on complicity even though the defendant was charged as a principal. *O'Neal v. Morris*, 3 F.3d 143, 145 (6th Cir. 1993), *rev'd on other grounds, O'Neal v. McAninch*, 513 U.S. 432, 115 S. Ct. 992, 130 L. Ed. 2d 947 (1995). The penalty for complicity is punishment as if the defendant were a principal offender of the offense charged. Ohio Rev. Code § 2923.03(F).

However, charging a defendant with complicity as an aider and abetter does not alter the government's responsibility to establish the culpability required for commission of the principal offense. *O'Neal*, 3 F.3d at 145. Specifically, under Ohio law, purpose to kill must be proven by the government in situations where a defendant is charged as an aider and abetter to the crime of aggravated murder. *Clark v. Jago*, 676 F.2d 1099, 1102 (6th Cir. 1982), *cert. denied*, 466 U.S. 977, 104 S. Ct. 2360, 80 L. Ed. 2d 832 (1984).

In this case, before instructing on aggravated murder, the judge instructed on complicity. The first complicity instruction was with regard to the testimony of Lance Carter, who pled guilty midway through the trial and testified against Thompson. The jury instructions then indicated that Thompson was charged as an aider and abetter under the complicity statute.

. . . Specifically, the jury instructions regarding complicity provide that aiding and abetting occurs when two or more persons have a common purpose to commit a crime and when one does one part and the other performs the other part.

Following the complicity instruction, the judge indicated that, "If you determine that the defendant acted in concert with others, then you shall refer to this instruction on aiding and abetting as I reviewed the elements of the crime charged." He then reviewed the elements aggravated murder. The issue is whether a reasonable juror could have interpreted these instructions to mean that Thompson could be guilty of aggravated murder, the crime charged, without the state proving that he had the requisite mental state for aggravated murder. The answer is "no."

The jury was first instructed regarding the credibility of the testimony of Lance Carter as an accomplice. The jury was then instructed as to the meaning of the complicity statute and specifically the meaning of an aider and abetter under the complicity statute. The jury instructions are clear that aiding and abetting is not a crime unto itself but is when two or more persons have a common purpose to commit a crime.

The instructions then provide that a person who purposely aids and abets or assists another person in the commission of a crime is just as guilty as if he personally performed the act constituting the crime. This instruction, taken alone, could cause some confusion. However, there is no confusion when this instruction is considered within the context of all of the instructions given.

[Text omitted]

. . . In *Laird v. Horn*, the Third Circuit affirmed the district court's grant of a writ of habeas corpus on the basis that Laird was denied due process because the jury was not required to find a specific intent in order to convict him for accomplice liability. 414 F.3d 419 (3d Cir. 2005). However, *Laird* is factually distinguishable from this case.

In *Laird*, the jury was instructed on accomplice liability as set forth in Pennsylvania law and then was instructed on first-degree murder. *Id.* at 422–23. Since Pennsylvania's accomplice liability is similar to Ohio's complicity liability, the order of instructions in this case is similar to the order in which the instructions were given in *Laird*. However, this is where the similarity ends.

The accomplice-liability charge in *Laird* concluded with the instruction that, "you may find the defendant guilty of a particular crime on the theory that he was an accomplice so long as you are satisfied beyond a reasonable doubt that the crime was committed and the defendant was an accomplice of the person who committed it." *Id.* Here, no such instruction was given. Here the jury instructions require that the aider and abetter has a common purpose to commit a crime and that Thompson must have committed the elements of aggravated murder, the crime charged, to be found guilty.

The instruction on intent with regard to first-degree murder in *Laird* was given in the context of a charge on a diminished-capacity defense to first-degree murder. *Id.* at 427–28. In this case, there is no record of a diminished-capacity defense. In this case, the instruction on intent was clearly given as part of the aggravated murder instruction.

In *Laird*, the court had no way to know which of the two "irreconcilable" instructions the jurors applied in reaching their verdict of first-degree murder. *Id.* at 428. In this case, the instructions are not irreconcilable. The aiding and abetting instruction ends with the statement that the jury is to refer to the aiding and abetting instruction as the elements of aggravated murder are reviewed, and aggravated murder is the crime charged.

Further, the jury in this case was not given the option of findings other than guilty or not guilty of aggravated murder, and they clearly found aggravated murder. In the case of *Laird*, kidnaping, aggravated assault, false imprisonment, unlawful arrest and second and third degree murder were also charged and the jury could have found accomplice liability for either or any of those charges. *Id.* at 422.

III. CONCLUSION

Thompson has failed to establish that the jury instructions are unconstitutional. His ineffective assistance of counsel claim must, therefore, fail. The district court's denial of Thompson's petition for a writ of habeas corpus due to ineffective assistance of counsel is affirmed.

Source: 170 Fed. Appx. 945. Reprinted with permission from Westlaw.

Chapter 9

Inchoate Crimes

CHAPTER OBJECTIVES

Upon completion of this chapter, you will be able to:

- Discuss the theory of punishment for inchoate crimes.
- Explain the crime of attempt.
- Understand the crime of solicitation.
- Identify the elements of the crime of conspiracy.

Most people can identify most crimes. One person kills another and it is a crime. Someone robs a bank and it is a crime. A woman is raped and it is a crime. However, the law recognizes that criminal liability can exist when a crime has been attempted but not completed. An attempted but incomplete crime is called an **inchoate crime**. Inchoate is pronounced *in-koh-it*. This chapter will discuss the inchoate crimes.

inchoate crime
An incipient crime; an act that generally leads to a crime.

INCOMPLETE CRIMES

Inchoate crimes are crimes that were never completed. A criminal's failed efforts to complete a crime do not excuse the criminal behavior or provide a defense to criminal liability. Inchoate crimes are considered to be dangerous conduct that should be prohibited, punished, and deterred before harm can ensue. Inchoate crimes also are known as anticipatory, incomplete, incipient, preliminary, and preparatory crimes. The word "inchoate" comes from the Latin word that means "to begin." It also has the meanings of underdeveloped and unripened. An inchoate crime goes beyond the mere thought of the crime but stops short of the completion of the crime.

The purpose of the identification and punishment of inchoate crimes is to prevent a defendant from committing the substantive crime that is the intention of the preparatory action. Due to society's need to prevent crimes before they actually occur, statutes were created that determined what preparatory actions committed by a defendant constituted an anticipatory crime. If the preparatory actions are punished, the commission of the criminal offense can be prevented. To leave anticipatory criminal actions unpunished would lead to an injustice to society.

Three distinct inchoate crimes were defined under common law and are still valid today. Those crimes are

- Attempt;
- Conspiracy; and
- Solicitation.

There are three elements connected with inchoate crimes:

- A specific intent or purpose to commit the crime or to cause harm must be present;
- Some action must have occurred in furtherance of that intent or purpose; and
- Lesser penalties should typically be charged for inchoate crimes.

ATTEMPT

attempt
To actually try to commit a crime and have the actual ability to do so.

One of the most familiar inchoate crimes is that of **attempt**. Attempt is, in many ways, a failure of a crime. A criminal attempt occurs when a defendant intends to commit a criminal offense and performs a substantial step toward the commission of the crime and the crime is not completed. The Model Penal Code, section 5.01, defines the crime of attempt as follows:

1. *Definition of Attempt. A person is guilty of attempt if he:*
   a. *purposely engages in conduct that would constitute the crime if the attendant circumstances were as he believes them to be; or*
   b. *when causing a particular result is an element of the crime, he does or omits to do anything with the purpose of causing or with the belief that it will cause such result without further conduct on his part; or*
   c. *purposely does or omits to do anything that, under the circumstances as he believes them to be, is an act or omission constituting a substantial step in a course of conduct planned to culminate in his commission of the crime.[1]*

The elements of a criminal attempt are

- An intent or purpose to commit a specific crime;
- An act or acts taken to carry out the intent to commit the crime; and
- Failure to complete the crime.

History has recognized the need to punish a person who attempts to commit a crime. Suppose that John tries to kill Sally but fails in his attempt. John is obviously a dangerous person and it would be desirable to punish such actions; otherwise John may try again to kill Sally and might succeed.

Mens Rea of Attempt

As was discussed in Chapter 2, every criminal action has a mens rea and an actus reus. In the crime of attempt, the mens rea is the intent or purpose to commit a specific crime. In the example of John above, he possessed the intent to kill Sally. His intent to kill Sally is the mens rea of the crime of attempt. The intent must be to commit a specific criminal activity. Attempt is a specific-intent crime even if the offense that is attempted is a general-intent crime. It is not enough that a person intends to commit some unspecified crime; if that is the case, then the necessary mens rea does not exist. In order to fulfill the mens rea requirement for the crime of attempt, the person must intend to commit a specific crime and have the intent necessary to commit a substantive act in furtherance of that specific crime. In other words, a person cannot be guilty of the crime of attempt unless his/her actions are in furtherance of the specific crime and are committed with the specific purpose of causing the unlawful result.

Actus Reus of Attempt

Perhaps the most difficult question in an attempt case is when does the defendant cross the line between mere preparation and the actual attempt. The defendant must take some action that is in substantial furtherance of committing the crime. For example, Tony decides that he is going to rob a bank. He goes out and buys a handgun, but he never takes

---

[1] Model Penal Code, copyright 1985 by the American Law Institute. Reprinted with permission.

any other steps toward the robbing of the bank. Tony's actions would be considered preparation. However, suppose that Tony bought the gun, specified a target bank, formulated a plan, went to the bank with the handgun, and was stopped by the security guard. Tony's actions would have moved beyond mere preparation into attempt.

Various courts and statutes have established certain tests in order to determine when a defendant's actions cross the line between mere preparation and substantial furtherance. The four main tests that are used in most jurisdictions are

- Physical proximity test.
- Probable desistance test.
- Equivocality test.
- Substantial step test.

The physical proximity test involves how close the defendant came to completing the crime. This does not mean that the defendant must have completed every act necessary to commit the crime. The courts will examine the actions of the defendant to determine what actions still needed to be taken in order for the defendant to have completed the crime. The closer the defendant was to successfully completing the crime, the more likely it is that he/she crossed the line between preparation and substantial furtherance. Courts will sometimes use what is considered the last act by the defendant. The court will focus on the remaining acts necessary by the defendant in order to commit the crime. In the example of Tony, all that stopped Tony from robbing the bank was the security guard. Tony was only one act away from committing the crime. His actions would satisfy the physical proximity test.

In addition to the last act, courts also will look to see if the defendant had achieved a dangerous proximity to success. For example, suppose that John decided to slowly kill Sally by poisoning her. If the court waited for the last act by John in order to find attempt, then Sally would be dead because the last act would be the final dose of poisoning. Therefore, the courts will look to see how dangerously close the defendant was to achieving success. Once John administered the first dose of poisoning, he would have committed enough of an action to be charged with the crime of attempt under the physical proximity test.

Another test, the probable desistance test, examines the defendant's conduct to see if it meets the requirement that the conduct has gone beyond the point at which the defendant would voluntarily, on his/her own without any interference from an outside source, stop short of completing the crime. It is no longer probable that the defendant would **desist** once he/she has met the act requirements of this test. In the example of John poisoning Sally, John's actions of administering the first dose of poisoning have gone beyond the point at which he would voluntarily have desisted. At this point, interference from an outside source would be necessary to stop the commission of the killing.

desist
To cease an activity.

The physical proximity test and the probable desistance test both examine the defendant's action in order to determine how close he/she came to succeeding with the crime. The equivocality test is different in that it examines the defendant's conduct in order to determine if the conduct unequivocally manifested the defendant's criminal intent. The test examines whether the conduct has no other purpose than a commission of the crime. If the conduct could be indicative of a noncriminal intent as well as of a criminal intent, then the conduct is not sufficient under this test. In the example of John's poisoning Sally, if John had obtained some obscure type of poison that is not used by ordinary people for other noncriminal purposes such as rat poison might be, the action by John of simply obtaining the obscure poison would be considered as manifesting his criminal intent under the equivocality test as there could be no other purpose for the use of the poison. Under this test, a confession to the police is not considered conduct that manifests the defendant's criminal intent.

The Model Penal Code incorporates elements of both the physical proximity test and the equivocality test and utilizes what is known as the substantial step test. The Model Penal Code, section 5.01, states:

> 2. *Conduct That May Be Held Substantial Step Under Subsection (1)(c).* Conduct that may be a substantial step under Subsection (1)(c) must be strongly corroborative of the defendant's criminal purpose. Each of the following acts may be considered a substantial step as a matter of law:
> a. *lying in wait, searching for, or following the victim,*
> b. *enticing or seeking to entice the victim to go to the place where the crime is to be committed,*
> c. *reconnoitering the place where the crime is to occur,*
> d. *unlawfully entering a structure, vehicle, or enclosure that is the contemplated scene of the crime,*
> e. *possessing materials to be used in a crime that were designed for the crime or that under the circumstances serve no lawful purpose,*
> f. *possessing, collecting, or fabricating material to be used in the commission of a crime at or near the scene of the crime, where such possession, collection, or fabrication serves no lawful purpose, and*
> g. *soliciting an innocent agent to engage in conduct constituting an element of the crime.*[2]

The substantial step test states that a defendant's act or omission to act constitutes a substantial step if the course of conduct planned by the defendant would lead to the defendant's commission of the crime. The Model Penal Code approach also looks for corroborating evidence in the form of conduct that tends to confirm or verify the criminal intent possessed by the defendant. Most states have adopted some version of the Model Penal Code into their statutes.

Failure to Complete the Crime

The courts will look at the reasons why the crime failed in determining whether or not this element is present. If the crime failed because of the interference of an outside source, then the defendant's acts probably constitute an attempt. However, there are some cases in which the reasons the crime of attempt failed can remove liability or lessen the punishment that the defendant might face.

Sometimes the defendant can take every action necessary to commit a crime, but, due to external circumstances, he/she is unable to complete the crime. There are two types of impossibility: legal and factual.

Legal Impossibility

Legal impossibility is a defense to attempt because a person cannot be guilty of attempting an action that is not a crime. It does not matter if the defendant believes that the actions he/she is taking are a crime or if he/she misunderstands the law. For example, a man may intend to steal the wallet of an unsuspecting victim out of her purse, but once he reaches into the purse, he realizes that nothing is inside the purse. It is not illegal to steal from an empty purse. However, most jurisdictions no longer recognize pure legal impossibility as a defense to the crime of attempt. For example, a thief broke into a jewelry store and stole a watch. Unbeknownst to him, the watch was actually his. His wife had purchased the watch for him earlier that day and had left it to be engraved. The traditional approach would say that the thief could defend a charge of larceny because it is legally impossible to steal one's own property. The modern approach punishes defendants for their mens rea rather than for the target crime. This approach basically eliminates the defense of legal impossibility.

Factual Impossibility

Factual impossibility occurs when the defendant is mistaken about an issue of fact. If the defendant had not been mistaken, he/she would have known that the attempted crime

---

[2] Model Penal Code, copyright 1985 by the American Law Institute. Reprinted with permission.

had no possibility of being successful. Factual impossibility is not a defense to the crime of attempt except in Minnesota. For example, John intends to poison Sally, but instead of purchasing poison, he purchases sugar in order to accomplish the task. The method is not one that would be considered adequate by most people unless Sally was a severe diabetic. The reason that factual impossibility is not a defense is that if the facts had been as the defendant believed them to be, then a crime would have occurred.

For example, suppose Todd decides to shoot Muncy. Todd picks up a gun from a drawer in Muncy's home, points it at Muncy, and pulls the trigger. The gun is not loaded, so no killing occurred. Todd was mistaken as to the fact that he believed the gun was loaded. However, had the gun been loaded, Todd would have shot Muncy and either killed or injured him. Todd exhibited dangerous behavior for which a punishment needs to be issued.

RESEARCH THIS

The law can be very different from one jurisdiction to another. It is very important to know the law in your jurisdiction. As stated above, factual impossibility is recognized in Minnesota under certain circumstances. Research the law in Minnesota as to factual impossibility being a defense to attempt. If you were in this jurisdiction, what are the circumstances in which factual impossibility might be used as a defense to the crime of attempt?

Renunciation

Suppose a defendant has intent or purpose, takes a substantial step toward the completion of the crime, but changes his/her mind and abandons his/her plan to commit the crime. This is known as **renunciation**. In order for the defense of abandonment or renunciation to succeed, the defendant must demonstrate that he/she abandoned the crime for moral reasons and not just because he/she thought the crime would be thwarted. Common law is not decisive on whether withdrawal or abandonment relieves a defendant of liability. The Model Penal Code, section 5.01(4), states that a person is not guilty of the crime of attempt if he:

renunciation
Abandonment of effort to commit a crime.

1. *abandons his effort to commit the crime or prevents it from being committed; and*

2. *his conduct manifests a complete and voluntary renunciation of his criminal purpose.[3]*

CONSPIRACY

A **conspiracy** may be found where no substantive crime has been committed. The crime is thwarted before any criminal act can take place. Therefore, conspiracy is considered an inchoate crime. A conspiracy is the only inchoate crime that a person can be charged with in addition to the substantive crime. For example, a person can be charged with murder and, if more than one person is involved, conspiracy to commit murder.

conspiracy
By agreement, parties work together to create an illegal result, to achieve an unlawful end.

The legal theory behind the law of conspiracy is that people working together can be more dangerous than people working alone because they can support and encourage each other in their criminal endeavor. Conspiracy is typically a crime that occurs in secrecy. The conspirators hatch a plan and try to bring it to fruition before it is discovered and thwarted by others. It is to the benefit of society that such dangerous and secret acts be punished no matter whether or not the actual crime was ever committed.

The elements of a conspiracy are as follows:

- An agreement between two or more persons to commit the crime.
- A specific intent or purpose to commit the crime.
- An **overt act** in furtherance of the agreement.

overt act
Identifiable commission or omission, an intentional tort requirement.

---

[3] Model Penal Code, copyright 1985 by the American Law Institute. Reprinted with permission.

The Model Penal Code at section 5.03 defines conspiracy as follows:

1. A person is guilty of conspiracy if he:
   a. enters into an agreement with another person,
      i. to engage in criminal conduct or attempts or solicits another to commit a crime, or
      ii. agrees to aid such person in planning or committing a crime or an attempt or solicitation of such crime . . .[4]

The fundamental nature of a conspiracy is the agreement between two or more persons. The agreement does not have to be in writing; usually it is not. It can be inferred from the circumstances. Also, it is not necessary for all of the conspirators to have knowledge of every detail of the act. If the participants are aware of the essential nature of the crime, it is a conspiracy. For example, a person who is driving the getaway car in a bank robbery may not know all of the details of the planned robbery, but he/she will know that the bank robbery is going to occur and has agreed to assist. The Model Penal Code as stated above recognizes four types of agreements that can be considered conspiratorial:

- An agreement to commit an offense.

- An agreement to attempt to commit an offense.

- An agreement to solicit someone else to commit an offense.

- An agreement to aid another person in the planning or commission of the offense.

A prosecutor in a conspiracy case merely has to present evidence to suggest that one of the above circumstances has occurred and then let the judge or jury determine whether or not the conspiracy existed. The evidence can be, and usually is, circumstantial. Typically, if a prosecutor can submit enough evidence to demonstrate that at least one of the conspirators has the intent to commit the substantive offense, a conspiracy will be found to have existed. The bar for proving the existence of a conspiracy is not as high as the one used to prove an attempted crime.

The intent requirement of conspiracy can take on two forms: the unilateral or the bilateral (or plurality) approach. In the **unilateral** approach, the specific intent necessary to commit the crime must be found to have existed on the part of at least one of the conspirators. In every conspiratorial agreement, at least one of the conspirators must have demonstrated an intent to bring about the criminal result. The Model Penal Code specifically states that the agreement must have been developed "with the purpose of promoting or facilitating" the commission of the actual crime. The Model Penal Code supports the unilateral approach. In the **bilateral** or plurality approach, at least two or more persons must have possessed the requisite intent or purpose to commit the crime in order to find that a conspiracy existed.

In addition to the unilateral and bilateral approaches, there is a third approach, known as Wharton's rule. **Wharton's rule** states that a conspiracy needs to have at least three people involved in order to be considered a conspiracy. Therefore, crimes such as dueling, adultery, incest, or bigamy that require only two persons cannot be charged as conspiratorial crimes. For example, If White Knight and Black Knight engage in a duel, they are guilty of dueling but not of conspiracy to duel.

At common law, there was no requirement that the partners to a conspiracy commit an overt act toward the commission of the crime. However, most statutes now have an element that requires proof of the commission of an overt act in furtherance of the conspiracy in order to prove that a conspiracy existed among the potential partners. The federal rule in most circumstances requires an overt act. The general reason for requiring an overt act toward the conspiracy is to verify that there was a realistic intent by the conspirators to complete the crime. The Model Penal Code requires an overt act only to more serious crimes. An overt act can be considered to be any action that is taken in

unilateral
One-sided; relating to only one of two or more persons or things.

bilateral
Affecting or obligating both parties.

Wharton's rule
The doctrine that an agreement by two or more persons to commit a particular crime cannot be prosecuted as a conspiracy if the crime could not be committed except by the actual number of participants involved.

---

[4] Model Penal Code, copyright 1985 by the American Law Institute. Reprinted with permission.

A DAY IN THE LIFE OF A REAL PARALEGAL

Your boss, *the head partner of the firm*, Mr. Moneyshoes, comes to you one day and says he has been invited to speak at the town's new law school, ABCs of LAW, on the topic of conspiracy. He tells you that he got "corralled" into it by his wife, Ms. Solicitation Sally, the main board member at the school. Your assignment is to come up with three very distinct reasons as to why conspiracies rarely work. Look back at the elements of the crime to help you form the answers.

furtherance of the conspiracy and not necessarily the commission of the crime, although sometimes the act could be the same for both. Typically, only one defendant needs to demonstrate the overt act for a conspiracy to be found to have existed. Acts of mere preparation will suffice as overt acts when dealing with a charge of conspiracy. For example, if the conspirators were planning a bank robbery, the purchase of a gun by one of the conspirators would be considered an overt act that establishes the conspiracy.

Parties to a Conspiracy

In a conspiracy, every person involved in the conspiracy is liable for every offense committed by every other person who is a party to the conspiracy. Using the example of the commission of a bank robbery, suppose that during the commission of the robbery, a security guard is shot and killed by one of the conspirators. At that point, each conspirator can be charged with the homicide as well as the robbery and conspiracy.

In addition, as stated above, only one conspirator need commit an overt act in furtherance of the conspiracy in order for that action to be attributed to the group. Conspiracies that involve multiple parties can be characterized as either a wheel or a chain conspiracy. A **wheel conspiracy** applies to an agreement in which there is a ringleader or central person who deals with each of the other parties in the conspiracy, but the other parties don't deal with each other. The ringleader is thought of as the hub and the other conspirators are the spokes of the wheel. The co-conspirators do not have contact or deal with each other, but only with the ringleader or hub. A shared criminal intent exists among all the parties to the conspiracy.

> **wheel conspiracy**
> A conspiracy in which a single member or group separately agrees with two or more other members or groups.

In a **chain conspiracy**, there is a sequence of events or links that have to be successfully performed within the agreement. In a chain conspiracy theory, the participants do not always know or deal with each other. An example of a chain conspiracy could involve the distribution of illegal drugs into the country. In order for the drugs to reach the consumer, a series of actions must take place among the suppliers, distributors, and sellers of the illegal substance before it reaches the consumer. If the conspiracy is discovered, all parties would be guilty of it based on their intent and actions in the chain that led to the ultimate sale.

> **chain conspiracy**
> A single conspiracy in which each person is responsible for a distinct act within the overall plan.

Defenses

Certain defenses are applicable to the crime of conspiracy. For example, as stated above, Wharton's rule may require that three people be involved in the agreement in order for a conspiracy to exist. The specific law for the jurisdiction may not provide for a charge of conspiracy if it would inhibit the prosecution of the substantive crime. If an individual conspirator drops out of the plan, he/she may avoid being charged

A DAY IN THE LIFE OF A REAL PARALEGAL

One of a paralegal's most important responsibilities is legal research. Research your home state's and the federal definitions of conspiracy and then compare those definitions to the Model Penal Code's definition. A good paralegal is aware that there may be more than one applicable definition.

EYE ON ETHICS

Remember that ethics are a very important element of being a legal assistant, especially in areas of criminal defense. Your potential client may reveal facts to you about his/her case in the course of your attorney's representation of him/her. Those facts could be very incriminating. It is important that you, as a legal assistant, hold those facts in confidence. Every person is entitled to a defense, whether he/she is guilty of the offense or not. It is the attorney's job to provide that defense. It is unethical for you to breach that confidence. Such a breach can jeopardize not only the case but also the license of your supervising attorney. It is always important to keep in mind that, as a legal assistant, you are an extension of the attorney who is your supervisor.

with a conspiracy if he/she communicates his/her withdrawal from the plan to each co-conspirator. Also, he/she will be considered to have withdrawn from the conspiracy if he/she notifies the police of the plan.

SOLICITATION

solicitation
The crime of inducing or encouraging another to commit a crime.

The last major inchoate crime that will be discussed in this chapter is **solicitation**. The elements for the crime of solicitation are

- The intent that another party commit the crime and
- Asking, encouraging, or requesting another party to commit a crime.

In simple terms, a solicitation occurs when someone asks someone else to commit a crime for him/her. The person who is being asked does not have to agree to commit the crime in order for the solicitation to have occurred (see Figure 9.1).

The intent required for a solicitation to occur is not the intent to commit the crime but rather the intent to have someone else commit the crime. The defendant must have intended to induce or encourage someone else to commit the specific crime. The mere utterances of words without the specific intent do not constitute a solicitation, even if the crime is committed. For example, if John jokingly says to Muncy that John wished that someone would kill Sally, and Muncy kills Sally, John may not have been guilty of solicitation because he was only joking and did not have any intent to have Sally killed.

Under Model Penal Code, section 5.02, a person is guilty of solicitation if

1. *his purpose is to promote or facilitate the commission of a substantive offense; and*
2. *with such purpose, he commands, encourages, or requests another person to engage in conduct which would constitute the crime, or attempted commission.*[5]

inducement
The act or process of enticing or persuading another person to take a certain course of action.

The specific actus reus required for the crime of solicitation involves words. Words that create an **inducement** for another person to commit the crime are the act committed by the defendant. Those words must command, counsel, encourage, entice,

FIGURE 9.1
Inchoate Crimes: Solicitation and Conspiracy

Solicitation	Conspiracy
Defendant entices, advises, encourages, orders, or requests another to commit a crime.	The crime consists of an agreement between two or more persons to commit a crime and the intent to achieve the criminal objective.
The crime solicited need not be committed.	The agreement is the "essence" of the crime.
The crime requires no agreement or action by the person solicited.	The crime does not require a substantial step in the commission of the crime.

---

[5] Model Penal Code, copyright 1985 by the American Law Institute. Reprinted with permission.

CASE FACT PATTERN

The strange story of Wanda Holloway, a seemingly typical suburban mom from Texas, provides a startling example of the crime of solicitation. Obsessed with the idea of her daughter Shanna being a cheerleader, and distraught after Shanna failed to make the squad, Wanda decided that her next-door neighbor Verna Heath and Verna's daughter Amber, who had made the cheerleading squad, were largely to blame for Shanna's failure. Determined that Shanna would make the squad,

Wanda plotted to eliminate the competition before the next tryout session. She approached her brother-in-law about hiring a hitman to kill Verna. Holloway was arrested and charged with solicitation when her conversations about hiring a hitman were recorded. She was convicted of solicitation of capital murder. Strangely, Holloway was released six months later when her conviction was overturned because it was revealed that one of her original jurors had been on probation.

incite, instigate, urge, or induce someone else to commit the crime. Remember that the words without the intent do not constitute solicitation. It does not matter whether the words are conveyed orally, in writing, or electronically such as through e-mail. It is also important to remember that solicitation merges into conspiracy; if the conspiracy is successful, a conspirator may be convicted of both conspiracy and the actual crime, but may not be convicted of solicitation and conspiracy.

The Model Penal Code has established a defense to the crime of solicitation if the person renounces his/her criminal purpose. The Model Code under section 5.02(3) provides that a renunciation has occurred if there is a complete and voluntary renouncement of the criminal intention and the defendant either persuades the solicited party not to commit the criminal act or prevents him/her from doing so.

PRACTICE TIP

Martin is married to Dawn. He has been married for over 15 years and most of those years have not been happy. Martin knows that he and Dawn obtain a divorce, it will be nasty and Dawn will be entitled to half of his very substantial wealth. Martin begins to have an affair with Dana. The affair lasts for three years, during which time Martin and Dana fall in love. Martin wants to be with Dana. Dawn is beginning to become suspicious and her watchfulness is making it more difficult for Dana and Martin to be together. Martin decides that the simplest solution to the problem is to have Dawn killed and to have the murder made to look like an accident. Martin devises a plot to hire someone to enter his house, kill Dawn, and make it look like a killing as a result of a robbery attempt. Martin sets out

on his quest to find someone to commit the murder. During his inquiries, Martin is directed to Dan as a potential person who would commit the killing. Unbeknownst to Martin, Dan is an undercover police officer. Martin arranges to meet Dan at the local park to discuss the plan. Dan is wearing a wire. Martin discusses the plan with Dan and offers Dan $50,000 for the successful completion of the murder of Dawn. Dan agrees and Martin prepares to leave the park in order to obtain the money and bring it to Dan. Martin is arrested for the crime of solicitation to commit murder for trying to solicit Dan to kill Dawn. Remember, with solicitation the crime itself does have to occur nor does it matter that the guilty person would not have committed the criminal act.

SURF'S UP

To research more about the crimes of attempt, conspiracy, and solicitation, look into the following Internet resources:

- Haeji Hong's Lecture Notes: Inchoate Crimes.
- Kent Law School: A Brief History of Conspiracy.

- Quid Pro Quo's Criminal Law Outline.
- ALIOS Online: Renunciation of Attempt, Conspiracy and Solicitation.

Summary

Inchoate crimes are crimes that were never completed. The fact that a criminal's efforts to complete a crime failed does not excuse the criminal behavior or provide a defense to criminal liability. Inchoate crimes are considered to be dangerous conduct that should be prohibited, punished, and deterred before harm can ensue. Inchoate crimes also are known as anticipatory, incomplete, incipient, preliminary, and preparatory crimes. The word *inchoate* comes from the Latin word that means "to begin." It also has the meanings of underdeveloped and unripened. An inchoate crime goes beyond the mere thought of the crime but stops short of the completion of the crime.

One of the most familiar inchoate crimes is that of attempt. Attempt is, in many ways, a failure of a crime. A criminal attempt occurs when a defendant intends to commit a criminal offense and performs a substantial step toward the commission of the crime and the crime is not completed. The elements of a criminal attempt are (1) an intent or purpose to commit a specific crime, (2) an act or acts taken to carry out the intent to commit the crime, and (3) failure to complete the crime.

The courts will look at the reasons why the crime failed in determining whether or not this element is present. If the crime failed because of the interference of an outside source, then the defendant's acts probably constitute an attempt. However, there are some cases in which the reasons the crime of attempt failed can remove liability or lessen the punishment that the defendant might face.

A conspiracy may be found where no substantive crime has been committed. The crime is thwarted before any criminal act can take place. Therefore, conspiracy is considered an inchoate crime. A conspiracy is the only inchoate crime that a person can be charged with in addition to the substantive crime. The elements of a conspiracy are as follows: (1) an agreement between two or more persons to commit the crime, (2) a specific intent or purpose to commit the crime, and (3) an overt act in furtherance of the agreement.

The last major inchoate crime is solicitation. The elements for the crime of solicitation are (1) the intent that another party commit the crime and (2) asking, encouraging, or requesting another party to commit a crime. In simple terms, a solicitation occurs when someone asks someone else to commit a crime for him/her. The person who is being asked does not have to agree to commit the crime in order for the solicitation to have occurred.

Key Terms

Attempt	Overt act
Bilateral	Renunciation
Chain conspiracy	Solicitation
Conspiracy	Unilateral
Desist	Wharton's rule
Inchoate crime	Wheel conspiracy
Inducement	

Review Questions

1. Why are attempt, conspiracy, and solicitation referred to as inchoate crimes?
2. List the elements of attempt.
3. List the elements of conspiracy.
4. List the elements of solicitation.
5. How does solicitation differ from conspiracy?

6. What is the difference between unilateral and bilateral conspiracy?

7. What are the differences between the wheel theory of conspiracy and chain conspiracy? What are the similarities?

8. What is public policy behind punishing people for an attempted crime?

9. What is the proximity test and when does it apply?

10. What is the difference between a legal impossibility and a factual impossibility? Give an example of each that is not used in the chapter.

11. What is a renunciation and when can it be used as a defense?

12. In order to withdraw from a conspiracy and possibly escape liability, what does a conspirator need to do?

13. What is the substantial step test and where can you find the elements of this test?

14. What is the equivocality test?

15. Identify the societal justifications for punishing people involved in a conspiracy.

Exercises

1. Joan, Paula, and Samantha are college girls who live in a dormitory. One evening, Nancy, the director of the dormitory, knocked on the door of Joan and Paula's room and demanded that they turn down their music immediately because it was too loud. Joan and Paula were furious as it was still early in the evening and they did not see a reason to turn down the music. They decided to get even with Nancy. Joan and Paula knew that Nancy had a severe allergy to peanuts. They decided to place peanut oil in Nancy's food at the cafeteria. Joan and Paula did not know for sure whether or not Nancy would die, but they hoped that she would. Samantha, who also disliked Nancy, overheard Joan and Paula's conversation. She also hoped that the plan would succeed. She decided to help Joan and Paula but did not let anyone know that she was helping. Later that night, all parties went to the cafeteria to eat. Paula changed her mind about going through with the plan but did not tell anyone. Paula left for the bathroom as she and Joan walked toward the cafeteria. Samantha decided to provide a diversion and dropped her purse on the floor next to Nancy while Nancy was eating. Nancy proceeded to help Samantha pick up the contents of her purse while Joan poured peanut oil onto Nancy's food. Nancy ate the food, had a severe allergic reaction, and died.

   If Samantha is charged with conspiracy, a court will probably find her
   a. Guilty because she knowingly aided in the commission of the crime.
   b. Guilty because she committed an overt act in furtherance of the agreement between Joan and Paula to pour peanut oil onto Nancy's food.
   c. Not guilty because she did not agree to commit any crime.
   d. Not guilty because Paula withdrew from the conspiracy.

2. Aida decides to pick the pocket of Manny. She reaches into Manny's pocket intending to steal money that she believes Manny has in his pocket. Unbeknownst to Aida, Manny has removed the money from his pocket before she tries to pick it. Is Aida guilty of a crime? If not, why? If so, what defense might she try to assert and will it be successful?

3. Bobby was present when Paul, Gregory, and Pat decided to rob the U.S. National Bank. Paul, Gregory, and Pat committed the robbery and were arrested and charged with both the robbery and conspiracy to commit robbery. Bobby was arrested and charged with conspiracy to commit the bank robbery. Is Bobby guilty of conspiracy? Why or why not?

4. Pete, an ex-con who had recently been released from the state penitentiary, approached Patty and Steve and asked if they wanted to be involved in a bank robbery he was planning. They both said "yes." Pete continued to plan for the robbery. As part of his plan, he stole two handguns he intended to use in the robbery. According to Pete's plan, he would pick Patty and Steve up on Monday morning and drive to the Valley State Bank. The day before the planned robbery, Pete was arrested for assaulting his girlfriend. Despite the fact that Pete was in jail, Patty and Steve decided to proceed with the robbery. An undercover police officer was in the bank when they attempted to rob it and they were both arrested. Is Pete guilty of solicitation? Conspiracy? Both?

5. Travis and Tim both work in a profitable electronics store and are upset about their low wages. One day during their cigarette break, they decide they will rob the store that night after everyone has gone home. Travis and Tim know that the store manager keeps a large amount of cash in his office and they also plan on stealing whatever electronic equipment they can fit in the trunk of Tim's car. Before carrying out their plan, Travis and Tim approach Andy, another employee, who has a key to the manager's office, about joining them. At first, Andy tells the two that he is not interested. Then, Travis and Tim tell Andy he can have a share of their loot if he "accidentally" leaves the key in the break room when he leaves for the day. Andy agrees and leaves the key. That night, Travis and Tim come back to the store after it has closed for the day and, using Andy's key, enters the manager's office. Suddenly an alarm goes off and the two frightened men run back to their car and drive off without stealing anything. Is Andy criminally liable for conspiracy? Why or why not?

6. Susan and Annie are co-workers, but when Susan sees Annie stealing office supplies and turns her in, Annie is fired. Because Annie has lost her job, she fails to make her car payment and her car is repossessed. She also can't pay rent and is informed she has 48 hours to get out of her apartment. Annie blames all of her problems on Susan and decides to kill her. One morning she takes her boyfriend's gun, goes to Susan's house, hides in some bushes, and waits for Susan to leave for work. When Susan comes out of the house, Annie attempts to fire the gun at her. Unbeknownst to Annie, the gun is unloaded. Is Annie still guilty of the attempted murder of Susan? Why or why not?

 PORTFOLIO ASSIGNMENT

Research and list five different examples of solicitation, explaining how the elements are met in each.

Vocabulary Builders

Instructions

Use the key terms from this chapter to fill in the answers to the crossword puzzle.

NOTE: When the answer is more than one word, leave a blank space between words.

ACROSS

1. The crime of inducing or encouraging another to commit a crime.
6. An incipient crime; an act that generally leads to a crime.
9. The act or process of enticing or persuading another person to take a certain course of action.
11. By agreement, parties work together to create an illegal result, to achieve an unlawful end.
12. Affecting or obligating both parties.
13. A single conspiracy in which each person is responsible for a distinct act within the overall plan.

DOWN

2. Identifiable commission or omission, an intentional tort requirement.
3. A conspiracy in which a single member or group separately agrees with two or more other members or groups.
4. The doctrine that an agreement by two or more persons to commit a particular crime cannot be prosecuted as a conspiracy if the crime could not be committed except by the actual number of participants involved.
5. One-sided, relating to only one of two or more persons or things.
7. Abandonment of effort to commit a crime.
8. To actually try to commit a crime and have the actual ability to do so.
10. To cease an activity.

STATE of North Carolina

v.

Dalton Osborn BRUNSON.

599 S.E.2d 576

Court of Appeals of North Carolina.

Aug. 3, 2004

Background: Defendant was convicted by jury in the Superior Court, Durham County, A. Leon Stanback, Jr., J., of drug-related offenses. Defendant appealed.

Holdings: The Court of Appeals, Calabria, J., held that:

1. statute setting forth prohibition against subsequent prosecution by state barred prosecution by state for trafficking offenses;

2. prohibition against subsequent prosecution by state was not applicable to offense of conspiracy to traffic in cocaine by sale; and

3. evidence showed only a single conspiracy to traffic cocaine rather than multiple conspiracies.

Affirmed in part, reversed and vacated in part.

CALABRIA, Judge.

In March 2001, a detective from the Durham County Sheriff's Department initiated an undercover drug operation. After numerous purchases of prescription controlled substances from Nancy Ashley ("Ashley"), the undercover officer negotiated to purchase one and one-half ounces of cocaine from her. On 5 April 2001, the undercover officer met Ashley and went to her sister's house to arrange a deal.

Thereafter, Dalton Osborn Brunson ("defendant") arrived and greetings were exchanged. Defendant sold the undercover officer a bag of white powder between the size of a golf ball and a tennis ball. Later, the State Bureau of Investigation ("SBI") confirmed the bag of white powder contained 41.5 grams of cocaine hydrochloride ("cocaine"). On 17 April and again on 1 May 2001, two additional purchases for approximately one and one-half ounces of cocaine occurred. Immediately following defendant's 1 May 2001 sale to the undercover officer, law enforcement officials apprehended and arrested defendant after he attempted to flee.

On 6 August 2001, defendant was indicted by the Durham County Grand Jury of, *inter alia*, three counts of conspiracy to traffic in cocaine, nine counts of trafficking in cocaine, and four counts of possession of cocaine with intent to sell or deliver. On 27 August 2001, after state prosecutors supplied the pertinent information to federal prosecutors, defendant was also charged, *inter alia*, with three counts of unlawful distribution of cocaine under federal law for the same three drug transactions. Defendant pled guilty in the United States District Court for the Middle District of North Carolina on one count of unlawful distribution of cocaine and was sentenced to 166 months' imprisonment for that charge. The State subsequently proceeded on the charges upon which defendant had been indicted by the Durham County Grand Jury. Defendant moved to dismiss the drug-related charges, contending "that the North Carolina Constitution, the law of the land provision, does not permit the State to [exact] double punishment for the same conduct." The trial court denied defendant's motion. The jury found defendant guilty of all drug-related offenses and of being a habitual felon. The trial court arrested judgment on the four counts of possession with intent to sell and deliver cocaine and sentenced defendant on the remaining charges relating to the transactions between the undercover officer and defendant. Defendant appeals.

On appeal, we consider defendant's assertions that (I) the trial court erred in failing to dismiss the State charges relating to the transactions between defendant and the undercover officer and (II) the evidence was insufficient to show three separate conspiracies.

I. NORTH CAROLINA GENERAL STATUTES § 90–97

Many of defendant's assignments of error turn on the issue of whether the federal charges and the state charges constitute the same offense. At trial, defendant argued only constitutional double jeopardy grounds as a bar to his prosecution by the State. Defendant, for the first time on appeal, argues N.C. Gen. Stat. § 90–97 (2001) barred prosecution by the State for the drug-related offenses. Because the transcript reveals defendant failed to raise this argument in the trial court, the question is not properly before us . . . Nonetheless, we choose to address this argument in our discretion pursuant to Rule 2 of the North Carolina Rules of Appellate Procedure.

North Carolina General Statutes § 90–97 provides, in pertinent part, as follows: "[i]f a violation of [the North Carolina Controlled Substances Act] is a violation of a federal law . . ., a conviction or acquittal under federal law . . . *for the same act* is a bar to prosecution in this State." (Emphasis added) . . .

[Text omitted]

Applied to the case *sub judice*, we hold that "the same act" as used in N.C. Gen. Stat. § 90–97 focuses the relevant analysis on the underlying actions for which defendant is prosecuted at the state and federal levels and operates as a bar to the State's prosecution of defendant's trafficking offenses under N.C. Gen. Stat. § 90–95. We need not reach defendant's constitutional argument.

Defendant also asserts, on the basis of N.C. Gen. Stat. § 90–97, that the three counts of conspiracy to traffic in cocaine by sale were barred. We disagree. Under 21 U.S.C. § 841, only the acts of manufacturing, distributing, dispensing, or possession with intent to engage in one of those acts are criminalized. Conspiracy is separately prohibited in 21 U.S.C. § 846 (2001), with which defendant was not charged. Accordingly, the prohibition against subsequent prosecution by the State found in N.C. Gen. Stat. § 90–97 is not applicable under these facts to the offense of conspiracy to traffic in cocaine by sale, and defendant's argument is without merit.

II. NUMBER OF CONSPIRACIES

Defendant asserts the evidence at trial showed defendant was guilty of only one conspiracy to traffic in cocaine rather than three separate conspiracies. Specifically, defendant contends that, although there was a series of agreements and acts, they constituted a single conspiracy.

"A criminal conspiracy is an agreement, express or implied, between two or more persons to do an unlawful act or to do a lawful act by unlawful means." *State v. Burmeister*, 131 N.C. App. 190, 199, 506 S.E.2d 278, 283 (1998). A "conspiracy is complete upon formation of the unlawful agreement [but] continues until the conspiracy comes to fruition or is abandoned." *State v. Griffin*, 112 N.C. App. 838, 841, 437 S.E.2d 390, 392 (1993). However, "[a] single conspiracy is not transformed into multiple conspiracies simply because its members vary occasionally and the same acts in furtherance of it occur over a period of time." In determining the propriety of multiple conspiracy charges, we look to "the nature of the agreement or agreements" in light of the following factors: "time intervals, participants, objectives, and number of meetings. . . ." *State v. Tabron*, 147 N.C. App. 303, 306, 556 S.E.2d 584, 586 (2001).

In the instant case, these factors support the existence of a single conspiracy. Initially, the three drug transactions involved the same principal participants engaging in virtually identical conduct for each transaction. In each transaction, the undercover officer contacted Ashley by phone and asked her to arrange a meeting in which he would purchase one and one-half ounces of cocaine. Each time, Ashley then contacted defendant and arranged for herself, the undercover officer, and defendant to meet and make the exchange. After each transaction between defendant and the undercover officer, the undercover officer paid Ashley a "commission" for arranging the transfer.

Regarding the objective sought to be accomplished, the undercover officer testified his private motivation was to identify Ashley's source in the first transaction, confirm the source in the second, and close down the source in the third; however, it could easily be stated that the undercover officer's objective was, at all times, to identify and apprehend Ashley's source. Certainly with respect to Ashley and defendant, the objective remained the same. Ashley's objective was to arrange a drug transaction and receive a "commission" for doing so, and defendant's objective was the sale of drugs to a purchaser. Additionally, the indictments all aver the same objective: trafficking by sale in a controlled substance.

Looking at the time interval, we note that each transaction was temporally separated from the preceding transaction by no more than fourteen days and "all transactions transpired over a short period of time, a one month period." *See Griffin*, 112 N.C. App. at 841, 437 S.E.2d at 392 (rejecting the argument that multiple conspiracies existed "because the offenses occurred one to two weeks apart").

Additionally, we note the undercover officer testified that he continued to contact Ashley throughout the time the transactions were being planned and "told her . . . that [he] did want to make another purchase of cocaine, buy another one-and-a-half ounces." This statement indicates the transaction was not a separate or discreet transaction but was to be part of an ongoing agreement for the continued purchase and supply of cocaine. The State's arguments, that there were some discrepancies in how Ashley was paid her commission or that one of the transactions took place at a different location, are unavailing. Admittedly, each transaction was not a mirror image of the other transactions; however, we have never required, and do not herein adopt, absolute precision in examining the similarities of the surrounding circumstances in order to determine the number of conspiracies. In short, we find the transactions sufficiently similar in consideration of the factors set forth in *Tabron* and the surrounding circumstances to hold that the transactions were part of a single conspiracy entered into by the same parties for the same purpose.

[Text omitted]

In summary, defendant's prosecution by the State for cocaine trafficking convictions, but not for conspiracy to traffic in cocaine convictions, were barred by operation of N.C. Gen. Stat. § 90–97. Furthermore, the trial court erred in denying defendant's motion to dismiss two counts of conspiracy to traffic cocaine. We remand for further proceedings consistent with this opinion.

Affirmed in part, reversed and vacated in part.

[Footnotes omitted]

Source: Reprinted with the permission of Westlaw.

Chapter 10

Defenses

CHAPTER OBJECTIVES

Upon completion of this chapter, you will be able to:

- Understand defenses that involve criminal responsibility.
- Identify the different insanity tests.
- Explain the justification and excuse defenses.
- Discuss procedural defenses.

The theory of defenses involves avoiding criminal liability for a crime that has been committed. Under certain circumstances, it is permissible to commit a crime and society will not punish the perpetrator. This chapter will examine the various defenses available to a person who commits a crime that may enable him/her to avoid criminal liability.

CRIMINAL RESPONSIBILITY

defense
Legally sufficient reason to excuse the complained-of behavior.

A **defense** is a legal justification or excuse that enables a person who appears to be guilty of a crime to avoid punishment and walk away from criminal liability free and clear to continue his/her life. Defenses play an important and essential part in criminal law and are used every day in criminal courts.

Some defenses raised in a criminal proceeding concern the perpetrator's state of mind. The mental status of the defendant can negate a person's criminal accountability for a crime. Criminal responsibility defenses relate to whether or not a defendant possessed the necessary mental capacity to form the intent to commit the criminal act. Without the ability to form the requisite mens rea to commit a crime, the defendant will be provided with an excuse for his/her criminal action. In a case using a criminal responsibility defense, the defendant will admit to committing the criminal act but will assert that, due to his/her lack of mental capacity, he/she was incapable of forming the requisite intent necessary for criminal prosecution. Typically, there are four types of defenses that fall under criminal responsibility:

- Infancy
- Insanity
- Diminished capacity
- Intoxication

Infancy

Perhaps one of the defenses most associated with lack of criminal responsibility is that of **infancy**. Infancy deals with whether or not a minor child has the mental capacity to be able to form the requisite mental intent to formulate criminal responsibility. Under civil law, a minor child is any child under the age of 18. In criminal law, the definition of a minor child is far murkier. Children are generally not held criminally responsible for their actions until they reach an age when they understand the difference between right and wrong and the nature of their actions. Children under seven are conclusively presumed to lack the capacity to commit a crime. From the age of 7 to the age of 14, children are presumed incapable of committing a crime, but this presumption is not conclusive and can be rebutted by the prosecution by the evidence that the child was aware that what she or he was doing was wrong. A minor over the age of 14 is presumed to be capable of committing a crime, but this presumption also may be rebutted. In recent times, some children who have committed particularly heinous crimes such as gang slayings and murder have been tried as adults due to the inherently dangerous nature of the crimes they have committed; however, minors are not subject to the death penalty. Most states have statutes that determine when a minor child should or should not be criminally responsible for his/her actions.

Generally, under common law, criminal responsibility for a minor was determined under the following guidelines:

1. Children under seven years of age are convincingly assumed not to possess the mental capacity necessary to form the requisite mens rea for criminal responsibility to attach.

2. Children between the ages of 7 and 14 are generally presumed not to have the mental capacity required for criminal responsibility. However, as stated above, if the crime committed by the minor is particularly malicious or the child shows awareness of the wrongfulness of the conduct, then the child may be held to have formulated the required mens rea for criminal responsibility to be found.

3. Children over the age of 14 can be treated the same as an adult for purposes of mental capacity and criminal responsibility.

Typically, the chronological age of a child is used in order to determine criminal responsibility rather than mental capacity. In most states, a child who is accused of a crime will fall under the jurisdiction of the juvenile division of the criminal courts until he/she is the age of 17. After the age of 17, a child will be tried as an adult and will fall under the general jurisdiction of the criminal court.

Insanity

The first thing to remember is that insanity as a defense is a legal term and not a medical diagnosis. The medical diagnosis of insanity is relevant in the legal sense only if insanity impairs one's ability to form the criminal intent necessary to commit a crime. If the defendant is unable to form the requisite mens rea, then the elements of a crime fail and insanity becomes a defense to the commission of the criminal act. Someone raising a defense of insanity is stating that he or she should be excused from criminal liability because of mental impairment.

A defendant may plead insanity at the time the act was committed, at the time of trial, during the period of incarceration, as well as at the time of execution.

If a person is determined to be legally insane at the time the crime was committed, then he/she is not criminally responsible for his/her actions because the law seeks to punish criminals and not people who are mentally ill. Insanity can be a full defense to some crimes. However, just because a person is found to be legally insane and

infancy
The state of a person who is under the age of legal majority.

incapable of committing a crime does not mean that the person is set free. Typically, the legally insane person is committed to some type of institution for treatment and observation. He/she is still considered to be a danger to society and could pose a substantial risk if he/she remains free.

If a defendant chooses to assert insanity at the time of trial, then the court must determine if the defendant is mentally competent to stand trial. The defendant must possess the mental capacity necessary to assist his/her attorney in his/her defense. Insanity pled at the time of trial does not negate the commission of the criminal act. If the court determines that the defendant is not mentally competent to stand trial, then the state must delay the trial until such time that the defendant is determined to be mentally competent. If the defendant is never determined to be mentally competent to stand trial, then the trial may never be held due to the fact that the defendant's mental state remained unchanged.

If insanity is pled at the time of execution, then the execution will be stayed until such time as the defendant is determined to be sane. There are two reasons why the execution of an insane defendant is delayed. First, the defendant should be sane so that he/she understands the nature and gravity of his/her criminal conduct and the punishment being inflicted upon him/her. Second, the defendant should be sane so that he/she might offer some reason or explanation that could lead to a permanent stay of execution.

Determining legal sanity can be difficult. The law has developed various tests to assist in determining the mental capacity of a defendant. The main tests for determining a defendant's sanity are

- M'Naghten Rule
- Irresistible impulse
- Durham
- Substantial capacity
- Federal standard

M'Naghten Rule

M'Naghten Rule
The defendant alleges he or she lacked capacity to form criminal intent.

The **M'Naghten Rule** is the oldest rule used to determine the sanity of a defendant and is used in approximately one-half of the states. The M'Naghten Rule is also known as the "right-wrong" test. This test focuses on whether or not a defendant can distinguish between right and wrong. The M'Naghten Rule came from an 1843 English case in which defendant Daniel M'Naghten was delusional and thought the then–prime minister of England was involved in a conspiracy to kill M'Naghten. M'Naghten shot at the prime minister but killed his secretary instead. During the trial, the court ruled that a defendant should be presumed to be legally sane unless the defendant can prove that, at the time he committed the offense, he was "labouring under such a defect of reason, from disease of the mind, as not to know the nature and quality of the act he was doing; or, if he did know it, that he did not know he was doing what was wrong." The M'Naghten test requires that the defendant (not the prosecution) prove two elements:

- The defendant suffered a mental disease, causing a defect in his reasoning powers.
- As a result of the defendant's mental disease, he/she either (1) did not understand the "nature and quality" of his/her act or (2) did not know that his/her act was wrong.

In other words, if, because of a diseased condition, you are unable to understand the nature of your act (you did not know what you were doing), or if you knew what you were doing but lacked the mental capacity to distinguish right from wrong, you may be found legally insane under the M'Naghten test. There is a split of authority in M'Naghten jurisdictions as to whether a "wrong" includes both legal and moral wrongs. Some jurisdictions will hold that a defendant is not insane if the defendant realizes an act is illegal even if the defendant believes an action to be morally acceptable.

Irresistible Impulse

Many states that follow the M'Naghten Rule also have added the **irresistible impulse** test. The irresistible impulse test looks at a person's will. In other words, the defendant may know that his/her actions are right or wrong, but he/she may not be able to control his/her actions. For example, you may know that smoking is bad for you, but you cannot help lighting up another one. A defendant can claim an insanity defense if his/her mental disease damages his/her willpower. The irresistible impulse test has the following elements:

irresistible impulse
An impulse to commit an unlawful or criminal act that cannot be resisted or overcome because mental disease has destroyed the freedom of will, the power of self-control, and the choice of actions.

* The defendant was afflicted with a disease of the mind at the time of the commission of the crime.
* The defendant could distinguish between right and wrong, but an insanity defense may excuse his/her behavior if (1) the mental disease caused the defendant to lose his/her willpower to choose between right and wrong and the disease destroyed the defendant's ability to assert his/her willpower to stop his/her actions even though he/she knew it was wrong and (2) the mental disease was the sole cause of the defendant's act.

The irresistible impulse test takes the M'Naghten test and adds the focus on the defendant's impaired willpower.

 RESEARCH THIS

The landmark case for the irresistible impulse test was *Parsons v. State*, 81 Ala. 577, 2 So. 854 (1886). Research the case of *Parsons v. State*. What were the legal elements of criminal responsibility that the *Parsons* court determined were necessary in this type of defense?

Durham

In the case of *Durham v. U.S.*, 214 F.2d 862 (D.C. Cir. 1954), the U.S. Court of Appeals for the District of Columbia provided the legal world with a new test of insanity that encompasses persons who might fall under both the M'Naghten Rule and irresistible impulse tests as well as other circumstances. The *Durham* court determined that

> The science of psychiatry now recognizes that a man is an integrated personality and that reason, which is only one element in that personality, is not the sole determinant of his conduct. The right-wrong test, which considers knowledge or reason alone, is therefore an inadequate guide to mental responsibility for criminal behavior. [214 F.2d at 871.]

The court determined that a defendant might be entitled to an insanity acquittal "if his unlawful act was the product of mental disease or defect." The purpose of the Durham rule was to enable psychiatrists to testify as expert witnesses as to the mental capacity of the defendant. The test was not widely accepted and was left in effect only in New Hampshire.

SURF'S UP

To learn more about the John Hinckley Jr. trial, use search engines such as www.google.com, www.msn.com, and www.yahoo.com and search "John Hinckley." A myriad of information concerning the trial and the subsequent enactment of the Insanity Defense Reform Act of 1984 can be found by this search.

Substantial Capacity

substantial capacity
The term used in the definition of legal insanity proposed by the Model Penal Code.

The **substantial capacity** test was developed by the authors of the Model Penal Code in an effort to broaden the M'Naghten and irresistible impulse tests. The Model Penal Code section 4.01(1) defined substantial capacity as follows:

A person is not responsible for criminal conduct if at the time of such conduct as a result of mental disease or defect he lacks substantial capacity either to appreciate the criminality [wrongfulness] of his conduct or to conform his conduct to the requirements of the law.[1]

The main distinction in the substantial capacity test is that if a defendant is unable to have an emotional understanding of the wrongfulness of his/her conduct, he/she may be legally insane. The Model Penal Code uses the word *appreciate* as opposed to the word *know* to make this distinction. It is not the total capacity test, but the substantial capacity test. The substantial capacity test has been adopted in a minority of jurisdictions.

Federal Standard

The federal courts now abide by an insanity defense that was established by Congress in 1984 after John Hinckley Jr. was acquitted for the attempted assassination of Ronald Reagan. The federal standard developed due to a jury instruction that was given in the Hinckley trial. The jury was instructed that it must acquit Hinckley if there was reasonable doubt about whether Hinckley could appreciate the wrongfulness of his conduct or could not conform his conduct to the law. The jury found Hinckley not guilty by reason of insanity due to this jury instruction. There was a public outcry as a result of the trial's verdict.

clear and convincing
Evidence that indicates that a thing to be proved is highly probable or reasonably certain.

As result of the verdict, Congress enacted the Insanity Defense Reform Act of 1984, Pub. L. No. 98-473, 18 U.S.C. § 4241. This statute narrows the insanity defense of M'Naghten in federal criminal cases. The defense is allowed to be asserted if the defendant essentially meets the elements of M'Naghten; that is, primarily "as a result of a severe mental disease or defect, [the defendant] was unable to appreciate the nature and quality or the wrongfulness of his acts." This mental disease needs to have been in effect at the time the criminal offense was committed. The burden is on the defendant to prove his/her insanity by **clear and convincing** evidence.

diminished capacity
The doctrine that recognizes that an accused does not have to be suffering from a mental disease to have impaired mental capacities at the time the offense was committed.

Diminished Capacity

Another defense that claims impaired reasoning on the part of the defendant is **diminished capacity**. Diminished capacity is similar to a defense of insanity except that it is not a complete defense to a crime. A defendant who is found to have diminished

A DAY IN THE LIFE OF A REAL PARALEGAL

The practicing paralegal should be aware of what test the jurisdiction in which he or she resides applies to determine if a defendant may be adjudicated insane. Research your home state and determine which of the tests are applicable.

[1] Model Penal Code, copyright 1985 by the American Law Institute. Reprinted with permission.

capacity suffers from a mental impairment that makes him/her unable to formulate the requisite mens rea for the crime. Due to this impairment, the defendant is not insane, but he/she is not completely criminally responsible for his/her actions.

Usually, when a defense of diminished capacity is allowed to be asserted by the defendant, it will lead to the defendant's being charged with a lesser crime instead of the original crime. For example, if a defendant is accused of first degree murder, a successful defense of diminished capacity could lead to a reduction of the charge to second degree murder or from murder to manslaughter. Unlike an insanity defense, a diminished capacity defense does not lead to the defendant's being acquitted of the charges. Typically, when a diminished capacity defense is asserted by the defendant, it is up to the prosecution to prove all the elements of the crime, including the mens rea. The defendant does not have the burden of proof to prove diminished capacity. Although still a valid defense in many jurisdictions, other jurisdictions have abolished the defense of diminished capacity.

Intoxication

Another defense that seeks to negate the intent of a crime is the defense of **intoxication**. Whether or not the defendant was voluntarily or involuntarily intoxicated may determine to what extent the intoxication defense is successful. The Model Penal Code section 2.08(4) provides for an involuntary intoxication defense that states: "[i]f by reason of such intoxication, the actor, at the time of his conduct, lacks substantial capacity either to appreciate its criminality or to conform his conduct to the requirements of law."[2]

Perhaps you are wondering how the law determines when someone is involuntarily intoxicated. One instance involves when a person is tricked into drinking or ingesting alcohol or drugs to the extent that he/she is incapable of forming the necessary intent to commit a crime. For example, someone could be tricked into drinking an alleged fruit punch that actually contains a drug. The drug makes the person hallucinate and, during his/her hallucination, the person attacks a person whom he/she thinks is trying to kill him/her. The person was incapable of forming the requisite intent to commit a battery. The second situation in which a person can legally be recognized as having been involuntarily intoxicated is when the defendant is forced to consume a substance. The law recognizes that a person who is forced to consume such a substance would usually be forced to do so under duress and, therefore, should be provided with a defense to a crime that he/she may have committed under both the duress and the involuntary intoxication.

Typically, someone who voluntarily becomes intoxicated is not provided a defense. However, voluntary intoxication can negate a specific intent. In other words, if a defendant's voluntary intoxication renders him/her unable to form the necessary intent required for a specific criminal act, then the defendant may have a defense of intoxication. Voluntary intoxication that impedes a person's ability to form the requisite mens rea for a particular crime also may reduce the degree of the crime that may be charged.

JUSTIFICATION AND EXCUSE

Some defenses are classified into either justifications or excuses. With a **justification**, a defendant commits an offense, accepts responsibility for his/her actions, but asserts that his/her actions were necessary under the circumstances. With an **excuse**, the defendant may admit that his/her actions were wrong, but he/she claims not to be responsible for those actions. The following defenses are considered justification and excuse defenses:

- Consent.
- Self-defense.

PRACTICE TIP

Competency to stand trial is different from mental incapacity. "Incompetency" generally refers to a doctrine that prevents defendants from being tried, convicted, or punished unless they have a sufficient present mental capacity to consult with an attorney and have a reasonable and rational understanding of the legal proceedings taking place. A minority of states have the "defense of diminished capacity." For example, mental illness may be used in a murder case to mitigate the criminal charges.

intoxication
Under the influence of alcohol or drugs which may, depending on the degree of inebriation, render a party incapable of entering into a contractual relationship or of acting in the manner in which an ordinarily prudent and cautious person would have acted under similar circumstances.

justification
A lawful reason for acting or failing to act.

excuse
A reason alleged for doing or not doing a thing.

- Defense of others.
- Defense of property.
- Force in making an arrest.
- Necessity.
- Duress.
- Entrapment.
- Mistake of fact.

Consent

consent
Voluntarily yielding the will to another.

Generally, **consent** by a victim does not negate criminal liability. Crimes are wrongs against society and victims cannot generally consent to their commission. However, consent may be a defense to a crime in two instances. The first instance is one in which the lack of consent of the victim is an element of the crime. For example, at common law, a rape could not have occurred if the victim consented; it was considered rape only if there was a lack of consent by the victim. Therefore, lack of consent was an element of the crime. The other instance is limited to circumstances in which the victim's consent negates the harm that resulted; this is typically limited to activities where the participants implicitly or expressly consent to the risks inherent to the activity. For example, when two boxers are engaged in a legally sanctioned boxing event, the death of one of the boxers due to blows to the head will not be prosecuted as a crime. The boxer's consent to step into the ring and engage in the match negates the resulting harm he/she sustained.

There are certain crimes in which a victim cannot consent or in which the victim's consent will not constitute a defense. Crimes for which consent is not a defense are statutory rape (rape of a minor child), larceny, murder, mayhem, prostitution, and sale of narcotics. In addition, if the defendant obtains the victim's consent by fraudulent methods, the victim's consent will be determined to be invalid.

Self-Defense

self-defense
A defendant's legal excuse that the use of force was justified.

Self-defense, or protecting oneself from being injured, can be a defense to a crime. However, the amount of allowable force that is acceptable when preventing injury can be only that which would be considered reasonably necessary when it appears that the defendant was in danger of immediate harm from someone else. The following elements generally must be present in order to assert a defense of self-defense:

- The defendant must have been resisting the imminent or present use of unlawful force against him/her.
- The degree of force that is used by the defendant to protect himself/herself must not be more than is reasonably necessary to protect him/her from the threatened harm.
- The defendant must not have used deadly force in defense of himself/herself unless threatened with deadly force.
- The defendant should not have been the aggressor.

The defense of self-defense is available only to those who do not provoke an attack. However, if an initial aggressor to an attack completely withdraws from the attack and then is attacked himself/herself, he/she can use force to defend himself/herself from the attack, and the defense of self-defense may be available to him/her. Suppose that Johnny attacks Marty in a fistfight. Johnny decides to cease fighting and turns to walk away from the fight. If Marty then grabs a pipe and attacks Johnny, Johnny may be entitled to use force to protect himself after he had withdrawn from his initial attack of Marty.

The defendant must be defending himself/herself against imminent bodily injury. A defense of self-defense cannot be used for a threat of future harm. The harm must be present or imminent.

Deadly force is acceptable only if the defendant is in immediate danger of death or serious injury and the use of deadly force is reasonably necessary for the defendant's own protection. The test to determine if the use of deadly force is reasonable is whether the force used was that which a reasonably prudent person would use in the same or similar circumstances.

Some states follow the **retreat rule** and require that the victim of a crime must choose a safe retreat over using deadly force in self-defense unless the victim is in his or her own home or place of business or if the assailant is a person the victim is attempting to arrest.

Defense of Others

A person may be entitled to assert the **defense of others** when using force to protect someone else, even a stranger, from being injured in an attack. If the defendant is defending someone else, the defendant must (figuratively speaking) step into the shoes of the other person that he/she is protecting. At that time, the defendant will have the same rights as the person that he/she is defending. If the defendant is mistaken as to the situation and uses deadly force when it was not necessary to use deadly force in the defense of the other person, then the defendant could be charged with a severe crime such as a homicide should the attacker be killed in the defense. The defendant must assess the situation and be sure that he/she understands the circumstances and the amount of force that is reasonably necessary in order to protect and defend the person who is in danger.

Defense of Property

A person is allowed to defend his/her property from being taken. However, the defendant will be allowed to use only reasonable force to defend his/her property. Deadly force in the defense of property is not considered reasonable. Deadly force may be permissible if the intrusion into a dwelling poses a serious threat of bodily injury to

deadly force
Defense available in cases involving the defense of persons, oneself, or another. It is a violent action known to create a substantial risk of causing death or serious bodily harm.

retreat rule
The doctrine holding that the victim of a crime must choose to retreat instead of using deadly force if certain circumstances exist.

defense of others
A justification defense available if one harms or threatens another while defending a third person.

A DAY IN THE LIFE OF A REAL PARALEGAL

Fran loves working as a criminal law paralegal. Recently, she was given an assignment to research and investigate a client's (Pedro) killing of a police officer. Pedro was arrested and is currently being held downtown at the county jail. The supervising attorney gave Fran the following fact pattern based on the client's viewpoint of the killing:

Pedro was walking down the street on his way to the local grocery store to pick up some items for dinner. Pedro lives in a rough area downtown and often carries a small handgun, for which he has a license. He hears a commotion in the alley between two apartment buildings. Pedro walks slowly down the alley and sees a man and a woman struggling over a knife. The man is grabbing the woman when Pedro walks toward them. The man, holding the woman with one hand, turns toward Pedro with the knife and begins to walk toward Pedro. Pedro becomes afraid, takes out the gun, and shoots the man. The man turns out to be an undercover police officer who was apprehending the woman who had just robbed a liquor store and was fleeing the scene with a deadly weapon.

Fran immediately begins to outline the case with facts from Pedro. Fran must determine what issues are present including the charges pending against Pedro, any defenses Pedro may have, and finding any witnesses that haven't come forward as yet.

the inhabitants. Any mechanical devices used to defend property must be nondeadly. For example, barbed wire or spiked fences are considered nondeadly. However, the use of an electric fence or some type of trip-gun may be considered deadly force. If the perpetrator is injured or killed by the use of such an item, the defendant probably would not be able to successfully assert a defense of property.

A person is allowed to pursue his/her property and use reasonable force to retrieve it. The pursuit and retrieval have to be done immediately. A defendant is not entitled to use reasonable force to pursue his/her property if, after learning of his/her property's whereabouts, he/she waits days before retrieving it.

Force in Making an Arrest

A law enforcement officer is entitled to use reasonable force in making an arrest. Due to the privilege of their job, law enforcement officers may be excused in breaking the law if such violation is in connection with making an arrest, preventing the occurrence of a crime, or keeping a suspect from escaping. If a law enforcement officer reasonably believes that he/she is in danger of serious bodily harm or even death, he/she is entitled to use deadly force to protect himself/herself.

If a suspect is fleeing, a law enforcement officer typically is entitled to use only nondeadly force to stop the flight as the officer would not be considered to be under threat of bodily injury or harm.

Necessity

necessity
A justification defense for a person who acts in an emergency and commits a crime that is less harmful than the harm that would have occurred but for the person's actions.

Necessity is a valid defense where the defendant has committed a crime while acting under the reasonable belief that the criminal act was necessary to avoid an occurrence of a greater harm. For example, a mountain climber is hiking when a sudden snowstorm hits. The climber comes upon a small cabin. If the climber breaks into the cabin for shelter and eats some food out of the cupboards, his or her crimes would likely be justified by necessity.

Duress

duress
Any unlawful threat or coercion used by a person to induce another to act (or to refrain from acting) in a manner that he or she otherwise would not do.

One is not usually liable for criminal acts committed under **duress**. A defendant may have committed a criminal act under threat of, or use of, force by a third person that was so overwhelming that it overpowered the defendant's will. The elements required for a defense of duress are

- A threat by a third person.
- A reasonable fear possessed by the defendant as a result of the threat.
- The defendant's fear that he/she will suffer immediate or imminent harm.
- The harm threatened is of serious bodily injury or death.

To a person under duress, the threat of harm facing him/her if he/she does not commit the offense is greater than the harm faced by him/her for committing the offense. For example, Martin is threatened by a local gang that if he does not participate in a robbery, they will kill him. The harm of committing the robbery is not as great for Martin as is the harm of death.

However, duress is not a defense to committing murder or manslaughter. If the defendant is charged with murder or manslaughter, the killer is still liable for killing done under duress, threat, or coercion. Modern trends favor mitigating murder to voluntary manslaughter if a reasonable person in the same situation would have killed rather than die. Common law rules did not allow duress as a defense to murder because it was considered honorable to choose death rather than intentionally kill another person. A mistake of fact, although not a classic defense, will be a defense where such mistake negates an element of a crime.

CASE FACT PATTERN

Patty Hearst, granddaughter of publishing giant William Randolph Hearst, was kidnapped in February of 1974 by the revolutionary group called the Symbionese Liberation Army (SLA). Patty was allegedly kept in a closet and "brainwashed" for two months by the radical group, who targeted wealthy capitalists as their enemies. The Hearst family agreed to the group's initial demands, including the distribution of millions of dollars in food, but negotiations subsequently broke off. Then a photo of Patty, machine gun in hand, was published. It appeared she was a willing participant in the criminal activities of the group. Specifically, she took part in the robbery of a San Francisco bank. Suddenly Patty Hearst had gone from a victim to being on the FBI's Ten Most Wanted List. A 1974 assault by law enforcement left most SLA members dead, but Patty managed to escape. For about a year she remained a fugitive. She was finally arrested in 1975 and charged with bank robbery. Patty's legal team raised the defense of duress; however, Patty was convicted of bank robbery. In 1979 her sentence was commuted by President Jimmy Carter.

EYE ON ETHICS

The purpose of an entrapment defense is to protect the public from law enforcement. While it is important for law enforcement to thwart crimes, it is not legal for them to form the criminal intent and induce a person to commit a crime under color of authority.

Entrapment

Entrapment occurs when a law enforcement officer or government agent talks the defendant into committing a crime that the defendant was not otherwise predisposed to commit. This can be a valid defense to crimes such as solicitation, prostitution, selling drugs, and others. The majority of jurisdictions utilize a subjective test in order to determine if an entrapment has occurred. The defendant must prove that before an undercover agent approached him/her, he/she was not inclined to do the act. The court must determine where the criminal intent originated. Did the criminal intent originate with the defendant or from the officers? If it is found that the criminal intent originated with the officers or agents, then the defendant may be able to successfully assert an entrapment defense. An entrapment defense is usually used for lesser crimes and is not available for more serious crimes such as murder, rape, arson, robbery, and other violent crimes.

entrapment
An act of a law enforcement official to induce or encourage a person to commit a crime when the defendant expresses no desire to proceed with the illegal act.

Mistake of Fact

A mistake of fact, although not a classic defense, will be a defense where such mistake negates an element of a crime. For example, a mistake of fact may negate the specific intent required for a crime. Even an unreasonable mistake, if made in good faith, can negate a specific-intent crime.

A defense is a legal justification or excuse that enables a person who appears to be guilty of a crime to avoid punishment and walk away from criminal liability free and clear to continue his/her life. Defenses play an important and essential part in criminal law and are used every day in criminal courts.

Perhaps one of the defenses most associated with lack of criminal responsibility is that of infancy. Infancy deals with whether or not a minor child has the mental capacity to be able to form the requisite mental intent to formulate criminal responsibility. Under civil law, a minor child is any child under the age of 18. In criminal law, the

Summary

definition of a minor child is far murkier. Most states have statutes that determine when a minor child should or should not be criminally responsible for his/her actions.

The first thing to remember is that insanity as a defense is a legal term and not a medical diagnosis. The medical diagnosis of insanity is relevant in the legal sense only if it impairs one's ability to form the criminal intent necessary to commit a crime. If the defendant is unable to form the requisite mens rea, then the elements of a crime fail and insanity becomes a defense to the commission of the criminal act. Someone raising a defense of insanity is stating that he/she is not legally criminally responsible for his/her actions because he/she was mentally impaired at the time he/she committed the criminal act.

The M'Naghten test requires that the defendant (not the prosecution) prove two elements: (1) the defendant suffered a mental disease causing a defect in his/her reasoning powers and (2) as a result of the defendant's mental disease, he/she either (a) did not understand the "nature and quality" of his/her act or (b) did not know that his/her act was wrong.

A defendant can claim an insanity defense if his/her mental disease damages his/her willpower. The irresistible impulse test has the following elements: (1) the defendant was afflicted with a disease of the mind at the time of the commission of the crime and (2) the defendant could distinguish between right and wrong. An insanity defense may excuse his/her behavior if (a) the mental disease caused the defendant to lose his/her willpower to choose between right and wrong and the disease destroyed the defendant's ability to assert his/her willpower to stop his/her actions even though he/she knew it was wrong and (b) the mental disease was the sole cause of the defendant's act.

Another defense that claims impaired reasoning on the part of the defendant is diminished capacity. Diminished capacity is similar to a defense of insanity except that it is not a complete defense to a crime. A defendant who is found to have diminished capacity suffers from a mental impairment that makes him/her unable to formulate the requisite mens rea for the crime.

Another defense that seeks to negate the intent of a crime is the defense of intoxication. Whether the defendant was voluntarily or involuntarily intoxicated may determine to what extent the intoxication defense is successful. Typically, someone who voluntarily becomes intoxicated is not provided a defense. However, voluntary intoxication can negate a specific intent. Voluntary intoxication that impedes a person's ability to form the requisite mens rea for a particular crime also may reduce the degree of the crime that may be charged.

There are certain crimes in which a victim cannot consent or in which the victim's consent will not constitute a defense. Crimes where consent is not a defense are statutory rape (rape of a minor child), larceny, murder, mayhem, prostitution, and sale of narcotics. In addition, if the defendant obtains the victim's consent by fraudulent methods, the victim's consent will be determined to be invalid.

Protecting oneself from being injured can be a defense to a crime. However, the amount of force that is acceptable when preventing injury can be only that which would be considered reasonably necessary when it appears that the defendant is in danger of immediate harm from someone else. The following elements generally must be present in order to assert a defense of self-defense: (1) the defendant must have been resisting the imminent or present use of unlawful force against him/her, (2) the degree of force that is used by the defendant to protect himself/herself must not be more than is reasonably necessary to protect him/her from the threatened harm, (3) the defendant must not have used deadly force in defense of himself/herself unless threatened with deadly force, and (4) the defendant should not have been the aggressor.

A person may be entitled to assert the defense of others when using force to protect someone else, even a stranger, from being injured in an attack. If the defendant is defending someone else, the defendant must step into the shoes of the person that he/she is protecting. At that time, the defendant will have the same rights as the person that he/she is defending. If the defendant is mistaken as to the situation and uses deadly force when it is not necessary to use deadly force in the defense of the other person, then the defendant could be charged with a severe crime such as a homicide should the attacker be killed in the defense.

A person is allowed to defend his/her property from being taken. However, the defendant will be allowed to use only reasonable force to defend his/her property. Deadly force in the defense of property is not considered reasonable. Mechanical devices that are used to defend property must be nondeadly.

One is not usually liable for criminal acts committed under duress. A defendant may have committed a criminal act under threat of, or use of, force by a third person that was so overwhelming that it overpowered the defendant's will. Duress is not a defense to homicide.

A mistake of fact, although not a classic defense, can be a defense where such mistake negates an element of a crime. Even an unreasonable mistake, if made in good faith, may qualify as a valid defense.

Key Terms

Clear and convincing
Consent
Deadly force
Defense
Defense of others
Diminished capacity
Duress
Entrapment
Excuse
Infancy
Intoxication
Irresistible impulse
Justification
M'Naghten Rule
Necessity
Retreat rule
Self-defense
Substantial capacity

Review Questions

1. List the elements of the M'Naghten Rule and give an example of how they might be applied to a situation.
2. What is the test for substantial capacity?
3. Why is defense important?
4. What is the difference between a justification and an excuse?
5. When can intoxication be a defense?
6. List the elements of the defense of self-defense and explain why a person asserting a defense of self-defense cannot be the aggressor.
7. Give an example of entrapment and explain why the entrapment defense might be applicable to the situation.
8. When can somebody use deadly force in defense of property and why?
9. What are the elements for a defense of duress? Give an example of a situation in which a duress defense might be applied.
10. Give an example of a situation in which someone might assert a defense of others and explain how each element of the defense applies to your example.
11. Why is insanity a legal issue and not a medical issue?
12. Explain the elements of the irresistible impulse test.
13. What is the difference between voluntary and involuntary intoxication?
14. Who has the burden of proof in an insanity defense?
15. When can consent be asserted as a defense and when is it not permitted as a defense?

Exercises

1. Joanna is a college student in the middle of finals week. Joanna has been studying incessantly for many nights. She is exhausted and goes to bed. In the middle of the night, Joanna is awakened by the sound of glass being smashed. Joanna grabs a gun that she keeps in her bedside table and fires a shot at the front door of the dormitory. The person standing at the door is killed. Is Joanna justified in using deadly force? Suppose that the alleged intruder was Joanna's roommate? What if the intruder were Joanna's ex-husband against whom Joanna had a restraining order because he had beaten her on previous occasions? What if Joanna could have escaped easily out the window, thereby avoiding the intruder? What if the intruder possessed a knife?

2. Using whatever legal resources available to you, research the case of *Virginia v. Lorena Bobbitt,* the infamous case of a wife who cut off the penis of her husband, John Wayne Bobbitt, in 1994. What were the facts regarding Lorena's insanity defense? What was the insanity test that was applied in Lorena's case?

3. Dan was caught shoplifting a Rolex watch from a local jewelry store. At his trial for the theft, Dan asserted a defense of insanity. Dan had been diagnosed as a kleptomaniac since childhood and brought forth evidence to support the diagnosis. Despite years of psychotherapy, Dan could not be cured and continued to steal. In a jurisdiction applying the M'Naghten test for insanity, may Dan be convicted of larceny? Why or why not?

4. Nancy is visiting her good friend Michelle when she sees a jacket that she believes in good faith she had let Michelle borrow. Before she leaves, Nancy takes the jacket. May Nancy be convicted of larceny? Why or why not?

5. Danny believes a higher power has directed him to kill his neighbor Ned. Danny waits outside Ned's house to kill him. Danny knows it is illegal to kill people but believes he has the moral authority to kill Ned. Explain how jurisdictions employing the M'Naughten rule could differ in deciding whether or not Danny should be relieved of criminal liability due to insanity.

6. Fred and Frankie have been drinking at a local pub. Suddenly Frankie pulls out a revolver and shoots the bartender. He then points the gun at Diane, who is sitting at the other side of the bar. Fred jumps up and knocks Frankie to the ground. Frankie hits his head on the corner of the bar and dies instantly. May Fred be convicted of homicide? Why or why not?

7. Donnie robs a store clerk at knife point. The store clerk points a gun at Donnie to stop the robbery. If Donnie responded by stabbing the store clerk and the store clerk was killed, could Donnie claim self-defense? Why or why not?

8. Bruce was flying his small plane over a large urban area when both engines suddenly died. Rather than put the plane down in a crowded city park, he maneuvered the plane and managed to put it down in a cornfield. His plane struck and killed Bob, who was in the field preparing to harvest his crops. Will Bruce be held criminally liable for killing Bob? Why or why not?

PORTFOLIO ASSIGNMENT

Create for your portfolio a chart depicting the different insanity tests and which states use each of the tests.

Instructions

Use the key terms from this chapter to fill in the answers to the crossword puzzle.

NOTE: When the answer is more than one word, leave a blank space between words.

ACROSS

2. Defense available in cases involving the defense of persons, oneself, or another. It is a violent action known to create a substantial risk of causing death or serious bodily harm.
8. Any unlawful threat or coercion used by a person to induce another to act (or to refrain from acting) in a manner that he or she otherwise would not do.
9. An act of a law enforcement official to induce or encourage a person to commit a crime when the defendant expresses no desire to proceed with the illegal act.
11. A defendant's legal excuse that the use of force was justified.
14. The term used in the definition of legal insanity proposed by the Model Penal Code.
15. The state of a person who is under the age of legal majority.
16. A lawful reason for acting or failing to act.
17. Evidence that indicates that a thing to be proved is highly probable or reasonably certain.

DOWN

1. An impulse to commit an unlawful or criminal act that cannot be resisted or overcome because mental disease has destroyed the freedom of will, the power of self-control, and the choice of actions.
3. A reason alleged for doing or not doing a thing.
4. A justification defense available if one harms or threatens another while defending a third person.
5. The doctrine that recognizes that an accused does not have to be suffering from a mental disease to have impaired mental capacities at the time the offense was committed.
6. Voluntarily yielding the will to another.
7. The defendant alleges he or she lacked capacity to form criminal intent.
8. Legally sufficient reason to excuse the complained-of behavior.
10. The doctrine holding that the victim of a crime must choose to retreat instead of using deadly force if certain circumstances exist.
12. A justification defense for a person who acts in an emergency and commits a crime that is less harmful than the harm that would have occurred but for the person's actions.
13. Under the influence of alcohol or drugs which may, depending on the degree of inebriation, render a party incapable of entering into a contractual relationship or of acting in the manner in which an ordinarily prudent and cautious person would have acted under similar circumstances.

The PEOPLE of the State of Colorado, Petitioner

v.

Larry G. FLIPPO, Respondent.

159 P.3d 100

Supreme Court of Colorado,

No. 05SC794.

May 21, 2007.

As Modified on Denial of Rehearing June 11, 2007.

Background: Defendant was convicted in the District Court, Weld County, of felony sexual assault. He appealed. The Court of Appeals, 134 P.3d 436, reversed and remanded. The Supreme Court granted certiorari.

Holding: The Supreme Court, held that expert testimony proposed by defendant about his intellectual disability and its effect on reliability or credibility of his statements to police officers was expert testimony on a "mental condition" within meaning of statute establishing notice and evaluation requirements before a defendant may offer expert testimony on his or her "mental condition."

Reversed and remanded. . . .

I. FACTS AND PROCEDURAL HISTORY

Larry Flippo ("Flippo") was convicted at trial of felony sexual assault. The evidence presented at trial included statements made by Flippo directly to the police during a videotaped interrogation. Before trial, Flippo challenged the admissibility of those statements as the product of an involuntary confession. The judge ruled his statements voluntary and the videotape admissible. Flippo then requested that the court allow him to introduce testimony at trial about his intellectual disability for the purpose of challenging the credibility of his statements made to the police. Flippo endorsed three experts to testify about his intellectual disability and its effect on the reliability or credibility of the statements he gave to police. In response, the prosecution filed a motion in limine to exclude such evidence. The trial court held a hearing in which a social worker testified and scientific and legal journal articles were introduced together with the resumes and proposed testimony of the other two experts.

The substance of the proposed expert testimony, supported by the literature, was that people with intellectual disabilities are more suggestible in a police interview than a person without those disabilities and that they will agree with statements made by the police, even if those statements are not true. The purpose of the proposed evidence was to undermine the reliability and credibility of Flippo's statements on a videotape showing officers making incriminating statements ending with "Correct?" to which Flippo would agree. The social worker testified that Flippo had an intellectual disability and he also "idealized" police officers. She expressed concern that during the interrogation, Flippo gave incriminating responses he thought would satisfy the police officers.

The prosecution argued that Flippo was required to give notice of his proposed evidence at arraignment and submit to a court-ordered evaluation pursuant to both section 16-8-103.5 (controlling the procedure for raising impaired mental condition as an affirmative defense) and section 16-8-107(3)(b). Flippo argued that an intellectual disability is not a "mental condition" for purposes of section 16-8-107(3)(b) and thus the procedural requirements should not apply. The trial court ruled that "mental retardation is a *mental condition* . . . within the meaning of [section] 16-8-107(3)." The court then found that Flippo had not given notice at arraignment of his intent to introduce expert testimony. The court also held that Flippo's proposed expert testimony would not be relevant or helpful to the jury and therefore Flippo would not be allowed to present any expert evidence of his I.Q. at trial.

[Text omitted]

On appeal, Flippo challenged the exclusion of both his expert testimony and his lay opinion testimony. The court of appeals concluded that Flippo's proposed expert testimony did not fall within section 16-8-107(3)(b) because Flippo was not introducing the evidence as part of a defense. *Flippo*, 134 P.3d at 441–42. It held the trial court's exclusion of the expert evidence was error and ordered a new trial. *Id.* The court of appeals did not address whether it was error to exclude his lay opinion testimony.

We granted certiorari to consider whether the court of appeals was correct in finding that the trial court improperly excluded Flippo's expert testimony under section 16-8-107. We now reverse and remand for further consideration of Flippo's remaining issues including the exclusion of his lay opinion testimony.

II. ANALYSIS

[Text omitted]

Flippo argues that the term "mental condition" as used contextually in section 16-8-107 is limited to evidence introduced for only two purposes: (1) in support of an insanity or impaired mental condition defense; and (2) a defense that the defendant lacked the requisite mens rea. Here, Flippo's evidence was offered to attack the weight a jury should give to his statements. Because Flippo was not offering the evidence to directly challenge an element or to advance an affirmative defense, he argues his expert testimony falls outside of the statute. We disagree.

Based on the language of the statute, "mental condition" includes intellectual disabilities, even though section 16-8-107(3)(b) itself provides no definition of "mental condition." The first line of subsection 107(3)(b) begins: "[r]egardless of whether a defendant enters a plea of not guilty by reason of insanity. . . ."

These words, in this context, unambiguously state that the statute is meant to apply in those situations where insanity is *not* the reason the evidence is being introduced, such as evidence of an intellectual disability.

In *People v. Requejo,* the court of appeals noted that intellectual disabilities were not included within the definition of "mental condition" as used in section 16-8-107(1). *Requejo* was decided in 1996; three years later, the General Assembly amended section 16-8-107 and added subsection 107(3)(b) with the "regardless of whether" language. Due to the gap in time, we cannot say that the General Assembly was directly responding to *Requejo.* However, the added language did fill a statutory gap identified by that case.

Despite this, Flippo argues that in other parts of the statute, the term "mental condition" refers exclusively to a mental impairment affecting a defendant's sanity or ability to form a culpable mental state. *Requejo,* 919 P.2d at 878. Though Flippo's interpretation is correct as to those parts of the statute relating to mental condition evidence as a defense, subsection 107(3)(b) uses "mental condition" in a notably different manner.

The language of section 16-8-107(3)(b) evinces the General Assembly's desire to address evidence that relates to the condition of a defendant's mind beyond just issues of insanity. We agree that the term is used differently in other parts of the statute . . . However, since subsection 107(3)(b) applies regardless of whether a defendant enters a plea of insanity, "mental condition," as used in that subsection, unambiguously includes the introduction of expert evidence of a defendant's intellectual disability. We therefore hold that the term "mental condition," as used in section 16-8-107(3)(b), includes expert testimony regarding a defendant's intellectual disability.

In reaching the opposite conclusion, the court of appeals relied on a Wyoming decision holding that exclusion of expert testimony regarding a defendant's low I.Q., offered to challenge the circumstances of his confession, was reversible error. *See Hannon v. State,* 2004 WY 8, 84 P.3d 320 (2004) . . .

We agree with the Wyoming court's assessment that, unless the expert opinion evidence is flatly unreliable, its exclusion risks deprivation of a defendant's right to present a defense. However, including intellectual disabilities within the requirements of the statute is not to say that such expert testimony is inadmissible. To the contrary, our case law has made clear that evidence of a defendant's intellectual disability is admissible when relevant. In *Vanrees,* we held that evidence of "mental slowness" is admissible on the issue of whether the defendant was able to form the required mens rea for the offense. In *People v. Lopez,* we held that a defendant has the right to present expert psychological evidence to show the jury his confession was unworthy of belief. 946 P.2d 478, 482 (Colo. App. 1997) . . .

Therefore, generally speaking, defendants may attack the credibility or reliability of a confession and allow the jury to determine any weight that should be given to such statements. *Crane,* 476 U.S. at 690 (noting that: "an essential component of procedural fairness is an opportunity to be heard. . . . That opportunity would be an empty one if the State were permitted to exclude competent, reliable evidence bearing on the credibility of a confession when such evidence is central to the defendant's claim of innocence.").

Although a defendant is entitled to present evidence in his or her defense, the manner in which the evidence is presented may be controlled by statute. In Colorado, when a defendant wishes to introduce expert testimony about his mental condition, he must comply with section 16-8-107. According to the requirements of the statute, a defendant must provide notice and permit a court-ordered examination before offering expert testimony regarding the effect of his mental condition on a relevant issue at trial. § 16-8-107(3)(b). If a defendant does not provide notice at arraignment, the trial court must allow the defendant to argue good cause has been shown as to why the defendant should be allowed to give notice at a later date. *Id.* Once notice has been given, the court may order an evaluation. *Id.* After these procedural requirements have been met, the only remaining issue is admissibility. Admissibility of this expert testimony must be determined under the Colorado Rules of Evidence and in light of the constitutional considerations we have identified here. However, failure to comply with the procedural prerequisites of the statute may prevent such evidence from being admitted.

Under the facts of this case, the trial court properly determined that Flippo's proposed expert testimony was subject to the requirements of the statute. Flippo did not provide timely notice and therefore the trial court did not order an examination. Flippo therefore failed to comply with the procedural requirements of the statute and the trial court was correct in excluding Flippo's expert testimony. However, our opinion here does not reach any conclusions about the admissibility of Flippo's proposed lay opinion testimony or whether its exclusion was error by the trial court.

The court of appeals' conclusion, that exclusion of Flippo's expert testimony at trial was error, is therefore reversed. On remand, the court of appeals should address Flippo's remaining issues including whether Flippo's lay opinion testimony was wrongfully excluded and, if so, whether such exclusion was error.

III. CONCLUSION

The judgment of the court of appeals is reversed. We remand to the court of appeals to resolve Flippo's remaining appellate issues.

Source: 159 P.3d 100 (Colo. 2007). Reprinted by permission of Westlaw.

Chapter 11

Crimes against the State, Public Order, and Morality

CHAPTER OBJECTIVES

Upon completion of this chapter, you will be able to:

- Identify common crimes against the state.

- Identify issues surrounding the public order.

- Explain crimes that affect the quality of life.

- Discuss crimes that affect the public morals.

- Understand how laws enacted for these crimes protect the public.

Crimes against the state vary in their severity and breadth. These crimes can run the gamut from threatening the administration of justice to threatening national security. Because of the disruption and menace that these crimes pose, they can be a serious threat to social order.

In addition to crimes against the state, there are also laws to uphold public order and morality. These laws are designed to provide a minimum standard for civility and decency in society. The purpose of these laws is to provide a better quality of life for citizens located in the jurisdiction that establishes these laws. Most crimes of this type are crimes of **general intent**.

This chapter will explore crimes against the administration of justice, crimes against the state, as well as crimes against public order and morality.

general intent
An unjustifiable act; reckless conduct.

BRIBERY

bribery
The offering, giving, receiving, or soliciting of something of value for the purpose of influencing the action of an official in the discharge of his or her public or legal duties.

Bribery is a crime against justice that is common practice in many societies across the globe. In some countries, bribing public officials is a common business practice and is expected in order to conduct business in that country. Bribery dates back to ancient times and was intended to influence judges and public officials. The benefit of bribery is not necessarily one of monetary value. When bribery occurs, a payment of something is offered to a person in return for a favor that is typically connected to the person's public duty or office.

The elements of bribery are

- The tender
- Of anything of value

- To a public official
- With the intent that the public office holder will be influenced in the performance of his or her official duties.

The element of tender in the crime of bribery means to receive something. It does not matter under the law how the thing of value is transferred or received by the public official. Bribery either occurs or it does not. There is no such crime as an attempted bribery.

Laws vary by state as to which officials can be bribed under the law. Examples of the types of public office holders that may be identified in state bribery laws are

- Legislators.
- Judges.
- Jurors.
- Law enforcement officers.
- Corporate officers.
- Athletes.

It is a crime to give a public official a bribe as well as to receive a bribe. However, the giving and receiving of bribes are not mutually dependent crimes. A person can be charged and convicted of one of the crimes without another party being convicted.

Bribery is usually thought of as a general-intent crime. The intent requirement of bribery is the intent to influence. Some states require that there be a mutual intent between the giver and the receiver of a bribe. In order to be convicted of bribery in a federal crime, according to 18 U.S.C. § 201(b)(1) the prosecutor must prove beyond a reasonable doubt the following:

> - *That the defendant directly or indirectly gave [offered, promised] something of value to the person to be bribed [i.e. public official]; and*
> - *That the defendant did so corruptly with intent to:*
>   - *Influence an official act by the public official; or*
>   - *Persuade the public official to omit an act; or*
>   - *Persuade the public official to do an act in violation of his lawful duty.*

The Foreign Corrupt Practices Act of 1977 was enacted by Congress to eliminate the bribery of foreign officials, which was destroying the public confidence in corporate America. The act was amended in 1998 by the International Anti-Bribery Act of 1998. Federal anti-bribery legislation tends to be more focused on the intent of the bribery rather than the amount.

PERJURY

Another crime against the administration of justice is the crime of **perjury**. All states as well as federal laws make perjury a crime. Perjury is defined under federal law 18 U.S.C.A. § 1621 as follows:

> *Whoever—*
> 1. *having taken an oath before a competent tribunal, officer, or person, in any case in which a law of the United States authorizes an oath to be administered, that he will testify, declare, depose, or certify truly, or that any written testimony, declaration, deposition, or certificate by him subscribed, is true, willfully and contrary to such oath states or subscribes any material matter which he does not believe to be true;*
>
> . . .
>
> *is guilty of perjury and shall, except as otherwise expressly provided by law, be fined under this title or imprisoned not more than five years, or both.*

PRACTICE TIP

Under federal law, remember that there are two types of crimes that involve political officials' receiving money in exchange for influencing the political official's duties. These two crimes are *bribery* and the lesser crime of *receiving illegal gratuities*. The federal cases in which the court distinguished between these two types of crimes are *United States v. Brewster*, 506 F.2d 62 (D.C. Cir. 1974), and *United States v. Anderson*, 509 F.2d 312 (D.C. Cir. 1974). Both of these cases involved a political action committee receiving monies from a lobbyist for the benefit of a senator.

perjury
The willful assertion as to a matter of fact, opinion, belief, or knowledge, made by a witness in a judicial proceeding as part of his/her evidence, either upon oath or in any form allowed by law to be substituted for an oath, whether such evidence is given in open court, in an affidavit, or otherwise, such assertion being material to the issue or point of inquiry and known to such witness to be false.

Most perjury laws have the following elements in common:

- The willful taking of a false oath
- In a judicial proceeding
- In regard to a material matter at issue.

oath
Any form of attestation by which a person signifies that he/she is bound in conscience to perform an act faithfully and truthfully.

An **oath** is an essential element for the crime of perjury. The defendant must have taken an oath and then lied after having taken the oath. The crime of perjury can be completed when it involves lying under oath in a judicial proceeding. Besides lying in open court, perjury can be committed by lying on an affidavit, in a deposition, or in testimony or other sworn proceedings.

It is important that the person lies about a subject matter that is important to the outcome of the legal proceeding. The outcome does not necessarily have to be significant to the guilt or innocence of the defendant in the case or the liability of the defendant, but it does have to be more than just a social lie such as lying about your age. A person does not need to know definitely that he/she is lying. If he/she is uncertain about the truth of his/her statement and makes the statement anyway, that recklessness toward the truth may be sufficient to satisfy the elements for perjury.

The federal law states the following elements for perjury:

- False testimony under oath or affirmation
- Regarding a material matter
- With willful intent to provide false testimony.

CONTEMPT

contempt
A willful disregard for or disobedience of a public authority.

Contempt is the willful disobedience to the authority of a court or legislative body. The crime of contempt cannot occur without a willful disregard or some type of intentional wrongdoing. Contempt can be committed directly by conducting some direct act against the court during a judicial proceeding. A disruption of court proceedings is an example

CASE FACT PATTERN

In 1987, Dr. Elizabeth Morgan was imprisoned on civil contempt charges. Morgan had accused her ex-husband of sexually abusing their daughter and refused to permit an unsupervised court-ordered visit. Morgan instead put her daughter into hiding and was subsequently jailed for contempt. She was released 25 months later, only when Congress passed a bill that limited the time judges in the District of Columbia could incarcerate a person on civil contempt charges.

EYE ON ETHICS

When dealing with the legal industry, a legal professional is placed in a position of trust repeatedly. As officers of the court, attorneys take an oath to uphold the judicial system and processes in which they work and practice. Unfortunately, there are times when attorneys cross the line. Attorneys have been prosecuted and disbarred for committing perjury or being in contempt in various cases. For example, in 2005, in Providence, Rhode Island, a defense attorney pled guilty to perjury and contempt for violating a court order not to release video footage of a political official accepting a bribe and then lying about it under oath. By releasing the videotape against court orders, the attorney had satisfied the elements for contempt. By lying about his actions in court, the attorney committed perjury. Attorneys and their legal assistants are held to the same standard–if not a higher standard –as other citizens by virtue of the nature of their profession.

of direct contempt. Contempt can be committed indirectly when the disobedience happens outside of the hearing process. For example, a juror may leak information concerning a case to family or friends.

Under penal statutes, criminal contempt is punished by imposing some type of sentence on the perpetrator in order to punish him/her for disobeying a judicial directive. The perpetrator has committed a crime against the public's right to peace, security, and order. The ability of our judicial system to function as prescribed is one of the fundamental rights of all Americans. Those who thumb their noses at the system and commit crimes against its administration breach the public security.

TREASON

Treason is the only crime that is actually identified in the U.S. Constitution. The Constitution refers to treason as a breach of the allegiance to the United States and names it as one of the most serious felonies that can be committed by a citizen. The Constitution handles treason in Article III, Section 3[1] as follows:

> *Treason against the United States, shall consist only of levying War against them, or, in adhering to their Enemies, giving them Aid and Comfort. No Person shall be convicted of Treason unless on the Testimony of two Witnesses to the same overt Act, or on Confession in open Court.*

treason
A breach of allegiance to one's government, usually committed through levying war against such government or by giving aid or comfort to the enemy.

The U.S. Code also discusses treason. In Title 18, Part I, Chapter 115, section 2381 handles treason as follows:

> *Whoever, owing allegiance to the United States, levies war against them or adheres to their enemies, giving them aid and comfort within the United States or elsewhere, is guilty of treason and shall suffer death, or shall be imprisoned not less than five years and fined under this title but not less than $10,000; and shall be incapable of holding any office under the United States.*

The elements of treason are

- A breach of allegiance.
- Overt act of betrayal.
- Intent to betray.

The allegiance to the United States must be as a citizen of the United States or naturalized alien, nationals who are not aliens such as Samoans or Puerto Ricans, individuals on temporary visas in the United States, or foreign nationals who are permitted to reside in the United States.

In order to satisfy the next element, the person must commit some sort of overt act of betrayal that constitutes material aid or comfort to the enemy. Disloyalty by itself is not enough to satisfy the element. For example, in 2006, Adam Pearlman, a citizen of the United States and former resident of Southern California, appeared on several Al Qaeda videos making direct appeals to American citizens and soldiers to turn against the government of the United States. His actions on the videos constituted an overt act of betrayal against the United States.

The last element, intent to betray, is essential to the crime of treason. Treason is a specific-intent crime. The government must establish that the perpetrator's actions were done purposefully and knowingly. Treason is not committed without the actor knowing exactly what he/she is doing.

American history provides only a few cases of treason. The most famous treason trial in American history was that of Aaron Burr in 1807; he, however, was acquitted. After the Civil War, several Confederate leaders, including Jefferson Davis and Robert E. Lee, were indicted for treason, but they along with all the others received amnesty when President Andrew Johnson left office.

ESPIONAGE

Espionage is the crime against the state that is the subject matter for many suspense thriller movies in the entertainment industry. It is a crime against the state that has proved to be very destructive to the United States. Espionage is spying or being a party to spying. More often than not, espionage is conducted by the perpetrator for monetary gain.

Espionage can be conducted in a variety of ways such as the following:

- Selling governmental secrets.
- Identifying other U.S. spies to other foreign powers.
- Obstructing or accessing governmental buildings.
- Disrupting governmental functions.

The U.S. Criminal Code identifies two types of espionage: espionage during peacetime and espionage during war. Espionage during peacetime is defined as the turning or attempting to turn over information or documentation about national defense to any foreign power with the intent or with reason to believe that information will be used to help the foreign power in its dealings with the United States or to actually injure the national security of the United States. Espionage during war is the collecting, recording, publishing, or communicating, or the attempt to do so, of any information about U.S. troop movements, or the location of ships and aircraft as well as any other information that might prove useful to the enemy. The penalty for espionage during war can be death or life imprisonment as it poses such a breach to the national security and seriously jeopardizes both troop safety and public safety.

TERRORISM

Americans did not pay much attention to **terrorism** before 2001. Since that tragic day in American history, terrorism has been considered one of the biggest threats to public order. On September 11, 2001, Islamic militants hijacked several U.S. airliners and slammed them into the World Trade Center towers and the Pentagon. Thousands of innocent citizens were killed. September 11, 2001, changed the lives of Americans forever. The existence of terrorism is now a harsh reality for Americans.

Terrorism is used to accomplish the goals of the terrorists. Some typical goals are

- To intimidate the civilian population of an area.
- To retaliate against the government for its conduct or policies.
- To influence or coerce a government to take or not to take a particular action.

Various criminal activities make up a terrorist act. Some examples of terrorist activity are car bombings, plane hijackings, and money laundering, as well as suicide bombers. Due to the breadth and depth of activities that are considered terrorism, it is not practical to provide an exhaustive list in this discussion. In addition, terrorists are continuing to think of new methods with which to attack the civilian population.

The United States acted to make terrorism a crime within its borders when Congress enacted the USA PATRIOT Act in 2001. The USA PATRIOT Act (18 U.S.C.A. §§ 2331–2339) delineates items, activities, and punishments that are to be used for people who are convicted of terrorism in the United States. The act specifies the types of weapons, targets, and jurisdictions that can be considered to be acts of terrorism. The act also sets punishments such as the death penalty if deaths occur as a result of such criminal activity. The act prohibits financial transactions with any country that supports terrorism, harbors or conceals terrorists, or knowingly provides support to terrorist organizations that could pose a threat to the United States.

A DAY IN THE LIFE OF A REAL PARALEGAL

Since the terrorist strike that occurred on U.S. soil on September 11, 2001, the United States has struggled to protect the homeland as well as preserve individual freedoms. The scope of the USA PATRIOT Act has been called into question as to whether or not it results in an **infringement** on individual rights and freedoms upon which the United States has with pride based its government. Items such as electronic surveillance, the compiling and storing of personal information of individuals on a broad scale, the detainment of people who are labeled "enemy combatants," and the suspension of detainees' habeas corpus rights have been challenged in the Congress and the U.S. Supreme Court. There is no doubt that in the future the need of the United States to protect the homeland and its citizens from the threat of terrorism will be challenged more as it continues to call into question whether or not individual rights and freedoms should be infringed upon in order to accomplish that goal.

infringement
An act that interferes with an exclusive right.

The USA PATRIOT Act also broadens the scope of law enforcement and government officials when conducting electronic surveillance and other types of electronic information gathering or seizures. The law also enables the government to detain individuals, including American citizens, as enemy combatants if they have conducted or planned to conduct activities that may threaten the public order in the United States. The cases of these prospective enemy combatants are then heard under the secrecy of a military tribunal. The government's activities in this regard have come under scrutiny as it is believed by some that people being detained by the United States are being denied their **habeas corpus** rights.

There is no doubt that, with the War on Terror waged by the Bush administration as well as continuing terrorist activities taking place around the world, the crimes to the public order that make up a terrorist act will only be expanded in the future.

habeas corpus
A writ employed to bring a person before a court, most frequently to ensure that the party's imprisonment or detention is not illegal.

RESEARCH THIS

Terrorism also can be caused by domestic terrorists or American-born citizens against their own fellow citizens. Such was the case with the bombing of the Murrah Federal Building in Oklahoma City on April 19, 1995, by Timothy McVey. Research the USA PATRIOT Act (18 U.S.C.A. § 2331) and determine if domestic terrorism is covered in the act. Also, how does the act define domestic terrorism and what are the penalties for conducting such activities in the United States?

DISORDERLY CONDUCT

The types of conduct that are considered **disorderly conduct** are normally considered minor crimes or misdemeanors. The laws that govern them are typically local ordinances. There are a variety of conducts that are considered disorderly conduct, but they have a common feature: the acts are public in nature. The Model Penal Code at section 250.2 defines disorderly conduct as follows:

disorderly conduct
Behavior that tends to disturb the public peace, offend public morals, or undermine public safety.

1. *Offense Defined. A person is guilty of disorderly conduct if, with purpose to cause public inconvenience, annoyance or alarm, or recklessly creating a risk thereof, he:*
   (a) engages in fighting or threatening, or in violent or tumultuous behavior; or
   (b) makes unreasonable noise or offensively course utterance, gesture or display, or addresses abusive language to any person present; or
   (c) creates a hazardous or physically offensive condition by any act which serves no legitimate purpose of the actor.

2. *Grading. An offense under this section is a petty misdemeanor if the actor's purpose is to cause substantial harm or serious inconvenience, or if he persists in disorderly conduct after reasonable warning or request to desist. Otherwise disorderly conduct is a violation.[1]*

---

[1] Model Penal Code, copyright 1985 by the American Law Institute. Reprinted with permission.

Types of conduct that are considered disorderly conduct in many jurisdictions are

- Fighting in public.
- Unreasonably loud noise.
- Disruption of a lawful assembly.
- Obstruction of traffic.

Some of these crimes disturb the public peace or could possibly cause injury or damage to people or properties who are innocently subjected to the conduct.

RIOT

riot
An unlawful disturbance of the peace by an assembly of usually three or more persons acting with a common purpose in a violent or tumultuous manner that threatens or terrorizes the public.

A **riot** is considered group disorderly conduct. The Model Penal Code defines riot in section 250.1(1) as follows:

1. *Riot. A person is guilty of riot, a felony of the third degree, if he participates with [two] or more others in a course of disorderly conduct:*
   (a) with purpose to commit or facilitate the commission of a felony or misdemean or;
   (b) with purpose to prevent or coerce official action; or
   (c) when the actor or any other participant to the knowledge of the actor uses or plans to use a firearm or other deadly weapon.[2]

In order to constitute a riot, there typically must be three or more people who have gathered together for an unlawful purpose or to carry out a lawful purpose in an unlawful manner. The most important element of a riot is an action by a group. A riot does not have to take place in public. However, the actions of the riot need to disrupt or disturb the public order in some manner. For example, the Los Angeles riots were a series of group actions that vandalized and terrorized the city of Los Angeles after the police officers who were accused of beating Rodney King were acquitted at trial. People who disagreed with the verdicts rioted throughout the city of Los Angeles in protest.

Sometimes, people say and do things to incite a riot. Inciting a riot does not need to lead to an actual riot. The urging of others to partake in actions and behaviors that could cause people to riot is enough.

VAGRANCY AND LOITERING

vagrancy
The act of going about from place to place by a person without visible means of support, who is idle, and who, though able to work for his/her maintenance, refuses to do so, but lives without labor or on the charity of others.

loitering
To stand around or move about slowly; to linger or spend time idly.

Vagrancy and **loitering** are crimes that are somewhat based on economic status. If someone is unemployed and homeless, then he/she has satisfied the elements for vagrancy or loitering. The person's economic status rather than his/her acts satisfies the elements for this crime. Society wants anyone who is capable of working to do so and not live on the streets or linger on street corners. Therefore, to protect the public quality of life, vagrancy and loitering have been declared minor crimes in some states; other states do not have laws forbidding such behavior, while others might have such laws but not enforce them.

GANG ACTIVITY

It is obvious that gang activity seriously impacts the quality of life of the citizens who are exposed to the tactics and antics of the members of the gang. Gang activity can constitute everything from a group of loitering teenagers to organized cartels that terrorize neighborhoods.

Many states and cities have passed laws in an effort to regulate gang activities and behavior. The idea behind such legislation is to deter individuals from wanting to participate in gangs. Penalties for gang activities are becoming stiffer as gang activities have become more violent. Large cities have had to deal with gangs such

[2] Model Penal Code, copyright 1985 by the American Law Institute. Reprinted with permission.

as the Crips and the Bloods, who have terrorized neighborhoods, trafficked in drugs, and committed drive-by shootings. Rural areas that were once gang-free are now being exposed to gang activity as drug activities reach every corner of the United States.

Laws that seek to regulate gang activity seek to protect quality-of-life interests such as peace, quiet, order, and individual security. However, these laws have been challenged in recent times as the members of the gangs assert their rights to congregate, assemble, and express themselves.

OBSCENITY

Obscenity is a crime that affects the public morals. Obscenity typically refers to the distribution or display of material depicting sexual activity knowing that the material may offend a reasonable person's sensibilities. The Miller test, from *Miller v. California,* 413 U.S. 15 (1973), defines obscenity using a three-prong test. The elements of the crime of obscenity are

- An average person applying contemporary sensibilities would find that the work, taken as a whole, appeals to the **prurient interest**.
- The work depicts or describes, in a patently offensive way, sexual conduct specifically defined by state law.
- The work, taken as a whole, lacks serious literary, artistic, political, or scientific value.

The Model Penal Code at section 251.4 defines obscenity as follows:

> *Material is obscene if, considered as a whole, its predominant appeal is to prurient interest, that is, a shameful or morbid interest, in nudity, sex, or excretion, and if in addition it goes substantially beyond customary limits of candor in describing or representing such matters. Predominant appeal shall be judged with reference to ordinary adults unless it appears from the character of the material or the circumstances of the dissemination to be designed for children or other specially susceptible audience. Undeveloped photographs, molds, printing plates, and the like, shall be deemed obscene notwithstanding that processing or other acts may be required to make the obscenity patent or to disseminate it.[3]*

The federal law covering obscenity is found at 18 U.S.C.A. §§ 1460–1470 and covers the possession, sale, mailing, transportation, broadcasting, and transfer to minors of obscene material. Obscene material falls outside the protections of the First Amendment right of freedom of expression. Obscene speech is subject to criminal punishment.

PROSTITUTION

Prostitution is another crime against public morals. Prostitution is an industry that has been around for thousands of years. It is even referenced in the Bible. It is condemned both religiously and morally by most people and societies. The following elements make up the crime of prostitution:

- Soliciting or engaging in
- Any sexual activity, including deviate sex,
- For the purpose of commercial gain.

The crime of prostitution typically punishes both the prostitute and the person who solicits and engages in sexual activity with a prostitute for money. Any sexual act may satisfy the element of sexual activity such as masturbation, sexual intercourse, or sodomy, and it includes any sex, heterosexual sex as well as homosexual sex. The

obscenity
The quality or state of being morally abhorrent or socially taboo, especially as a result of referring to or depicting sexual or excretory functions.

prurient interest
Characterized by or arousing inordinate or unusual sexual desire.

prostitution
The act of performing, or offering or agreeing to perform, a sexual act for hire.

---

[3] Model Penal Code, copyright 1985 by the American Law Institute. Reprinted with permission.

A DAY IN THE LIFE OF A REAL PARALEGAL

Bambi works on the street. She is a prostitute and sells her body for sex. Bambi is also a single mom and this is how she supports her family. Every night, Bambi goes out to a selected street corner to sell sexual favors for money. Bambi works under the protection of her pimp, Edward. Edward will solicit johns for Bambi to service at a local motel. Edward's job is to try to keep Bambi safe as well as to ensure that she gets paid. For his services, Edward gets paid a large portion of all monies that Bambi earns.

One night, Edward solicits a john from a different area to have sex with Bambi. Once inside the motel, Bambi begins to strip down when the door bursts open and the motel room is raided by law enforcement. Apparently, the john was an undercover law enforcement officer. Both Bambi and Edward are arrested.

Bambi and Edward are taken to the police station, booked, and then arraigned the next morning. They post bail and are scheduled to return for a future court hearing. Edward retains the services of the firm you work in, known in the prostitution industry to be competent at handling these types of cases. You and your supervising attorney tell Edward and Bambi that they will probably have to pay a fine and perhaps spend a few days in jail if convicted or they can plead **nolo contendere** and try to be released on probation. Bambi and Edward decide to plead nolo contendere and the judge sentences them to six months' probation since they have not had a prior arrest record before this incident. Bambi decides to move to Nevada where legalized prostitution exists.

nolo contendere
Latin for "I do not wish to contend"; to plead no contest.

sexual activity must be done for pay. Asking someone for sex without the exchange of something of value such as money does not constitute prostitution.

GAMBLING

gambling
Making a bet. Such occurs when there is a chance for profit if a player is skillful and lucky.

Gambling is engaging in games of chance. Gambling is typically not considered a crime until it becomes a public nuisance or offends the public morality. Many people gamble and see nothing wrong with it. States even host state lotteries and promote gambling in an effort to provide money for the state coffers.

There are several federal laws that regulate gambling. A couple of them are

- 18 U.S.C.A § 1955 prohibits conducting, financing, managing, supervising, directing, or owning an interest in an illegal gambling business that is in violation of a state or local law.

- 18 U.S.C.A. § 1084 prohibits the interstate or foreign transmission by wire communications facility of wagering information by persons engaged in betting or wagering activities that are illegal by state or local law. This law has been used to indict people on gambling charges using the Internet. The use of telephone lines during interstate sports betting to connect to the Internet brought those indictments under the federal law.

States also have gambling statutes, but they vary from state to state. Some states allow betting at horse racing tracks and off-track facilities. Other states allow bingo and state lotteries. In addition, many Indian tribes own and operate casinos. On the basis of their identity as their own sovereign, gambling on Indian land in Indian-owned casinos is legal.

Typically, gambling becomes a public problem when it leads to members of society being tricked or defrauded by gambling establishments or individuals who take and place bets.

Summary

Bribery is a crime against justice that is common in many societies across the globe. In some countries, bribing public officials is a common business practice and is actually an expected business activity. Bribery dates back to ancient times and developed as a way to influence the decisions of judges and public officials. The benefit of bribery is not necessarily one of monetary value. When bribery occurs, a payment of something is offered to a person in return for a favor that is typically connected with the person's public duty or office.

The elements of bribery are the tender of anything of value to a public official with the intent that the public office holder will be influenced in the performance of his/her official duties.

Most perjury laws have the following elements in common: the willful taking of a false oath in a judicial proceeding in regard to a material matter at issue. An oath is an essential element for the crime of perjury. The defendant must have taken an oath and then lied after having taken the oath. The crime of perjury can be completed when it involves lying under oath in a judicial proceeding. Besides by lying in open court, perjury can be committed by lying on an affidavit, in a deposition, or in testimony or other sworn proceedings.

Contempt is the willful disobedience of the authority of a court or legislative body. The crime of contempt cannot occur without a willful disregard or some type of intentional wrongdoing. Contempt can be committed directly by conducting some direct act against the court during a judicial proceeding. A disruption of court proceedings is an example of direct contempt. Contempt can be committed indirectly when the disobedience happens outside of the hearing process.

The elements of treason are a breach of allegiance with an overt act of betrayal and an intent to betray.

The U.S. Criminal Code identifies two types of espionage: espionage during peace time and espionage during war. Espionage during peace time is defined as the turning or attempting to turn over information or documentation about national defense to any foreign power with the intent or with reason to believe that information will be used to help the foreign power in its dealings with the United States or to actually injure the national security of the United States. Espionage during war is the collecting, recording, publishing, or communicating, or the attempt to do so, of any information about U.S. troop movements, or the location of ships and aircraft as well as any other information that might prove useful to the enemy. The penalty for espionage during war can be death or life imprisonment as it poses such a breach to the national security and seriously jeopardizes both troop safety as well as public safety.

Terrorism is the use of criminal activity to accomplish certain goals. Some typical goals of terrorists are to intimidate the civilian population of an area, to retaliate against the government for its conduct or policies, and to influence or coerce a government to take or not to take a particular action.

The United States acted to make terrorism a crime within its borders when Congress enacted the USA PATRIOT Act in 2001. The USA PATRIOT Act (18 U.S.C.A. §§ 2331–2339) delineates items, activities, and punishments that are to be used for people who are convicted of terrorism in the United States. The act specifies the types of weapons, targets, and jurisdictions that can be considered to be acts of terrorism. The act also sets punishments such as the death penalty if deaths occur as a result of such criminal activity. The act prohibits financial transactions with any country that supports terrorism, harbors or conceals terrorists, or knowingly provides support to terrorist organizations that could pose a threat to the United States.

Types of conduct considered to be disorderly conduct are normally considered minor crimes or misdemeanors. The laws that govern them are typically local ordinances. There are a variety of actions that are considered disorderly conduct, but they have a common feature: they are public in nature.

In order to constitute a riot, there typically must be three or more people who have gathered together for an unlawful purpose or to carry out a lawful purpose in an unlawful manner. The most important element of a riot is an action by a group. A riot does not have to take place in public. However, the actions of the riot need to disrupt or disturb the public order in some manner.

Vagrancy and loitering are crimes often related to economic status. If someone is unemployed and homeless, then he/she has satisfied the elements for vagrancy or loitering. Economic status rather than acts satisfies the elements for this crime. Society wants anyone who is capable of working to do so and not live on the streets. Therefore, to protect the public quality of life, vagrancy and loitering have been declared minor crimes.

It is obvious that gang activity seriously impacts the quality of life of the citizens who are exposed to their tactics and antics. Gang activity can constitute everything from a group of loitering teenagers to organized cartels that terrorize neighborhoods.

Obscenity is a crime that affects the public morals. It typically refers to the distribution or display of material depicting sexual activity knowing that the material may offend a reasonable person's sensibilities. The elements of the crime of obscenity are (1) an average person applying contemporary sensibilities would find that the work, taken as a whole, appeals to the prurient interest; (2) the work depicts or describes, in a patently offensive way, sexual conduct specifically defined by state law; and (3) the work, taken as a whole, lacks serious literary, artistic, political, or scientific value.

Prostitution is another crime against public morality. The following elements make up the crime of prostitution: soliciting or engaging in any sexual activity, including deviate sex, for the purpose of commercial gain.

Gambling is engaging in games of chance. It is typically not considered a crime until it becomes a public nuisance or offends the public morality. Many people gamble and see nothing wrong with it. States even host state lotteries and promote gambling in an effort to provide money for the state coffers.

Key Terms

Bribery	Oath
Contempt	Obscenity
Disorderly conduct	Perjury
Espionage	Prostitution
Gambling	Prurient interest
General intent	Riot
Habeas corpus	Terrorism
Infringement	Treason
Loitering	Vagrancy
Nolo contendere	

1. What are the elements of perjury according to the U.S. Code?
2. List three types of activities in which someone can commit perjury.
3. What is contempt and why is it a crime?
4. Give an example of direct contempt.
5. What distinguishes vagrancy and loitering from other crimes?
6. List the elements for obscenity.
7. What constitutes a gang?
8. List five things that the USA PATRIOT Act regulates in its efforts to control terrorism in the United States.
9. Why is gambling an activity that offends the public morals?
10. What does it mean to be a quality-of-life crime?
11. List five activities that can be considered disorderly conduct.
12. Why would it be considered illegal to place a bet on a game over the Internet?
13. What are the elements of prostitution?
14. Give a current example that has been in the news recently of a riot or inciting a riot.
15. Why is it not a crime to ask someone to have sex for free?
16. List three activities that would be considered sexual activity to satisfy the elements for prostitution.
17. Give five examples of materials that would be considered obscenity.
18. What is the difference between vagrancy and loitering?
19. Why is it important to have laws that protect the public order?

Review Questions

1. Judge Julie is presiding over a highly publicized murder trial. Both the public and the press are in the courtroom. The courtroom becomes noisy and unruly, so Judge Julie clears the courtroom to calm everything down. When people are readmitted to the courtroom, a man enters the room who had not been in the courtroom earlier when it had become disruptive. The man was unaware that there had been any previous issue. After Judge Julie asked the courtroom for quiet so that the proceedings could resume, the man begins talking quietly to his neighbor. Judge Julie immediately charges the man with contempt of court. Was the man guilty of contempt of court? Why or why not?

2. Joe and Jake are American citizens who are disillusioned with the divisiveness in the Congress between the Republican and Democratic Parties. In their opinion, every vote in Congress comes down along party lines and nothing ever seems to get to done. Joe and Jake think that the Communist Party provides a better form of government. Joe and Jake begin recruiting and teaching high school seniors to overthrow the U.S. government by violence and force and to replace it with communism. Have Joe and Jake committed a crime? Explain your answer in detail.

3. Josephine is a witness in a murder trial. She is being called to identify the defendant as the man that she saw running away from the scene of the crime. Josephine is not certain that the defendant was in fact the man that she observed that night, although she thinks it might be. Knowing that she is not certain about her recollection, Josephine goes ahead and states in court under oath that the man that she saw that night was in fact the defendant. When the prosecutor asks her if she is certain in her recollection of the events of that evening, Josephine responds in the affirmative. Has Josephine committed a crime? Explain your answer.

Exercises

4. Jorge is at a party with his friends. From across the room, he sees a very nice looking lady. He goes up to her and finds out that her name is Mona. Jorge and Mona seem to get along, and, as the night grows older and Jorge has had a few more drinks, Jorge decides that he would like to have sex with Mona. Unbeknownst to Jorge, Mona is a prostitute. Mona likes Jorge too and also would like to have sex with him. Jorge asks Mona if she would like to go somewhere private and have sex. Mona agrees. If Jorge and Mona are arrested, they would be charged with
   a. Jorge with soliciting a prostitute and Mona with no crime.
   b. Mona with prostitution, but Jorge would have committed no crime.
   c. Jorge with solicitation and Mona with prostitution.
   d. Neither one of them has committed a crime.

5. Wayne is a chief executive officer for a major corporation. He met Stacy in a local strip club. Stacy was one of the dancers. Wayne has to go on a business trip to New York and he asks Stacy to accompany him. Stacy agrees. Wayne is hoping that on the trip he will be able to have Stacy provide him with sexual favors. Once in New York, Wayne buys Stacy a pearl necklace worth about $2,000 with the expectation that she will provide him sexual services in exchange for the expensive gift. Stacy is aware of Wayne's expectations and is willing to oblige. Does the purchase of an expensive gift in exchange for sex satisfy the elements of prostitution? Why or why not? Give a detailed analysis in your answer.

6. Research your local city, county, and state jurisdictions. What laws are in place to curb gang activity in these jurisdictions? How do these laws differ from each other? What type of activities do they seek to deter?

7. Research punishments for treason against the federal government. Has the federal government every put anyone to death for treason?

8. Research the following case and brief it: *People v. Heidi Fleiss*. Find the main issue and then subissues along with the law or code used to prosecute Heidi Fleiss and the decision made in the case.

PORTFOLIO ASSIGNMENT

When judging obscenity, the trial court may instruct the jury to apply "community standards" without specifically defining the term. States are allowed to establish statewide standards for judging obscenity. Research the standards for your home state and write a memo discussing them to include in your portfolio.

Vocabulary Builders

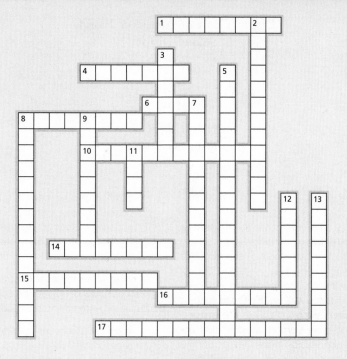

Instructions

Use the key terms from this chapter to fill in the answers to the crossword puzzle.

NOTE: When the answer is more than one word, leave a blank space between words.

ACROSS

1. A willful disregard for or disobedience of a public authority.
4. The willful assertion as to a matter of fact, opinion, belief, or knowledge, made by a witness in a judicial proceeding as part of his/her evidence, either upon oath in any form allowed by law to be substituted for an oath, whether such evidence is given in open court, in an affidavit, or otherwise, such assertion being material to the issue or point of inquiry and known to such witness to be false.
6. Any form of attestation by which a person signifies that he/she is bound in conscience to perform an act faithfully and truthfully.
8. Making a bet. Such occurs when there is a chance for profit if a player is skillful and lucky.
10. An act that interferes with an exclusive right.
14. The act of going about from place to place by a person without visible means of support, who is idle, and who, though able to work for his/her maintenance, refuses to do so, but lives without labor or on the charity of others.
15. The use of threat of violence to intimidate or cause panic, especially as a means of affecting political conduct.
16. The quality or state of being morally abhorrent or socially taboo, especially as a result of referring to or depicting sexual or excretory functions.
17. Latin for "I do not wish to contend"; to plead no contest.

DOWN

2. The act of performing, or offering or agreeing to perform, a sexual act for hire.
3. A breach of allegiance to one's government, usually committed through levying war against such government or by giving aid or comfort to the enemy.
5. Characterized by or arousing inordinate or unusual sexual desire.
7. A writ employed to bring a person before a court, most frequently to ensure that the party's imprisonment or detention is not illegal.
8. An unjustifiable act; reckless conduct.
9. To stand around or move about slowly; to linger or spend time idly.
11. An unlawful disturbance of the peace by an assembly of usually three or more persons acting with a common purpose in a violent or tumultuous manner that threatens or terrorizes the public.
12. The offering, giving, receiving, or soliciting of something of value for the purpose of influencing the action of an official in the discharge of his or her public or legal duties.
13. Spying or the gathering, transmitting, or losing of information respecting the national defense with intent or reason to believe that the information is to be used to the injury of the United States, or to the advantage of any foreign nation.

District Court of Appeal of Florida,
Second District.
Henry Brian BARRY, Appellant,

v.

STATE of Florida, Appellee.
934 So. 2d 656
No. 2D05-2667.
Aug. 4, 2006.

Affirmed in part and reversed in part.

STRINGER, Judge.

Henry Brian Barry challenges his convictions and sentences for aggravated assault on a law enforcement officer with a deadly weapon and disorderly conduct, contending that the evidence was insufficient to support either conviction. We affirm the aggravated assault conviction without further comment. However, because we agree that the evidence was insufficient to support the disorderly conduct conviction, we reverse as to that charge.

The charges against Barry arise from an incident that occurred between him and Lake Placid Police Officer Bonnie Pruitt. After dropping their daughter off at school, Barry and his wife were walking back to their car, which was parked in front of the elementary school. While returning to their car, Barry and his wife exchanged words with three young girls who were walking toward the school. While the content of these words was never definitively established at trial, whatever was said was sufficient to upset the girls and make at least one of them cry. The three girls approached Officer Pruitt, who was acting as the school crossing guard that day, and told her what Barry had said. Officer Pruitt decided to discuss the matter with Barry and his wife in an effort to resolve the problem.

When Officer Pruitt approached Barry to ask about the incident with the girls, Barry loudly told Officer Pruitt to mind her "own f—ing business." When Officer Pruitt continued to try to speak with Barry, he again told her to mind her "own f—ing business." After Barry started to get into his car, Officer Pruitt attempted to speak with Barry's wife about the incident with the girls. At that point, Barry got out of his car, came around to the passenger side, and began screaming obscenities at Officer Pruitt while pointing and shaking his finger in her face.

According to Officer Pruitt, while this confrontation was occurring, traffic along the road in front of the elementary school was slowing and stopping to watch the confrontation. One motorist allegedly yelled something about Barry preparing to hit Officer Pruitt. However, there was no testimony that any of the motorists got out of their cars or otherwise reacted to the scene itself. Based on this evidence, the trial court denied Barry's motion for judgment of acquittal on this count, and the jury subsequently found Barry guilty. Barry now appeals this conviction.

Section 877.03, Florida Statutes (2004), states, in pertinent part:

> **Breach of the peace; disorderly conduct**.—Whoever commits such acts as are of a nature to corrupt the public morals, or outrage the sense of public decency, or affect the peace and quiet of persons who may witness them, or engages in brawling or fighting, or engages in such conduct as to constitute a breach of the peace or disorderly conduct, shall be guilty of a misdemeanor of the second degree. . . .

In order to avoid possible constitutional problems, the supreme court has narrowed the scope of the conduct that may be punished under section 877.03:

> In light of these considerations, we now limit the application of Section 877.03 so that it shall hereafter only apply either to words which "by their very utterance . . . inflict injury or tend to incite an immediate breach of the peace," or to words, known to be false, reporting some physical hazard in circumstances where such a report creates a clear and present danger of bodily harm to others. We construe the statute so that no words except "fighting words" or words like shouts of "fire" in a crowded theatre fall within its proscription, in order to avoid the constitutional problem of overbreadth, and "the danger that a citizen will be punished as a criminal for exercising his right of free speech." With these two exceptions, Section 877.03 should not be read to proscribe the use of language in any fashion whatsoever.

. . . [I]t is clear that speech alone will not generally support a conviction for disorderly conduct. For example, in *Miller v. State*, 780 So. 2d 197 (Fla. 2d DCA 2001), the defendant's actions involved only loud and aggressive speech directed at a police officer who had come to her residence. This court reversed the conviction for disorderly conduct, noting that Miller's conduct was entirely verbal until after the officer initiated the arrest.

On the other hand, protected speech can be rendered unprotected by a defendant's additional physical actions. For example, in *C.L.B. v. State*, 689 So. 2d 1171, 1172 (Fla. 2d DCA 1997), C.L.B. not only engaged in loud verbal protests and name-calling, but he also repeatedly approached the officer and an arrestee so closely that the officer repeatedly had to push C.L.B. aside and tell him to stay away. This court noted that while C.L.B.'s words alone would be insufficient to support the adjudication for disorderly conduct, the combination of the words and his actions, which hindered the officer's ability to complete the arrest, was sufficient to support the adjudication.

Here, the only evidence presented at the trial to support the disorderly conduct charge was that Barry yelled obscenities at

Officer Pruitt concerning her actions. No evidence was presented that the words used were "fighting words" or words that would tend to incite an immediate breach of the peace. Further, the State presented no evidence that Barry engaged in any physical conduct toward Officer Pruitt that affected Officer Pruitt's ability to do her job or that breached the peace or otherwise incited others to act. Therefore, the State did not prove that Barry was guilty of disorderly conduct as that offense has been defined and limited.

The State contends that Barry's conviction should be upheld because drivers along the roadway slowed or stopped while Barry was yelling, thus causing a "crowd" to gather and causing Officer Pruitt to fear for the safety of children crossing the street. The State correctly points out that when a defendant's words are sufficient to cause a crowd to gather to such an extent that officers develop safety concerns, convictions for disorderly conduct have been affirmed. *See, e.g., Marsh v. State*, 724 So. 2d 666 (Fla. 5th DCA 1999).

However, the mere fact that other people come outside or stop to watch what is going on is insufficient to support a conviction for disorderly conduct. Instead, there must be some evidence that the crowd is actually responding to the defendant's words in some way that threatens to breach the peace. *See, e.g., Gonzales v. City of Belle Glade*, 287 So. 2d 669, 670 (Fla. 1973).

Here, the State presented some evidence that motorists slowed down to watch the interaction between Barry and Officer Pruitt. However, the State presented no evidence that these individuals actually responded to Barry's words or that anyone in the area was actually incited into engaging in an immediate breach of the peace. At most, the State proved that onlookers slowed because they were curious or annoyed. Thus, the evidence that onlookers stopped or slowed to watch Barry yell obscenities at Officer Pruitt, without more, is insufficient to support the conviction.

Because the State's evidence was insufficient to support Barry's conviction for disorderly conduct, we reverse that conviction. In all other respects, we affirm.

Affirmed in part; reversed in part.

[Footnotes omitted]

CASANUEVA and VILLANTI, JJ., Concur.

Source: 934 So. 2d 656 (Fla. 2d DCA 2006). Reprinted with permission of Westlaw.

Chapter 12

Criminal Procedures Leading Up to Trial

CHAPTER OBJECTIVES

Upon completion of this chapter, you will be able to:

- Explain the arrest and booking procedures.
- Discuss the types of pretrial appearances.
- Understand the plea bargaining process.
- Recognize the various types of pretrial motions.

Once a person has been identified as a suspect and accused of having committed a crime, he/she enters a world ruled by procedural laws. Our judicial system is structured in such a manner as to try to provide the defendant with an opportunity to justly and fairly defend himself/herself against the charges that have been brought against him/her. Criminal procedural law is a systematically proscribed process toward that end. This chapter will provide an overview of the criminal procedural process prior to trial. Not all procedural matters are handled in the same manner for all jurisdictions. This chapter provides a general overview of the types of criminal processes that are typically found in most jurisdictions.

ARREST

arrest
The formal taking of a person, usually by a police officer, to answer criminal charges.

bench warrant
The process issued by the court itself for the attachment or arrest of a person.

According to the *Restatement (Second) of Torts,* an arrest involves the taking of an individual into custody in order to bring that individual before a court or to otherwise assist in the administration of the law. The first step in the criminal procedural process is the **arrest**. When a suspect is taken into custody, he/she may be searched and then taken to the police station to be formally charged with the crime. If the suspect is not apprehended or absconds before arrest, then an arrest warrant will be issued for the suspect. If he/she is arrested for the commission of a misdemeanor, then the suspect may be released with a citation. The citation instructs the defendant that he/she must appear in court at a later date to respond to the charges that have been made against him/her. Failure to appear in court will result in a **bench warrant** being issued for the defendant. At that time, he/she may not be released from incarceration pending charges due to the fact that he/she failed to appear in court.

As stated in Chapter 2, before a person can be arrested, the requirement of probable cause must be met. *Martinez v. People,* 168 Colo. 314, 451 P.2d 293 (1969), held that a valid arrest without a warrant is one based on probable cause. This means that the arresting officer had "reasonable grounds" to believe that the individual he or she arrested was guilty. Remember, probable cause exists if there is a substantial likelihood that (1) a crime was committed and (2) the suspect committed the crime. Sometimes the police have time to try to gather more information before making an arrest. In those cases, they must first obtain an arrest warrant prior to arresting the suspect. If the arrest comes as a result of one of the Fourth Amendment exceptions that have been discussed previously, then an arrest warrant may not be necessary. A general power to arrest without a warrant generally exists (1) for a felony or a breach of the peace committed in the arresting officer's presence, (2) when that officer has had a private person accuse another of a felony, (3) if reasonable grounds exist to believe that a felony has been committed, and (4) for felonies committed by the arrestee even if not committed in the arresting officer's presence. However, it is important to always keep in mind that an arrest without a warrant and not supported by reasonable grounds is unlawful.

BOOKING

After having arrested a suspect, the law enforcement officer will take him/her to the station or other facility to complete the process of **booking** him/her. Booking involves entering the suspect's name, offense, and time of arrival on a log kept by law enforcement that lists all persons who are detained by law enforcement. The log is also known as the blotter. The suspect is fingerprinted and photographed. A number is given to the suspect so that he/she can be tracked through the criminal justice detention system. The reason for the arrest is stated on the blotter and made known to the defendant. The accused is then allowed to make a telephone call to notify someone of his/her detention or to seek assistance of legal counsel. A suspect cannot refuse to submit to booking procedures on Fifth Amendment grounds. The procedures involved in booking compel only physical evidence, not testimonial; they are therefore not prohibited by the Fifth Amendment.

booking
Administrative step taken after an arrested person is brought to the police station that involves entry of the person's name, the crime for which the arrest was made, and other relevant facts on the police blotter.

After booking, the suspect may be released if he/she was arrested for a lesser offense such as a misdemeanor. As stated above, if a release occurs, the suspect will have to return and appear before a magistrate or judicial officer in the future. However, if the crime is of a more serious nature, then he/she will be detained in a detention facility pending **arraignment**. The suspect's place of detention is often called a *holding cell*. In some jurisdictions, the defendant may be released on bail prior to the arraignment and the bail is set by a bail commissioner or other judicial officer who possesses the authority to do so.

arraignment
A court hearing where the information contained in an indictment is read to the defendant.

INVESTIGATION AFTER ARREST

In many criminal cases, law enforcement officers must find and interview witnesses; conduct searches; and hold a lineup, photo spread, or videotaped lineup in order to obtain the identification of the suspect as well as perform further investigation in order to solidify their case against the defendant. Once law enforcement officers have reviewed the evidence that has been gathered during the investigation, they, along with the prosecuting attorney, may decide that there is insufficient evidence to prosecute the defendant. If this occurs, the suspect will be released and the case is either closed or placed in a pending status so that if more evidence is gathered at a future date, it may be reopened. If, after reviewing the evidence, law enforcement officers believe they do not have enough evidence for the originally charged crime, but they do have enough evidence to demonstrate that the defendant committed a lesser crime, then they may decide to change the charge and reduce it to the lesser offense. Unless the suspect is released, at this point in the criminal process, control over the case moves to the prosecutor's office for future handling of the matter.

IDENTIFICATION

A pretrial identification of the suspect by a witness or victim is often one of the first steps taken by police as they pursue their investigation of a suspect after an arrest. The most often used methods of identification are lineups, show-ups, and photo identifications. These identification procedures have been held to not violate the Sixth Amendment right to counsel or the right to procedural due process guaranteed under the Fifth and Fourteenth Amendments. A pretrial identification will typically only be held invalid in one of two situations. First, it may be invalid if the defendant's Sixth Amendment right to counsel was violated. For example, the right to counsel at lineups and show-ups attaches after formal charges have been filed against a suspect. However, even if formal charges have been filed, there still would be no right to counsel at a photo identification. The other instance where a pretrial identification may be held invalid is where the defendant's due process rights were violated. For example, where a lineup includes a group of people whose appearance is drastically different than the suspect's, the identification procedure may be held to violate due process.

THE COMPLAINT

The criminal litigation process may begin with the filing by the prosecutor of an accusatory pleading known as **complaint**, **indictment**, or **information**, depending on the jurisdiction. The complaint includes a statement of the charges that are being brought against the suspect, and the suspect is now a criminal defendant. The complaint also will specify if any **enhancements** are being brought along with the charges. For example, murder with special circumstances could evidence enhancements to the charge of murder. Prosecutors must demonstrate that probable cause existed that a crime was committed and that the defendant was the one who committed it. In other cases, a **grand jury** may be called in at this point to determine if probable cause exists.

INITIAL APPEARANCE

In most jurisdictions, defendants are taken before a magistrate within 24 to 72 hours after the arrest. During this initial appearance or arraignment, the magistrate makes sure that the person charged is the same person named in the complaint. The magistrate informs the defendant of the charges, explains to the defendant his/her constitutional rights, and asks the defendant if he/she needs legal counsel. If the defendant does need legal counsel, the magistrate will then appoint counsel if the defendant indicates that he/she cannot afford legal counsel. The defendant may enter a plea at this time or request more time in which to enter a plea so that he/she can consult with legal counsel.

If the initial appearance is based on either the information or the indictment, the prosecutor will submit a motion to the court to order the defendant to appear for an arraignment or initial appearance. At this court appearance, the defendant can move to have the charges dismissed, as defendants often do. As stated before, the defendant can enter a plea at the initial appearance. The typical pleas that are entered by a defendant are **not guilty**, **guilty**, or **nolo contendere**. Not guilty means that the defendant asserts that he is not liable for the criminal activity or criminal results for which he is charged.

complaint
A charge, preferred before a magistrate having jurisdiction, that a person named has committed a specified offense, with an offer to prove the fact, to the end that a prosecution may be instituted.

indictment
A written list of charges issued by a grand jury against a defendant in a criminal case.

information
States that the magistrate determines there is sufficient cause to make an arrest and also sets forth the formal charges sought by the prosecution.

enhancements
Added factors to a criminal charge that make the charge carry greater weight.

grand jury
A jury of inquiry who are summoned and returned by the sheriff to each session of the criminal courts and whose duty is to receive complaints and accusations in criminal cases, hear evidence, and decide if the defendant should stand for trial.

guilty
A verdict only available in criminal cases in which the jury determines that the defendant is responsible for committing a crime.

nolo contendere
Latin for "I do not wish to contend"; to plead no contest.

Nolo contendere is a plea in which the defendant does not contest the charge. A defendant would plead nolo contendere when the defendant wants to admit to committing the act but denies that the act was a crime. Originally, a plea of nolo contendere was used only as the preliminary plea or if there was a strong expectation that the punishment for the act admitted to would be no more than a fine. However, the use of nolo contendere pleas has evolved and today such a plea has essentially the same effect as a plea of guilty. Most often, a defendant will plead nolo contendere when he does not want to admit guilt due to the possibility of exposure to a civil lawsuit that might be brought from the same event.

Guilty means that the defendant accepts criminal liability. A guilty plea means that the defendant admits to every element of the offense and can be considered equivalent to a conviction at trial. However, a court may not accept a defendant's guilty plea if it is not entered voluntarily and intelligently. To make sure that a defendant's guilty plea is entered voluntarily and intelligently, the trial judge will generally personally inform the defendant of four things: (1) the nature of the charges, (2) the potential penalty, (3) the fact that the guilty plea is a waiver of all constitutional challenges other than lack of jurisdiction and double jeopardy, and, finally, (4) the right to counsel. Entering a guilty plea always requires the assistance of counsel unless the defendant has expressly and voluntarily waived the right.

Most frequently, the defendant pleads guilty to the charge or a lesser charge that has been agreed to in a **plea bargain**. A plea bargain is the process by which the accused and the prosecutor negotiate a satisfactory disposition of the case, subject to court approval. It is important to note that the defendant's plea agreement may be accepted by the prosecutor, but the judge may refuse to accept it. Usually, a plea bargain involves the defendant's pleading guilty to a lesser offense in return for a lighter sentence. A prosecutor must honor a promise made to the defendant if the defendant's entered plea was based upon that promise. If a prosecutor fails to honor such a promise, he or she must allow the defendant to withdraw the plea. Other important facts to remember with regard to plea bargains is that prosecutors decide what charges will be filed and judges decide appropriate sentences; therefore, any promises by the police of reduced charges or light sentences in return for cooperation are not legally binding. Additionally, Rule 32(e) of the Federal Rules of Criminal Procedure allows a defendant to withdraw his or her guilty plea any time before a sentence is imposed if a fair and just reason can be demonstrated.

The magistrate may release the defendant from jail pending further proceedings. Defendants arrested for misdemeanors are often released on their own recognizance. Defendants arrested for more serious crimes will be released only on **bail**. The word *bail* comes from an old French term, *baillier,* which means "to deliver." Bail is used for the purposes of ensuring that the defendant will show up for his/her trial. Every defendant is entitled to a hearing before a judge, magistrate, or bail commissioner to determine if bail should be established and, if so, in what amount. Bail is usually arranged for the defendant by his or her attorney through a bail bonds person. Bail can take the form of bail bonds, property deposits, third-party supervision, or other conditions as may be necessary to ensure that the defendant shows up for his/her trial. The Constitution does not guarantee a person the right to bail, only the right to due process under the Fourteenth Amendment. Both the federal government and the majority of states have enacted laws that allow for the denial of bail to an individual suspected of committing a capital crime. If bail is set, the Eighth Amendment prohibits the court from setting excessive bail, but the Eighth Amendment is not binding on the states. However, most states, through their constitutions, have provided a guarantee to the right to bail.

plea bargain
The process whereby the accused and the prosecutor in a criminal case work out a mutually satisfactory disposition of the case subject to court approval.

bail
Court-mandated surety or guarantee that the defendant will appear at a future date if released from custody prior to trial.

When determining a person's bail, the court will consider the following factors in determining the bail amount:

- The seriousness of the charge against the defendant.
- The weight of the evidence against the defendant.
- The defendant's ties to the community, family, and employment.
- The defendant's prior criminal record.
- The defendant's history, that is, whether the defendant has previously failed to appear at court.

The amount of bail will vary from defendant to defendant. Some courts allow for a partial bond to be posted directly with the court, effectively eliminating the need for a bail bonds person. The bail bonds person will keep a percentage of the bond in payment for his/her services. If a person violates his/her conditions of bail, he/she will be rearrested and bail may not be established the second time so the defendant might be held throughout the proceedings. If the defendant fails to appear in court following the issuance of a cash bond, that will result in the forfeiture of the cash. Some defendants are released without bail or on their own recognizance.

PRELIMINARY HEARING

preliminary hearing
A hearing by a judge to determine whether a person charged with a crime should be held for trial.

In some jurisdictions, a **preliminary hearing** replaces the need for a grand jury. Generally, a preliminary hearing is a hearing where a judge decides if sufficient evidence exists to make the accused stand trial on the charges that have been filed against him/her. The judge's decision at a preliminary hearing is considered to be the equivalent of the decision that a grand jury would make in deciding whether to return an indictment. There is no constitutionally guaranteed right to a preliminary hearing; however, if a preliminary hearing takes place, it is a stage to which the defendant's Sixth Amendment right to counsel has attached. The defendant and his/her legal counsel appear before a magistrate or judge for a preliminary hearing. During this hearing, another determination of probable cause is made. At the preliminary hearing, the prosecution must introduce evidence to demonstrate to the court why the case against the defendant should be set for trial. This may be an adversarial proceeding with the prosecution presenting witnesses. The rules of evidence are more relaxed at a preliminary hearing than they are at a trial as the purpose of the hearing is to establish if probable cause exists to order the accused to stand trial. Hearsay is allowed. Evidence can be introduced at the hearing without consideration of whether it was legally collected.

The defense attorney usually has the opportunity to cross-examine the witnesses at the preliminary hearing. If the defendant intends to plead guilty, the preliminary hearing is usually waived. If the defense decides to waive the preliminary hearing, a written document or form is usually required to do so.

The defendant may be released if the magistrate finds that the evidence is insufficient. If the evidence is found to be sufficient, the magistrate has the option to reduce the charges against the defendant if he/she feels it is warranted. If the magistrate finds sufficient evidence to establish probable cause, then the prosecutor issues an information. As stated before, the information is a formal accusation that replaces the complaint and binds the defendant over for trial.

GRAND JURY

Unlike a preliminary hearing, a grand jury is a group of citizens, not a judge, who are called upon to decide whether probable cause exists to try the defendant. In federal court, the Fifth Amendment guarantees defendants the right to a grand jury indictment in any felony case. Many states also have a grand jury process; however, the number of jurors called varies from jurisdiction to jurisdiction. The grand jury convenes in a closed session and hears only evidence presented by the prosecutor. The defendant is not allowed to present evidence before the grand jury. Grand juries have the ability to **subpoena** evidence. The grand jury can subpoena people to testify before it or it can subpoena evidence such as documents, tape recordings, photographs, and other pertinent evidence to be brought to it.

If the grand jury finds probable cause, it issues a bill of indictment against the defendant. The indictment is then filed with the trial court and becomes the formal charge against the defendant. If the information is insufficient to charge the suspect, the grand jury will not issue a bill of indictment. The federal government and about half of the states require a grand jury. It is important to remember that grand jury proceedings are not adversarial. A defendant has no right to counsel and no right to examine opposing witnesses.

subpoena
An order issued by the court clerk directing a person to appear in court.

PRACTICE TIP

Each state determines the exact number of people who should sit on its grand jury. In addition, some states require that a preliminary hearing be held first and that the judge or magistrate just recommend to the grand jury whether or not probable cause exists. It is very important to be familiar with the rules and procedures of the jurisdiction that you are dealing with so that you will understand the criminal process that is required there.

RESEARCH THIS

The pretrial procedures in a criminal matter vary from jurisdiction to jurisdiction. Research your jurisdiction to determine if a preliminary hearing or grand jury is used to determine if there is sufficient probable cause to hold a defendant for trial. In addition, does your jurisdiction use a complaint, information, or indictment?

PRETRIAL MOTIONS

Pretrial motions are made to request the judge to take some particular action on specified matters in a case. The motions may be made orally in a court appearance or in writing for consideration by the court. Many pretrial motions are based on alleged violations of the defendant's constitutional rights and serve as defenses against the charges. Some of the possible pretrial motions that may be made to the court are

- Motion to dismiss. This type of motion asserts that one of the defendant's constitutional rights has been violated. For example, evidence against the defendant has been obtained illegally. Therefore, this motion asserts that the charges against the defendant, or some of the charges, be thrown out and not asserted against the defendant. If the defendant wins a motion to dismiss all charges, he/she is released and the case is dropped. However, if the prosecutor establishes more evidence that was not available at the time the motion to dismiss was heard, the charges can be reestablished against the defendant at a later date.

- Motion to suppress evidence. This is a request to the court that certain evidence be excluded, or suppressed, from consideration during the trial. Motions to suppress are typically used for illegally seized evidence or evidence that may be extremely prejudicial to the defendant as it attacks his/her character and is not necessarily relevant to the case at bar.

- Motion challenging sufficiency of the indictment. This is a motion claiming that the evidence submitted by the prosecutor was insufficient to establish probable cause that the defendant committed the crime with which he/she has been charged.

- Motion in limine. This is a motion to limit the use of certain evidence.

CASE FACT PATTERN

Judith is representing Keith in a murder trial. Keith is 28 years old. However, when Keith was a juvenile, he was arrested twice for aggravated assault. Judith knows that if this information is admitted at trial, it will seriously prejudice the jury in Keith's murder trial. In an attempt to have the evidence excluded at trial, Judith files a motion in limine asking the judge to exclude the prior arrests from being admitted at trial due to the fact that they happened when Keith was a minor, that he never stood trial for the accusations after the arrests, and that such information will prejudice the jury. How would you rule on the motion in limine if you were the judge?

- Motion for a change of venue. This type of motion requests that the trial be moved to a different location to ensure that the defendant receives a fair and impartial proceeding. Sometimes a motion for change of venue can be made for the convenience of the parties or for some other acceptable reason.

- Motion for severance as to a party or an offense. This type of motion is made when the defendant is charged with more than one offense or when multiple parties are charged with the same crime and the defendant wants to be tried separately for each offense or separately from the other defendants. The premise behind such a motion is that if the defendant is tried together with all of the other defendants in the case or with all of the charges together, the defendant will not receive a fair trial.

- Motion for exculpatory evidence ("Brady motion"). This is a motion made by the defendant directing the prosecution to swear under oath that the prosecution has turned over to the defendant's counsel all exculpatory information that may prove the defendant's innocence.

DISCOVERY

discovery
The pretrial investigation process authorized and governed by the rules of civil procedure; process in which the opposing parties obtain information about the case from each other.

Discovery is allowed in criminal cases, although it is allowed to a much lesser extent than in civil cases. During discovery in a criminal case, a defendant is entitled to obtain any evidence in the possession of the prosecutor that relates to his/her case. This evidence can include statements previously made by the defendant, objects used in the crime or that are otherwise incriminating, documents, reports of tests, and examinations. Discovery in a criminal case might include a confession, a weapon, reports of scientific information such as a DNA report, photographs of persons and places, and other materials pertinent to the case. To obtain evidence from the prosecutor's office, a motion for discovery and inspection is prepared and submitted to the court. The court then orders the prosecutor to turn over to the defense attorney the requested evidence. It is important to remember, however, that work product material is not generally considered to be discoverable. Rule 16 of the Federal Rules of Criminal Procedure gives defendants their rights to pretrial discovery (see Figure 12.1). Beyond the requirements of the Federal Rules of Criminal Procedure, the American Bar Association Model Rules of Professional Conduct require a prosecutor to disclose to the defense all known evidence and information that tends to either negate or mitigate the guilt of the defendant.

Constitutional rights of the accused affect the discovery process in criminal cases. As stated in the Chapter 2 the Fifth Amendment sets forth that an accused has the right against compulsory self-incrimination as well as due process. The Sixth Amendment guarantees the right to effective assistance of counsel in criminal proceedings. All of these rights are applicable to the states via the Fourteenth Amendment. The right against compulsory self-incrimination means that, at some point in time, discovery against the accused will be restricted so as not to incriminate him/her. The prosecution

FIGURE 12.1
Federal Rules of Criminal Procedure: Discovery

Sources: FED. R. CRIM. P. 16(a)(1)(c) (1997). FED. R. CRIM. P. 16(a)(1)(A) and (B) (2002).

Rule 16. Discovery and inspection. (a) Governmental Disclosure of Evidence.
(1) *Information Subject to Disclosure.*
  (A) *Statement of Defendant.* Upon request of a defendant the government must disclose to the defendant and make available for inspection, copying, or photographing: any relevant written or recorded statements made by the defendant, or copies thereof, within the possession, custody, or control of the government, the existence of which is known, or by the exercise of due diligence become known, to the attorney for the government; that portion of any written record containing the substance of any relevant oral statement made by the defendant whether before or after arrest in response to interrogation by any person then know[n] to the defendant to be a government agent; and recorded testimony of the defendant before a grand jury the substance of any other relevant oral statement made by any person then known by the defendant to be a government agent if the government intends to use that statement at trial.

Rule 16. Discovery and Inspection. (a) Government's Disclosure.
(1) *Information Subject to Disclosure.*
  (A) *Defendant's Oral Statement.* Upon a defendant's request, the government must disclose to the defendant the substance of any relevant oral statement made by the defendant, before or after arrest, in response to interrogation by a person the defendant knew was a government agent if the government intends to use the statement at trial.
  (B) *Defendant's Written or Recorded Statement.* Upon a defendant's request, the government must disclose to the defendant, and make available for inspection, copying, or photographing, all of the following:
    (i) any relevant written or recorded statement by the defendant if:
      • the statement is within the government's possession, custody, or control; and
      • the attorney for the government knows—or through due diligence could know—that the statement exists;
    (ii) the portion of any written record containing the substance of any relevant oral statement made before or after arrest if the defendant made the statement in response to interrogation by a person the defendant knew was a government agent; and
    (iii) the defendant's recorded testimony before a grand jury relating to the charged offense.

is obligated to provide to the defense all exculpatory information and to avoid the use of false testimony. The defense counsel is not required to turn over to the prosecution the defense counsels' preparation or defendants' communications. In most criminal cases, the prosecutor allows the defense attorney to review the government's file. As a result of this review, discovery is normally kept at a minimum between the parties.

A DAY IN THE LIFE OF A REAL PARALEGAL

Paralegals who work in criminal law play an integral part in the prosecution or defense of the case. More often than not, the supervising attorneys spend all day in court in hearings and trials on the numerous cases in which they are involved. The paralegal is left handling the documentation of the case. Paralegals who are employed in the area of criminal law can expect to research case law concerning bringing motions in limine, motions to dismiss, motions for severance, and other pretrial motions. Many times the paralegal will be responsible for drafting these motions for review by the supervising attorney upon his/her return from court. In addition, the paralegal is responsible for classifying and organizing all discovery in the matter. It would not be unusual for a paralegal working on a murder case to be interviewing witnesses to the incident or organizing autopsy photographs.

EYE ON ETHICS

The prosecutor is an officer of the court. As such, he/she is responsible to protect and serve the judicial system. A prosecutor is required to turn over evidence to the defense attorneys so the defense attorneys can properly prepare the defense of their client. Every person is entitled to a proper and adequate defense. If the prosecution fails to turn over evidence to the defense, the entire case against the defendant can be in jeopardy and may be dismissed. It is very important for prosecutors to act ethically and to be diligent in dealing with the turning over of evidence to the defense. To withhold evidence in a criminal matter is a serious ethical offense. Paralegals who work for prosecutors must be very aware of these requirements as it is the paralegal who is often gathering evidence that is ultimately going to be provided to the defense.

TRIAL

Most trials involving felonies are tried by a jury. Trials involving misdemeanors are typically tried by a judge without a jury. Criminal trials differ from civil trials in a number of ways, such as the right to a speedy and public trial, unanimous agreement by the jury on the verdict, the presumption that a defendant is innocent until proven guilty, a higher burden of proof because the defendant must be proven guilty beyond a reasonable doubt, the privilege against self-incrimination, as well as complex evidence rules.

A DAY IN THE LIFE OF A REAL PARALEGAL

Marcus belongs to an inner-city gang. The gang decides to give a demonstration of its strength and power and claim a block of a neighboring gang's turf. One night, Marcus and his gang members drive through the residential block of a neighboring gang, firing their weapons randomly. One of the bullets from one member's gun pierces through the wall of a house on the street and strikes a woman in the head, killing her instantly. Marcus is arrested, along with other members of his gang who were also in the vehicle that night. Marcus is brought to the police station and booked for murder. His fingerprints are taken, his information is entered into the police blotter, and his photograph is taken. He is issued prison clothing, searched, and detained in the county jail.

Marcus is brought to the court for an arraignment before a judge within 24 hours of his arrest. The judge reads his name and the charges of murder that have been filed against Marcus. He asks Marcus if he understands the charges that have been levied against him. Marcus understands. Marcus is scared. The judge asks Marcus if he has legal counsel or would he like to have legal counsel appointed. Marcus tells the judge that he needs to have a lawyer appointed on his behalf. The judge appoints one of the public defenders in the courtroom that day to represent Marcus. The public defender asks the judge for a moment and converses with Marcus. The public defender says that he needs time to examine Marcus's case and asks Marcus if it would be okay to defer his plea until he has time to review the evidence. Marcus agrees. The judge asks the public defender if Marcus wishes to enter a plea at this arraignment. The public defender states that Marcus would like to defer his plea until a later date.

After the hearing, the public defender and his paralegal gather and review the evidence that the prosecutor will be presenting at trial. The paralegal organizes and categorizes all of the evidence so that it can be easily referenced. The evidence against Marcus is substantial. The public defender then visits Marcus at the county jail. He tells Marcus that there is substantial evidence against him as the prosecutors have numerous witnesses who have identified the gang members in the car that night, including Marcus. In addition, the car had been impounded and Marcus's fingerprints were found in the car as well as on the gun. The public defender indicates that the prosecutor has offered a plea bargain that he will drop the murder charges if Marcus pleads guilty to manslaughter. Instead of facing life in prison, Marcus will be facing a possible sentence of 10 to 12 years and could get out earlier for good behavior. Marcus agrees to the deal and the court affirms the arrangement.

Each criminal trial is different as the evidence presented against each defendant differs. However, most trials involve the following basic processes:

- Opening statements by the prosecutor and defense attorneys.
- The prosecution presenting its case.
- The defense attorneys cross-examining prosecutorial witnesses.
- The defense presenting its case.
- The prosecutors cross-examining defense witnesses.
- Closing arguments by both the prosecution and the defense.
- Jury instructions being given by the judge to the jury.
- Jury deliberations.
- Verdict.

If the defendant is found guilty, then he/she is sentenced. If an **acquittal** is obtained, the defendant is released from all charges.

acquittal
The legal and formal certification of the innocence of a person who has been charged with a crime.

Summary

The first step in the criminal procedural process is the arrest. When a suspect is taken into custody, he/she may be searched and then taken to the police station to be formally charged with the crime. A pretrial identification of the suspect by a witness or victim is often one of the first steps taken by police as they pursue their investigation of a suspect after an arrest. The most often used methods of identification are lineups, show-ups, and photo identifications. If the suspect has been arrested for the commission of a misdemeanor, then he/she may be released with a citation. The citation instructs the defendant that he/she must appear in court at a later date to respond to the charges that have been made against him/her. Failure to appear in court will result in another warrant being issued for his/her arrest. At that time, he/she may not be released from incarceration pending charges due to the fact that he/she failed to appear in court.

After having been arrested, the law enforcement officer will take a suspect to the station or other facility to complete the process of booking. Booking involves entering the suspect's name, offense, and time of arrival on a log, also known as the blotter, kept by law enforcement that lists all persons who are detained by law enforcement. The suspect is fingerprinted and photographed. A number is given to the suspect so that he/she can be tracked through the criminal justice detention system. The reason for the arrest is stated on the blotter and made known to the defendant. The accused is then allowed to make a telephone call in order to notify someone of his/her detention or to seek assistance of legal counsel.

The criminal litigation process may begin with the filing by the prosecutor of an accusatory pleading known as a complaint, indictment, or information, depending on the jurisdiction. The complaint includes a statement of the charges that are being brought against the suspect, and the suspect is now a criminal defendant. The complaint also will specify if any enhancements are being brought along with the charges. For example, murder with special circumstances could evidence enhancements to the charge of murder. Prosecutors must demonstrate that probable cause existed that a crime was committed and that the defendant was the one who committed it. In other cases, a grand jury may be called in at this point to determine if probable cause exists.

In most jurisdictions, defendants are taken before a magistrate within 24 to 72 hours after the arrest. During this initial appearance or arraignment, the magistrate makes sure that the person charged is the same person named in the complaint. The magistrate informs the defendant of the charges, explains to the defendant his/her constitutional rights and asks the defendant if he/she needs legal counsel. If the defendant does need legal counsel, the magistrate will then appoint counsel. The defendant may enter a plea at this time or request more time in which to enter a plea so that he/she can consult with legal counsel.

In some jurisdictions, a preliminary hearing replaces the need for a grand jury. The defendant and his/her legal counsel appear before a magistrate or judge for a preliminary hearing. During this hearing, another determination of probable cause is made. At the preliminary hearing, the prosecution must present evidence to demonstrate to the court why the case against the defendant should be set for trial. This may be an adversarial proceeding with the prosecution presenting witnesses. The defense attorney usually has the opportunity to cross-examine the witnesses at the preliminary hearing. If the defendant intends to plead guilty, the preliminary hearing is usually waived. The defendant may be released if the magistrate finds that the evidence is insufficient. If the evidence is found to be sufficient, the magistrate has the option to reduce the charges against the defendant. If the magistrate finds sufficient evidence to establish probable cause, then the prosecutor issues an information. As stated before, the information is a formal accusation that replaces the complaint and binds the defendant over for trial.

A grand jury is a group of citizens called to decide whether probable cause exists to try the defendant. Many states have a grand jury process; however, the number of jurors called varies from jurisdiction to jurisdiction. The grand jury convenes in a closed session and hears only evidence presented by the prosecutor. The defendant is not allowed to present evidence before the grand jury. If the grand jury finds probable cause, it issues an indictment against the defendant. The indictment is then filed with the trial court and becomes the formal charge against the defendant. The federal government and about half of the states require a grand jury.

Discovery is allowed in criminal cases, although it is allowed to a much lesser extent than in civil cases. During discovery in a criminal case, a defendant is entitled to obtain any evidence in the possession of the prosecutor that relates to his/her case. This evidence can include statements previously made by the defendant, objects used in the crime or that are otherwise incriminating, documents, reports of tests, and examinations. To obtain evidence from the prosecutor's office, a motion for discovery and inspection is prepared and submitted to the court. The court then orders the prosecutor to turn over to the defense attorney the requested evidence.

Key Terms

Acquittal	Grand jury
Arraignment	Guilty
Arrest	Indictment
Bail	Information
Bench warrant	Nolo contendere
Booking	Plea bargain
Complaint	Preliminary hearing
Discovery	Subpoena
Enhancements	

1. What is the purpose of bail?
2. List some of the items that are examined when determining bail and state why those issues are important.
3. What is the purpose of discovery?
4. Explain the difference between a preliminary hearing and a grand jury.
5. What is nolo contendere?
6. Why is it important for a defense attorney to be given all the evidence that the prosecution might have against his/her client?
7. What happens during the booking process?
8. If a defendant is charged with a misdemeanor, what can happen to him/her after his/her initial appearance?
9. What is a plea bargain?
10. What is the purpose of a pretrial motion?
11. List four criminal procedures that need to occur prior to commencement of criminal trial.
12. Why do police sometimes keep investigating after a defendant has been charged with a crime?
13. What is an enhancement and why is it important?
14. What is a grand jury?
15. What can the defense do at a preliminary hearing?

Review Questions

1. In the example given in "A Day in the Life of a Real Paralegal," suppose that Marcus confessed to the shooting while he was being interrogated by the police without legal counsel. Suppose that Marcus had never been read his *Miranda* rights at the time that he was arrested. What type of pretrial motion might his public defender bring to try to get the court not to allow the confession into evidence at trial and why?
2. Using the same example, suppose that Marcus decided not to take the plea bargain offered by the prosecutor and decided to enter a plea of not guilty? What would happen at the preliminary hearing? Describe in great detail a scenario of how you think the preliminary hearing would unfold. Make sure to include evidence presented, witness testimony, and the cross-examination that might be conducted by the public defender.
3. Locate a local criminal case that has appeared in the newspaper recently. What was the plea entered by the defendant? What types of pretrial motions have been or are being brought? Was a preliminary hearing or grand jury used to bring the defendant to trial? Prepare a two-page, typewritten, double-spaced paper describing the case and the questions above in detail for presentation to the class. Prepare a motion to suppress evidence that would have been brought for the case.
4. Why would a defense attorney opt for a preliminary hearing versus a grand jury? Provide three reasons with explanations.
5. What are the due process amendments? Give five reasons, with analysis, as to how the due process amendments are applied when arresting, booking, and arraigning a prisoner after arrest?
6. Does a bail bonds person and/or a bounty hunter need a warrant to make an arrest of someone at his/her dwelling? Explain.

Exercises

7. Provide five reasons why a prosecutor/state would offer a plea bargain to a prisoner, affording the prisoner an earlier release from incarceration, when the prisoner may be a dangerous threat to the public?

8. Provide three reasons and scenarios as to when a bench warrant will be issued for someone's arrest.

PORTFOLIO ASSIGNMENT

Interview a director or manager of a local county jail. Have him/her give you a tour and interview him/her on the process of cataloging and processing a prisoner. How long does it take on average to process someone? Are proper procedure and safety the main concerns? How much turnover in employees is there? Apply what you have learned in this chapter when formulating questions. Document and report back on your findings to the class.

Vocabulary Builders

Instructions
Use the key terms from this chapter to fill in the answers to the crossword puzzle.
NOTE: When the answer is more than one word, leave a blank space between words.

ACROSS

2. Added factors to a criminal change that make the charge carry greater weight.
5. The pretrial investigation process authorized and governed by the rules of civil procedure; process in which the opposing parties obtain information about the case from each other.
8. Court-mandated surety or guarantee that the defendant will appear at a future date if released from custody prior to trial.
9. The process whereby the accused and the prosecutor in a criminal case work out a mutually satisfactory disposition of the case subject to court approval.
11. A verdict only available in criminal cases in which the jury determines that the defendant is responsible for committing a crime.
12. The formal taking of a person, usually by a police officer, to answer criminal charges.
13. The legal and formal certification of the innocence of a person who has been charged with a crime.
14. States that the magistrate determines there is sufficient cause to make an arrest and also sets forth the formal charges sought by the prosecution.
15. An order issued by the court clerk directing a person to appear in court.
16. A charge, preferred before a magistrate having jurisdiction, that a person named has committed a specified offense, with an offer to prove the fact, to the end that a prosecution may be instituted.

DOWN

1. A hearing by a judge to determine whether a person charged with a crime should be held for trial.
3. Administrative step taken after an arrested person is brought to the police station, that involves entry of the person's name, the crime for which the arrest was made, and other relevant facts on the police blotter.
4. A jury of inquiry who are summoned and returned by the sheriff to each session of the criminal courts and whose duty is to receive complaints and accusations in criminal cases, hear evidence and decide if the defendant should stand for trial.
6. A written list of charges issued by a grand jury against a defendant in a criminal case.
7. The process issued by the court itself for the attachment or arrest of a person.
10. A court hearing where the information contained in an indictment is read to the defendant.

COMMONWEALTH vs. JAMES F. WERMERS.
61 Mass. App. Ct. 182; 808 N.E.2d 326; 2004 Mass. App. LEXIS 521
No. 03-P-563
APPEALS COURT OF MASSACHUSETTS
January 14, 2004, Argued May 13, 2004, Decided

CASE SUMMARY

PROCEDURAL POSTURE: The Commonwealth appealed a decision of the Suffolk Superior Court Department (Massachusetts), which dismissed defendant's indictment for armed robbery without prejudice.

OVERVIEW: In grand jury testimony, the victim, a pharmacy employee, testified that he observed tattoos on the forearms of a man who robbed the pharmacy. The same man entered the store several months later and was identified by the victim. The man was wearing long sleeves at the time, and the victim did not see any tattoos. The victim identified defendant later that day as he sat in a police cruiser. Although defendant was no longer wearing long sleeves, the victim did not see any tattoos but stated that he had identified defendant from a distance. A booking form indicated defendant had "tattoos/symbols/upper left arm." The booking form was not provided to the defense. The trial court deemed the failure to provide the booking form to be an impairment that warranted dismissal of the indictment. The court reversed. The victim's testimony was plausible, and there was no evidence that the booking form was knowingly withheld because it tended to show that the victim's testimony was false. There was no indication that the prosecution had a purpose to procure the indictment by improper means and it was highly unlikely that presentation of the booking form would have prevented the indictment.

OUTCOME: The dismissal of the indictment was reversed.

OPINION: KAPLAN, J. On the ground that there had been a material fault in the prosecutor's presentation of evidence to the grand jury, a judge of the Superior Court dismissed without prejudice an indictment for armed robbery. The Commonwealth appeals from the order of dismissal.

Grand jury testimony. About 2:30 p.m., September 17, 2001, Shamta Patel and Anthony Chen were at work behind the pharmacy counter at a CVS store on Morrissey Boulevard, in the Dorchester section of Boston. A man appeared at the counter and handed Patel a note, which she in turn handed to Chen. Chen read (paraphrased): "I have a gun. Put all your Oxycontin in a bag, you have thirty seconds to do this or I can shoot. Put this note in the bag, too." Chen opened the safe, took up some 600 Oxycontin tablets and put them into a brown paper CVS bag together with the note, and passed the bag to the waiting man. The man walked about ten feet toward the exit, then broke out into a run. According to Chen's observation, the man had had his hand in his jeans pocket. He had a tattoo on each forearm. He wore a gray T-shirt. Chen figured the man was 5'4" or 5'5" tall because his head was level with Chen's eyes.

Chen was working at the same CVS store on December 5, 2001. From behind the counter Chen saw a man approaching whom he recognized at once as the perpetrator of September 17, this time wearing a green sweatshirt, sunglasses, and a baseball cap. Chen bluffed, telling the man he needed to make a telephone call; he went to the phone and pretended to make the call. At this point, the man turned and started toward the exit. Chen alerted Paul Sweeney, a manager who was present, and told another worker to call the police. Sweeney got to the fleeing man but the man shook Sweeney off and exited the place, with Sweeney in pursuit. Sweeney caught up to the man to the point of grabbing his shoulder. The man drew out a black weapon and pointed it at Sweeney's head. The man ran off. Sweeney returned to the store.

Police arrived at once. Sweeney told Officers Steven Charbonnier and Christopher Ross of the Boston police, who had responded to the report of a man with a gun, that the man involved was 5'7" or up to 5'10" tall and was wearing a blue sweatshirt, sunglasses, blue jeans, and a blue baseball cap. The officers invited Sweeney into the backseat of their cruiser and drove about the nearby streets in hopes of finding the man.

At the same time, other officers were looking for the man on the basis of Sweeney's description. Officer Lee Chau noticed a white vehicle located across the street from the CVS, with its door open, no person inside, keys in the ignition, the hood warm, blue sweatshirt and blue baseball hat lying on a seat. Unmarked police units that waited in the vicinity finally saw a man trying to enter the vehicle. He was apprehended and taken to the CVS store for possible immediate identification. There Chen identified the man as the robber of the September 17 incident and the fleeing customer of that day, December 5. Sweeney identified the man as the one who put the gun to him. The man was James Wermers (the defendant herein).

Under arrest, Wermers was brought to the police station and booked. Waiving Miranda rights, he led the police to the hiding place of his pellet handgun and the police recovered it. Wermers, however, denied any knowledge of the events of September 17.

On the day following the arrest, Detective Richard Atwood, who was assigned to all Oxycontin robberies in Dorchester and had been informed of Wermers's involvement, displayed to Chen a photographic array of nine men. From the array, Chen made a positive identification of one as picturing the actor of the two dates; the photograph was that of Wermers.

After Chen, in the course of his testimony, told the grand jury that on September 17 he had seen tattoos on the man's forearms, he was asked whether he had made a similar observation on December 5 when the man came into the store. Chen said he had not; the man was then wearing a long-sleeved sweatshirt. When later that day the man left the cruiser to be viewed by Sweeney and Chen, he was not wearing a sweatshirt, rather he showed a short-sleeved T-shirt. Chen said, however, that he had viewed the man at a distance, as he did not want to encounter him face to face.

The grand jury, having met and heard testimony on January 22 and February 14, 2002, on the latter date brought in indictments of Wermers for armed robbery (incident of September 17, 2001) and assault with a dangerous weapon (December 5, 2001). On the day of the indictments, the Commonwealth tendered to the defense the first certificate of discovery. Thereby the defense received the "Arrest Booking Form" for Wermers together with police incident reports. On the booking form Wermers's height is given as 5'8"; clothing: gray T-shirt, blue jeans, white Nike sneakers, and gray Bruins hat. Following the caption "Scars/Marks/Tattoos," we read the booking officer's entry "Tattoos/Symbols/Upper Left Arm."

On November 8, 2002, the defense filed a motion to dismiss the armed robbery indictment with prejudice on the ground of an alleged "impairment" of the grand jury proceedings by reason of "improper prosecutorial conduct resulting in the indictment of the defendant," citing *Commonwealth v. O'Dell*, 392 Mass. 445, 450, 466 N.E.2d 828 (1984). The impairment came about, according to the defendant's claim, by reason of the prosecution's failure to disclose to the grand jury the booking form with the notation about tattoos.

After a short hearing on February 13, 2003, and submission of briefs, a judge of the Superior Court on February 20, 2003, allowed the motion to dismiss the armed robbery indictment, the dismissal to be without prejudice. The Commonwealth's motion to reconsider was denied, and the Commonwealth appeals to this court under Mass. R. Crim. P. 15(a)(1), as amended, 422 Mass. 1501 (1996).

Appealability. The defendant contends, first, that the Commonwealth has no right of appeal from the without-prejudice dismissal of an indictment; the defendant would confine the rule 15(a)(1) appeal to dismissals with prejudice, where the criminal prosecution is at an end except as saved by a successful appeal. There is no basis in the words or theme of the rule for such a restriction, and the Commonwealth points out there are plenty of decided cases in which appeals have been entertained from nonfinal dismissals. Respect for the prosecutor in his executive function counts against pressing him to reindict (and suppose there is no conscientious way of correcting the defect supposed to justify the dismissal?) and eliminating his choice of a prompt test of validity of the indictment by means of the interlocutory appeal.

Merits. The judge ruled there was in the presentation to the grand jury an impairment of the integrity of the proceeding that called for dismissal of the challenged indictment (although not foreclosing reindictment). The judge relied on *Commonwealth v. Salman*, 387 Mass. 160, 439 N.E.2d 245 (1982); *Commonwealth v. O'Dell*, 392 Mass. 445, 466 N.E.2d 828 (1984); and *Commonwealth v. Mayfield*, 398 Mass. 615, 500 N.E.2d 774 (1986).

In *Salman*, 387 Mass. at 166, 168, thirty-seven indictments were dismissed, allowing reindictment on other evidence, where police testimony was (questionably) false and (questionably) given with knowledge of falsity and the Commonwealth

could not furnish additional information required by the judge. In *O'Dell*, 392 Mass. at 448–449, an indictment was ordered dismissed without prejudice where the prosecution offered police testimony about an inculpatory statement by the accused suggesting his guilt, but knowingly withheld an exculpatory portion of the same statement, thus distorting it. In *Mayfield*, 398 Mass. at 624–626, a murder case, a police officer gave false testimony that he had found in the area of the victim's body a cigarette lighter from a gym bag that had been stolen by the accused, when in fact the lighter was found by another officer farther from the body; dismissal was not warranted, as the false testimony was not given recklessly or intentionally and was not likely to have influenced the grand jury's decision to indict.

These cases offer nice questions and answers about alleged ethical lapses in the presentation of evidence to a grand jury and it is perhaps already evident on the face of things that the present case does not come near deserving dismissal. This is verified when we examine the record by reference to the three-part standard set out in the *Mayfield* case, 398 Mass. at 621:

> "To sustain a claim that the integrity of the grand jury proceeding has been impaired, not only must the evidence have been given with knowledge that it was false or deceptive, but the false or deceptive evidence must probably have been significant in the view of the grand jury and must have been presented with the intention of obtaining an indictment."

The defendant's contention in this case is not that the Commonwealth presented evidence with knowledge it was false or deceptive, but rather that it knowingly withheld evidence (the booking form) that would tend to show the victim's testimony (about the tattoos) to be false. The contention falters. Chen's testimony is plausible, complete, and without any inner inconsistencies. The booking in its staccato or telegraphic style does not contradict Chen's testimony, for it refers to "tattoos" in the plural, and the reference to "upper left arm" may well relate to the unspecified "symbols," rather than the tattoos. If the words on the form are susceptible of a different reading that puts the tattoos on the upper left arm, rather than on the forearms as mentioned by Chen, the discrepancy seems the stuff of ultimate cross-examination, not a ground for dismissing an indictment. As to the "knowledge" point of the *Mayfield* formulation, there is no extrinsic material that points directly to malice prepense on the part of the prosecutor, and any inference in that respect must be circumstantially weak.

It is highly unlikely that disclosure of the booking form would have affected the grand jury's decision to indict. It is perhaps enough to note that Chen identified the defendant as the September 17 culprit on three occasions without reliance on tattoos: in the store on December 5, at the show-up the same day, and during the photographic display session the following day. An omission to offer the booking form does not seem important in weighing the congeries of factors with a bearing on probable cause.

The third clause of *Mayfield* may conceivably add as a requirement to justify dismissal, that the prosecutor shall be shown to have had a set purpose to procure an indictment by improper means. Such an imputation of motive, if a condition of dismissal, would be quite hard to sustain on this record.

Conclusion. Thus we conclude that any claim of an ethical lapse on the part of the prosecution is without material support. For the rest, there is no doubt the record herein "supplied the standard elements of an adequate presentation to a grand jury as understood in this Commonwealth—evidence identifying the accused and furnishing probable cause to believe that he or she committed the crime to be charged." *Commonwealth v. Biasiucci*, 60 Mass. App. Ct. 734, 736–737, 806 N.E.2d 104 (2004), citing *Commonwealth v. McCarthy*, 385 Mass. 160, 163, 430 N.E.2d 1195 (1982). If the booking form is taken as having some exculpatory value, then we need recall that it is when the prosecution possesses information that would gravely undermine evidence supporting probable cause that the prosecutor is duty bound to furnish it to the grand jury," *Commonwealth v. Biasiucci, supra* at 738, citing cases, and such was not the situation here, as already indicated.

The order dismissing the indictment for armed robbery is reversed.

So ordered.

[Footnotes omitted]

Source: 61 Mass. App. Ct. 182; 808 N.E.2d 326; 2004 Mass. App. LEXIS 521 (2004). Reprinted with permission of LexisNexis.

Chapter 13

An Overview of a Criminal Trial

CHAPTER OBJECTIVES

Upon completion of this chapter, you will be able to:

- Understand the steps and procedures necessary to the workings of a criminal trial.

- Recognize the importance of jury selection.

- Identify the different types of evidence that can be presented at trial.

- Explain the differences between direct examination and cross examination.

- Know and understand how jury instructions, jury deliberations, and verdicts work.

In Chapter 12, you learned about criminal procedures from arrest and booking up through discovery and to trial. As pointed out in that chapter, most criminal trials contain the following processes: jury selection, opening statements, prosecution presenting its case, defense presenting its case, evidence issues, closing arguments, jury instructions, jury deliberations, and, finally, the verdict. This chapter explores these stages of the criminal trial itself beginning with jury selection. Representation of a client in court must be done by a licensed attorney. However, paralegals can aid the attorney in the representation of a defendant by preparing documents, doing research, assisting the attorney, interviewing and preparing witnesses, and performing a myriad of other tasks.

DIFFERENCES BETWEEN CRIMINAL AND CIVIL TRIALS

Criminal trials and civil trials are similar in many ways procedurally, yet each offers different aspects and nuances as well. Both types of trials contain adversary parties to an action that is decided by either a judge or jury. The adversary parties may each have legal representation at trial, if they opt to, or, in each type, represent themselves. Each kind of trial has evidence presented and decided upon at trial, *both* having standards of proof, albeit different, by which to judge the offending party. In criminal trials, the standard for finding the defendant guilty must be **beyond a reasonable doubt**. At a civil trial, finding the defendant liable must be **by a preponderance of evidence**. In layman's terms, *beyond a reasonable doubt* means that you must be 90 to 95 percent sure of a person's guilt before convicting. You don't have to be 100 percent positive,

beyond a reasonable doubt
The requirement for the level of proof in a criminal matter in order to convict or find the defendant guilty. It is a substantially higher and more-difficult-to-prove criminal matter standard.

by a preponderance of evidence
The weight or level of persuasion of evidence needed to find the defendant liable as alleged by the plaintiff in a civil matter.

FIGURE 13.1
Similarities and Differences between Criminal Trials and Civil Trials

	Criminal Trial	Civil Trial
Similarities	Adverse parties at trial	Adverse parties at trial
	Outcome decided by a judge or jury (*jury option—for gross misdemeanors and felonies*)	Outcome decided by a judge or jury
	May have legal representation or not	May have legal representation or not
	Evidence presented	Evidence presented
Differences	Burden of proof: "beyond a reasonable doubt"	Burden of proof: "by a preponderance of evidence"
	State brings the action	Individual brings the action
	Penalties: fines, prison, or death	Penalties: monetary damages

PRACTICE TIP

In your professional career as a paralegal, remember to always refer to the criminal standard of judgment as "beyond a *reasonable doubt*." Many people, including persons working in the legal field, refer to the standard as "beyond a *shadow of a doubt*." This is incorrect and can skew how people look at the standard, the legal system, and the defendant.

prosecutor
Attorney representing the people or plaintiff in criminal matters.

impartial jury
A jury that is unbiased and does not favor one party or the other.

bench trial
A case heard and decided by a judge.

as that would imply you have "no doubt at all" of the person's guilt. The civil standard, *by a preponderance of evidence,* means you must be at least 51 percent sure of the person's responsibility before finding liability. The standard for convicting a person in a criminal trial is higher than the standard of finding a person liable in a civil trial. This is because the penalties potentially involved with a criminal trial are incarceration (loss of freedom) or death. Both are extreme penalties. With a loss in the civil system, the worst reprimand for the defendant is simply a monetary one. Finally, both types of trials impose some sort of penalty on the responsible party upon conviction or being held liable.

Differences between the two forms of trials abound too. Criminal trials are embodied in the notion that the *state* serves and protects the *people* and it is the state that represents the community at large and prosecutes offenders that have broken the law. The victims of criminal behavior neither prosecute the alleged offender nor are they individually represented by the state and/or **prosecutor**. Civil trials deal with individuals bringing actions against each other for an injury or harm suffered. Another difference is the penalties that are handed out by each. Civil lawsuits place a monetary burden on the offending party, but no jail or prison time is served. Penalties handed out at criminal trials may range from a monetary fine to the death penalty. (See Figure 13.1.)

JURY SELECTION

The Sixth Amendment to the U.S. Constitution guarantees the following rights to the accused in a criminal prosecution by the federal government with the Fourteenth Amendment applying the same standards to the states in state prosecutions:

- Right to a speedy and public trial by an **impartial jury**.
- Right to be confronted with witnesses against him/her.
- Right to call his/her own witnesses in defense of him/her.
- Right to counsel.

(See Appendix A for the full text of the Constitution.)

It should be noted that the *right* to a jury trial is constitutionally required in a state case only where the potential penalty is greater than six months of incarceration. The defendant in those circumstances has the *right* to a jury but may still elect to waive a jury and have a judge make the decision. For our purposes, we shall proceed through the steps of a trial as though the defendant has opted for a jury trial.

Offenses that carry sentences of six months or more up to a year are called *gross misdemeanors*. Offenses that carry sentences of one year or more are called *felonies*. Petty offenses for which six months or less is the maximum penalty are called *misdemeanors* and will always be tried by a judge. A trial decided by a judge is called a **bench trial**. (See Figure 13.2.)

Classification	Description	Possible Penalty
Misdemeanor	Minor crime	6 months incarceration or less in county jail
		Fine
		Both incarceration and fine
Gross misdemeanor	Semimajor crime	6 months or more, up to a year in state prison
		Fine
Felony	Major crime	Both incarceration and fine
		1 year or more in state prison or federal penitentiary
		Death penalty
		Fine
		Both incarceration and fine

FIGURE 13.2
Possible Penalties for Crimes

The first step in prosecuting a defendant at the trial level is to select a jury. This is presuming the defendant has been charged with a gross misdemeanor or felony and has opted for a jury trial.

In order to satisfy constitutional requirements, the jury must be selected from a cross section of the community where the trial is being held. The selection must not be discriminatory in nature and the defendant and/or state cannot exclude or include anyone based on any particular grouping of the community. Choosing potential jurors, and ultimately the actual jurors, based on race, gender, age, ethnicity, and national origin is not only discriminatory in nature and illegal but would preclude certain individuals from participating in the American civic experience of sitting on a **jury panel** and eventually perhaps the jury.

For this impartiality to occur in selecting a jury panel, the **jurisdiction** must utilize methods to ensure that a true cross section of the community is represented. Accepted contact methods to find suitable jurors throughout the United States include voter registration records, motor vehicle records, and, in some areas, utility records/bills. Each means of contact possesses the inherent quality sought in achieving a fair representation within the community, that of impartial jurors. There is a presumption in law that voting should be done by everyone who meets the requirements of voting and most people have a driver's license. Hence, these two methods are used quite frequently. Tax returns, as an example, would not be a fair method. Many people do not pay taxes and/or do not file tax returns. If this method was employed, many would be excluded, resulting perhaps in a jury that is not truly representative of the community.

Most criminal trials will have 12 jurors with some alternate jurors as well just in case a sitting juror gets sick or is taken off the case. All federal criminal trials have 12 jurors and the decision must be a unanimous one. There are caveats, however, to this federal requirement. Exceptions that may be acted upon, as long the judge and both parties agree to that change, include decreasing the number of jurors and not concluding with unanimity. State requirements vary from state to state. Jurors in all cases must be citizens, impartial, and from the community. (See Figure 13.3.)

jury panel
Group of people called to court from which a jury is chosen.

jurisdiction
The place or court that may hear a case, based on subject matter and/or geographic area.

- Must be a U.S. citizen
- Chosen from a cross section of the community
- Chosen in a nondiscriminatory manner
- Chosen by common records found in society:
  - Voter registration records
  - Department of Motor Vehicles
- Federal criminal case:
  - 12 jurors
  - Unanimous decision
- State criminal case:
  - Requirements vary from state to state

FIGURE 13.3
Jury Selection Requirements

FIGURE 13.4
Sample Juror Questions Asked at First Stage of Jury Selection

1. What is your age?
2. What is your race?
3. What is your marital status?
4. Are you a male or female?
5. Do you have children?
6. Where do you live?
7. What do you do for a living?
8. Have you ever been a victim of crime?
9. Do you know anyone that has been a victim of crime?
10. Did your parents divorce or remain married?
11. Do you own a gun?
12. What is your highest completed grade level?
13. Do you speak any foreign languages?
14. Do you drive a car?
15. How do you feel about violence?

voir dire
The process of selecting a jury for trial.

excused for cause
Process of excusing jurors for bias, prejudices, and legitimate reasons as well, such as sickness, job commitment, or others.

peremptory challenges
An attorney's elimination of a prospective juror without giving a reason; limited to a specific number of strikes.

Once a potential jury panel has been solicited, they are called to court to answer questions, usually provided in a written questionnaire. It is important to find an impartial jury to sit at trial. Because of this, many are called to complete the questionnaire to see who will make it to the next step, which includes questioning by the judge and the attorneys in the case. (See Figure 13.4 for some examples of written questions asked of a potential jury.)

After some have been excluded based on answers provided in the written questionnaire, the attorneys and judge begin to question the remaining jury panel to sift out more people that have biases or for other reasons such as illness, job commitments, and others. This questioning stage of the proceeding is known as **voir dire**. It is the judge who has the power to remove possible jurors for those reasons. That process is called **excused for cause**. Questions asked at the voir dire level may be like this: Do you know anyone involved in this case? Have you ever been involved in a case as a defendant?

Excused for cause can be related to bias, interest, and prejudice. Both parties also have what are called **peremptory challenges** allowing each party to excuse a juror while not having to provide a reason as to why the juror was excused.

SURF'S UP

Demand has created burgeoning careers for jury consultants and jury experts on how to pick winning juries. Research the following Web sites for information on jury selection.

- Jury selection information: http://web.info.com/infocom.us2/search/web/Jury%20Selection?CMP=3343&itkw=Jury%20
- Federal jury selection: www.uscourts.gov/jury/selection.html

A DAY IN THE LIFE OF A REAL PARALEGAL

Susan was new to the field of criminal law. She had worked as a real property paralegal for seven years and wanted a change. She wanted to continue being a paralegal but wanted to expand her knowledge and venture into the world of criminal law. As the practice of defending clients can have the life of another at risk for incarceration or death, it is truly necessary that any paralegal or attorney working in the criminal law field know his/her stuff inside and out. This being the case, Susan's new managing attorney assigned her to observe the goings on of criminal court proceedings for an entire month at the local courthouse. Susan dutifully followed through, checking the court dockets daily for criminal trials occurring throughout the month.

Once the jurors and alternates have been selected (varies from 6 to 12 depending on the state), they are then sworn in to evaluate only the facts of the case, solely based on the evidence presented at trial.

OPENING STATEMENTS

After a jury has been chosen, it's time to begin the trial by having opening statements delivered to the court by the prosecutor and defense attorney. The prosecution delivers its opening statement first. The defense then follows with its opening statement. However, the defense can opt for giving its opening statement at the beginning of the defense's presentation. It's important to always remember that the complaint was brought by the state and the **burden of proof** is on them to prove the facts in order to convict. The defense never has to say anything at any time.

burden of proof
Standard for assessing the weight of the evidence.

Opening statements provide an outline of sorts for each side's case that they expect to prove. It also describes the different pieces of evidence each side intends to show to prove the facts of its story.

Because neither side wants to look bad in front of a jury, it usually will not promise more than it can deliver. Keep in mind that each side should not be opinionated, use hyperbole, falsify, or give grandiose sermons during the opening statements. Such tactics could lead to a mistrial or an appeal later on after the trial has ended. It's not supposed to be a soapbox for attorneys to pontificate. Rather, any opinionating going on during the opening statements should be tempered with a statement such as, "The evidence will show the defendant is guilty and murdered those people," not "I know the defendant is guilty." Returning always to what the evidence will show during trial is what wins cases and only evidentiary statements should be made to the jury.

EVIDENCE

At this juncture, it is important to cover evidentiary rules and definitions before moving on to the prosecution's and defense's presentations, covering both direct and cross-examinations of witnesses.

Evidence in all of its forms attempts to demonstrate and make clear the truth of a fact at issue for one side or the other. It is evidence that decides the outcomes of cases. Before we discuss the types of evidence available, it's important to note that much of the evidence to be used at trial is established in the discovery, the investigative phase before the case comes to trial (see Chapter 12). The judge determines what evidence will be allowed into the trial. Before trial, both sides present their exhibits of evidence and their witness lists to each other and the court. The prosecution must turn all of its evidence over to the defense. The defense must turn all of its evidence over to the prosecution except for anything that can be deemed confidential that has transpired between the defendant and his/her attorney.

evidence
Any fact, testimony, or physical object that tends to prove or disprove allegations raised in a case; must be reasonably calculated to lead to the discovery of admissible evidence.

Consequently, the practice of sharing evidence is less stringent for the defense as much of it may fall under the scope of attorney-client privilege of confidentiality. As an example, if the defendant told the attorney, "Yes, I shot her with the gun." The attorney, bound

EYE ON ETHICS

Remember that although paralegals are not attorneys and are not part of a licensing body, they still owe the client the duty of confidentiality and cannot divulge any information that may be deemed part of the attorney–client privilege. The mere fact that the paralegal is not an attorney does not preclude the paralegal from abiding by the same standards set for the attorney.

A DAY IN THE LIFE OF A REAL PARALEGAL

Dan just received the assignment to compile a possible witness list for the prosecution in a case in which the state is prosecuting a homeless person for being a serial killer and taking the lives of 32 people over a span of 13 years. Some of the witnesses on which the prosecution will rely are having difficulty recollecting facts and details, particularly the witnesses that observed an occurrence many years ago. Dan must now sift through the discovery information and produce a list of witnesses to review, with the prosecutor, ensuring that the witnesses they call will benefit the state's case.

by confidentiality, must keep it confidential and not divulge that information. However, if the defendant said "Yes, I shot her with the gun and after this mess of a trial is over I intend to kill the prosecutor," the defense attorney in that instance would have to notify the prosecution and police only about the future threat and not the information regarding the defendant's admittance of guilt to the attorney about the past shooting.

probative evidence
Evidence that tends to or actually proves the fact.

Evidence used at trial must be **probative** in nature and **relevant** to the case at hand. In part, to uphold the speedy trial requirement of the Sixth Amendment, the courts do not want to waste time with evidence that has no bearing on the issue at hand or on the outcome of the trial. As an example, if evidence was brought in to prove the weather was sunny on the day the crime was committed, it would not be probative or relevant, unless somehow the sun's shining led to the crime at hand and would affect the decision to acquit or find guilt. It would normally not be entered as evidence, even though it may be a fact.

relevant evidence
Evidence that makes the existence of any fact more probable or less probable than it would be without the evidence.

Evidentiary rules governing the admittance of evidence are embodied in a number of documents including the Federal Rules of Evidence, the Uniform Rules of Evidence, and the numerous statutes that govern evidence rules found throughout the states. Both the prosecution and defense must follow the rules of evidence found in their jurisdictions.

direct evidence
Evidence that establishes a particular fact without resort to other testimony or evidence.

Types of Evidence

Both the prosecution and the defense may enter evidence into court to bolster their side of the issue. As mentioned, the evidence each decides to enter is usually determined during the discovery stage (see Chapter 12). Again, only the prosecution must enter evidence, as the burden of proof falls upon the prosecution. The defense need not enter anything if it so chooses.

circumstantial evidence
Evidence that suggests a conclusion.

There are many types, forms, and categories of evidence available to each side. There is **direct evidence** and **circumstantial** (indirect) **evidence**. Direct and circumstantial evidence can take the form of firsthand witness testimony, expert witness testimony, and **tangible evidence**. There is also **demonstrable evidence** and **hearsay** as well.

tangible evidence
Evidence that can be touched, picked up.

Direct evidence is actual evidence. It is the evidence both the prosecution and the defense seek, as it is almost always the best evidence to have at trial. It proves a direct point. Witness testimony is direct evidence. It is testimony about a subject of which the witness has personal knowledge. Expert testimony is also direct evidence. It is testimony about conclusions drawn based on his or her expertise. A tangible item such as a gun or a set of fingerprints or DNA results can be direct evidence. The purse stolen and recovered can be direct evidence as well. Direct evidence can help the prosecution hammer home its points but also can serve the defense by proving, or many times disproving, an assertion made by the prosecution.

demonstrative evidence
Any object, visual aid, model, scale drawing, or other exhibit designed to help clarify points in the trial.

hearsay
An out-of-court statement offered to prove a matter in contention in the lawsuit.

Circumstantial evidence is evidence that is inferred from direct evidence, usually not present at trial. It is the most common form of evidence presented at criminal trials. Circumstantial evidence is good evidence and can, alone, convict someone for a crime. An example of circumstantial evidence can be powder burns on the hands of the defendant. The gun (direct evidence) that murdered the victim was never found, but clearly

Encompassing Rules of Evidence	Types of Evidence
Must demonstrate the truth of a fact	Direct evidence
Must be probative	Circumstantial evidence
Must be relevant	Tangible evidence
Exclusion of evidence is judge's decision	Demonstrative evidence
Prosecution must give all of its evidence to defense	Hearsay—falling within an exception to the hearsay rule.
Defense must give all of its evidence to prosecution, less anything related to attorney–client privilege of confidentiality	

FIGURE 13.5
Evidentiary Rules:
Types of Evidence
Allowed in Court

the powder burns on the hands of a defendant act as evidence leading to the conclusion that, at a minimum, the defendant fired a gun. The same example can help the defense if there were no powder burns on the hands of the defendant. The defense could easily argue that as long as no powder burns were visible, the defendant did not fire a gun.

Demonstrative evidence is created by either side for use in court to strengthen a point. It can take the form of diagrams, photos, charts, and others.

Hearsay is evidence of a statement that was made outside of court other than by the witness while testifying at the trial. An example would be this statement made by the witness on the stand, "I overheard John tell Susie about the murder." This is not admissible as both John and Susie are not present to deny or affirm that the statement was made and the witness was not a party to the conversation. Hearsay is generally not admissible in court. However, there are currently 23 exceptions to the hearsay rule. (See Appendix B for a list of hearsay exceptions and explanations.) The underlying rationale for many of the hearsay exceptions is that the circumstances of a particular statement make them reliable enough to be heard by the jury. Please review Figure 13.5 for a summary of evidentiary rules and types of evidence allowed in court.

RESEARCH THIS

Surf the Web and find out which criminal case in your state contained the most hearsay exceptions, allowing hearsay evidence into the proceeding.

Begin by trying www.findlaw.com and www.allaw.com to see what you can find.

PROSECUTION AND DEFENSE PRESENTATIONS AND EXAMINATION OF WITNESSES

Because the prosecution has the burden of proof in a criminal trial, it is the responsibility and duty of the state to present its case first, immediately following opening statements. The prosecution will begin by entering exhibits of evidence and calling state witnesses to testify on behalf of the prosecution. The prosecutor will begin **direct examination** of those witnesses. On direct examination of the state's witnesses, the prosecutor may not ask leading questions. This is because, theoretically, the state's witnesses are not hostile to the prosecutor. An example of a direct question, which is proper in this instance, would be "Where were you on February 1st?" An improper leading question would be "So, on February 1st you were at the saloon, weren't you?" After the prosecutor finishes examining each witness on direct examination, the defense is then allowed to proceed with **cross-examination** of the same witnesses.

direct examination
Occurs when the attorney questions his or her own witness.

cross-examination
Occurs when the opposing attorney asks the witness questions.

The defense in this illustration may ask leading questions, as the prosecution witnesses may be hostile to the defense and the defense may not be able to illicit answers without asking leading questions. After the defense finishes cross examination of the prosecution witnesses, the prosecution may approach the witness again for a redirect question to clarify a certain point.

Once the prosecution rests with its evidence and witnesses, it is now the defense's opportunity to present its side of the story with its own submission of evidence and witnesses. If the defense did not participate in an opening statement at the beginning of the trial, now is its opportunity to do so. As the defense doesn't have to prove anything one way or the other, it will immediately ask the judge for a directed verdict in its favor arguing that the prosecution did not prove anything at all, based on the evidence produced. Sometimes the judge will rule in favor of the defense at this point, dismiss the jury, and drop the charge against the defendant. If not, it now becomes the defense's burden to either provide a legal, appropriate defense to the action or argue effectively against the charge. The same procedures apply to the defense in the presentation of its case as was found in the presentation of the prosecution's case, including direct and cross-examinations of witnesses and the asking of leading questions. In the defense's presentation, it cannot ask leading questions, but the prosecution may for the same reasons as stated above when reviewing the prosecution's presentation.

With both instances, there will be a flurry of objections by the opposing side regarding submission of evidence and the asking of certain questions. In both examples, it is the judge who will decide to overrule the objection or sustain it.

One element of the Sixth Amendment notes that the defendant must have the opportunity to confront witnesses against him/her. This is satisfied by the cross-examination of the state's witnesses by the defense. The Sixth Amendment also calls for the defendant to call his/her own favorable witnesses to testify on his/her behalf. This is satisfied by the defense calling its own witnesses to testify. (See Appendix A.)

When the defense brings forth its version of the facts, the defendant may elect to testify as his/her own witness. The Fifth Amendment does not require the defendant to testify. It is the defendant's sole choice as to whether to testify or not. His/her attorney can advise him/her what to do but cannot make that very important decision for him/her: whether to testify or not.

One of the dangers of having the defendant testify is that the prosecution may cross-examine him/her and, by doing so, the state may attack the defendant's own testimony by addressing issues that the defendant himself/herself brought into the testimony.

Once both sides have finished presenting their versions of the action, each is allowed to have a closing statement, a closing argument. Closing statements are much like the opening statements except now worded in the past tense. An example of this would be the following:

Opening statement: "The evidence will show that the defendant murdered those two people."

Closing statement: "In conclusion, the evidence clearly showed that the defendant murdered those two people."

Closing statements are the last opportunities for each side to summarize facts, issues, evidence, and conclusions that can be drawn from the evidence presented.

JURY INSTRUCTIONS, DELIBERATIONS, AND VERDICT

After each side has given its closing argument, the judge is ready to instruct the jury. The purpose of the instruction is to inform and explain to the jury the applicable rule of law when deciding the fate of the defendant. It's not merely enough to convict the defendant based on how someone feels or because there may be a mountain of evidence. The jurors can only convict if the evidence fits properly into the rule of law based on the instruction.

Before the judge instructs the jury, he/she has already met with the attorneys for each side, together, to inform them of the law and how it will be applied in the jury instruction. In that meeting, each side can give their opinions regarding how the law should be interpreted.

Part of the instruction stage also includes the explanation as to the role of the jury and its purpose. See Figure 13.6 for an example of a general jury instruction.

After instructions have been made, the jury now begins its deliberation process. Jury deliberations are always done in private. Many times, there is a jury room adjacent to the courtroom where the trial took place. Some juries are sequestered, meaning they are confined to a hotel and are not allowed to watch television, read newspapers, and discuss the facts and evidence with anyone, including themselves when they are not deliberating at the courthouse. This is to ensure that an impartial jury is considering only the evidence that was raised at trial. Sequestering a jury usually happens in high-profile cases.

Once the jury reaches a **verdict**, the court reconvenes. The judge is shown the verdict first and then it is read into the court record. If the defendant is **acquitted**, he/she is free to leave immediately. If the defendant is found **guilty**, that is, **convicted**, he/she

verdict
Decision of the jury following presentation of facts and application of relevant law as they relate to the law presented in the jury instructions.

acquittal
The legal and formal certification of the innocence of a person who has been charged with a crime.

guilty
A verdict only available in criminal cases in which the jury determines that the defendant is responsible for committing a crime.

conviction
Results from a guilty finding by the jury in a criminal trial.

Instruction No. 1
- In deciding what the facts are, you may have to decide what testimony you believe and what testimony you do not believe. You may believe all of what a witness said, or only part of it, or none of it.
- In deciding what testimony to believe, consider the witness's intelligence, the opportunity the witness had to have seen or heard the things testified about, the witness's memory, any motives that the witness may have for testifying a certain way, the manner of the witness while testifying, whether that witness said something different at an earlier time, the general reasonableness of the testimony, and the extent to which the testimony is consistent with any evidence that you believe.
- In deciding whether or not to believe a witness, keep in mind that people sometimes hear or see things differently and sometimes forget things. You need to consider, therefore, whether a contradiction is an innocent misrecollection or lapse of memory or an intentional falsehood, and that may depend on whether it has to do with an important fact or only a small detail.

Instruction No. 2
- I have mentioned the word "evidence." The "evidence" in this case consists of the testimony of witnesses, the documents and other things received as exhibits, and the facts that have been stipulated—this is, formally agreed to by the parties.
- You may use reason and common sense to draw deductions or conclusions from facts that have been established by the evidence in the case.
- Certain things are not evidence. I shall list those things again for you now:
  1. Statements, arguments, questions, and comments by lawyers representing the parties in the case are not evidence.
  2. Objections are not evidence. Lawyers have a right to object when they believe something is improper. You should not be influenced by the objection. If I sustained an objection to a question, you must ignore the question and must not try to guess what the answer might have been.
  3. Testimony that I struck from the record, or told you to disregard, is not evidence and must not be considered.
  4. Anything you saw or heard about this case outside the courtroom is not evidence. Finally, if you were instructed that some evidence was received for a limited purpose only, you must follow that instruction.

Instruction No. 3
- There is no burden upon a defendant to prove that he is innocent. Accordingly, the fact that a defendant did not testify must not be considered by you in any way, or even discussed, in arriving at your verdict.

FIGURE 13.6   Sample Jury Instructions

CASE FACT PATTERN

Bob was on trial for robbery. The prosecution presented its case and the defense followed with its presentation. Many witnesses were called to the stand by both parties. A lot of exhibits of evidence were submitted to the court. Each side gave a closing argument and the jury was instructed on how to proceed with deliberations. The jury spent many hours and days deciding Bob's fate. After two weeks of deliberations, the jury was deadlocked and could not come back with a unanimous decision, which was required in this proceeding. As a result, the judge had to call a **mistrial** and let the defendant leave. It will now be up to the prosecutor to decide whether or not to retry Bob for robbery.

mistrial
A trial that has been terminated prior to a normal conclusion.

is usually handcuffed and escorted to the county jail for processing and will eventually be sent to a state prison or federal penitentiary.

Appeals and post-trial formalities and issues are covered in Chapter 14.

Summary

Both criminal and civil trials have common procedures as well as differences. Their standards of judgment are different as well as their penalties. The parties are also different between the examples, with a prosecutor and defense attorney present in criminal proceedings while civil trials have an attorney for the person suing and a defense attorney for the defendant.

Jury selection must be a serious task to ensure impartiality toward the defendant. Juries are chosen by providing written answers to questions asked by the court as well as their being interviewed by the judge and the attorneys in the proceeding.

Opening statements begin the trial and both the prosecutor and the defense attorney are allowed an opening statement. The defense, however, never has to present an opening statement or evidence, as the burden to convict is on the prosecution.

Both sides present evidence to bolster their positions. The prosecution goes first and the defense follows. Both sides are allowed to call witnesses and both sides are allowed to cross-examine the other side's witnesses.

There are many types of evidence that can be brought into court. The parties must share evidence with each other. The defense, however, does not have to share anything that may be deemed confidential, invoking the attorney–client privilege.

Jury instructions from the judge to the jury begin the final process of the trial. After instructions are given, the jury deliberates and hopefully returns with a unanimous verdict.

The verdict when returned is read and allowed into the record either acquitting the defendant or convicting him/her.

Key Terms

Acquittal
Bench trial
Beyond a reasonable doubt
Burden of Proof
By a preponderance of evidence
Circumstantial evidence
Conviction
Cross examination
Demonstrative evidence
Direct evidence
Direct examination
Evidence
Excused for cause

Guilty
Hearsay
Impartial jury
Jurisdiction
Jury panel
Mistrial
Peremptory challenges
Probative evidence
Prosecutor
Relevant evidence
Tangible evidence
Verdict
Voir dire

1. What is the standard for convicting in a criminal trial?
2. What is the standard for convicting in a civil trial?
3. What is a bench trial?
4. What is the difference between a jury panel and a jury?
5. Why is hearsay not allowed in court, except if it fits into one of the accepted exceptions?
6. Research and find out what person has taken part as an expert witness in criminal trials more times than anyone else.
7. Provide three examples of demonstrative evidence that might be used in a sexual assault case.
8. Is direct evidence the same as actual evidence?
9. List three reasons why courts will allow only probative and relevant evidence to be entered into court.
10. Give three examples of circumstantial evidence that might be presented in a case when the victim was strangled and killed.
11. Why is jurisdiction so important in a criminal trial?
12. Explain how jury instructions may lead to an appeal by the defendant should he/she be found guilty.
13. Why might a judge dismiss the charge and let the jury leave, ending the trial?
14. What is a hostile witness?
15. Why does the Fifth Amendment to the U.S. Constitution allow the option for the defendant to testify against himself/herself? Come up with three possible answers.

1. Explain how circumstantial evidence can convict someone if there is no direct evidence to judge from?
2. Why does the court system frown upon mistrials? Provide five reasons.
3. Spend a week, when you can, at the criminal courthouse in your area. Provide five examples of an attorney's objecting to a statement made by a witness and whether or not the judge sustained or overruled the objection. Can you spot any patterns?
4. Investigate the jurisdiction of the criminal court in your area. What geographic area does that jurisdiction cover?
5. Explain how opening and closing statements can sway a jury. Provide three examples of such.

PORTFOLIO ASSIGNMENT

Research the evidentiary rules that govern the laws of evidence in your state. Compare them with the federal rules of evidence for similarities and differences. Keep your research and comparisons in your portfolio for future reference.

Vocabulary Builders

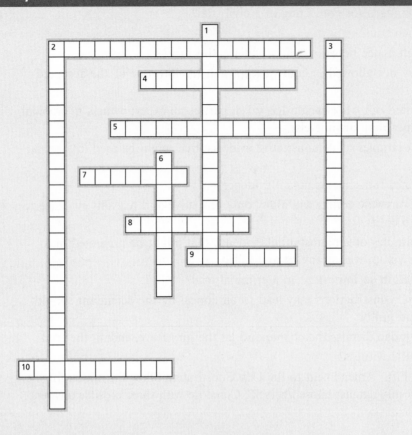

Instructions

Use the key terms from this chapter to fill in the answers to the crossword puzzle.

NOTE: When the answer is more than one word, leave a blank space between words.

ACROSS

2. Occurs when the opposing attorney asks the witness questions.
4. Attorney representing the people or plaintiff in criminal matters.
5. Occurs when the attorney questions his or her own witness.
7. Decision of the jury following presentation of facts and application of relevant law as they relate to the law presented in the jury instructions.
8. Any fact, testimony, or physical object that tends to prove or disprove allegations raised in a case must be reasonably calculated to lead to the discovery of admissible evidence.
9. An out-of-court statement offered to prove a matter in contention in the lawsuit.
10. Results from a guilty finding by the jury in a criminal trial.

DOWN

1. Evidence that establishes a particular fact without resort to other testimony or evidence.
2. Evidence that suggests a conclusion.
3. A jury that is unbiased and does not favor one party or the other.
6. The legal and formal certification of the innocence of a person who has been charged with a crime.

STATE of West Virginia, Plaintiff Below, Appellee

v.

Michael DOONAN, Defendant Below, Appellant

640 S.E.2d 71

Supreme Court of Appeals of

West Virginia.

No. 33052.

Submitted: Nov. 1, 2006.

Decided: Dec. 1, 2006.

Background: Defendant was convicted in the Magistrate Court of driving under influence of alcohol (DUI). He appealed. The Circuit Court, Wood County, George W. Hill, J., affirmed. Defendant appealed.

Holdings: The Supreme Court of Appeals, Davis, C.J., held that:

1. magistrate court could not impose a duty of reciprocal discovery on defendant based on statute governing a prosecutor's duties to disclose certain evidence to a defendant upon request;
2. defendant had no duty to provide his expert-witness list to the state, and thus magistrate court could not exclude defense expert from testifying at trial as sanction for defendant's failure to provide list;
3. error in magistrate court's exclusion of defense expert's testimony was reversible error;
4. copy of printout of defendant's breath-test results was inadmissible under rule governing admissibility of duplicates; and
5. error in magistrate court's admission of copy of printout was harmless.

Reversed and remanded.

DAVIS, Chief Justice.

The defendant and appellant herein, Michael Doonan (hereinafter "Mr. Doonan"), appeals from an order entered July 8, 2005, by the Circuit Court of Wood County. By that order, the circuit court found that the errors committed by the magistrate court amounted to harmless errors, and further, that there was sufficient evidence to support the magistrate jury's finding of guilt for the charge of driving under the influence (hereinafter "DUI"). On appeal to this Court, Mr. Doonan argues that the magistrate court errors were not harmless and that there was insufficient evidence to support his conviction. Based upon the parties' arguments, the record designated for our consideration and the pertinent authorities, we reverse the decision by the circuit court, and further, we remand the case for a new trial.

I. FACTUAL AND PROCEDURAL HISTORY

In this case, Mr. Doonan was charged with driving under the influence of alcohol. On March 21, 2004, Mr. Doonan was pulled over by a member of the Parkersburg Police Department for speeding. The officer testified that when he approached the car, he noticed an odor of alcohol on Mr. Doonan's breath, blood shot eyes, and slightly slurred speech. Mr. Doonan was then requested to perform three different field sobriety tests: walk and turn, horizontal gaze nystagmus, and the one-legged stand. After Mr. Doonan failed all three tests, he was transported to the police station where his blood alcohol content was measured by breathalyzer at .134, which was over the legal limit.

Mr. Doonan was charged with first offense of driving under the influence pursuant to W. Va. Code § 17C-5-2 (2004) (Repl. Vol. 2004). On November 5, 2004, Mr. Doonan was found guilty by a magistrate court jury of first offense of driving under the influence, and was sentenced to serve forty-eight hours in the North Central Regional Jail. Mr. Doonan appealed his conviction to the circuit court, arguing it was improper to exclude his expert witness and that it was error to admit an illegible copy of his DUI printout. The circuit court recognized that some errors existed in the underlying court, but found that the errors were harmless and that there was sufficient evidence to uphold Mr. Doonan's conviction. This appeal then followed.

[Text omitted]

III. DISCUSSION

On appeal to this Court, Mr. Doonan sets forth three assignments of error: (1) the magistrate court's refusal to allow Mr. Doonan's expert witness testimony violated the Sixth Amendment to the United States Constitution and Article III, Section 14 of the West Virginia Constitution and constituted more than harmless error; (2) the admission into evidence of an illegible copy of a certified copy of the breathalyzer printout was more than harmless error; and (3) the evidence was insufficient to support the jury's verdict of driving under the influence. The State originally filed a written response wherein it challenged Mr. Doonan's three assignments of error. Subsequent to the State's written response and during oral argument, the State abandoned its challenges and conceded error on the issue of the preclusion of Mr. Doonan's expert witness, and admitted that such preclusion was more than harmless error and necessitated a reversal for a new trial.

We applaud and appreciate the candor of the State in admitting that it was error to preclude Mr. Doonan's expert witness. This Court has previously recognized that "[t]his Court is not obligated to accept the State's confession of error in a criminal case. We will do so when, after a proper analysis, we believe error occurred." Syl. pt. 8, *State v. Julius,* 185 W. Va. 422, 408 S.E.2d 1 (1991). Therefore, we will conduct our own analysis of the case, which will concentrate on the preclusion of Mr. Doonan's expert witness. Because we find error and determine that this case should be reversed and remanded for a new trial, we offer some guidelines on remand by also addressing the issue of the admission of the illegible copy of the DUI printout. This opinion will first address the exclusion of Mr. Doonan's expert witness, then will turn to the issue of the illegible copy of the DUI printout.

A. Exclusion of Expert Witness

In the present case, Mr. Doonan planned on introducing testimony by an expert, Mr. White, who was a former chemist with the West Virginia State Police. After the expert was excluded, Mr. Doonan's counsel proffered to the court that the subject of the testimony was that Mr. White would have addressed the horizontal gaze nystagmus test, and would have further addressed the issue of Mr. Doonan's alleged level of intoxication and the breathalyzer results. The State objected to the use of Mr. White as a witness because he had not been disclosed by Mr. Doonan. The magistrate court relied on W. Va. Code § 62-1B-2 (1965) (Repl. Vol. 2005) to sustain the objection and preclude Mr. White's testimony. We find this statute wholly inapplicable as it only addresses the duties of the prosecuting attorney to disclose to the defendant and is silent on the issue of a defendant's duty of disclosure to the State. Thus, it was improper for the magistrate court to impose a duty of "reciprocal discovery" on the defendant based on this statutory provision. The circuit court found that it was error to exclude the witness, but that it was harmless error. We cannot agree and find that the exclusion of Mr. White's testimony constituted more than simply harmless error.

There is some discussion by the parties and the magistrate court as to which rules and statutes apply to criminal proceedings in magistrate court. Turning for direction to the Rules of Criminal Procedure for Magistrate Courts, we note that Rule 14 is titled "Discovery and inspection; bill of particulars." However, this rule provides no guidance because it is reserved for later delineation. Thus, our analysis must take another turn.

We note that it is within the inherent authority of this Court to promulgate rules governing discovery procedures. W. Va. Const., art. VIII, § 3 provides, in part, that "[t]he court shall have power to promulgate rules for all cases and proceedings, civil and criminal, for all of the courts of the State relating to writs, warrants, process, practice and procedure, which shall have the force and effect of law." To this end, we previously held that "[u]nder article eight, section three of our Constitution, the Supreme Court of Appeals shall have the power to promulgate rules for all of the courts of the State related to process, practice, and procedure, which shall have the force and effect of law." Syl. pt. 1, *Bennett v. Warner*, 179 W. Va. 742, 372 S.E.2d 920 (1988). Moreover, it is well-settled that "[g]eneral supervisory control over all intermediate appellate, circuit, and magistrate courts resides in the Supreme Court of Appeals. W. Va. Const., art. VIII, § 3." Syl. pt. 1, *Carter v. Taylor*, 180 W. Va. 570, 378 S.E.2d 291 (1989).

In addition to our inherent authority to promulgate rules governing discovery, we also recognize that there are other instances when magistrate courts are instructed to look to the procedure employed in circuit courts for direction. Thus, it is not exceptional for the Rules of Criminal Procedure for Magistrate Courts to look to guidance from the West Virginia Rules of Criminal Procedure for circuit courts. Rule 16 of the Rules of Criminal Procedure is titled "Discovery and inspection," and sets forth the discovery procedure to be used in criminal matters in circuit court. Because Rule 14 of the Rules of Criminal Procedure for Magistrate Courts is silent on discovery issues, it is necessary

and appropriate to look to the West Virginia Rules of Criminal Procedure for discovery guidelines. Thus, we now hold that, until an appropriate rule is adopted in the Rules of Criminal Procedure for Magistrate Courts, the provisions of Rule 16 of the West Virginia Rules of Criminal Procedure shall govern the procedures and requirements for discovery in criminal cases which are to be heard on their merits in magistrate courts.

Now that we have determined that Rule 16 of the West Virginia Rules of Criminal Procedure applies to magistrate court proceedings, we will apply the same to the particular case before us. Rule 16 states, in pertinent part, as follows:

> (b) Disclosure of evidence by the defendant.—(1) Information subject to disclosure.... (C) Expert witnesses.— *If the defendant requests disclosure under subdivision (a)(1)(E) of this rule and the state complies, the defendant, at the state's request, must disclose to the state a written summary of testimony the defendant intends to use* under Rules 702, 703, and 705 of the Rules of Evidence as evidence at trial. The summary must describe the opinions of the witnesses, the bases and reasons therefor, and the witnesses' qualifications.
>
> ....
>
> (2) Failure to comply with a request.—If at any time during the course of the proceedings it is brought to the attention of the court that a party has failed to comply with this rule, the court may order such party to permit the discovery or inspection, grant a continuance, or prohibit the party from introducing evidence not disclosed, or it may enter such other order as it deems just under the circumstances. The court may specify the time, place and manner of making the discovery and inspection and may prescribe such terms and conditions as are just.

(Emphasis added).

The language of the rule is very clear that the defendant may request disclosure from the State. The State only has the option to request reciprocal discovery if the defendant has made an initial request and then, only if the State complied with such request. In the present case, the defendant did make a motion for discovery from the State pursuant to Rule 16. The State did not make a reciprocal request for discovery, and conceded this point in the record. The State argues, however, that an equitable principle of reciprocity should apply, and the magistrate court agreed. Under the statute and the caselaw, this decision by the magistrate court was more than harmless error.

It has been explained that

> Under Rule 16(b) of the West Virginia Rules of Criminal Procedure the State's right to request discovery from a defendant is triggered only if the defendant initially seeks discovery, and is confined to the particular area in which the defendant has sought discovery. Additionally, the State must have complied with the defendant's initial discovery request before it can request discovery.

Syl. pt. 1, *Marano v. Holland*, 179 W. Va. 156, 366 S.E.2d 117 (1988). Prosecutors can discover a defendant's expert witnesses only when triggered first by a defense request. Even then, the rule is not automatically reciprocal and applies only when the State makes a specific request. When a request is not made regarding an expert witness, then there is no basis to exclude the proposed expert. *See Taylor v. Illinois*, 484 U.S. 400, 108 S. Ct. 646, 98 L. Ed. 2d 798 (1998)...

In this case, the defendant made a request of the State for discovery pursuant to Rule 16. In turn, the State was allowed to make a similar request from the defendant only if the State complied with Mr. Doonan's request. However, not only did the State fail to make any discovery request, but it failed to respond to Mr. Doonan's discovery request and was, therefore, precluded from making any such reciprocal request. Therefore, Mr. Doonan was under no duty to provide his expert witness list, and it was error for the magistrate court to preclude the defense witness. Thus, the case must be reversed and remanded for a new trial.

B. Admission of Illegible Copy of the DUI Printout

During the jury trial before the magistrate court, the arresting officer testified, without objection, to the results of the breathalyzer test. However, at the point when the State wanted to submit into evidence a copy of the DUI printout, counsel for Mr. Doonan objected on the basis that the copy was not the original certified copy and, further, that it was illegible. The magistrate court allowed the admission into evidence of the DUI printout while acknowledging the difficulty in deciphering the numbers on the printout. On appeal to the circuit court, the trial court stated that

> [c]learly such evidence should not have been admitted because the probative value of such an exhibit would be far outweighed by the danger of unfair prejudice, confusion of the issues or misleading the jury. However, the admission of the printer ticket was not necessary given the jury was already aware of the results of the test. Only harmless error has been committed given that the jury had already heard the results of the intoxilyzer without objection.

We have long held that "[e]rrors involving deprivation of constitutional rights will be regarded as harmless only if there is no reasonable possibility that the violation contributed to the conviction." Syl. Pt. 20, *State v. Thomas*, 157 W. Va. 640, 203 S.E.2d 445 (1974). If the alleged error is not constitutionally based, then the harmless error analysis is governed by a different standard. We previously explained the following:

> Where improper evidence of a non-constitutional nature is introduced by the State in a criminal trial, the test to determine if the error is harmless is: (1) the inadmissible evidence must be removed from the State's case and a determination made as to whether the remaining evidence is sufficient to convince impartial minds of the defendant's guilt beyond a reasonable

doubt; (2) if the remaining evidence is found to be insufficient, the error is not harmless; (3) if the remaining evidence is sufficient to support the conviction, an analysis must then be made to determine whether the error had any prejudicial effect on the jury.

Syl. pt. 2, *State v. Atkins*, 163 W. Va. 502, 261 S.E.2d 55 (1979). Applying this legal principle to the current case, we agree that the introduction of the illegible printout was harmless error because the same information had already been introduced, without objection, through the officer's testimony. Further, we conceive of no way that the officer's testimony had a prejudicial effect on the jury.

However, because this case is being remanded, the evidentiary issue regarding the DUI printout should be resolved differently during the course of the new trial. The West Virginia Rules of Evidence apply to criminal proceedings in magistrate court. See R. Crim. Proc. for Magis. Cts. 17. In the present case, the DUI printout that was admitted into evidence was a copy of a certified copy. It was not the certified copy of the printout. Rule 1003 of the West Virginia Rules of Evidence states that "[a] duplicate is admissible to the same extent as an original unless (1) a genuine question is raised as to the authenticity of the original or (2) in the circumstances it would be unfair to admit the duplicate in lieu of the original." Under the present circumstances, we agree that it was unfair to admit an illegible copy of the DUI printout into evidence. More direction is obtained from Rule 403 of the West Virginia Rules of Evidence, which provides that "[a]lthough relevant, evidence may be excluded if its probative value is substantially outweighed by the danger of unfair prejudice, confusion of the issues, or misleading the jury, or by considerations of undue delay, waste of time, or needless presentation of cumulative evidence." An illegible printout, as its condition was conceded by all parties and by the magistrate court judge, can have no probative value to a jury. Thus, under normal circumstances, its admission would have been an abuse of discretion. However, under the present circumstances, the error was harmless based on the introduction of the officer's testimony, without objection, regarding the breathalyzer results.

IV. CONCLUSION

For the reasons set out in the body of this opinion, the order of the Circuit Court of Wood County, entered on July 8, 2005, is reversed, and this case is remanded for a new trial.

Reversed and Remanded.

[Footnotes omitted]

Source: 640 S.E.2d 71 (W. Va. 2006). Reprinted with permission from Westlaw.

Chapter 14

Sentencing and Post-Trial Procedures

CHAPTER OBJECTIVES

Upon completion of this chapter, you will be able to:

- Understand the goals of sentencing.
- Identify the different types of sentencing systems.
- Discuss the death penalty and other types of sentences.
- Explain other post-trial procedures.

Ultimately, at the end of a criminal trial, if a person is determined to be guilty of committing a crime, a punishment must be imposed by the judge. Sentences vary from state to state, but all states recognize that those who pose a threat to society must face some sort of punishment. This chapter examines the sentencing process as well as other processes that can occur after the criminal trial has concluded.

SENTENCING

sentencing
The post-conviction stage of the criminal justice process in which the defendant is brought before the court for imposition of sentence.

sentence
The judgment formally pronounced by the court or judge upon the defendant after his/her conviction in a criminal prosecution, imposing the punishment to be inflicted, usually in the form of a fine, incarceration, or probation.

After a trial, a defendant who has been found guilty has a punishment imposed upon him/her by the judge. This process is called **sentencing** and the punishment is known as the **sentence**. Some states may have separate proceedings for the sentencing portion of the criminal proceeding and will allow hearsay and witness testimony to be admissible at the sentencing hearing, testimony that otherwise would not have been admissible at trial. The judge must decide what punishment is within legal limits to impose upon the defendant. The judge will look at the totality of the circumstances when trying to decide what sentence to give. Some of those factors include, but are not limited to:

- The seriousness of the criminal offense committed by the defendant.
- The prior criminal record of the defendant.
- Standard operating procedures that regularize sentences.
- The threat posed to society by the defendant.

Sentencing laws are often passed by the legislature under pressures by a society that believes that a certain punishment should be imposed upon a person found guilty of a particular criminal activity. Sentencings for misdemeanor cases usually involve the imposition of a **fine**, a short jail sentence, **community service** or super-vision, or **probation**.

As discussed in Chapter 1, sentencing the defendant to a form of punishment has certain goals. As a review, some of the goals of sentencing are

- Incapacitation. Society seeks to counteract the defendant's ability to commit further criminal activity by restricting his/her freedom and minimizing his/her contact with people. By incarcerating the defendant, the public safety is protected because the defendant has been removed from society.

- Deterrence. Punishment offered as deterrence seeks to try to stop future criminal behavior. It is hoped that punishment can deter criminal behavior in the specific defendant who is being punished as well as deterring others in society who may contemplate committing the same type of crime in the future.

- Retribution. The theory behind retribution is to give justice to the victim, to avenge the wrong done to society, and to exact punishment from the specific defendant who committed the crime.

- Rehabilitation. It is thought that if a punishment is imposed upon the defendant, he/she will change his/her attitude or behavior and be able to reenter society as a productive citizen.

fine
A pecuniary punishment or penalty imposed by lawful tribunal upon a person convicted of a crime or misdemeanor.

community service
A criminal sentence requiring that the offender perform some specific service to the community for some specified period of time.

probation
A court-imposed criminal sentence that, subject to stated conditions, re-leases a convicted person into the community in-stead of sending the criminal to prison.

PROCEDURAL RIGHTS DURING SENTENCING

A defendant is guaranteed certain procedural rights during the sentencing process. An indigent defendant has the right to appointed counsel. A defendant also is entitled to a sentencing hearing; however, the right of confrontation is limited to testimony that reveals new facts, and matters covered in the original trial may not be revisited. A judge also may choose to consider at the sentencing hearing evidence that was objectionable or inadmissible during the original trial. For example, the judge may consider hearsay or the judge's own personal belief that the defendant gave false testimony. There is no right to have a jury determine a sentence. A death penalty may be imposed by a judge acting alone; however, if a jury acting as the sentencing body does choose to impose the death penalty, the defendant has additional procedural rights that must be protected.

A state law cannot exclude from the jury all individuals who express some opposition to the death penalty, but such a law may exclude potential jurors who indicate they would never impose the death penalty on anyone no matter what the crime.

Additional procedural requirements include the right to appellate review to prevent the imposition of the death penalty for discriminatory or arbitrary reasons, as well

CASE FACT PATTERN

A recent case handed down by the U.S. Supreme Court severely limits how state court judges sentence defendants. In *Crawford v. Washington*, 541 U.S. 36 (2004), the outcome of the case hung on the admissibility of a police statement made by Sylvia Crawford with regard to the nature of the attack by her husband, Michael, on Kenneth Lee. Defense counsel objected to the admissibility of the statement because Michael Crawford was not able to confront his wife on the statement without waiving spousal privilege. At trial, the objection was overruled, the statement was received into evidence, and Michael Crawford was convicted. The Washington Court of Appeals then overturned the case, only to have the decision reinstated by the Washington Supreme Court. The U.S. Supreme Court granted certiorari. The majority held that the use of the spouse's recorded statement did indeed violate the defendant's Sixth Amendment right to confrontation. Essentially, *Crawford v. Washington* determined that whenever testimonial evidence is at issue, the Sixth Amendment's guaranteed right to confrontation requires both unavailability and a prior opportunity to cross-examine the witness.

as the right to remain silent. The Fifth Amendment gives a defendant undergoing sentencing the right to remain silent and no adverse inference is to be drawn from a defendant's choosing to do so.

SENTENCING SYSTEMS

Sentencing systems vary by jurisdiction. The following is a brief description of the various types of sentencing systems.

A **mandatory sentence** is one in which the legislature of a state or Congress enacts laws that prescribe specific sentences for certain types of crimes. In other words, the sentence is a mandate of the law. A judge has no discretion to deviate from the mandated punishment. For example, some states have enacted a "three strikes" sentence for people who are convicted of three felonies. If a person has been convicted of three felonies, there is a mandatory life imprisonment punishment imposed, no matter what the level of seriousness of the felonies.

A **determinate sentence** is one that is fixed by the law. The punishment is determined proportionate to the seriousness of the crime. Determinate sentencing has a goal of regularizing sentences so that disparities do not occur between defendants who have been convicted of the same crime. Determinate sentences typically have three designations for the amount of time that can be imposed upon a defendant: presumptive, aggravated, and mitigated.

Think of these three designations as being time periods on a scale. The presumptive term is the middle-of-the-road sentence. It is the middle of the scale. It is the presumed sentence that a judge will bestow on a criminal. It is not extreme at either end of the scale. On the far right side of the scale is the aggravated term. If the defendant committed a crime that was aggravated or enhanced, a judge may impose an aggravated term, which would represent the upper time limit allowed by law for that particular crime. At the lower end of the spectrum is the mitigated term, which represents the least amount of time that a defendant can serve by law for that particular crime. A judge may impose the lowest time limit if the crime was committed with factors that are less serious than other factors or where the defendant may not have had a prior criminal record. For example, the crime of rape may carry a determinate term of between 10 and 20 years. A presumptive term may be 15 years. An aggravated term could be 20 years, while a mitigated term might be 10 years.

Indeterminate sentencing involves both a prison sentence and then the opportunity for the offender to be paroled after a certain period of time. The purpose of providing an offender with the opportunity to be paroled after a certain period of time is so that a rehabilitated defendant will have the opportunity to reenter society once his/her rehabilitation has been achieved. Using the rape example above, suppose that the law had a provision that allowed for the possibility of parole every two years beginning after year 12. At year 12, a parole board conducts a review of the defendant's progress toward being rehabilitated in order to determine the appropriate time for his/her release.

Concurrent sentences apply when a defendant is convicted of multiple crimes and each crime carries a separate sentence. A defendant can serve his/her sentences all at the same time. For example, suppose that a defendant is convicted of rape and battery. Rape has a sentence of 10 years and battery a sentence of 5 years. If the defendant serves his/her sentences concurrently, then he/she will serve the maximum of 10 years and will be given credit for time served toward the five-year battery sentence.

Consecutive sentences also apply to a defendant who has been convicted of multiple offenses; however, the sentences do not run concurrently. Instead, they run back

mandatory sentence
A sentence set by law with no discretion for the judge to individualize punishment.

determinate sentence
A sentence for a fixed length of time rather than for an unspecified duration.

indeterminate sentence
A sentence of an unspecified duration such as one for a term of 5 to 10 years.

concurrent sentences
Two or more sentences of jail time to be served simultaneously.

consecutive sentences
Two or more sentences of jail time to be served in sequence.

to back. So, in the example given above for rape and battery, the defendant would serve 10 years for rape and then 5 years for battery for a total of 15 years.

In a **split sentence** part of the time served is spent in confinement, to expose the offender to the unpleasantness of prison life, and the rest is spent on probation, outside of prison and back within the community. A **suspended sentence** is a sentence postponed so that the defendant is not required to spend time in prison unless he or she commits an additional crime or violates a court-imposed condition for the suspended sentence. Sometimes a defendant may be sentenced to time served: a criminal defendant is sentenced to prison but is credited with time served in an amount equal to the sentence given. A suspended sentence is essentially a type of probation.

split sentence
A sentence in which part of the time is served in confinement and the rest is spent on probation.

suspended sentence
A sentence postponed so that the defendant is not required to serve time in the absence of certain circumstances.

DEATH PENALTY

In some instances, a crime is so heinous that the law imposes a punishment of death. The Eighth Amendment prohibits a judge from imposing a sentence that amounts to cruel and unusual punishment. However, in 1972, the Supreme Court ruled that a sentence of death is not cruel and unusual punishment in instances in which the crime is aggravated. But, a death sentence can be imposed only under a statutory framework that enables a judge to use reasonable discretion when examining the full information concerning a defendant and gives guidance to the making of such a grave decision of death. The Eighth Amendment is made applicable to the states through the Fourteenth Amendment. A sentence must comply with the Fourteenth Amendment and provide a defendant with **procedural due process**.

Judges are permitted to look at aggravating and mitigating factors when trying to make a determination of whether or not to put a defendant to death. Whether a judge or a jury, the sentencing body must have a reasonable opportunity and guidelines to consider mitigating factors. **Mitigating factors** are background factors that work in the defendant's favor to help lessen the punishment, and the sentencing body must be allowed to hear any aspect of the defendant's character or record that suggests the defendant deserves a sentence of less than death. Examples might include

- The defendant had no significant prior criminal record.
- The defendant suffered extreme mental or emotional disturbance.
- The defendant was a minor participant in the crime.
- The defendant was a minor at the time of the crime.

Aggravating factors also are considered. These are characteristics of the defendant or the crime that work against the defendant during the sentencing determination. Types of aggravating factors are

- The defendant has a prior criminal record of felonies.
- The crime committed was a felony murder.
- The crime involved more than one victim.
- The victim was a law enforcement officer or other public official.
- The crime was one that was heinous or involved torture.
- The defendant tried to avoid arrest.
- The defendant tried to escape.

The death penalty is very controversial. It has been enacted in certain states, repealed, and then enacted again. Some people believe that the death penalty is inhumane.

procedural due process
These requirements mandate scrupulous adherence to the method or mechanism applied. Notice and fair hearing are the cornerstones of due process, though certainly not the only consideration.

mitigating factor
A fact or situation that does not justify or excuse a wrongful act or offense but that reduces the degree of culpability and thus may reduce the damages in a civil case or the punishment in a criminal case.

aggravating factor
A fact or circumstance that increases the degree of liability or culpability for a criminal act.

appeal
Tests the sufficiency of the verdict under the legal parameters or rules.

question of law
An issue to be decided by the judge concerning the application or interpretation of the law.

question of fact
An issue that has not been predetermined and authoritatively answered by the law; a disputed issue to be resolved by the jury in a jury trial or by the judge in a bench trial.

Certain countries such as Mexico may not extradite criminals back to the United States to stand trial for crimes committed in the United States unless an agreement is made that the defendant will not be put to death. It is certain that this type of punishment will continue to raise discussion in the future.

RESEARCH THIS

In 1972, in the case of *Furman v. Georgia*, 408 U.S. 238 (1972), the U.S. Supreme Court ruled that the death penalty was not cruel and unusual punishment. However, there were problems with the manner in which it was applied. Later, in the case of *Gregg v. Georgia*, 428 U.S. 153 (1976), the Supreme Court allowed judges to take into consideration aggravating and mitigating factors when considering a punishment of death. Recently, in *Roper v. Simmons*, 543 U.S. 551 (2005), the Supreme Court held that juveniles under age 18 may not be sentenced to death. Research the above cases and compare and contrast the decisions in each. Why did the Supreme Court rule that the death penalty was not cruel and unusual punishment? In each of the three cases, what did they hope their ruling would achieve?

A DAY IN THE LIFE OF A REAL PARALEGAL

Willie Martin had been convicted of the armed robbery of a local convenience store approximately six months ago and was sentenced to 10 years in the state prison. Willie had been plotting his escape for many months. He had taken one of the spoons from his lunch tray back to his cell and had sharpened it into a knifelike instrument. Willie knew that at night, between the hours of 1:00 a.m. and 4:00 a.m., the prison kept a skeleton crew of guards due to the late hour. He also had watched as one of the inmates had been taken to the infirmary by only one guard when he had fallen ill with food poisoning. Willie decided that his method of escape would be to fake an illness in the early morning hours, wait until he got to the infirmary, kill the medical aide, and escape through the door that leads to the medical portion of the prison.

At 2:00 a.m., Willie began to moan. The guard came to his cell and determined that Willie needed to go to the infirmary. Once there, Willie stabbed and killed both the guard and the medic. After taking the guard's weapon and changing into his uniform, Willie let himself out the door of the facility and made his way to the guard gate at the entrance to the prison. The guard on duty thought that Willie was another guard and welcomed him into the guard gate. Willie stabbed the second guard and made his escape out of the gate.

Three days later, Willie was captured at a motel near the state line. He stood trial for the murder of the two guards and the medic. Willie was sentenced to death because the murders were premeditated, involved law enforcement personnel, involved more than one victim, and were committed during an escape. Willie is scheduled to die by lethal injection next year. Your firm has taken Willie's case to attempt an appeal of his death sentence. Your task is to begin researching any means by which Willie can bring a successful appeal, exploring questions of both law and fact as issues to raise an appeal.

SURF'S UP

The death penalty is a controversial topic and always sparks great debate as to the humanity of killing another human being. To learn more about the death penalty and the issues and controversies surrounding it, visit the following Web sites:

- www.deathpenaltyinfo.org
- www.deathpenalty.org

- www.prodeathpenalty.com
- www.aclu.org
- http://web.amnesty.org/pages/deathpenalty

APPEAL

If the defendant loses a trial and is convicted and sentenced, he/she has the opportunity to file an **appeal** of his/her conviction and sentence to a higher court. An appeal is not a new trial. Instead, in an appeal, a higher court examines the trial record to ensure that all trial proceedings were conducted in a fair manner and that no judicial errors occurred during the trial. A defendant needs to have a valid legal reason for filing an appeal. The appeals court focuses on **questions of law** rather than **questions of fact**. For example, if a witness testified to seeing the defendant buy the gun that was later used to commit a crime and the jury believed the statement to be truthful, the appeals court will not revisit the issue of whether or not the defendant purchased the gun in question. The appeals court will examine the trial court record to ensure that the defendant's rights were not violated in some manner. In addition, the appeals court will look to see if the trial court misapplied the law in some manner that led to an adverse outcome for the defendant. There is no right to appeal a criminal conviction guaranteed in the U.S. Constitution. The right to appeal has been created by the federal government and the states via statute or state constitutions.

The types of errors that might be discovered as having been committed in the trial court are fundamental or plain errors, harmful errors, harmless errors, and reversible errors.

A fundamental or **plain error** is the type of error that goes to the heart of the case. It is in the interest of justice to reconsider the error even if the defendant fails to properly raise the issue himself/herself in the appeal. For example, the court misapplied the law so a misuse of justice occurred.

A **harmful error** is an error that the higher court concludes probably impacted the outcome of the trial in a negative manner. For example, some type of evidence was admitted that might have been prejudicial to the defendant such as a former conviction for an unrelated crime.

A **harmless error** is an error that the higher court concludes had no negative effect on the outcome of the trial. A small amount of evidence was admitted into court against the defendant that otherwise should have been deemed inadmissible. However, the overwhelming evidence against the defendant deemed the error harmless.

A **reversible error** is an error that is so serious that the higher court overturns the lower court's decision as a reversible error. If a reversible error occurs, then the appellate court may remand or reverse the case. **Reversal** occurs when the appellate court overturns the lower court's decision. **Remand** involves sending the case back to the lower court so that the prosecutor may retry the case against the defendant.

If the higher court agrees with the lower court's decision, then they will **affirm** the decision of the lower court.

In a typical appeals process, a defendant will appeal his/her case from the state court to an intermediary state court to a state supreme court and finally to the U.S. Supreme Court. Just because a defendant appeals his/her case does not mean that the court will agree to hear the appeal. A review panel of lawyers who work for the appellate courts will review the case to make a preliminary determination of whether the case should be heard on appeal. If the review committee believes that the case has merit, then the appeal may be heard.

A DAY IN THE LIFE OF A REAL PARALEGAL

Paralegals are often instrumental in preparing cases for appeal. Keeping in mind the difference between questions of law and questions of fact, and acknowledging which are the focus of an appeal, provide a list of a few appropriate legal reasons for an appeal.

---

plain error
A decision or action by the court that appears to a reviewing court to have been unquestionably erroneous.

harmful error
An error by the court that has an identifiable negative impact on the trial to such a degree that the constitutional rights of a party are compromised.

harmless error
Standard of review that has not caused legal error requiring reversal of the trial court's decision.

reversible error
An error that affects a party's substantive rights or the case's outcome, and thus is grounds for reversal if the party properly objected.

reversal
Disposition in which the appellate court disagrees with the trial court.

remand
Disposition in which the appellate court sends the case back to the lower court for further action.

affirm
Disposition in which the appellate court agrees with the trial court.

PRACTICE TIP

If a state has guaranteed a first appeal as a right, the state also must provide counsel to indigent defendants. There is, however, no right to appointed counsel for discretionary appeals or applications for revision to the U.S. Supreme Court.

EYE ON ETHICS

Lately, habeas corpus has made its way into the news. With the War on Terror, the rights of detainees who have shown hostility toward the United States have been severely tested. The Military Commissions Act of 2006 effectively suspended a prisoner who is detained as a result of his/her hostility toward the United States from challenging his/her detention. Some proponents state that this new act enables the United States to effectively defend itself against terrorism. Others suggest that it has eliminated the writ of habeas corpus, a concept that dates back to the Magna Carta. So long as the United States feels pressure from terrorism, habeas corpus rights may be suspended for those who threaten homeland security.

HABEAS CORPUS

writ of habeas corpus
Literally "you should have the body"; application for extraordinary relief or a petition for rehearing of the issue on the basis of unusual facts unknown at the time of the trial.

writ
A written order of a judge requiring specific action by the person or entity to whom the writ is directed.

habeas corpus
A writ employed to bring a person before a court, most frequently to ensure that the party's imprisonment or detention is not illegal.

Sometimes a defendant may want to challenge the legality surrounding his/her imprisonment. In order to accomplish this, a defendant must file a post-conviction **writ of habeas corpus**. This effectively appeals his/her case directly from the state trial court to the federal district court and proceeds through the federal appellate system. A **writ** is an order from a higher court to a lower court. A **habeas corpus** is usually filed by a person who objects to being in custody. He/she must demonstrate in the writ that his/her incarceration is due to either legal or factual error.

Many state constitutions as well as the U.S. Constitution provide for the filing of a writ of habeas corpus when the imprisonment of a defendant may have been illegal or in error. The U.S. Supreme Court recognized the importance of a habeas corpus action when it stated that a writ is "the fundamental instrument for safeguarding individual freedom against arbitrary and lawless state action" (*Harris v. Nelson,* 394 U.S. 286, 290–91 (1969)).

A defendant is entitled to habeas corpus relief if he/she can demonstrate that a constitutional error occurred that had a substantial and injurious effect or in some way influenced the jury negatively so that he/she was imprisoned on the verdict. In a habeas corpus proceeding, the federal court typically will not review a question of federal law if it is decided under state law. For example, if a petitioner asserts federal claims in his/her habeas corpus proceeding, but he/she failed to meet state requirements, the federal court will not review the proceeding. The federal courts do not supervise the state courts. The federal courts can only review standards of the states that are delineated to the federal courts by way of the Constitution. Whether or not a constitutional violation occurred is usually determined by the evidence presented during the case as well as the jury instructions that were given at the time of deliberation.

Summary

After a trial, a defendant who has been found guilty has a punishment imposed upon him/her by the judge. This process is called sentencing and the punishment is known as the sentence. Some states may have separate proceedings for the sentencing portion of the criminal proceeding and will allow hearsay and witness testimony to be admissible at the sentencing hearing, testimony that otherwise would not have been admissible at trial. The judge must decide what punishment is within the legal limits to impose upon the defendant. A defendant is guaranteed certain procedural rights during the sentencing process. For example, an indigent defendant has the right to appointed counsel and a defendant also is entitled to a sentencing hearing.

Sentencing laws often are passed by the legislature under pressure by a society of people who believe that a certain punishment should be imposed upon a person found guilty of a particular criminal activity. Sentences for misdemeanor cases usually involve the imposition of a fine, a short jail sentence, community service work, or probation.

A determinate sentence is one that is fixed by the law. The punishment is determined proportionate to the seriousness of the crime. Determinate sentencing has a goal of regularizing sentences so that disparities do not occur between defendants who have been convicted of the same crime.

Indeterminate sentencing involves both a prison sentence and then the opportunity for the offender to be paroled after a certain period of time. The purpose of providing an offender with the opportunity to be paroled after a certain period of time is so that a rehabilitated defendant will have the opportunity to reenter society once his/her rehabilitation has been achieved.

In some instances, a crime is so heinous that the law imposes a punishment of death. The Eighth Amendment prohibits a judge from imposing a sentence that amounts to cruel and unusual punishment. However, in 1972, the Supreme Court ruled that a sentence of death is not cruel and unusual punishment in instances in which the crime is aggravated. However, a death sentence can be imposed only under a statutory framework that enables a judge to use reasonable discretion when examining the full information concerning a defendant and gives guidance in making such a grave decision of death.

If the defendant loses a trial and is convicted and sentenced, he/she has the opportunity to file an appeal of his/her conviction and sentence to a higher court. An appeal is not a new trial. Instead, in an appeal, a higher court examines the trial record to ensure that all trial proceedings were conducted in a fair manner and that no judicial errors occurred during the trial. A defendant needs to have a valid legal reason for filing an appeal. The appeals court focuses on questions of law. The appeals court will examine the trial court record to ensure that the defendant's rights were not violated in some manner. In addition, the appeals court will look to see if the trial court misapplied the law in some manner that led to an adverse outcome for the defendant.

Sometimes a defendant may want to challenge the legality surrounding his/her imprisonment. In order to accomplish this, a defendant must file a writ of habeas corpus, which effectively appeals his/her case directly from the state trial court to the federal district court and proceeds through the federal appellate system. A writ is an order from a higher court to a lower court. A post-conviction writ of habeas corpus is usually filed by a person who objects to being in custody. He or she must demonstrate in the writ that his or her incarceration is due to either legal or factual error.

Key Terms

Affirm	Plain error
Aggravating factor	Probation
Appeal	Procedural due process
Community service	Question of fact
Concurrent sentences	Question of law
Consecutive sentences	Remand
Determinate sentence	Reversal
Fine	Reversible error
Habeas corpus	Sentence
Harmful error	Sentencing
Harmless error	Split sentence
Indeterminate sentence	Suspended sentence
Mandatory sentence	Writ
Mitigating factor	Writ of habeas corpus

Review Questions

1. List the reasons that a defendant might be sentenced to death.
2. How does a defendant learn what his/her punishment is to be?
3. List the factors that a judge might look at in deciding what type of sentence to give a defendant.
4. What is a fine?
5. When might a defendant be sentenced to community service?
6. What is the concept behind rehabilitation?
7. What is the difference between a mandatory sentencing system and a determinate sentencing system?
8. What is the difference between an aggravated and a presumptive term?
9. What is a concurrent sentence?
10. What happens to the defendant when he/she is sentenced to serve consecutive sentences and what are consecutive sentences?
11. List some of the mitigating factors that a judge may consider in a death penalty case.
12. Under what circumstances can a defendant file an appeal?
13. What happens in an appeal?
14. What is the difference between an appeal and a writ of habeas corpus?
15. When a higher court remands a decision to the lower court, what does that mean?

Exercises

1. Research the law in your state. Does your state sanction the use of the death penalty in certain types of criminal cases? What does the law state? Do you agree or disagree with the law and why?
2. Bert was a driver for an illegal immigrant smuggling ring. On one particular run, the smugglers loaded 70 illegal immigrants into a trailer to transport them across the Texas/Mexico border during the summer. Due to the excessively high heat and lack of air conditioning in the trailer, 19 of the illegal immigrants died from dehydration. Bert did not know the people in the back of the trailer were dying until it was too late. Bert was found guilty on 58 counts of illegally transporting aliens across the border as well as the 19 deaths. Should Bert be sentenced to death or not for his role in the deaths of the illegal aliens? Why or why not?
3. Twenty years ago, Elias was convicted of raping, beating, and killing a teenage girl. Due to the severity of the crime, Elias was sentenced to life in prison without the possibility of parole. Elias has always stated that he did not commit the crime and that an innocent man has been convicted. Now, 20 years later, Juno is arrested for a similar crime. While in custody, Juno confesses to the rape and murder of the teenage girl whose death Elias had been found guilty of some 20 years before. Hearing this news, what should Elias do?
   a. Nothing as he was convicted of circumstances as they stood 20 years ago.
   b. File an appeal alleging that an error was committed during his trial.
   c. File a writ of habeas corpus.
4. If a defendant receives concurrent sentences of 10 years and 12 years, what is the total amount of jail time?
5. If a defendant receives consecutive sentences of 10 years and 12 years, what is the total amount of jail time?
6. Using the Internet, research the sentencing guidelines for your home state.

7. Read and write a brief summary of Model Penal Code section 210.6 discussing the death penalty.

8. After shooting and killing her abusive husband, Molly is given a suspended sentence by the court. Under what circumstances might Molly have to actually spend time in prison?

PORTFOLIO ASSIGNMENT

Using the Internet, including the sites suggested within the chapter, research which states allow the death penalty. Prepare a list to keep in your portfolio for future reference.

Vocabulary Builders

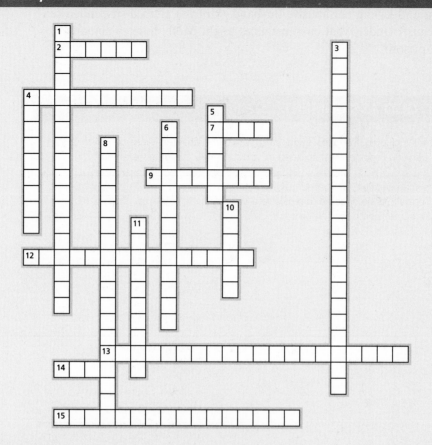

Instructions
Use the key terms from this chapter to fill in the answers to the crossword puzzle.
NOTE: When the answer is more than one word, leave a blank space between words.

ACROSS
2. Tests the sufficiency of the verdict under the legal parameters or rules.
4. A decision or action by the court that appears to a reviewing court to have been unquestionably erroneous.
7. A pecuniary punishment or penalty imposed by lawful tribunal upon a person convicted of a crime or misdemeanor.
9. Disposition in which the appellate court disagrees with trial court.
12. An issue to be decided by the judge concerning the application or interpretation of the law.
14. A written order of a judge requiring specific action by the person or entity to whom the writ is directed.
15. An issue that has not been predetermined and authoritatively answered by the law; a disputed issue to be resolved by the jury in a jury trial or by the judge in a bench trial.

DOWN
1. A sentence set by law with no discretion for the judge to individualize punishment.
3. These requirements mandate scrupulous adherence to the method or mechanism applied. Notice and fair hearing are the cornerstones of due process, though certainly not the only consideration.
4. A court-imposed criminal sentence that, subject to stated conditions, releases a convicted person into the community instead of sending the criminal to prison.
5. Disposition in which the appellate court agrees with the trial court.
6. A writ employed to bring a person before a court, most frequently to ensure that the party's imprisonment of detention is not illegal.
8. A fact or situation that does not justify or excuse a wrongful act or offense but that reduces the degree of culpability and thus may reduce the damages in a civil case or the punishment.
10. Disposition in which the appellate court sends the case back to the lower court for further action.
11. The post-conviction stage of the criminal justice process in which the defendant is brought before the court for imposition of sentence.

CASE IN POINT

Commonwealth Court of Pennsylvania.
Michael GRIFFIN, Petitioner

v.

PENNSYLVANIA DEPARTMENT OF CORRECTIONS, Respondent.
Submitted on Briefs Oct. 15, 2004.
862 A.2d 152
Decided Nov. 22, 2004.

Background: Parolee filed petition for mandamus requesting that Department of Corrections be directed to recalculate state sentences imposed for crimes committed on parole by crediting time served in federal prison. The Department filed objections in nature of demurrer.

Holdings: The Commonwealth Court, No. 347 M.D. 2004, Pellegrini, J., held that:

1. parolee was required to serve new federal sentence before he could serve backtime on original sentence;
2. parolee was required to finish backtime on original sentence after release from federal prison before beginning to serve time on new state sentences;
3. federal court had no authority to order that parolee's federal sentence for crimes committed on parole be served concurrent with new state sentences; and
4. parolee was entitled to have time served in federal prison credited against new state sentences.

Objections granted in part.
OPINION BY Judge PELLEGRINI.

Before this Court are preliminary objections in the nature of a demurrer filed by the Commonwealth of Pennsylvania, Department of Corrections (Department) in response to a petition for a writ of mandamus filed by Michael Griffin (Griffin) requesting this Court to direct the Department to recalculate his state sentence to give him credit for time served in a federal correctional institution.

The facts pled are as follows. While on parole from a state prison sentence, Griffin committed further criminal acts which resulted in both state and federal charges. On December 10, 1992, Griffin pled guilty to two state robbery charges. For each conviction, he received a sentence of five to 10 years at a state correctional facility to run concurrently. Griffin also pled guilty to the federal charges, and on May 21, 1993, he was sentenced to 293 months of incarceration and five years of supervised release, which was subsequently reduced to 121 months of incarceration and five years of supervised release purportedly to run concurrent with his state sentence. After being sentenced on his federal charges, federal authorities took custody of Griffin and he was removed to a federal correctional facility.

On September 19, 1994, Griffin returned to the Philadelphia County Court of Common Pleas and pled guilty to two more state robbery charges for which he was sentenced to serve five to 10 years and 10 to 20 years. Both of these charges were to be served concurrently with each other and with any other state or federal sentences Griffin was serving at the time. Griffin returned to federal custody after being sentenced on these charges where he remained until April 27, 2001, at which time he was released to a detainer lodged by the Pennsylvania Board of Probation and Parole (Board).

After being returned to state custody, the Board issued a recommitment order assessing Griffin 14 years, six months and one day of backtime on his original state sentence. Based upon the recommitment order, the Department recalculated Griffin's sentence to reflect the completion of his federal sentence on April 27, 2001, and the commencement of his backtime on that same date. The Department also recalculated Griffin's new state sentence to begin running concurrently with his previous sentences after the completion of his backtime.

Claiming that the Department improperly recalculated his sentence and after exhausting his administrative remedies, Griffin filed a petition for review in the nature of a writ of mandamus arguing that the Department failed to credit the time he served in federal prison toward his state court prison terms as provided for in both his federal sentence and his 1994 state court sentence. The Department filed preliminary objections in the nature of a demurrer arguing that Griffin had no clear legal right to the relief requested because a federal court could not order time served in a federal prison to count against state court time, and the 1994 state court sentence could not run against federal time because he had to serve his backtime first.

Section 21.1(a) of the Act commonly known as the Parole Act governs the order in which sentences and backtime are served. Backtime is served before the commencement of the new sentence in two instances: (1) if the parolee was paroled from a state penal institution and the new sentence is to be served in a state penal institution; or (2) if the parolee was paroled from a county penal institution and the new sentence is to be served there. In all other cases, Section 21.1(a) provides that the new sentence is to be served before backtime.

In this case, because Griffin was directed to serve his federal sentence in a federal rather than a state correctional institution, under Section 21.1(a) of the Parole Act, he was required to serve the new federal sentence before he could begin serving the backtime on his original sentence. Additionally, pursuant to Section 21.1(a) of the Parole Act, after being returned to state custody, Griffin was required to begin serving his backtime before the commencement of either of his new state sentences.

The issue in this case then is what effect did the federal court and state court orders have on the calculation of the time

215

Griffin would ultimately have to spend incarcerated because the federal court ordered Griffin's federal sentence to run concurrent with his state sentence, and the state court ordered his 1994 state sentences to run concurrent with each other and with any other state or federal sentence he was serving at the time.

As to his federal sentence being credited against his state court sentence, it is clear that "[a] federal court has no power to direct that a federal sentence shall run concurrently with a state sentence." *Gomori v. Arnold*, 533 F.2d 871, 875 (3rd Cir. 1976), *certiorari denied*, 429 U.S. 851, 97 S. Ct. 140, 50 L. Ed. 2d 125 (1976). Rather, a federal judge may only recommend to the Attorney General that he designate a state institution as the place of service of a federal sentence in order to make it concurrent with a state sentence being served at that institution. *See United States v. Devino*, 531 F.2d 182 (3rd Cir. 1976). In this case, based upon the facts alleged in Griffin's petition for mandamus, the federal judge did not recommend that Griffin serve his federal sentence in a state institution, but rather only designated that his federal sentence be served concurrent to any state sentence. Accordingly, because the federal judge had no power to direct that the time Griffin spent incarcerated in a federal prison would count against his 1992 state sentences, the Department properly concluded that the time Griffin served on his federal sentence should not have been credited against his state time.

This brings us to the second and more difficult issue, i.e., what was the effect of the state court's order that Griffin's 1994 state sentences run concurrent with each other and with any other state or federal sentence Griffin was serving at the time. As to state time running against federal time, Section 9761(b) of the Sentencing Code, 42 Pa. C.S. § 9761(b), provides:

> (b) SENTENCES IMPOSED BY OTHER SOVEREIGNS.—
> *If the defendant is at the time of sentencing subject to imprisonment under the authority of any other sovereign, the court may indicate that imprisonment under such other authority shall satisfy or be credited against both the minimum and maximum time imposed under the court's sentence.* If the defendant is released by such other authority before the expiration of the minimum time imposed by the court, he shall be returned to a correctional institution of the Commonwealth to serve the time which remains of the sentence. If the defendant is released after the minimum time has elapsed, he shall be considered for parole on the same basis as a prisoner who has served his minimum time in a correctional institution of the Commonwealth. If the defendant is released after the maximum time imposed under the sentence of imprisonment he shall be deemed to have served his sentence.

42 Pa. C.S. § 9761(b). (Emphasis added.)

Based upon the facts alleged in Griffin's petition for mandamus, after pleading guilty to two more state robbery charges in 1994, he received state sentences of five to 10 years and 10 to 20 years to run concurrently with each other and with any other state or federal sentences Griffin was serving at the time. Pursuant to 42 Pa. C.S. § 9761(b), the trial court was authorized to

credit any time Griffin spent in federal prison against his new 1994 state sentence.

The Department contends, however, that Section 21.1(a) of the Parole Act required Griffin's backtime to be served before the commencement of his new state sentences. Because he had to serve his approximately 14 years of backtime before he could begin to serve his state sentences, the Department argues that the 1994 state sentences could not run concurrently with his federal sentence, making the trial judge's order that they were to be served concurrently illegal under Section 21.1(a) of the Parole Act.

In *Parish v. Horn*, 768 A.2d 1214 (Pa. Cmwlth. 2001), *affirmed*, 569 Pa. 45, 800 A.2d 294 (2002), we addressed a similar issue, albeit involving credit for county time. In that case, a parolee was convicted of crimes during his parole period for which he received both a sentence on county charges in July of 1992 and a state sentence approximately three months later. At the state sentencing, the judge ordered that the inmate's state sentence was to run concurrently with any sentence he was serving. As in this case, the Department argued that giving the inmate three months and 20 days credit on his state sentence for the time he served concurrently on his county sentence was the same as allowing him to "serve" a portion of his state sentence before serving his backtime, which was contrary to Section 21.1(a) of the Parole Act. We wrote:

> We are guided in this matter by the well-established rule that, if a parolee remains incarcerated prior to trial because he has failed to satisfy bail requirements on new criminal charges, then the time spent in custody shall be credited to his new sentence. *See Gaito v. Pennsylvania Board of Probation and Parole*, 488 Pa. 397, 412 A.2d 568 (1980); *see also* section 9760(1) of the Sentencing Code, 42 Pa. C.S. § 9760(1). Respondents have cited no law, and we have found none, that prevents us from applying this rule in *Gaito* to the situation here.
>
> Indeed, we see no difference between a three-month and twenty-day credit for time spent in custody after failing to post bail and a three-month and twenty-day credit for time spent in custody serving a concurrent county sentence. In each instance, there is a valid legal basis other than the new state sentence for the parolee's confinement, viz., failure to meet bail requirements and a previously imposed sentence. *Thus, here, for purposes of section 21.1(a) of the Parole Act, Parish is not serving the new state sentence before serving his backtime. Rather, Parish is serving his county time, which, by court order, simultaneously reduces his new state sentence. Indeed, the reality of a concurrent sentence is that by serving one sentence, the inmate receives credit on the other sentence.* See section 9761(a) of the Sentencing Code, 42 Pa .C.S. § 9761(a).

Parish, 768 A.2d at 1216. (Emphasis added.)

Similarly, for the purpose of Section 21.1(a) of the Parole Act, Griffin is not serving his new 1994 state sentence before serving the backtime on his original sentence. Rather, when Griffin served his federal time, by court order he simultaneously reduced his 1994 sentence because the reality of a concurrent sentence was that by serving one sentence, he received credit on the other sentence. To hold otherwise would take away power from the state sentencing court granted under Section 9761(b) of the Sentencing Code to make state time run concurrently with federal time. Because there is no violation of Section 21.1(a) of the Parole Act, and concurrent sentences were authorized under 9761(b) of the Sentencing Code, under the facts pled, Griffin should have received credit against the time imposed on his 1994 state sentences for the time he served incarcerated in the federal institution on his federal sentence.

Accordingly, we grant in part the Department's preliminary objections in the nature of demurrer only in relation to the federal court's authority to order the time Griffin spent incarcerated in the federal prison to count against his 1992 state sentences.

[Footnotes omitted]

Source: 862 A.2d 152 (Pa. Commw. 2004). Reprinted with permission from Westlaw.

Appendix A

THE UNITED STATES CONSTITUTION AND BILL OF RIGHTS

In these pages, superseded text is presented like this: *(This is superseded text.)* Added text that is not a part of the Constitution is presented like this: [This is added text.]

CONTENTS

- Amendment 3. Quartering of Soldiers
- Amendment 4. Search and Seizure
- Amendment 5. Trial and Punishment, Compensation for Takings
- Amendment 6. Right to Speedy Trial, Confrontation of Witnesses
- Amendment 7. Trial by Jury in Civil Cases
- Amendment 8. Cruel and Unusual Punishment
- Amendment 9. Construction of Constitution
- Amendment 10. Powers of the States and People
- Amendment 11. Judicial Limits
- Amendment 12. Choosing the President, Vice-President
- Amendment 13. Slavery Abolished
- Amendment 14. Citizenship Rights
- Amendment 15. Race No Bar to Vote
- Amendment 16. Status of Income Tax Clarified
- Amendment 17. Senators Elected by Popular Vote
- Amendment 18. Liquor Abolished
- Amendment 19. Women's Suffrage
- Amendment 20. Presidential, Congressional Terms
- Amendment 21. Amendment 18 Repealed
- Amendment 22. Presidential Term Limits
- Amendment 23. Presidential Vote for District of Columbia
- Amendment 24. Poll Tax Barred
- Amendment 25. Presidential Disability and Succession
- Amendment 26. Voting Age Set to 18 Years
- Amendment 27. Limiting Congressional Pay Increases

THE CONSTITUTION OF THE UNITED STATES

Preamble

We the People of the United States, in Order to form a more perfect Union, establish Justice, insure domestic Tranquility, provide for the common defence, promote the general Welfare, and secure the Blessings of Liberty to ourselves and our Posterity, do ordain and establish this Constitution for the United States of America.

Article. I. The Legislative Branch

Section 1. The Legislature

All legislative Powers herein granted shall be vested in a Congress of the United States, which shall consist of a Senate and House of Representatives.

Section 2. The House

The House of Representatives shall be composed of Members chosen every second Year by the People of the several States, and the Electors in each State shall have the Qualifications requisite for Electors of the most numerous Branch of the State Legislature.

No Person shall be a Representative who shall not have attained to the Age of twenty five Years, and been seven Years a Citizen of the United States, and who shall not, when elected, be an Inhabitant of that State in which he shall be chosen.

(Representatives and direct Taxes shall be apportioned among the several States which may be included within this Union, according to their respective Numbers, which shall be determined by adding to the whole Number of free Persons, including those bound to Service for a Term of Years, and excluding Indians not taxed, three fifths of all other Persons.) **[The previous sentence in parentheses was modified by the 14th Amendment, section 2.]** The actual Enumeration shall be made within three Years after

the first Meeting of the Congress of the United States, and within every subsequent Term of ten Years, in such Manner as they shall by Law direct. The Number of Representatives shall not exceed one for every thirty Thousand, but each State shall have at Least one Representative; and until such enumeration shall be made, the State of New Hampshire shall be entitled to chuse three, Massachusetts eight, Rhode Island and Providence Plantations one, Connecticut five, New York six, New Jersey four, Pennsylvania eight, Delaware one, Maryland six, Virginia ten, North Carolina five, South Carolina five and Georgia three.

When vacancies happen in the Representation from any State, the Executive Authority thereof shall issue Writs of Election to fill such Vacancies.

The House of Representatives shall chuse their Speaker and other Officers; and shall have the sole Power of Impeachment.

Section 3. The Senate

The Senate of the United States shall be composed of two Senators from each State, *(chosen by the Legislature thereof,)* **[The preceding words in parentheses superseded by 17th Amendment, section 1.]** for six Years; and each Senator shall have one Vote.

Immediately after they shall be assembled in Consequence of the first Election, they shall be divided as equally as may be into three Classes. The Seats of the Senators of the first Class shall be vacated at the Expiration of the second Year, of the second Class at the Expiration of the fourth Year, and of the third Class at the Expiration of the sixth Year, so that one third may be chosen every second Year; *(and if Vacancies happen by Resignation, or otherwise, during the Recess of the Legislature of any State, the Executive thereof may make temporary Appointments until the next Meeting of the Legislature, which shall then fill such Vacancies.)* **[The preceding words in parentheses were superseded by the 17th Amendment, section 2.]**

No person shall be a Senator who shall not have attained to the Age of thirty Years, and been nine Years a Citizen of the United States, and who shall not, when elected, be an Inhabitant of that State for which he shall be chosen.

The Vice President of the United States shall be President of the Senate, but shall have no Vote, unless they be equally divided.

The Senate shall chuse their other Officers, and also a President pro tempore, in the absence of the Vice President, or when he shall exercise the Office of President of the United States.

The Senate shall have the sole Power to try all Impeachments. When sitting for that Purpose, they shall be on Oath or Affirmation. When the President of the United States is tried, the Chief Justice shall preside: And no Person shall be convicted without the Concurrence of two thirds of the Members present.

Judgment in Cases of Impeachment shall not extend further than to removal from Office, and disqualification to hold and enjoy any Office of honor, Trust or Profit under the United States: but the Party convicted shall nevertheless be liable and subject to Indictment, Trial, Judgment and Punishment, according to Law.

Section 4. Elections, Meetings

The Times, Places and Manner of holding Elections for Senators and Representatives, shall be prescribed in each State by the Legislature thereof; but the Congress may at any time by Law make or alter such Regulations, except as to the Place of Chusing Senators.

The Congress shall assemble at least once in every Year, and such Meeting shall *(be on the first Monday in December,)* **[The preceding words in parentheses were superseded by the 20th Amendment, section 2.]** unless they shall by Law appoint a different Day.

Section 5. Membership, Rules, Journals, Adjournment

Each House shall be the Judge of the Elections, Returns and Qualifications of its own Members, and a Majority of each shall constitute a Quorum to do Business; but a smaller number may adjourn from day to day, and may be authorized to compel the Attendance of absent Members, in such Manner, and under such Penalties as each House may provide.

Each House may determine the Rules of its Proceedings, punish its Members for disorderly Behavior, and, with the Concurrence of two-thirds, expel a Member.

Each House shall keep a Journal of its Proceedings, and from time to time publish the same, excepting such Parts as may in their Judgment require Secrecy; and the Yeas and Nays of the Members of either House on any question shall, at the Desire of one fifth of those Present, be entered on the Journal.

Neither House, during the Session of Congress, shall, without the Consent of the other, adjourn for more than three days, nor to any other Place than that in which the two Houses shall be sitting.

Section 6. Compensation

(The Senators and Representatives shall receive a Compensation for their Services, to be ascertained by Law, and paid out of the Treasury of the United States.) **[The preceding words in parentheses were modified by the 27th Amendment.]** They shall in all Cases, except Treason, Felony and Breach of the Peace, be privileged from Arrest during their Attendance at the Session of their respective Houses, and in going to and returning from the same; and for any Speech or Debate in either House, they shall not be questioned in any other Place.

No Senator or Representative shall, during the Time for which he was elected, be appointed to any civil Office under the Authority of the United States which shall have been created, or the Emoluments whereof shall have been increased during such time; and no Person holding any Office under the United States, shall be a Member of either House during his Continuance in Office.

Section 7. Revenue Bills, Legislative Process, Presidential Veto

All bills for raising Revenue shall originate in the House of Representatives; but the Senate may propose or concur with Amendments as on other Bills.

Every Bill which shall have passed the House of Representatives and the Senate, shall, before it become a Law, be presented to the President of the United States; If he approve he shall sign it, but if not he shall return it, with his Objections to that House in which it shall have originated, who shall enter the Objections at large on their Journal, and proceed to reconsider it. If after such Reconsideration two thirds of that House shall agree to pass the Bill, it shall be sent, together with the Objections, to the other House, by which it shall likewise be reconsidered, and if approved by two thirds of that House, it shall become a Law. But in all such Cases the Votes of both Houses shall be determined by Yeas and Nays, and the Names of the Persons voting for and against the Bill shall be entered on the Journal of each House respectively. If any Bill shall not be returned by the President within ten Days (Sundays excepted) after it shall have been presented to him, the Same shall be a Law, in like Manner as if he had signed it, unless the Congress by their Adjournment prevent its Return, in which Case it shall not be a Law.

Every Order, Resolution, or Vote to which the Concurrence of the Senate and House of Representatives may be necessary (except on a question of Adjournment) shall be presented to the President of the United States; and before the Same shall take Effect, shall be approved by him, or being disapproved by him, shall be repassed by two thirds of the Senate and House of Representatives, according to the Rules and Limitations prescribed in the Case of a Bill.

Section 8. Powers of Congress

The Congress shall have Power To lay and collect Taxes, Duties, Imposts and Excises, to pay the Debts and provide for the common Defence and general Welfare of the United States; but all Duties, Imposts and Excises shall be uniform throughout the United States;

To borrow money on the credit of the United States;

To regulate Commerce with foreign Nations, and among the several States, and with the Indian Tribes;

To establish an uniform Rule of Naturalization, and uniform Laws on the subject of Bankruptcies throughout the United States;

To coin Money, regulate the Value thereof, and of foreign Coin, and fix the Standard of Weights and Measures;

To provide for the Punishment of counterfeiting the Securities and current Coin of the United States;

To establish Post Offices and Post Roads;

To promote the Progress of Science and useful Arts, by securing for limited Times to Authors and Inventors the exclusive Right to their respective Writings and Discoveries;

To constitute Tribunals inferior to the supreme Court;

To define and punish Piracies and Felonies committed on the high Seas, and Offenses against the Law of Nations;

To declare War, grant Letters of Marque and Reprisal, and make Rules concerning Captures on Land and Water;

To raise and support Armies, but no Appropriation of Money to that Use shall be for a longer Term than two Years;

To provide and maintain a Navy;

To make Rules for the Government and Regulation of the land and naval Forces;

To provide for calling forth the Militia to execute the Laws of the Union, suppress Insurrections and repel Invasions;

To provide for organizing, arming, and disciplining the Militia, and for governing such Part of them as may be employed in the Service of the United States, reserving to the States respectively, the Appointment of the Officers, and the Authority of training the Militia according to the discipline prescribed by Congress;

To exercise exclusive Legislation in all Cases whatsoever, over such District (not exceeding ten Miles square) as may, by Cession of particular States, and the acceptance of Congress, become the Seat of the Government of the United States, and to exercise like Authority over all Places purchased by the Consent of the Legislature of the State in which the Same shall be, for the Erection of Forts, Magazines, Arsenals, dock-Yards, and other needful Buildings; And

To make all Laws which shall be necessary and proper for carrying into Execution the foregoing Powers, and all other Powers vested by this Constitution in the Government of the United States, or in any Department or Officer thereof.

Section 9. Limits on Congress

The Migration or Importation of such Persons as any of the States now existing shall think proper to admit, shall not be prohibited by the Congress prior to the Year one thousand eight hundred and eight, but a tax or duty may be imposed on such Importation, not exceeding ten dollars for each Person.

The privilege of the Writ of Habeas Corpus shall not be suspended, unless when in Cases of Rebellion or Invasion the public Safety may require it.

No Bill of Attainder or ex post facto Law shall be passed.

(No capitation, or other direct, Tax shall be laid, unless in Proportion to the Census or Enumeration herein before directed to be taken.) **[Section in parentheses clarified by the 16th Amendment.]**

No Tax or Duty shall be laid on Articles exported from any State.

No Preference shall be given by any Regulation of Commerce or Revenue to the Ports of one State over those of another: nor shall Vessels bound to, or from, one State, be obliged to enter, clear, or pay Duties in another.

No Money shall be drawn from the Treasury, but in Consequence of Appropriations made by Law; and a regular Statement and Account of the Receipts and Expenditures of all public Money shall be published from time to time.

No Title of Nobility shall be granted by the United States: And no Person holding any Office of Profit or Trust under them, shall, without the Consent of the Congress, accept of any present, Emolument, Office, or Title, of any kind whatever, from any King, Prince or foreign State.

Section 10. Powers Prohibited of States

No State shall enter into any Treaty, Alliance, or Confederation; grant Letters of Marque and Reprisal; coin Money; emit Bills of Credit; make any Thing but gold and silver Coin a Tender in Payment of Debts; pass any Bill of Attainder, ex post facto Law, or Law impairing the Obligation of Contracts, or grant any Title of Nobility.

No State shall, without the Consent of the Congress, lay any Imposts or Duties on Imports or Exports, except what may be absolutely necessary for executing its inspection Laws: and the net Produce of all Duties and Imposts, laid by any State on Imports or Exports, shall be for the Use of the Treasury of the United States; and all such Laws shall be subject to the Revision and Controul of the Congress.

No State shall, without the Consent of Congress, lay any duty of Tonnage, keep Troops, or Ships of War in time of Peace, enter into any Agreement or Compact with another State, or with a foreign Power, or engage in War, unless actually invaded, or in such imminent Danger as will not admit of delay.

Article. II. The Executive Branch

Section 1. The President

The executive Power shall be vested in a President of the United States of America. He shall hold his Office during the Term of four Years, and, together with the Vice President chosen for the same Term, be elected, as follows:

Each State shall appoint, in such Manner as the Legislature thereof may direct, a Number of Electors, equal to the whole Number of Senators and Representatives to which the State may be entitled in the Congress: but no Senator or Representative, or Person holding an Office of Trust or Profit under the United States, shall be appointed an Elector.

(The Electors shall meet in their respective States, and vote by Ballot for two persons, of whom one at least shall not be an Inhabitant of the same State with themselves. And they shall make a List of all the Persons voted for, and of the Number of Votes for each; which List they shall sign and certify, and transmit sealed to the Seat of the Government of the United States, directed to the President of the Senate. The President of the Senate shall, in the Presence of the Senate and House of Representatives, open all the Certificates, and the Votes shall then be counted. The Person having the greatest Number of Votes shall be the President, if such Number be a Majority of the whole Number of Electors appointed; and if there be more than one who have such Majority, and have an equal Number of Votes, then the House of Representatives shall immedi-

ately chuse by Ballot one of them for President; and if no Person have a Majority, then from the five highest on the List the said House shall in like Manner chuse the President. But in chusing the President, the Votes shall be taken by States, the Representation from each State having one Vote; a quorum for this Purpose shall consist of a Member or Members from two-thirds of the States, and a Majority of all the States shall be necessary to a Choice. In every Case, after the Choice of the President, the Person having the greatest Number of Votes of the Electors shall be the Vice President. But if there should remain two or more who have equal Votes, the Senate shall chuse from them by Ballot the Vice-President.) **[This clause in parentheses was superseded by the 12th Amendment.]**

The Congress may determine the Time of chusing the Electors, and the Day on which they shall give their Votes; which Day shall be the same throughout the United States.

No person except a natural born Citizen, or a Citizen of the United States, at the time of the Adoption of this Constitution, shall be eligible to the Office of President; neither shall any Person be eligible to that Office who shall not have attained to the Age of thirty-five Years, and been fourteen Years a Resident within the United States.

(In Case of the Removal of the President from Office, or of his Death, Resignation, or Inability to discharge the Powers and Duties of the said Office, the same shall devolve on the Vice President, and the Congress may by Law provide for the Case of Removal, Death, Resignation or Inability, both of the President and Vice President, declaring what Officer shall then act as President, and such Officer shall act accordingly, until the Disability be removed, or a President shall be elected.) **[This clause in parentheses has been modified by the 20th and 25th Amendments.]**

The President shall, at stated Times, receive for his Services, a Compensation, which shall neither be increased nor diminished during the Period for which he shall have been elected, and he shall not receive within that Period any other Emolument from the United States, or any of them.

Before he enter on the Execution of his Office, he shall take the following Oath or Affirmation:—"I do solemnly swear (or affirm) that I will faithfully execute the Office of President of the United States, and will to the best of my Ability, preserve, protect and defend the Constitution of the United States."

Section 2. Civilian Power over Military, Cabinet, Pardon Power, Appointments

The President shall be Commander in Chief of the Army and Navy of the United States, and of the Militia of the several States, when called into the actual Service of the United States; he may require the Opinion, in writing, of the principal Officer in each of the executive Departments, upon any subject relating to the Duties of their respective Offices, and he shall have Power to Grant Reprieves and Pardons for Offenses against the United States, except in Cases of Impeachment.

He shall have Power, by and with the Advice and Consent of the Senate, to make Treaties, provided two thirds of the Senators present concur; and he shall nominate, and by and with the Advice and Consent of the Senate, shall appoint Ambassadors, other public Ministers and Consuls, Judges of the supreme Court, and all other Officers of the United States, whose Appointments are not herein otherwise provided for, and which shall be established by Law: but the Congress may by Law vest the Appointment of such inferior Officers, as they think proper, in the President alone, in the Courts of Law, or in the Heads of Departments.

The President shall have Power to fill up all Vacancies that may happen during the Recess of the Senate, by granting Commissions which shall expire at the End of their next Session.

Section 3. State of the Union, Convening Congress

He shall from time to time give to the Congress Information of the State of the Union, and recommend to their Consideration such Measures as he shall judge necessary and expedient; he may, on extraordinary Occasions, convene both Houses, or either of them, and in Case of Disagreement between them, with Respect to the Time of Adjournment, he may adjourn them to such Time as he shall think proper; he shall receive Ambassadors and other public Ministers; he shall take Care that the Laws be faithfully executed, and shall Commission all the Officers of the United States.

Section 4. Disqualification

The President, Vice President and all civil Officers of the United States, shall be removed from Office on Impeachment for, and Conviction of, Treason, Bribery, or other high Crimes and Misdemeanors.

Article III. The Judicial Branch

Section 1. Judicial powers

The judicial Power of the United States, shall be vested in one supreme Court, and in such inferior Courts as the Congress may from time to time ordain and establish. The Judges, both of the supreme and inferior Courts, shall hold their Offices during good Behavior, and shall, at stated Times, receive for their Services a Compensation which shall not be diminished during their Continuance in Office.

Section 2. Trial by Jury, Original Jurisdiction, Jury Trials

(The judicial Power shall extend to all Cases, in Law and Equity, arising under this Constitution, the Laws of the United States, and Treaties made, or which shall be made, under their Authority; to all Cases affecting Ambassadors, other public Ministers and Consuls; to all Cases of admiralty and maritime Jurisdiction; to Controversies to which the United States shall be a Party; to Controversies between two or more States; between a State and Citizens of another State; between Citizens of different States; between Citizens of the same State claiming Lands under Grants of different States, and between a State, or the Citizens thereof, and foreign States, Citizens or Subjects.) **[This section in parentheses is modified by the 11th Amendment.]**

In all Cases affecting Ambassadors, other public Ministers and Consuls, and those in which a State shall be Party, the supreme Court shall have original Jurisdiction. In all the other Cases before mentioned, the supreme Court shall have appellate Jurisdiction, both as to Law and Fact, with such Exceptions, and under such Regulations as the Congress shall make.

The Trial of all Crimes, except in Cases of Impeachment, shall be by Jury; and such Trial shall be held in the State where the said Crimes shall have been committed; but when not committed within any State, the Trial shall be at such Place or Places as the Congress may by Law have directed.

Section 3. Treason

Treason against the United States, shall consist only in levying War against them, or in adhering to their Enemies, giving them Aid and Comfort. No Person shall be convicted of Treason unless on the Testimony of two Witnesses to the same overt Act, or on Confession in open Court.

The Congress shall have power to declare the Punishment of Treason, but no Attainder of Treason shall work Corruption of Blood, or Forfeiture except during the Life of the Person attainted.

Article. IV. The States

Section 1. Each State to Honor All Others

Full Faith and Credit shall be given in each State to the public Acts, Records, and judicial Proceedings of every other State. And the Congress may by general Laws prescribe the Manner in which such Acts, Records and Proceedings shall be proved, and the Effect thereof.

Section 2. State Citizens, Extradition

The Citizens of each State shall be entitled to all Privileges and Immunities of Citizens in the several States.

A Person charged in any State with Treason, Felony, or other Crime, who shall flee from Justice, and be found in another State, shall on demand of the executive Authority of the State from which he fled, be delivered up, to be removed to the State having Jurisdiction of the Crime.

(No Person held to Service or Labour in one State, under the Laws thereof, escaping into another, shall, in Consequence of any Law or Regulation therein, be discharged from such Service or Labour, But shall be delivered up on Claim of the Party to whom such Service or Labour may be due.) **[This clause in parentheses is superseded by the 13th Amendment.]**

Section 3. New States

New States may be admitted by the Congress into this Union; but no new States shall be formed or erected within the Jurisdiction of any other State; nor any State be formed by the Junction of two or more States, or parts of States, without the Consent of the Legislatures of the States concerned as well as of the Congress.

The Congress shall have Power to dispose of and make all needful Rules and Regulations respecting the Territory or other Property belonging to the United States; and nothing in this Constitution shall be so construed as to Prejudice any Claims of the United States, or of any particular State.

Section 4. Republican Government

The United States shall guarantee to every State in this Union a Republican Form of Government, and shall protect each of them against Invasion; and on Application of the Legislature, or of the Executive (when the Legislature cannot be convened) against domestic Violence.

Article V. Amendment

The Congress, whenever two thirds of both Houses shall deem it necessary, shall propose Amendments to this Constitution, or, on the Application of the Legislatures of two thirds of the several States, shall call a Convention for proposing Amendments, which, in either Case, shall be valid to all Intents and Purposes, as part of this Constitution, when ratified by the Legislatures of three fourths of the several States, or by Conventions in three fourths thereof, as the one or the other Mode of Ratification may be proposed by the Congress; Provided that no Amendment which may be made prior to the Year One thousand eight hundred and eight shall in any Manner affect the first and fourth Clauses in the Ninth Section of the first Article; and that no State, without its Consent, shall be deprived of its equal Suffrage in the Senate.

Article VI. Debts, Supremacy, Oaths

All Debts contracted and Engagements entered into, before the Adoption of this Constitution, shall be as valid against the United States under this Constitution, as under the Confederation.

This Constitution, and the Laws of the United States which shall be made in Pursuance thereof; and all Treaties made, or which shall be made, under the Authority of the United States, shall be the supreme Law of the Land; and the Judges in every State shall be bound thereby, any Thing in the Constitution or Laws of any State to the Contrary notwithstanding.

The Senators and Representatives before mentioned, and the Members of the several State Legislatures, and all executive and judicial Officers, both of the United States and of the several States, shall be bound by Oath or Affirmation, to support this Constitution; but no religious Test shall ever be required as a Qualification to any Office or public Trust under the United States.

Article VII. Ratification

The Ratification of the Conventions of nine States, shall be sufficient for the Establishment of this Constitution between the States so ratifying the Same.

Signatories

Done in Convention by the Unanimous Consent of the States present the Seventeenth Day of September in the Year of our Lord one thousand seven hundred and Eighty seven and of the Independence of the United States of America the Twelfth. In Witness whereof We have hereunto subscribed our Names. G°. Washington—President and deputy from Virginia

New Hampshire—John Langdon, Nicholas Gilman

Massachusetts—Nathaniel Gorham, Rufus King

Connecticut—Wm. Saml. Johnson, Roger Sherman

New York—Alexander Hamilton

New Jersey—Wil: Livingston, David Brearley, Wm. Paterson, Jona: Dayton

Pennsylvania—B Franklin, Thomas Mifflin, Robt Morris, Geo. Clymer, Thos. FitzSimons, Jared Ingersoll, James Wilson, Gouv Morris

Delaware—Geo: Read, Gunning Bedford jun, John Dickinson, Richard Bassett, Jaco: Broom

Maryland—James McHenry, Dan of St Thos. Jenifer, Danl Carroll

Virginia—John Blair, James Madison Jr.

North Carolina—Wm. Blount, Richd. Dobbs Spaight, Hu Williamson

South Carolina—J. Rutledge, Charles Cotesworth Pinckney, Charles Pinckney, Pierce Butler

Georgia—William Few, Abr Baldwin

Attest: William Jackson, Secretary

THE AMENDMENTS TO THE CONSTITUTION OF THE UNITED STATES

The following are the Amendments to the Constitution. The first ten Amendments collectively are commonly known as the Bill of Rights.

Amendment 1. Freedom of Religion, Press, Expression

Ratified 12/15/1791.

Congress shall make no law respecting an establishment of religion, or prohibiting the free exercise thereof; or abridging the freedom of speech, or of the press; or the right of the people peaceably to assemble, and to petition the Government for a redress of grievances.

Amendment 2. Right to Bear Arms

Ratified 12/15/1791.

A well regulated Militia, being necessary to the security of a free State, the right of the people to keep and bear Arms, shall not be infringed.

Amendment 3. Quartering of Soldiers

Ratified 12/15/1791.

No Soldier shall, in time of peace be quartered in any house, without the consent of the Owner, nor in time of war, but in a manner to be prescribed by law.

Amendment 4. Search and Seizure

Ratified 12/15/1791.

The right of the people to be secure in their persons, houses, papers, and effects, against unreasonable searches and seizures, shall not be violated, and no Warrants shall issue, but upon probable cause, supported by Oath or affirmation, and particularly describing the place to be searched, and the persons or things to be seized.

Amendment 5. Trial and Punishment, Compensation for Takings

Ratified 12/15/1791.

No person shall be held to answer for a capital, or otherwise infamous crime, unless on a presentment or indictment of a Grand Jury, except in cases arising in the land or naval forces, or in the Militia, when in actual service in time of War or public danger; nor shall any person be subject for the same offense to be twice put in jeopardy of life or limb; nor shall be compelled in any criminal case to be a witness against himself, nor be deprived of life, liberty, or property, without due process of law; nor shall private property be taken for public use, without just compensation.

Amendment 6. Right to Speedy Trial, Confrontation of Witnesses

Ratified 12/15/1791.

In all criminal prosecutions, the accused shall enjoy the right to a speedy and public trial, by an impartial jury of the State and district wherein the crime shall have been committed, which district shall have been previously ascertained by law, and to be informed of the nature and cause of the accusation; to be confronted with the witnesses against him; to have compulsory process for obtaining witnesses in his favor, and to have the Assistance of Counsel for his defence.

Amendment 7. Trial by Jury in Civil Cases

Ratified 12/15/1791.

In Suits at common law, where the value in controversy shall exceed twenty dollars, the right of trial by jury shall be preserved, and no fact tried by a jury, shall be otherwise re-examined in any Court of the United States, than according to the rules of the common law.

Amendment 8. Cruel and Unusual Punishment

Ratified 12/15/1791.

Excessive bail shall not be required, nor excessive fines imposed, nor cruel and unusual punishments inflicted.

Amendment 9. Construction of Constitution

Ratified 12/15/1791.

The enumeration in the Constitution, of certain rights, shall not be construed to deny or disparage others retained by the people.

Amendment 10. Powers of the States and People

Ratified 12/15/1791.

The powers not delegated to the United States by the Constitution, nor prohibited by it to the States, are reserved to the States respectively, or to the people.

Amendment 11. Judicial Limits

Ratified 2/7/1795.

The Judicial power of the United States shall not be construed to extend to any suit in law or equity, commenced or prosecuted against one of the United States by Citizens of another State, or by Citizens or Subjects of any Foreign State.

Amendment 12. Choosing the President, Vice-President

Ratified 6/15/1804.

The Electors shall meet in their respective states, and vote by ballot for President and Vice-President, one of whom, at least, shall not be an inhabitant of the same state with themselves; they shall name in their ballots the person voted for as President, and in distinct ballots the person voted for as Vice-President, and they shall make distinct lists of all persons voted for as President, and of all persons voted for as Vice-President and of the number of votes for each, which lists they shall sign and certify, and transmit sealed to the seat of the government of the United States, directed to the President of the Senate;

The President of the Senate shall, in the presence of the Senate and House of Representatives, open all the certificates and the votes shall then be counted;

The person having the greatest Number of votes for President, shall be the President, if such number be a majority of the whole number of Electors appointed; and if no person have such majority, then from the persons having the highest numbers not exceeding three on the list of those voted for as President, the House of Representatives shall choose immediately, by ballot, the President. But in choosing the President, the votes shall be taken by states, the representation from each state having one vote; a quorum for this purpose shall consist of a member or members from two-thirds of the states, and a majority of all the states shall be necessary to a choice. And if the House of Representatives shall not choose a President whenever the right of choice shall devolve upon them, before the fourth day of March next following, then the Vice-President shall act as President, as in the case of the death or other constitutional disability of the President.

The person having the greatest number of votes as Vice-President, shall be the Vice-President, if such number be a majority of the whole number of Electors appointed, and if no person have a majority, then from the two highest numbers on the list, the Senate shall choose the Vice-President; a quorum for the purpose shall consist of two-thirds of the whole number of Senators, and a majority of the whole number shall be necessary to a choice. But no person constitutionally ineligible to the office of President shall be eligible to that of Vice-President of the United States.

Amendment 13. Slavery Abolished

Ratified 12/6/1865.

Section 1.

Neither slavery nor involuntary servitude, except as a punishment for crime whereof the party shall have been duly convicted, shall exist within the United States, or any place subject to their jurisdiction.

Section 2.

Congress shall have power to enforce this article by appropriate legislation.

Amendment 14. Citizenship Rights

Ratified 7/9/1868.

Section 1.

All persons born or naturalized in the United States, and subject to the jurisdiction thereof, are citizens of the United States and of the State wherein they reside. No State shall make or enforce any law which shall abridge the privileges or immunities of citizens of the United States; nor shall any State deprive any person of life, liberty, or property, without due process of law; nor deny to any person within its jurisdiction the equal protection of the laws.

Section 2.

Representatives shall be apportioned among the several States according to their respective numbers, counting the whole number of persons in each State, excluding Indians not taxed. But when the right to vote at any election for the choice of electors for President and Vice-President of the United States, Representatives in Congress, the Executive and Judicial officers of a State, or the members of the Legislature thereof, is denied to any of the male inhabitants of such State, being twenty-one years of age, and citizens of the United States, or in any way abridged, except for participation in rebellion, or other crime, the basis of representation therein shall be reduced in the proportion which the number of such male citizens shall bear to the whole number of male citizens twenty-one years of age in such State.

Section 3.

No person shall be a Senator or Representative in Congress, or elector of President and Vice-President, or hold any office, civil or military, under the United States, or under any State, who, having previously taken an oath, as a member of Congress, or as an officer of the United States, or as a member of any State legislature, or as an executive or judicial officer of any State, to support the Constitution of the United States, shall have engaged in insurrection or rebellion against the same, or given aid or comfort to the enemies thereof. But Congress may by a vote of two-thirds of each House, remove such disability.

Section 4.

The validity of the public debt of the United States, authorized by law, including debts incurred for payment of pensions and bounties for services in suppressing insurrection or rebellion, shall not be questioned. But neither the United States nor any State shall assume or pay any debt or obligation incurred in aid of insurrection or rebellion against the United States, or any claim for the loss or emancipation of any slave; but all such debts, obligations and claims shall be held illegal and void.

Section 5.

The Congress shall have power to enforce, by appropriate legislation, the provisions of this article.

Amendment 15. Race No Bar to Vote

Ratified 2/3/1870.

Section 1.

The right of citizens of the United States to vote shall not be denied or abridged by the United States or by any State on account of race, color, or previous condition of servitude.

Section 2.

The Congress shall have power to enforce this article by appropriate legislation.

Amendment 16. Status of Income Tax Clarified

Ratified 2/3/1913.

The Congress shall have power to lay and collect taxes on incomes, from whatever source derived, without apportionment among the several States, and without regard to any census or enumeration.

Amendment 17. Senators Elected by Popular Vote

Ratified 4/8/1913.

The Senate of the United States shall be composed of two Senators from each State, elected by the people thereof, for six years; and each Senator shall have one vote. The electors in each State shall have the qualifications requisite for electors of the most numerous branch of the State legislatures.

When vacancies happen in the representation of any State in the Senate, the executive authority of such State shall issue writs of election to fill such vacancies: Provided, That the legislature of any State may empower the executive thereof to make temporary appointments until the people fill the vacancies by election as the legislature may direct.

This amendment shall not be so construed as to affect the election or term of any Senator chosen before it becomes valid as part of the Constitution.

Amendment 18. Liquor Abolished

Ratified 1/16/1919. Repealed by Amendment 21, 12/5/1933.

Section 1.

After one year from the ratification of this article the manufacture, sale, or transportation of intoxicating liquors within, the importation thereof into, or the exportation thereof from the United States and all territory subject to the jurisdiction thereof for beverage purposes is hereby prohibited.

Section 2.

The Congress and the several States shall have concurrent power to enforce this article by appropriate legislation.

Section 3.

This article shall be inoperative unless it shall have been ratified as an amendment to the Constitution by the legislatures of the several States, as provided in the Constitution, within seven years from the date of the submission hereof to the States by the Congress.

Amendment 19. Women's Suffrage

Ratified 8/18/1920.

The right of citizens of the United States to vote shall not be denied or abridged by the United States or by any State on account of sex.

Congress shall have power to enforce this article by appropriate legislation.

Amendment 20. Presidential, Congressional Terms

Ratified 1/23/1933.

Section 1.

The terms of the President and Vice President shall end at noon on the 20th day of January, and the terms of Senators and Representatives at noon on the 3rd day of

January, of the years in which such terms would have ended if this article had not been ratified; and the terms of their successors shall then begin.

Section 2.

The Congress shall assemble at least once in every year, and such meeting shall begin at noon on the 3rd day of January, unless they shall by law appoint a different day.

Section 3.

If, at the time fixed for the beginning of the term of the President, the President elect shall have died, the Vice President elect shall become President. If a President shall not have been chosen before the time fixed for the beginning of his term, or if the President elect shall have failed to qualify, then the Vice President elect shall act as President until a President shall have qualified; and the Congress may by law provide for the case wherein neither a President elect nor a Vice President elect shall have qualified, declaring who shall then act as President, or the manner in which one who is to act shall be selected, and such person shall act accordingly until a President or Vice President shall have qualified.

Section 4.

The Congress may by law provide for the case of the death of any of the persons from whom the House of Representatives may choose a President whenever the right of choice shall have devolved upon them, and for the case of the death of any of the persons from whom the Senate may choose a Vice President whenever the right of choice shall have devolved upon them.

Section 5.

Sections 1 and 2 shall take effect on the 15th day of October following the ratification of this article.

Section 6.

This article shall be inoperative unless it shall have been ratified as an amendment to the Constitution by the legislatures of three-fourths of the several States within seven years from the date of its submission.

Amendment 21. Amendment 18 Repealed

Ratified 12/5/1933.

Section 1.

The eighteenth article of amendment to the Constitution of the United States is hereby repealed.

Section 2.

The transportation or importation into any State, Territory, or possession of the United States for delivery or use therein of intoxicating liquors, in violation of the laws thereof, is hereby prohibited.

Section 3.

The article shall be inoperative unless it shall have been ratified as an amendment to the Constitution by conventions in the several States, as provided in the Constitution, within seven years from the date of the submission hereof to the States by the Congress.

Amendment 22. Presidential Term Limits

Ratified 2/27/1951.

Section 1.

No person shall be elected to the office of the President more than twice, and no person who has held the office of President, or acted as President, for more than two years of a term to which some other person was elected President shall be elected to the office of the President more than once. But this Article shall not apply to any person holding the office of President, when this Article was proposed by the Congress, and shall not prevent any person who may be holding the office of President, or acting as President, during the term within which this Article becomes operative from holding the office of President or acting as President during the remainder of such term.

Section 2.

This article shall be inoperative unless it shall have been ratified as an amendment to the Constitution by the legislatures of three-fourths of the several States within seven years from the date of its submission to the States by the Congress.

Amendment 23. Presidential Vote for District of Columbia

Ratified 3/29/1961.

Section 1.

The District constituting the seat of Government of the United States shall appoint in such manner as the Congress may direct: A number of electors of President and Vice President equal to the whole number of Senators and Representatives in Congress to which the District would be entitled if it were a State, but in no event more than the least populous State; they shall be in addition to those appointed by the States, but they shall be considered, for the purposes of the election of President and Vice President, to be electors appointed by a State; and they shall meet in the District and perform such duties as provided by the twelfth article of amendment.

Section 2.

The Congress shall have power to enforce this article by appropriate legislation.

Amendment 24. Poll Tax Barred

Ratified 1/23/1964.

Section 1.

The right of citizens of the United States to vote in any primary or other election for President or Vice President, for electors for President or Vice President, or for Senator or Representative in Congress, shall not be denied or abridged by the United States or any State by reason of failure to pay any poll tax or other tax.

Section 2.

The Congress shall have power to enforce this article by appropriate legislation.

Amendment 25. Presidential Disability and Succession

Ratified 2/10/1967.

Section 1.

In case of the removal of the President from office or of his death or resignation, the Vice President shall become President.

Section 2.

Whenever there is a vacancy in the office of the Vice President, the President shall nominate a Vice President who shall take office upon confirmation by a majority vote of both Houses of Congress.

Section 3.

Whenever the President transmits to the President pro tempore of the Senate and the Speaker of the House of Representatives his written declaration that he is unable to discharge the powers and duties of his office, and until he transmits to them a written declaration to the contrary, such powers and duties shall be discharged by the Vice President as Acting President.

Section 4.

Whenever the Vice President and a majority of either the principal officers of the executive departments or of such other body as Congress may by law provide, transmit to the President pro tempore of the Senate and the Speaker of the House of Representatives their written declaration that the President is unable to discharge the powers and duties of his office, the Vice President shall immediately assume the powers and duties of the office as Acting President.

Thereafter, when the President transmits to the President pro tempore of the Senate and the Speaker of the House of Representatives his written declaration that no inability exists, he shall resume the powers and duties of his office unless the Vice President and a majority of either the principal officers of the executive department or of such other body as Congress may by law provide, transmit within four days to the President pro tempore of the Senate and the Speaker of the House of Representatives their written declaration that the President is unable to discharge the powers and duties of his office. Thereupon Congress shall decide the issue, assembling within forty eight hours for that purpose if not in session. If the Congress, within twenty one days after receipt of the latter written declaration, or, if Congress is not in session, within twenty one days after Congress is required to assemble, determines by two thirds vote of both Houses that the President is unable to discharge the powers and duties of his office, the Vice President shall continue to discharge the same as Acting President; otherwise, the President shall resume the powers and duties of his office.

Amendment 26. Voting Age Set to 18 Years
Ratified 7/1/1971.

Section 1.

The right of citizens of the United States, who are eighteen years of age or older, to vote shall not be denied or abridged by the United States or by any State on account of age.

Section 2.

The Congress shall have power to enforce this article by appropriate legislation.

Amendment 27. Limiting Congressional Pay Increases
Ratified 5/7/1992.

No law, varying the compensation for the services of the Senators and Representatives, shall take effect, until an election of Representatives shall have intervened.

Appendix B

LIST OF HEARSAY EXCEPTIONS

Rule 803. Hearsay Exceptions; Availability of Declarant Immaterial

The following are not excluded by the hearsay rule, even though the declarant is available as a witness:

1. **Present sense impression.** A statement describing or explaining an event or condition made while the declarant was perceiving the event or condition, or immediately thereafter.

2. **Excited utterance.** A statement relating to a startling event or condition made while the declarant was under the stress of excitement caused by the event or condition.

3. **Then existing mental, emotional, or physical condition.** A statement of the declarant's then existing state of mind, emotion, sensation, or physical condition (such as intent, plan, motive, design, mental feeling, pain, and bodily health), but not including a statement of memory or belief to prove the fact remembered or believed unless it relates to the execution, revocation, identification, or terms of declarant's will.

4. **Statements for purposes of medical diagnosis or treatment.** Statements made for purposes of medical diagnosis or treatment and describing medical history, or past or present symptoms, pain, or sensations, or the inception or general character of the cause or external source thereof insofar as reasonably pertinent to diagnosis or treatment.

5. **Recorded recollection.** A memorandum or record concerning a matter about which a witness once had knowledge but now has insufficient recollection to enable the witness to testify fully and accurately, shown to have been made or adopted by the witness when the matter was fresh in the witness' memory and to reflect that knowledge correctly. If admitted, the memorandum or record may be read into evidence but may not itself be received as an exhibit unless offered by an adverse party.

6. **Records of regularly conducted activity.** A memorandum, report, record, or data compilation, in any form, of acts, events, conditions, opinions, or diagnoses, made at or near the time by, or from information transmitted by, a person with knowledge, if kept in the course of a regularly conducted business activity, and if it was the regular practice of that business activity to make the memorandum, report, record or data compilation, all as shown by the testimony of the custodian or other qualified witness, or by certification that complies with Rule 902(11), Rule 902(12), or a statute permitting certification, unless the source of information or the method or circumstances of preparation indicate lack of trustworthiness. The term "business" as used in this paragraph includes business, institution, association, profession, occupation, and calling of every kind, whether or not conducted for profit.

7. **Absence of entry in records kept in accordance with the provisions of paragraph (6).** Evidence that a matter is not included in the memoranda reports, records, or data compilations, in any form, kept in accordance with the provisions of paragraph (6), to prove the nonoccurrence or nonexistence of the matter, if the matter was of a kind of which a memorandum, report, record, or data compilation was regularly made and preserved, unless the sources of information or other circumstances indicate lack of trustworthiness.

8. **Public records and reports.** Records, reports, statements, or data compilations, in any form, of public offices or agencies, setting forth (A) the activities of the office or agency, or (B) matters observed pursuant to duty imposed by law as to which matters there was a duty to report, excluding, however, in criminal cases matters observed by police officers and other law enforcement personnel, or (C) in civil actions and proceedings and against the Government in criminal cases, factual findings resulting from an investigation made pursuant to authority granted by law, unless the sources of information or other circumstances indicate lack of trustworthiness.

9. **Records of vital statistics.** Records or data compilations, in any form, of births, fetal deaths, deaths, or marriages, if the report thereof was made to a public office pursuant to requirements of law.

10. **Absence of public record or entry.** To prove the absence of a record, report, statement, or data compilation, in any form, or the nonoccurrence or nonexistence of a matter of which a record, report, statement, or data compilation, in any form, was regularly made and preserved by a public office or agency, evidence in the form of a certification in accordance with rule 902, or testimony, that diligent search failed to disclose the record, report, statement, or data compilation, or entry.

11. **Records of religious organizations.** Statements of births, marriages, divorces, deaths, legitimacy, ancestry, relationship by blood or marriage, or other similar facts of personal or family history, contained in a regularly kept record of a religious organization.

12. **Marriage, baptismal, and similar certificates.** Statements of fact contained in a certificate that the maker performed a marriage or other ceremony or administered a sacrament, made by a clergyman, public official, or other person authorized by the rules or practices of a religious organization or by law to perform the act certified, and purporting to have been issued at the time of the act or within a reasonable time thereafter.

13. **Family records.** Statements of fact concerning personal or family history contained in family Bibles, genealogies, charts, engravings on rings, inscriptions on family portraits, engravings on urns, crypts, or tombstones, or the like.

14. **Records of documents affecting an interest in property.** The record of a document purporting to establish or affect an interest in property, as proof of the content of the original recorded document and its execution and delivery by each person by whom it purports to have been executed, if the record is a record of a public office and an applicable statute authorizes the recording of documents of that kind in that office.

15. **Statements in documents affecting an interest in property.** A statement contained in a document purporting to establish or affect an interest in property if the matter stated was relevant to the purpose of the document, unless dealings with the property since the document was made have been inconsistent with the truth of the statement or the purport of the document.

16. **Statements in ancient documents.** Statements in a document in existence twenty years or more the authenticity of which is established.

17. **Market reports, commercial publications.** Market quotations, tabulations, lists, directories, or other published compilations, generally used and relied upon by the public or by persons in particular occupations.

18. **Learned treatises.** To the extent called to the attention of an expert witness upon cross-examination or relied upon by the expert witness in direct examination, statements contained in published treatises, periodicals, or pamphlets on a subject of history, medicine, or other science or art, established as a reliable authority by the testimony or admission of the witness or by other expert testimony or by judicial notice. If admitted, the statements may be read into evidence but may not be received as exhibits.

19. **Reputation concerning personal or family history.** Reputation among members of a person's family by blood, adoption, or marriage, or among a person's associates, or in the community, concerning a person's birth, adoption, marriage, divorce, death, legitimacy, relationship by blood, adoption, or marriage, ancestry, or other similar fact of personal or family history.

20. **Reputation concerning boundaries or general history.** Reputation in a community, arising before the controversy, as to boundaries of or customs affecting lands in the community, and reputation as to events of general history important to the community or State or nation in which located.

21. **Reputation as to character.** Reputation of a person's character among associates or in the community.

22. **Judgment of previous conviction.** Evidence of a final judgment, entered after a trial or upon a plea of guilty (but not upon a plea of nolo contendere), adjudging a person guilty of a crime punishable by death or imprisonment in excess of one year, to prove any fact essential to sustain the judgment, but not including, when offered by the Government in a criminal prosecution for purposes other than impeachment, judgments against persons other than the accused. The pendency of an appeal may be shown but does not affect admissibility.

23. **Judgment as to personal, family or general history, or boundaries.** Judgments as proof of matters of personal, family or general history, or boundaries, essential to the judgment, if the same would be provable by evidence of reputation.

Source: http://judiciary.house.gov/

Glossary

A

accessory after the fact A person who, knowing a felony to have been committed by another, receives, relieves, comforts, or assists the felon in order to enable him/her to escape from punishment, or the like.

accessory before the fact One who orders, counsels, encourages, or otherwise aids and abets another to commit a felony and who is not present at the commission of the offense.

accomplice One who knowingly, voluntarily, and with common intent unites with the principal offender in the commission of a crime.

acquittal The legal and formal certification of the innocence of a person who has been charged with a crime.

actus reus The guilty act.

affiant The person who makes and subscribes an affidavit.

affirm(ed) Disposition in which the appellate court agrees with the trial court.

aggravated assault Criminal assault accompanied with circumstances that make it more severe such as the intent to commit another crime or the intent to cause serious bodily injury.

aggravated battery A criminal battery accompanied by circumstances that make it more severe such as the use of a deadly weapon or the fact that the battery resulted in serious bodily harm.

aggravated robbery Robbery committed by a person who either carries a dangerous weapon or inflicts bodily harm on someone during the robbery.

aggravating factor A fact or circumstance that increases the degree of liability or culpability for a criminal act.

aid and abet Help, assist, or facilitate the commission of a crime; promote the accomplishment thereof; help in advancing or bringing it about; or encourage, counsel, or incite as to its commission.

appeal Tests the sufficiency of the verdict under the legal parameters or rules.

arraignment A court hearing where the information contained in an indictment is read to the defendant.

arrest The formal taking of a person, usually by a police officer, to answer criminal charges.

arson At common law, arson had four requisites. First, there must be some actual burning (though this requirement did not include destruction of the building or even of any substantial part of the building). Second, the burning must be malicious (negligence is not sufficient). Third, the object burned must be a dwelling house. Fourth and finally, the house burned must be the habitation of another.

asportation The act of carrying away or removing property or a person.

assault Intentional voluntary movement that creates fear or apprehension of an immediate unwanted touching; the threat or attempt to cause a touching, whether successful or not, provided the victim is aware of the danger.

assisted suicide The intentional act of providing a person with the medical means or the medical knowledge to commit suicide.

attempt To actually try to commit a crime and have the actual ability to do so.

B

bail Court-mandated surety or guarantee that the defendant will appear at a future date if released from custody prior to trial.

battery An intentional and unwanted harmful or offensive contact with the person of another; the actual intentional touching of someone with intent to cause harm, no matter how slight the harm.

bench trial A case heard and decided by a judge.

bench warrant The process issued by the court itself for the attachment or arrest of a person.

beyond a reasonable doubt The requirement for the level of proof in a criminal matter in order to convict or find the defendant guilty. It is a substantially higher and more-difficult-to-prove criminal matter standard.

bilateral Affecting or obligating both parties.

Bill of Rights Set forth the fundamental individual rights government and law function to preserve and protect; the first ten amendments to the Constitution of the United States.

bodily injury Physical damage to a person's body.

booking Administrative step taken after an arrested person is brought to the police station that involves entry of the person's name, the crime for which the arrest was made, and other relevant facts on the police blotter.

brain death When the body shows no response to external stimuli, no spontaneous movements, no breathing, no reflexes, and a flat reading on a machine that measures the brain's electrical activity.

breaking In the law of burglary, the act of entering a building without permission.

bribery The offering, giving, receiving, or soliciting of something of value for the purpose of influencing the action of an official in the discharge of his or her public or legal duties.

burden of proof Standard for assessing the weight of the evidence.

burglary Breaking and entering into a structure for the purpose of committing a crime.

by a preponderance of evidence The weight or level of persuasion of evidence needed to find the defendant liable as alleged by the plaintiff in a civil matter.

C

carjacking The crime of stealing a motor vehicle while the vehicle is occupied.

case (common) law Published court opinions of federal and state appellate courts; judge-created law in deciding cases, set forth in court opinions.

causation Intentional act resulted in harm or injury to the complaining plaintiff.

chain conspiracy A single conspiracy in which each person is responsible for a distinct act within the overall plan.

circumstantial evidence Evidence that suggests a conclusion.

clear and convincing Evidence that indicates that a thing to be proved is highly probable or reasonably certain.

commingling A term for mixing a client's funds with the attorney's personal funds without permission; an ethical violation.

common law Judge-made law, the ruling in a judicial opinion.

community service A criminal sentence requiring that the offender perform some specific service to the community for some specified period of time.

complaint Document that states the allegations and the legal basis of the plaintiff 's claims. Also, a charge, preferred before a magistrate having jurisdiction, that a person named has committed a specified offense, with an offer to prove the fact, to the end that a prosecution may be instituted.

complicity A state of being an accomplice; participation in guilt.

concurrence Another view or analysis written by a member of the same reviewing panel. Also, a meeting or coming together of a guilty act and a guilty mind.

concurrent sentences Two or more sentences of jail time to be served simultaneously.

consecutive sentences Two or more sentences of jail time to be served in sequence.

consent All parties to a novation must knowingly assent to the substitution of either the obligations or parties to the agreement. Also, voluntarily yielding the will to another.

conspiracy By agreement, parties work together to create an illegal result, to achieve an unlawful end.

Constitution The organic and fundamental law of a nation or state, which may be written or unwritten, establishing the character and conception of its government, laying the basic principles to which its internal life is to be conformed, organizing the government, regulating functions of departments, and prescribing the extent to which a nation or state can exercise its powers.

contempt A willful disregard for or disobedience of a public authority.

conversion An overt act to deprive the owner of possession of personal property with no intention of returning the property, thereby causing injury or harm.

conviction Results from a guilty finding by the jury in a criminal trial.

corpus delicti [Latin "body of the crime"] The fact of the transgression or the physical evidence of a crime such as the body of a murder victim.

counterfeiting Forging, copying, or imitating without a right to do so and with the purpose of deceiving or defrauding.

court rules Regulations with the force of law governing practice and procedure in the various courts.

crime Any act done in violation of those duties that an individual owes to the community, and for the breach of which the law has provided that the offender shall make satisfaction to the public.

criminal trespass The offense committed by one who, without license or privilege to do so, enters or surreptitiously remains in any building or occupied structure.

cross-examination Occurs when the opposing attorney asks the witness questions.

curtilage Out buildings that are directly and intimately connected with the habitation and in proximity thereto and the land or grounds surrounding the dwelling that are necessary and convenient and habitually used for family purposes and carrying on domestic employment.

D

damages Money paid to compensate for loss or injury.

deadly force Defense available in cases involving the defense of persons, oneself, or another. It is a violent action known to create a substantial risk of causing death or serious bodily harm.

deadly weapon Any firearm or other device, instrument, material, or substance that, from the manner in which it is used or is intended to be used, is calculated or likely to produce death.

defendant The party against whom a lawsuit is brought.

defense Legally sufficient reason to excuse the complained-of behavior.

defense of others A justification defense available if one harms or threatens another while defending a third person.

demonstrative evidence Any object, visual aid, model, scale drawing, or other exhibit designed to help clarify points in the trial.

depraved heart murder A murder resulting from an act so reckless and careless of the safety of others that it demonstrates the perpetrator's complete lack of regard for human life.

desist To cease an activity.

detain To restrain, arrest, check, delay, hinder, hold, keep, or retain in custody.

detention The act of keeping back, restraining, or withholding, either accidentally or by design, a person or thing.

deter To turn aside, discourage, or prevent from acting.

determinate sentence A sentence for a fixed length of time rather than for an unspecified duration.

diminished capacity The doctrine that recognizes that an accused does not have to be suffering from a mental disease to have impaired mental capacities at the time the offense was committed.

direct evidence Evidence that establishes a particular fact without resort to other testimony or evidence.

direct examination Occurs when the attorney questions his or her own witness.

discovery The pretrial investigation process authorized and governed by the rules of civil procedure; the process of investigation and collection of evidence by litigants; process in which the opposing parties obtain information about the case from each other; the process of investigation and collection of evidence by litigants.

dismissal An order or judgment finally disposing of an action, suit, motion, or other without trial of the issues involved.

disorderly conduct Behavior that tends to disturb the public peace, offend public morals, or undermine public safety.

double jeopardy Being tried twice for the same act or acts.

Due Process Clause Refers to two aspects of the law: procedural, in which a person is guaranteed fair procedures, and substantive, which protects a person's property from unfair governmental interference or taking.

duress Unreasonable and unscrupulous manipulation of a person to force him to agree to terms of an agreement that he would otherwise not agree to. Also, any unlawful threat or coercion used by a person to induce another to act (or to refrain from acting) in a manner that he or she otherwise would not do.

dwelling A house or other structure that is used or intended for use as a residence.

E

elements of the crime Those constituent parts of a crime that must be proved by the prosecution to sustain a conviction.

embezzlement The fraudulent appropriation of property by one lawfully entrusted with its possession.

enhancements Added factors to a criminal charge that make the charge carry greater weight.

entrapment An act of a law enforcement official to induce or encourage a person to commit a crime when the defendant expresses no desire to proceed with the illegal act.

espionage Spying or the gathering, transmitting, or losing of information respecting the national defense with intent or reason to believe that the information is to be used to the injury of the United States, or to the advantage of any foreign nation.

evidence Any fact, testimony, or physical object that tends to prove or disprove allegations raised in a case; must be reasonably calculated to lead to the discovery of admissible evidence.

exclusionary rule Circumstances surrounding the seizure do not meet warrant requirements or exceptions; items seized deemed *fruit of the poisonous tree* are excluded from trial evidence.

excuse A reason alleged for doing or not doing a thing.

excused for cause Process of excusing jurors for bias, prejudices, and legitimate reasons as well, such as sickness, job commitment, or others.

extortion The obtaining of property from another induced by wrongful use of actual or threatened force, violence, or fear, or under color of official right.

F

false imprisonment Any deprivation of a person's freedom of movement without that person's consent and against his or her will, whether done by actual violence or threats.

false pretenses False representations of material past or present facts, known by the wrongdoer to be false, made with the intent to defraud a victim into passing title in property to the wrongdoer.

felony A crime punishable by more than a year in prison or death.

felony murder rule The doctrine holding that any death resulting from the commission or attempted commission of a dangerous felony is murder.

fiduciary One who owes to another the duties of good faith, trust, confidence, and candor.

fine A pecuniary punishment or penalty imposed by lawful tribunal upon a person convicted of a crime or misdemeanor.

forgery The process of making or adapting objects or documents with the intention to deceive.

fruit of the poisonous tree Evidence tainted based on illegal seizure may not be used in a trial.

G

gambling Making a bet. Such occurs when there is a chance for profit if a player is skillful and lucky.

general intent An unjustifiable act; reckless conduct.

grand jury A jury of inquiry who are summoned and returned by the sheriff to each session of the criminal courts and whose duty is to receive complaints and accusations in criminal cases, hear evidence, and decide if the defendant should stand for trial.

guilty A verdict only available in criminal cases in which the jury determines that the defendant is responsible for committing a crime.

H

habeas corpus A writ employed to bring a person before a court, most frequently to ensure that the party's imprisonment or detention is not illegal.

habitation Place of abode; dwelling place; residence.

harmful error An error by the court that has an identifiable negative impact on the trial to such a degree that the constitutional rights of a party are compromised.

harmless error Standard of review that has not caused legal error requiring reversal of the trial court's decision.

hate crime A crime motivated by the victim's race, color, ethnicity, religion, gender, sexual orientation, or national origin.

hearsay An out-of-court statement offered to prove a matter in contention in the lawsuit.

heat of passion Rage, terror, or furious hatred suddenly aroused by some immediate provocation.

homicide The killing of a human being by the act or omission of another.

I

impartial jury A jury that is unbiased and does not favor one party or the other.

incapacitation Punishment by imprisonment, mutilation, or death.

inchoate crime An incipient crime; an act that generally leads to a crime.

indeterminate sentence A sentence of an unspecified duration such as one for a term of 5 to 10 years.

indictment A written list of charges issued by a grand jury against a defendant in a criminal case.

indigent One who is needy and poor, or one who does not have sufficient property to furnish him a living or anyone able to support him or to whom he is entitled to look for support.

inducement The act or process of enticing or persuading another person to take a certain course of action.

infancy The state of a person who is under the age of legal majority.

inference A conclusion reached by considering other facts and deducing a logical consequence.

information States that the magistrate determines there is sufficient cause to make an arrest and also sets forth the formal charges sought by the prosecution.

infraction A violation of a statute for which the only sentence authorized is a fine and for which violation is expressly designated as an infraction.

infringement An act that interferes with an exclusive right.

intangible property Personal property that has no physical presence but is represented by a certificate or some other instrument such as stocks or trademarks.

interrogation The process of questions propounded by police to a person arrested or suspected to seek solution of crime.

intoxication Under the influence of alcohol or drugs which may, depending on the degree of inebriation, render a party incapable of entering into a contractual relationship or of acting in the manner in which an ordinarily prudent and cautious person would have acted under similar circumstances.

involuntary manslaughter Homicide in which there is no intention to kill or do grievous bodily harm but that is committed with criminal negligence or during the commission of a crime not included within the felony murder rule.

irresistible impulse An impulse to commit an unlawful or criminal act that cannot be resisted or overcome because mental disease has destroyed the freedom of will, the power of self-control, and the choice of actions.

J

judgment The court's final decision regarding the rights and claims of the parties.

jurisdiction The power or authority of the court to hear a particular classification of case. Also, the place or court that may hear a case, based on subject matter and/or geographic area.

jury panel Group of people called to court from which a jury is chosen.

justification A lawful reason for acting or failing to act.

K

kidnapping The unlawful confinement, removal, or hiding of a person against his/her will for the purpose of holding the person to obtain a ransom, to serve as a hostage, to facilitate the commission of a felony, to inflict harm or terrorize the victim, or to interfere with the performance of a governmental or political function.

L

larceny The common law crime of taking property of another without permission.

larceny by trick Larceny in which the taker misleads the rightful possessor, by a misrepresentation of fact, into giving up possession of the property in question.

loitering To stand around or move about slowly; to linger or spend time idly.

M

M'Naghten Rule The defendant alleges he or she lacked capacity to form criminal intent.

magistrate A public civil officer, possessing such power—legislative, executive, or judicial—as the government appointing him may ordain.

malice aforethought The prior intention to kill the victim or anyone else if likely to occur as a result of the actions or omissions.

malicious mischief The act of willfully damaging or destroying the personal property of another; sometimes referred to as criminal mischief.

malum in se An act that is prohibited because it is "evil in itself."

malum prohibitum An act that is prohibited by a rule of law.

mandatory sentence A sentence set by law with no discretion for the judge to individualize punishment.

manslaughter The unlawful killing of a human being without premeditation.

mayhem The maiming, dismembering, disabling, or disfigurement of the body part of another with the intent to harm or cause permanent injury.

mens rea "A guilty mind"; criminal intent in committing the act.

misdemeanor A lesser crime punishable by less than a year in jail and/or a fine.

mistrial A trial that has been terminated prior to a normal conclusion.

mitigating circumstance (mitigating factor) A fact or situation that does not justify or excuse a wrongful act or offense but that reduces the degree of culpability and thus may reduce the damages in a civil case or the punishment in a criminal case.

mitigating factor See *mitigating circumstance.*

moral turpitude An act or behavior that gravely violates the sentiment or accepted standard of the community.

motive Something such as willful desire that causes an individual to act.

murder The killing of a human being with intent.

N

necessity A justification defense for a person who acts in an emergency and commits a crime that is less harmful than the harm that would have occurred but for the person's actions.

nolo contendere Latin for "I do not wish to contend"; to plead no contest.

O

oath Any form of attestation by which a person signifies that he/she is bound in conscience to perform an act faithfully and truthfully.

obscenity The quality or state of being morally abhorrent or socially taboo, especially as a result of referring to or depicting sexual or excretory functions.

overt act Identifiable commission or omission, an intentional tort requirement.

owner One who has the right to possess, use, and convey something.

P

parental kidnapping The kidnapping of a child by one parent in violation of the other parent's custody or visitation rights.

parolee Ex-prisoner who has been released from jail, prison, or other confinement after having served part of a criminal sentence.

peremptory challenge (peremptory jury strike) An attorney's elimination of a prospective juror without giving a reason; limited to a specific number of strikes.

perjury The willful assertion as to a matter of fact, opinion, belief, or knowledge, made by a witness in a judicial proceeding as part of his/her evidence, either upon oath or in any form allowed by law to be substituted for an oath, whether such evidence is given in open court, in an affidavit, or otherwise, such assertion being material to the issue or point of inquiry and known to such witness to be false.

personal property Movable or intangible thing not attached to real property.

plain error A decision or action by the court that appears to a reviewing court to have been unquestionably erroneous.

plaintiff The party initiating legal action.

plea bargain The process whereby the accused and the prosecutor in a criminal case work out a mutually satisfactory disposition of the case subject to court approval.

possession Having or holding property in one's power; controlling something to the exclusion of others.

preliminary hearing An appearance by both parties before the court to assess the circumstances and validity of the restraining application. Also, a hearing by a judge to determine whether a person charged with a crime should be held for trial.

premeditation Conscious consideration and planning that precedes some act.

preponderance of the evidence The weight or level of persuasion of evidence needed to find the defendant liable as alleged by the plaintiff in a civil matter.

principal in the first degree The criminal actor; the one who actually commits the crime, either by his/her own hand, by an inanimate agency, or by an innocent human agent.

principal in the second degree The one who is present at the commission of a criminal offense and aids, counsels, commands, or encourages the principal in the first degree in the commission of that offense.

probable cause The totality of circumstances leads one to believe certain facts or circumstances exist; applies to arrests, searches, and seizures.

probation A court-imposed criminal sentence that, subject to stated conditions, releases a convicted person into the community instead of sending the criminal to prison.

probative evidence Evidence that tends to or actually proves the fact.

procedural due process These requirements mandate scrupulous adherence to the method or mechanism applied. Notice and fair hearing are the cornerstones of due process, though certainly not the only consideration.

prosecutor Attorney representing the people or plaintiff in criminal matters.

prostitution The act of performing, or offering or agreeing to perform, a sexual act for hire.

protective frisk A pat-down search of a suspect by police, designed to discover weapons for the purpose of ensuring the safety of the officer and others nearby.

prurient interest Characterized by or arousing inordinate or unusual sexual desire.

puffing The use of an exaggerated opinion—as opposed to a false statement—with the intent to sell a good or service.

Q

question of fact An issue that has not been predetermined and authoritatively answered by the law; a disputed issue to be resolved by the jury in a jury trial or by the judge in a bench trial.

question of law An issue to be decided by the judge concerning the application or interpretation of the law.

R

rape Unlawful sexual intercourse with a person without consent.

real property Land and all property permanently attached to it, such as buildings.

reasonable suspicion Such suspicion that will justify an officer, for Fourth Amendment purposes, in stopping a defendant in a public place, as having knowledge sufficient to induce an ordinarily prudent and cautious person under the circumstances to believe that criminal activity is at hand.

receiving stolen property The crime of acquiring or controlling property known to have been stolen by another person.

rehabilitation Restoring a person to his or her former capacity.

relevant evidence Evidence that makes the existence of any fact more probable or less probable than it would be without the evidence.

remand(ed) Disposition in which the appellate court sends the case back to the lower court for further action.

renunciation Abandonment of effort to commit a crime.

retreat rule The doctrine holding that the victim of a crime must choose to retreat instead of using deadly force if certain circumstances exist.

retribution Punishment based on just deserts.

reverse(d) (reversal) Disposition in which the appellate court disagrees with the trial court.

reversible error An error that affects a party's substantive rights or the case's outcome, and thus is grounds for reversal if the party properly objects.

riot An unlawful disturbance of the peace by an assembly of usually three or more persons acting with a common purpose in a violent or tumultuous manner that threatens or terrorizes the public.

robbery The direct taking of property from another through force or threat.

S

scienter A degree of knowledge that makes a person legally responsible for his or her act or omission.

search warrant Issued after presentation of an affidavit stating clearly the probable cause on which the request is based. In particular, it is an order in writing, issued by a justice or other magistrate, in the name of the state, and directed to a sheriff, constable, or other officer authorizing him to search for and seize any property that constitutes evidence of the commission of a crime, contraband, or the fruits of the crime.

self-defense A defendant's legal excuse that the use of force was justified.

self-incrimination Acts or declarations either as testimony at trial or prior to trial by which one implicates himself or herself in a crime.

sentence The judgment formally pronounced by the court or judge upon the defendant after his/her conviction in a criminal prosecution, imposing the punishment to be inflicted, usually in the form of a fine, incarceration, or probation.

sentencing The post-conviction stage of the criminal justice process in which the defendant is brought before the court for imposition of sentence.

serious bodily injury Serious physical impairment of the human body; especially, bodily injury that creates a substantial risk of death or that causes serious, permanent disfigurement or protracted loss or impairment.

settlement A negotiated termination of a case prior to a trial or jury verdict.

signatory A party that signs a document, becoming a party to an agreement.

sodomy Oral or anal copulation between humans.

solicitation The crime of inducing or encouraging another to commit a crime.

split sentence A sentence where part of the time is served in confinement and the rest is spent on probation.

stalking The act or offense of following or loitering near another with the purpose of annoying or harassing that person or committing a further crime.

standing Legally sufficient reason and right to object.

stare decisis (Latin) "Stand by the decision." Decisions from a court with substantially the same set of facts should be followed by that court and all lower courts under it; the judicial process of adhering to prior case decisions; the doctrine of precedent whereby once a court has decided a specific issue one way in the past, it and other courts in the same jurisdiction are obligated to follow that earlier decision in deciding cases with similar issues in the future.

statutory law Derived from the Constitution in statutes enacted by the legislative branch of state or federal government; Primary source of law consisting of the body of legislative law.

statutory rape The sexual intercourse with a female who is under a certain age (usually 14 to 18, depending on the state). The minor child is considered legally incapable of consenting.

stop and frisk The situation where police officers who are suspicious of an individual run their hands lightly over the suspect's outer garments to determine if the person is carrying a concealed weapon.

strict liability The defendant is liable without the plaintiff having to prove fault. Also, liability that is based on the breach of an absolute duty rather than negligence or intent.

subpoena A document that is served upon an individual under authority of the court, and orders the person to appear at a certain place and certain time for a deposition, or suffer the consequences; an order issued by the court clerk directing a person to appear in court.

substantial capacity The term used in the definition of legal insanity proposed by the Model Penal Code.

suppression hearing A pretrial proceeding in criminal cases in which a defendant seeks to prevent the introduction of evidence alleged to have been seized illegally.

suspended sentence A sentence postponed so that the defendant is not required to serve time in the absence of certain circumstances.

T

tangible evidence Evidence that can be touched, picked up.

tangible property Personal property that can be held or touched such as furniture or jewelry.

terrorism The use or threat of violence to intimidate or cause panic, especially as a means of affecting political conduct.

theft The taking of property without the owner's consent.

title The legal link between a person who owns property and the property itself; legal evidence of a person's ownership rights.

totality of the circumstances A legal standard that requires focus on the entire situation and not on one specific factor.

trade secret Property that is protected from misappropriation such as formulas, patterns, and compilations of information.

treason A breach of allegiance to one's government, usually committed through levying war against such government or by giving aid or comfort to the enemy.

trespassory taking The act of seizing an article from the possession of the rightful owner.

U

unilateral One-sided; relating to only one of two or more persons or things.

uttering The crime of presenting a false or worthless document with the intent to harm or defraud.

V

vagrancy The act of going about from place to place by a person without visible means of support, who is idle, and who, though able to work for his/her maintenance, refuses to do so, but lives without labor or on the charity of others.

vandalism Such willful or malicious acts are intended to damage or destroy property.

vehicular homicide The killing of another person by one's unlawful or negligent operation of a motor vehicle.

verdict Decision of the jury following presentation of facts and application of relevant law as they relate to the law presented in the jury instructions.

voir dire The process of selecting a jury for trial.

voluntary manslaughter An act of murder reduced to manslaughter because of extenuating circumstances such as adequate provocation or diminished capacity.

W

warrant Issued after presentation of an affidavit stating clearly the probable cause on which the request is based.

Wharton's rule The doctrine that an agreement by two or more persons to commit a particular crime cannot be prosecuted as a conspiracy if the crime could not be committed except by the actual number of participants involved.

wheel conspiracy A conspiracy in which a single member or group separately agrees with two or more other members or groups.

writ A written order of a judge requiring specific action by the person or entity to whom the writ is directed.

writ of habeas corpus Literally "you should have the body"; application for extraordinary relief or a petition for rehearing of the issue on the basis of unusual facts unknown at the time of the trial.

Index